1,000,000 Books

are available to read at

Forgotten Books

www.ForgottenBooks.com

Read online
Download PDF
Purchase in print

ISBN 978-0-265-03889-5
PIBN 10956781

This book is a reproduction of an important historical work. Forgotten Books uses state-of-the-art technology to digitally reconstruct the work, preserving the original format whilst repairing imperfections present in the aged copy. In rare cases, an imperfection in the original, such as a blemish or missing page, may be replicated in our edition. We do, however, repair the vast majority of imperfections successfully; any imperfections that remain are intentionally left to preserve the state of such historical works.

Forgotten Books is a registered trademark of FB &c Ltd.
Copyright © 2018 FB &c Ltd.
FB &c Ltd, Dalton House, 60 Windsor Avenue, London, SW19 2RR.
Company number 08720141. Registered in England and Wales.

For support please visit www.forgottenbooks.com

1 MONTH OF FREE READING

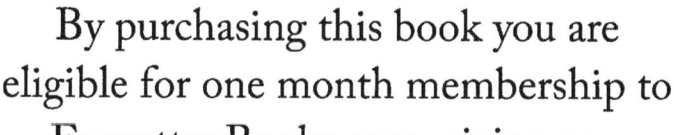

at
www.ForgottenBooks.com

By purchasing this book you are eligible for one month membership to ForgottenBooks.com, giving you unlimited access to our entire collection of over 1,000,000 titles via our web site and mobile apps.

To claim your free month visit: www.forgottenbooks.com/free956781

* Offer is valid for 45 days from date of purchase. Terms and conditions apply.

English
Français
Deutsche
Italiano
Español
Português

www.forgottenbooks.com

Mythology Photography **Fiction**
Fishing Christianity **Art** Cooking
Essays Buddhism Freemasonry
Medicine **Biology** Music **Ancient Egypt** Evolution Carpentry Physics
Dance Geology **Mathematics** Fitness
Shakespeare **Folklore** Yoga Marketing
Confidence Immortality Biographies
Poetry **Psychology** Witchcraft
Electronics Chemistry History **Law**
Accounting **Philosophy** Anthropology
Alchemy Drama Quantum Mechanics
Atheism Sexual Health **Ancient History**
Entrepreneurship Languages Sport
Paleontology Needlework Islam
Metaphysics Investment Archaeology
Parenting Statistics Criminology
Motivational

REPORT

OF THE

Executive Committee

OF THE

New York Civil Service Reform Association

Read at the Annual Meeting, May 13, 1903.

LIST OF MEMBERS, ETC.

NEW YORK
PUBLISHED FOR THE
CIVIL SERVICE REFORM ASSOCIATION
79 Wall Street
1903

CONTENTS.

	PAGE.
Annual Report of the Executive Committee, .	5
Annual Report of the Treasurer, . . .	21
Constitution and By-Laws, . .	23
Roll of Officers and Members, ...	31
Articles of Incorporation, ...	51

266628

enforcement of the civil service law in this city under the present administration over that under the last administration. Such criticism as it has felt bound to make in the past, and will make in this report, is due to the fact that the Committee has been unwilling to accept the unsympathetic and lax enforcement of the law under the last administration as a standard by which to judge, but has taken instead what it thought might reasonably be expected of an administration pledged to civil service reform and what it has seen actually accomplished under the Strong administration and in the Federal service.

In carrying on its work the Committee has pursued the same policy as in former years. Through its standing committees and through the Secretary's office it has closely followed the administration of the laws in the Federal offices in New York, in the State and in the City service. It has instituted important investigations and, from time to time, given the results to the public. It has carefully watched the course of legislation at Albany. Through its Law Committee it has conducted test cases involving the integrity of the service. It has received complaints and brought them to the attention of the proper authorities. It has suggested improvements and at all times has stood ready to aid in a constructive way in the enforcement of the laws.

THE FEDERAL SERVICE.

The advances made in the Federal service during the year 1902 were reviewed in the report of the National League at its annual meeting last December. The report of this Committee will deal with changes effected since that time, as well as with the enforcement of the law in the Federal offices in New York during the past year.

Congress adjourned without passing any act

that materially affected the merit system, although the House of Representatives, in the last days of the session, took up and passed a vicious veteran preference bill. On the other hand, both Houses approved, practically without debate, the clause in the appropriation bill providing for the much needed increase in the appropriation for the Civil Service Commission. The failure to provide a civil service system for the District of Columbia or to pass any legislation for the reform of the consular service was not, under the circumstances, unexpected.

The resignation of Commissioner Garfield in February, to take the position of Commissioner of Corporations in the newly created Department of Commerce, was felt to be a serious loss, not only by his colleagues, but by all who were familiar with his work as civil service commissioner. No definite appointment has as yet been made to fill the vacancy and the Association ventures to hope that the selection will be made with the same fidelity to the interests of civil service reform in the Federal service that was observed by President Roosevelt in his choice of Commissioners Foulke and Garfield.

Progress during the past four months has been marked by the preparation by the Commission of a careful revision of the Federal rules. This has resulted in greater brevity and clearness and in slight extensions of the competitive service. The most important of these extensions has been the restoration of shipping commissioners—withdrawn by President McKinley's order of May 29, 1899—to the competitive class. The revised rules were signed by the President on March 20th and went into effect April 15th.

On March 26th the President also signed an order providing for the extension of the regulations governing the appointment of laborers "as rapidly as may be found practicable" to Federal offices outside of Washington. The Civil Service Commission has had this subject under consideration for many months and was ready to proceed at once with the introduction of the system of labor registration in the Cities of Boston, New York, Philadelphia, Chicago, St. Louis and San Francisco. Objection has, however, been made by Collector Stranahan and, it is understood, also by Surveyor Clarkson, to the application of this system to the New York Custom House. We sincerely hope that these objections will be withdrawn—or will be overruled—as we can but feel that the exception of the New York Custom House, with over five hundred laborers, would be utterly unjustifiable.

In its last annual report the Committee criticised the appointment of James S. Clarkson, notorious as a spoilsman, as Surveyor of the Port of New York. Events during the past year have served to show the justness of this criticism. Mr. Clarkson has been reported by the press as a frequent absentee from his office, engaged in political work in other parts of the country; his department has once been the subject of investigation by the Civil Service Commission, while in the only two important appointments he has made—those of Deputy Surveyors—he has requested, and through his insistence has received—in one case by the order of President Roosevelt—permission to ignore the rules governing promotions in the New York Custom House.

The reports that have recently appeared in the press in regard to the investigation of the Post Office Department indicate a laxity in enforcing the rules in regard to the employment of laborers in classified positions to which the civil service reformers have repeatedly called attention. The investigation has not proceeded far enough as yet to justify the expression of an opinion in regard to other alleged violations of the civil service law. It will also be well to suspend judgment until the results of further investigation are known, on the sensational reports that have appeared in regard to the existence of a promotion syndicate in the New York Post Office. The Committee, however, is convinced that such scandals could not have arisen if the civil service law had been followed and proper regulations governing promotions had been introduced. It strongly recommends to the Civil Service Commission their introduction at this time.

NEW YORK STATE.

Realizing the importance to the integrity of the merit system in this State of the attitude of the Governor toward the civil service law, letters were addressed last autumn to the Republican and Democratic candidates. In each case satisfactory replies, announcing their intention to enforce the law, were received. At the time of the campaign, also, a circular letter was sent to the heads of departments and to the press generally, calling attention to the provisions of the civil service law in regard to political assessments. Governor Odell, the successful candidate, while open to criticism in his attitude toward the merit system for signing certain bills referred to in our last report and for using his influence, from time to time, to secure the approval by the State Commission of exemptions from competitive examination, has, nevertheless, in other respects, upheld the civil service law, and it has been felt that he could be relied upon to prevent the bills threatening to destroy the system from becoming laws.

The membership of the State Commission, except for the recent resignation of President Collier, has remained the same as during the previous year, and there has consequently been but little change in policy. The Commission has received the suggestions of the Association with unfailing courtesy, and has at all times granted requests for hearings on proposed changes in the rules and classification. It has materially aided the Association in its work of watching the enforcement of the law, by sending in advance of each meeting a list of the matters to come before them in which the Association was supposed to be interested.

William Miller Collier, who has just resigned from the Commission to take the position of Deputy Attorney-General attached to the Department of Commerce, in Washington, was appointed by Governor Roosevelt in 1899, and succeeded Colonel Silas W. Burt as President in 1901. His sympathy with the civil service reform movement and his experience in office—which he turned to good account in his book on the Civil Service Law—made him a valuable member of the Commission. In making an appointment to fill the vacancy, Governor Odell, who has publicly expressed himself as a believer in the civil service law, will, we hope, recognize the advisability of appointing someone who is in favor of its strict enforcement in the spirit of the Constitution.

Criticism of the State Commission's work attaches particularly to the number and character of exemptions from competitive examination granted both in the State service and in the various municipalities. Situated as the Commission is at Albany, strong political pressure is often brought to bear upon it, and, in several instances, the exemptions granted on the ground of the impracticability of competition have been sought, and used, for the purpose of making political appointments.

An important ruling has been obtained from the Commission which should have the effect of materially reducing the number of exemptions. At a meeting held in New York City Mr. Hardon, representing the Association, contended that, as the Constitution required that a position should be classified as competitive where competition is practicable, the burden of proof is upon the person requesting the exemption, and a prima facie case for the impracticability of competitive examination must be made out before those in opposition to the exemption are called upon. This contention was upheld.

MEASURES IN THE STATE LEGISLATURE.

The work of the Association in connection with the session of the legislature which closed on April 23 has been exacting, owing to the large number of bills affecting the merit system which were introduced and advanced. Copies of all bills were received and examined at the office and all those requiring action were passed upon by the Law Committee. As a rule these bills were harmful in character and were opposed by the Association by filing briefs with the appropriate committees or by personal appearances at hearings.

Exceptions to this rule were the bills introduced at the request of the State Civil Service Commission to carry out the recommendations contained in its last annual report. One of these was aimed to prevent collateral attacks through the courts upon the classification adopted by the Commission; another provided that reasons must be assigned and an opportunity to make explanation granted in cases of removal of competitive and non-competitive employees; a third was intended to correct certain ambiguities of language in the law and to give the Commission power, under strict limitations, to permit appointments to competitive positions without examination where it was proposed to appoint a person who was engaged in private business for occasional service. A fourth proposed to extend to municipal commissions power to make investigations and to administer oaths. Several conferences were held with the State Commission in regard to these bills with the result that they were slightly amended. They were advanced to third reading in the Assembly, but failed to pass.

The other bills watched by the Association may be divided into five classes: (1) bills to amend the civil service law; (2) bills to amend the City Charter; (3) bills to provide for rehearings and reinstatements in the service; (4) bills providing for payment for services rendered in violation of the civil service law; (5) miscellaneous bills.

Of the measures in the first class, all but two failed to pass the Assembly. A bill providing that crime committed before the age of sixteen should not be a bar to civil employment was vetoed by the Governor, before whom is still pending a bill—which is believed to be clearly unconstitutional—providing for a preference in appointment for veteran volunteer firemen.

From the standpoint of civil service reform, the most important of the bills amending the Charter which succeeded in passing the legislature were those introduced by Mr. McCarthy and Mr. Sullivan. The McCarthy bill provided that any person who had resigned or had been dismissed from the police force might be reappointed "upon the concurring vote of all members comprising the Board," which would appear to give the power to the single commissioner who has succeeded the Board, to reinstate all persons discharged under a previous administration. The Sullivan bill permitted the appointment without examination of volunteer firemen in Queens and Richmond upon the establishment of the paid fire department in those boroughs. The Mayor has refused to accept either of these bills.

Special bills providing for rehearings and reinstatements, and for the payment of persons for services rendered in violation of the civil service law were passed in large numbers. Very few, however, have secured the Mayor's approval.

Of the miscellaneous measures, the Remsen bill providing for the establishment of a pension fund for civil employees is particularly worthy of mention.

This bill was passed by the Assembly, but was not advanced in the Senate.

NEW YORK CITY.

The only change in the composition of the Municipal Civil Service Commission during the past year has been due to the resignation of Commissioner Vanderbilt, owing to illness. The Mayor has announced no appointment to fill the vacancy and the Commission has been proceeding for some months with only six members. Mr. George McAneny sent in his resignation as Secretary last May and has been succeeded in that position by Mr. S. William Briscoe, formerly Secretary under the Strong board.

As the Executive Committee has at various times during the past twelve months found it necessary to criticise publicly the course of the Municipal Commission, it is fitting that in this report it should lay before the members of the Association the reasons for such criticism and a brief account of its action.

In its last report the Committee called attention to the failure of the Commission, owing to the press of administrative work, to institute investigations into the condition of the service; to the protest which had been made against the number and character of exemptions from competitive examination which had been granted and to the vexatious delays in furnishing eligible lists to meet the pressing needs of the departments, caused, in part, by the continuance of the practice of employing persons as examiners at ten dollars per session of seven hours, who were engaged in private business and did their examining work away from the office of the Commission. The situation was considered so serious that a committee had appeared before the Mayor to lay the facts before him. At the time the report was made, however, it was understood that the Commission was to be reorganized with a salaried executive head and was to be reduced to three. From these changes a great improvement was expected. The Mayor, however, decided to retain the same Commission of seven, with Colonel Willis L. Ogden continued as President at a salary of $6,000.

The reclassification and regrading of the city service by the Commission was an important step in advance, in that it reduced the number of titles of competitive positions, provided a uniform classification of salaries for all departments and offered an opportunity—which, unfortunately, has not been improved—for instituting a thorough system of promotion by examination. At the same time, the large increase in the number of positions excepted from examination, which went with this plan of reclassification, led to a vigorous protest from the Association. This protest, upon the approval of the greater part of these exemptions by the State Commission, was embodied in resolutions which were given to the press in June. Exception was taken in particular to the twenty additional exempt places in the office of the Commissioners of Accounts and to the thirty-six new exemptions under the Comptroller, which brought the total number of excepted places in the Finance Department to one hundred and forty-two. It is beyond question that these new exemptions have been used, in certain instances, to make political appointments.

In order that the Commission might be made familiar with the reasons for opposing exemptions, as well as that the Association might have an opportunity to enter its protest—where it desired to protest—against them in the first instance, a request was made that the Commission should grant hearings on proposed changes in classification. This the Commission was unwilling at the time to do. The Mayor desired, however, that the City should have the opportunity to consider the protest of the Association, rather than that such protests should be made in the first instance before the State Commission at Albany, and courteously permitted a representative to appear before him before taking action on proposed changes. In June, at the Mayor's request, the Commission instituted the practice of granting public hearings on changes in classification, and this Committee cannot but feel that to this practice is due in part the striking diminution in the number of exemptions granted. In October, a further request was preferred that public hearings should be granted as to changes in the rules. The request was denied. As the Commission has not acted on the subsequent request of the Mayor to the same effect, his Honor has again adopted the plan of allowing a representative of the Association to appear before him.

At its October meeting, the Executive Committee appointed a special committee of eight to investigate the administration of the civil service in this city. Upon the report of the special committee in November, the Executive Committee authorized the sending of an open letter to Mayor Low. This letter was published on December 1, and received such widespread attention that members of the Association may be supposed to be familiar with its contents. The Commission made reply in a letter to the Mayor dated December 12, which was also given to the press. The correspondence closed with an answer to the Commission's letter, dated December 24.

In January, the Citizens' Union issued a statement, in which it urged an inquiry whether a Civil Service Commission of three paid members who would devote all their time to the work would not place the department upon a plane of greater efficiency. The Executive Committee of the Association at its January meeting, adopted and sent to the Mayor a resolution of similar import, in which it recommended that the Commission should be reorganized and in the interest of efficiency and expedition a new Commission of three should be appointed. The Mayor has, however, not considered it advisable to make any change.

The Committee is glad to be able to report that, in certain directions, the work of the Commission has shown a marked improvement since the publication of the Association's letter in December and distinctly on the lines indicated in that letter. Complaints are no longer heard in regard to delay in furnishing eligible lists and it is believed that serious delays no longer exist. The system of employing per session examiners to mark ordinary examination papers has been largely done away with. In January examinations were held for civil service examiners and for assistant chief examiner. The examinations were widely advertised and the papers were marked by experts. Adequate lists appeared on March 27, but no new appointments have been made. The number of appeals for re-rating of papers which have been granted has been greatly reduced. Since January 1 there have been 495 such appeals, of which 428 were denied and 67 granted. The number granted in these four months is, however, still in excess of the number granted by the Federal Commission during eleven months of 1902, in which 48,362 sets of papers were rated. Confirmation of the correctness of the statement in the Committee's open letter, that the Commission by its action had "invited a flood of appeals," is to be found in the fact that 233 appeals were made in regard to one examination. Only eight of these were granted, however, and the Commission's present course in regard to appeals will undoubtedly lead to a large reduction in the number of appeals made, as well as to an increased confidence in the integrity of the examinations.

On the other hand, little of a constructive character, along the lines mapped out by the Commission in its answer to the letter of the Association, has actually been accomplished, although it is understood that a sub-committee has in hand the proposed revision of the rules. The power of investigation conferred by the revised Charter, which it was thought a commission of seven could exercise to great advantage, has been, in practice, little used. Efficiency records for use in promotion examinations and the new plan for numbering examination papers so as to prevent possible disclosure of the candidate's identity—both matters referred to in the Commission's answer as under consideration—have not been introduced. Promotions by competition, outside of the uniformed forces, are still in a most unsatisfactory condition. The plan of instituting a salaried executive President has not worked out to so great advantage as was intended, the Commission apparently not having seen fit to confide to its President alone any extensive powers.

On the whole, however, the correspondence between the Association and the Civil Service Commission appears to have been fruitful of good results.

THE WORK OF THE LAW COMMITTEE.

The litigation conducted by the Law Committee has been of an exceedingly important character. Mr. Samuel H. Ordway and Mr. Edward M. Shepard, have conducted the case of Greene vs. Knox, a taxpayer's action instituted to set aside the promotion of nineteen police captains under the last administration, made as the result of an examination which the State Commission, upon investigation, pronounced to be illegal. This case has never come to trial on its merits, as the demurrer of the defense was sustained by the Appellate Division, which decided that the remedy must be sought through quo warranto proceedings. An appeal has been taken from this decision which will come before the Court of Appeals in a short time. The Corporation Counsel of the city obtained permission of Attorney General Davies to bring quo warranto proceedings, but as the present Attorney-General has shown considerable hesitation in approving the action, the matter appears to have been dropped. The Law Committee has strongly urged action by the city as the party most vitally interested in protecting the interests of the Police Department.

Even more important have been the cases brought by heads of departments and employees of the Sheriff's, Register's and County Clerk's offices in in New York and Kings Counties to compel the State Commission, by mandamus, to place in the exempt class certain offices which the Commission has classified as competitive. A decision favorable to the relators in these cases might involve the validity of the entire classification of these offices in all counties. In its earlier stages this litigation was conducted on behalf of the Attorney-General by Mr. Charles E. Hughes and Mr. Joseph P. Cotton Jr., of the Association. Mr. Ansley Wilcox, of Buffalo, was asked to represent the Association before the Court of Appeals, and, through the courtesy of Attorney-General Cunneen was permitted to submit an extended oral argument. This case has just been argued and a decision cannot be expected for some weeks, at least.

Aside from litigation, the Law Committee has passed on bills pending in the Legislature, and has opposed the granting of exemptions before the State Commission. It wishes to express its obligation to the Women's Auxiliary for the financial support it has given to the Association's legal work.

THE FINANCE COMMITTEE.

The Finance Committee calls attention to the improved state of the finances of the Association, as shown by the Treasurer's report, and to the absolute freedom from debt. The quota of the Association to the National League has been raised by means of a circular letter sent to all the members. The receipts from all sources during the past year —above the subscriptions to the League—have amounted to $7,617.55, and the disbursements to $7,169.11.

COMMITTEE ON PUBLICATION.

There has been no call for meetings of the Publication Committee, as the regular course has been followed in publishing and distributing material bearing on the merit system and its enforcement. Members of the Committee have contributed to the editorial columns of GOOD GOVERNMENT, which is sent to all members of the Association and which devotes considerable space to local matters.

COMMITTEE ON CORRESPONDENCE.

At a recent meeting, the Committee on Correspondence decided to establish correspondence committees in cities of the State which have civil service commissions, but in which no association exists for watching the enforcement of the law. To carry out this plan persons in these cities who are known to be interested in civil service reform will be urged to join the Association and to report to it at regular intervals.

COMMITTEE ON EXAMINATIONS.

The Committee on Examinations has investigated complaints in regard to the character of the examination papers used in the city service and has closely followed the course of the Commission in granting re-ratings. It has also made a number of practical suggestions looking toward the reorganization of the examining board and for facilitating its work.

COMMITTEE ON MEMBERSHIP.

The Membership Committee reports the number of members at the end of the year to be 757. In order to provide the Association with a source of regular income sufficient to its needs, the Committee feels that the regular membership should be increased to at least 1,000 and the sustaining membership to 100. To bring this about, it has secured the adoption of an amendment to the by-laws increasing the number of members of this Committee to fifteen.

The Executive Committee wishes to acknowledge its obligation to the members who have given their services in the litigation in which the Association has been engaged. It desires also to express its appreciation of the valuable work for the advancement of the merit system performed by the Women's Auxiliary to the Civil Service Reform Association, and to thank them, at the same time, for the assistance they have rendered to the Association's work.

Respectfully submitted,

JACOB F. MILLER,
Chairman.

ELLIOT H. GOODWIN,
Secretary.

ANNUAL REPORT OF THE TREASURER.

MAY 1, 1903.

Balance on hand, as per report, May 1, 1902.................. $37.35

RECEIPTS :

From Annual Dues......................	$3,075.00	
" Sustaining Membership Dues........	1,600.00	
" Subscriptions......................	1,667.00	
" Women's Auxiliary..................	500.00	
" National League, for rent advanced...	400.01	
" National League, subscription returned	375.00	
" Pamphlets sold.....................	.54	7,617.55
		$7,654.90

DISBURSEMENTS :

Salary of Secretary for Nov. 1901..........	$ 275.00	
Salary of Secretary for February, March and April, 1902.....	375.00	
Salary of Secretary......................	1,500.00	
" " Assistant-Secretary.	900.00	
" " Clerks........................	1,228.00	
Legislative Agent...	157.50	
Rent of Office............................	800.03	
Printing............................	162.78	
Postage and Stamped Envelopes...........	207.30	
Stationery................................	187.37	
Office Expenses.........................	269.86	
Traveling Expenses	60.05	
Telephone Service......................	181.50	
Expenses of Litigation....................	360.21	
Subscription to GOOD GOVERNMENT.......	504.51	7,169.11

Balance on hand, April 30, 1903....................... $ 485.79

E. & O. E.

A. S. FRISSELL,
Treasurer.

ORGANIZATION

OF

THE CIVIL SERVICE REFORM ASSOCIATION

(OF NEW YORK.)

CONSTITUTION.

ARTICLE I.

The name of this organization shall be The Civil Service Reform Association.

ARTICLE II.

The object of the Association shall be to establish a system of appointment, promotion, and removal in the Civil Service, founded upon the principle that public office is a public trust, admission to which should depend upon proven fitness. To this end the Association will demand that appointments to subordinate executive offices, with such exceptions as may be expedient, not inconsistent with the principle already mentioned, shall be made from persons whose fitness has been ascertained by competitive examinations open to all applicants properly qualified, and that removals shall be made for legitimate cause only, such as dishonesty, negligence, or inefficiency, but not for political opinion or refusal to render party service; and the Association will advocate all other appropriate measures for securing integrity, intelligence, efficiency, good order, and due discipline in the Civil Service.

ARTICLE III.

The Association will hold meetings, raise funds, publish and circulate appropriate information, correspond and cooperate with associations organized elsewhere for the objects

set forth in this Constitution, and support all executive and legislative action which promote its purposes.

Article IV.

The conditions of membership shall be wholly independent of party preference. Questions shall not be discussed in the debate or in the publications of the Association upon party grounds. Neither the name nor influence of the Association shall be used on behalf of any party, or for procuring office or promotion for any person. But nothing in this article shall be construed to prevent the Association from opposing any candidate when in its opinion, or in that of three-fourths of the members of the Executive Committee, such course is demanded by the objects of the Association.

Article V.

There shall be a President, to be elected by the Association at the annual meeting, who shall perform the usual and prescribed duties of that office. He shall be, ex-officio, a member of all committees, with a casting vote only, and he may call special meetings of the Executive Committee whenever he thinks it necessary, and, with the assent of two members of the Executive Committee, special meetings of the Association.

There shall be ten Vice-Presidents, to be annually elected by the Association.

There shall be a Treasurer and Secretary, who shall perform the usual and prescribed duties of such officers. They shall be respectively appointed by the Executive Committee, and may be removed by them. The Treasurer shall be, ex-officio, a member of the Finance Committee of the Association.

There shall be an Executive Committee of twenty five members, to be elected annually by the Association. Subject to these articles, the Executive Committee shall manage the affairs of the Association, direct and dispose of its funds, and from time to time make and modify by-laws for the Association and for its own action. The Executive Committee shall keep a record of its proceedings, and shall make a report to the

Association at the annual meeting. No appropriation of money by the Executive Committee beyond the amount in the hands of the Treasurer at the time shall bind any member of the Association, excepting those members of the Executive Committee who shall vote for it. Vacancies in the Executive Committee may be filled by the President for the remainder of the term. Other vacancies may be filled by the Executive Committee.

All the officers of the Association and members of the several Standing Committees shall be, ex-officio, members of the Executive Committee.

Article VI.

Each officer of the Association shall continue to hold office until his successor has been selected and is ready to enter upon the duties of the office.

Article VII.

There shall be an annual meeting of the Association on the second Wednesday of May, at which officers shall be elected for the ensuing year, and other appropriate business may be transacted; except in the year 1898, when the annual meeting shall be held on the second Wednesday of January.

Article VIII.

Any person may be proposed in writing for membership by any member of the Association, and shall be admitted upon approval of the Executive Committee. Members failing to pay their dues may be dropped from the roll by the Executive Committee.

Article IX.

The annual dues of each member shall be $5, payable on the 1st of May, and each member shall receive the annual report and all other publications of the Association. Sustaining members, on payment of twenty-five dollars annually, and Life members, exempt from annual dues on payment of one hundred dollars, may be elected by the Executive Committee at any regular meeting thereof.

Article X.

All provisions of this Constitution, except those relating to the rights of members, and the term of officers, may be suspended or amended by a vote of two-thirds of the Executive Committee, subject to the approval of the Association by a two-thirds vote of the members present either at the annual meeting or at a special meeting duly called. Due notice shall be given before any such annual or special meeting that the approval of the Association will, thereat, be asked for such action of the Executive Committee, and the notice shall clearly state the effect of such suspension or amendment in the text of the Constitution. Any member of the Association may propose amendments to the Constitution, which may be approved under the same conditions.

BY-LAWS.

FOR THE GOVERNMENT OF THE ASSOCIATION AND ITS COMMITTEES.

§ 1. The Annual meeting of the Association shall be held at such hour and place as the Executive Committee shall designate. The election of officers shall be by ballot, but any member not present may declare his vote by letter to the Secretary and it shall be counted.

§ 2. The meetings of each committee, unless otherwise especially provided for, shall be at half-past eight P. M., at which time the chairman shall direct the call of the names of its members and the Secretary shall record the names of those present and others as they appear.

§ 3. The order of business, before each committee shall be:

    1. The reading and correction of the records of the last meeting.

And, thereafter, unless otherwise ordered, as follows:

    2. Any statement due from the Treasurer.
    3. Unfinished business from the last meeting.
    4. Report from the Secretary's office.
    5. Reports of standing committees.
    6. Reports of special committees.
    7. Proposals of new members and their election.
    8. Miscellaneous business.

§ 4. Regular meetings of the Executive Committee shall be held on the second Wednesday of every month except July and August, but if that day be a holiday, then on the third Wednesday. Ten members of the Executive Committee shall constitute a quorum.

§ 5. Neither in the meetings of the Association nor of any committee shall any member speak more than once on any motion nor more than ten minutes at one time, without unanimous consent, nor shall any person, or his actions, be characterized on party grounds.

§ 6. Special meetings of any committee may be called by its chairman or by any three members, and due notice thereof shall be given by the Secretary.

§ 7. All notices to a member shall be sent to his address filed with the Secretary.

§ 8. On the demand of one-fifth of the members present, at any meeting of the Association or of a committee, the ayes and nays shall be called and recorded on any motion.

§ 9. All committees shall be appointed by the chair unless their selection shall be otherwise provided for.

§ 10. At each regular meeting of the Executive Committee, it shall be the duty of the Treasurer to make a statement of the amount of money in the treasury and of the place of its deposit, and, at the annual meeting, he shall state the source of all moneys received and the use made of the same during the past year.

§ 11. The Secretary shall keep a record of the proceedings of the Association and of the Executive Committee, and perform the other duties assigned him.

§ 12. Without the consent of three-fourths of the members present, no vote which will declare or fill a vacancy or elect a member of the Association shall be deemed carried, at the same meeting in which it was first moved.

§ 13. It shall require a vote of two-thirds of the members of the Executive Committee present to pass any vote under which more than $100 will be appropriated or the Association be pledged for more than that amount, and the Executive Committee alone shall have authority to create any charge upon the funds of the Association. But neither said committee nor any officer or officers of the Association shall be authorized to create a personal liability against any members but themselves.

§ 14. There shall be the following Standing Committees, of seven members each, which shall be selected annually by the Executive Committee:

(1) A Law Committee, whose duty it shall be to consider all legislation affecting the civil service, to promote such as may be approved, and to oppose such as may be disapproved by the Executive Committee, and to prepare and recommend

such amendments to the law as in their opinion will advance the purposes of the Association. The Law Committee shall have power to represent the Association in any legal proceedings which may be necessary in order to maintain or enforce the laws affecting the State or Municipal civil service.

(2) A Finance Committee, whose duty it shall be to devise and carry into effect, subject to the direction of the Executive Committee, suitable measures for raising funds, and to supervise and report upon the income and expenditures of the Association. The Finance Committee shall, in advance of each annual meeting of the Association, appoint an Auditing Committee from among its members, whose duty it shall be to examine all vouchers and audit the accounts of the Treasurer, and to report thereon at the annual meeting.

(3) A Publication Committee, whose duty it shall be to prepare and recommend matters suitable for publication by the Association, and to take charge of the printing and distribution of whatever may be ordered printed.

(4) A Committee on Correspondence, whose duty it shall be to promote the objects of the Association through correspondence and co-operation with other organizations.

(5) A Commitee on Examinations, whose duty it shall be to consider and recommend suitable methods of examination for admission to and promotion in the public service, and to investigate and report on the conduct of such examinations.

There shall also be a Standing Committee on Membership of fifteen members, which shall be selected annually by the Executive Committee. Its duties shall be to devise and carry into effect measures for increasing the membership of the Association.

Each Standing Committee shall be competent to fix the number of its own quorum; but such quorum shall in no case be less than three.

§ 15. These By-Laws may be amended, or new By-Laws added, by a four-fifths vote at any meeting of the Executive Committee; or by a two-thirds vote, provided a statement of the proposed change had been entered on the minutes at the last meeting.

§ 16. Amendments proposed under the last clause of the tenth section of the constitution shall be first submitted to the Executive Committee.

OFFICERS—1903-1904.

PRESIDENT:
CARL SCHURZ

VICE-PRESIDENTS:

JAMES C. CARTER	THEODORE ROOSEVELT
D. WILLIS JAMES	ELIHU ROOT
WILLIAM G. LOW	EDWARD M. SHEPARD
LEVI P. MORTON	OSCAR S. STRAUS
ALEXANDER E. ORR	EVERETT P. WHEELER

SECRETARY:
ELLIOT H. GOODWIN

ASSISTANT SECRETARY:
HENRY G. CHAPMAN

TREASURER:
A. S. FRISSELL

EXECUTIVE COMMITTEE:

JACOB F. MILLER, *Chairman.*	A. JACOBI
R. ROSS APPLETON	FRANKLIN B. LORD
SAMUEL P. AVERY	GEORGE McANENY
HENRY De FOREST BALDWIN	SAMUEL H. ORDWAY
CHARLES C. BURLINGHAM	GEORGE FOSTER PEABODY
SILAS W. BURT	WILLIAM JAY SCHIEFFELIN
EDWARD CARY	THOMAS R. SLICER
CHARLES COLLINS	HENRY SANGER SNOW
HORACE E. DEMING	ANSON PHELPS STOKES
SAMUEL B. DONNELLY	HENRY W. TAFT
J. WARREN GREENE	WILLIAM H. THOMSON
CHARLES W. WATSON	

Offices of the Association,
79 WALL STREET, NEW YORK

STANDING COMMITTEES.

LAW:

SAMUEL H. ORDWAY, *Chairman.* JOSEPH P. COTTON, JR.
HENRY DE FOREST BALDWIN J. WARREN GREENE
CHARLES C. BURLINGHAM HENRY W. HARDON
CHARLES E. HUGHES

FINANCE:

WILLIAM JAY SCHIEFFELIN, *Chairman.* JAMES J. HIGGINSON
JOHN G. AGAR JACOB W. MACK
L. T. CHAMBERLAIN SETH SPRAGUE TERRY
HORACE WHITE

PUBLICATION:

ROB'T UNDERWOOD JOHNSON, *Ch'n.* EDWARD CARY
GEORGE R. BISHOP RICHARD WATSON GILDER
R. C. E. BROWN B. LEARNED HAND
HENRY LOOMIS NELSON

CORRESPONDENCE:

WILLIAM POTTS, *Chairman.* HERBERT PARSONS
ALFORD WARRINER COOLEY WILLIAM H. RAND
WIRT HOWE CORNELIUS B. SMITH
WALTER U. TAYLOR

EXAMINATIONS:

SILAS W. BURT, *Chairman.* CHARLES COLLINS
CHARLES R. L. BARLOW JAY E. LAWSHE
HENRY G. CHAPMAN GEORGE McANENY
CLARENCE BISHOP SMITH

MEMBERSHIP:

EVERETT V. ABBOT, *Chairman.* ELLWOOD HENDRICK
ALBERT S. BARD FRANCIS H. KINNICUTT
EDWARDS S. CHILDS RUSSELL LOINES
R. BAYARD CUTTING WILLIS MUNRO
WINFRED T. DENISON J. H. C. NEVIUS
A. H. EASTMAN WILSON M. POWELL, JR.
GEORGE J. GREENFIELD CARL SCHURZ, JR.
J. G. PHELPS STOKES

MEMBERSHIP ROLL.

(May 1, 1903.)

SUSTAINING MEMBERS.

AMEND, BERNARD G.,	205 Third Avenue, New York City
AVERY, SAMUEL P.,	4 E. 38th Street, " " "
BOWKER, R. R.,	298 Broadway, New York City
BREWSTER, WILLIAM,	Broadway and 47th Street, " " "
BULL, WILLIAM LANMAN,	38 Broad Street, " " "
CARTER, JAMES C.,	54 Wall Street, New York City
CARY, EDWARD,	The "Times," " " "
CHAPLIN, DUNCAN D.,	64 Worth Street, " " "
CLYDE, WILLIAM P.,	5 Bowling Green, " " "
COLLINS, CHARLES,	33 E. 17th Street, " " "
CRANE, RICHARD T.,	2541 Michigan Avenue, Chicago, Ill.
CUTTING, R. FULTON,	32 Nassau Street, New York City
DAVISON, CHARLES STEWART,	56 Wall Street, New York City
DE COPPET, E. J.,	30 Broad Street, " " "
DEERING, JAMES,	Fullerton and Clybourne Avenues, Chicago, Ill.
DEMUTH, WILLIAM,	524 Fifth Avenue, New York City
DIMOCK, HENRY F.,	Pier 11, N. R., " " "
DODGE, WILLIAM E.,	11 Cliff Street, " " "
FRISSELL, A. S.,	530 Fifth Avenue, New York City
GILDER, RICHARD WATSON,	33 E. 17th Street, New York City
GOODWIN, J. J.,	11 W. 54th Street, " " "
HARRIOT, S. CARMAN,	454 W. 23rd Street, New York City
HEMENWAY, AUGUSTUS,	10 Tremont Street, Boston, Mass.
HUBER, JACQUES,	472 Broome Street, New York City
JACOBI, A.,	19 E. 47th Street, New York City
JOHNSON, ROBERT UNDERWOOD,	33 E. 17th Street, " " "
KENNEDY, JOHN S.,	31 Nassau Street, New York City
KUNHARDT, WILLIAM B.,	1 Broadway, " " "
LOEB, JAMES,	52 William Street, New York City
LOEB, SOLOMON,	P. O. Box 1193, " " "
LOW, SETH,	30 E. 64th Street, " " "
LOW, WILLIAM G.,	58 Remsen Street, Brooklyn

MACK, JACOB W., ... 92 Liberty Street, New York City
MACY, V. EVERIT, ... 68 Broad Street, " " "
MAITLAND, ALEXANDER, . . . 14 E. 55th Street, " " "
MAXWELL, ROBERT, ... 62 Worth Street, " " "
MILLER, JACOB F., ... 120 Broadway, " " "
MINTURN, ROBERT SHAW, . . 109 E. 21st Street, " " "
MORTON, LEVI P., ... 38 Nassau Street, " " "
MOSLE, GEORGE R., . . . 16–18 Exchange Place, " " "

McANENY, GEORGE, ... 19 E. 47th Street, New York City

OGDEN, ROBERT C. . . . . 784 Broadway, New York City
ORDWAY, SAMUEL H., ... 31 Nassau Street, " " "

PAGE, EDWARD D., ... 60 Worth Street, New York City
PAGE, WILLIAM H., Jr., . . 32 Liberty Street, " " "
PAGENSTECHER, A., ... P. O. Box 683, " " "
PEABODY, GEORGE FOSTER, . . 27 Pine Street, " " "
PINCHOT, JAMES W., ... 2 Gramercy Park, " " "
POWERS, NATHANIEL B., ..., Lansingburg, N. Y.

RANDOLPH, STUART F., ... 31 Nassau Street, New York City
RUSSELL, CHARLES H., ... 15 Broad Street, " " "

SANDS, B. AYMAR, ... 31 Nassau Street, New York City
SCHEFER, CARL, ... 476 Broome Street, " " "
SCHIEFFELIN, WILLIAM JAY, . . 5 E. 66th Street, " " "
SCHIFF, JACOB H., ... P. O. Box 1198, " " "
SCHWAB, GUSTAV H., ... 5 Broadway, " " "
SCRYMSER, JAMES A., ... 107 E. 21st Street, " " "
SHEPARD, EDWARD M., . . . 26 Liberty Street, " " "
SMITH, CORNELIUS B., . . . 101 E. 69th Street, " " "
SPENCER, NELSON S., ... 31 Nassau Street, " " "
SPEYER, JAMES, . . . 257 Madison Avenue, " " "
STETSON, FRANCIS LYNDE, . . 15 Broad Street, " " "
STOKES, ANSON PHELPS, . . 100 William Street, " " "
STRAUS, OSCAR S., ... 44 Warren Street, " " "

TRASK, SPENCER, ... 27 Pine Street, New York City

VOSS, F. G., ... 100 William Street, New York City

WARE, WILLIAM R., . . . Columbia University, New York City
WHITE, ALFRED T., ... 130 Water Street, " " "
WHITE, WILLIAM A., ... 130 Water Street, " " "
WUNDERLICH, F. W., ... 165 Remsen Street, Brooklyn

Abbot, Everett V., ... 59 Wall Street, New York City
Abbott, Lawrence F., ... "The Outlook," " " "
Abbott, Lyman, ... 287 Fourth Avenue, " " "
Achelis, John, ... 68 Leonard Street, " " "
Adams, Edward D., ... 35 Wall Street, " " "
Adams, Joseph, ... Union Stock Yards, Chicago, Ill.
Adams, Thatcher M., ... 36 Wall Street, New York City
Adler, Felix, ... 1524 Park Avenue, " " "
Affeld, Francis O., ... 873 President Street, Brooklyn
Agar, John G., ... 31 Nassau Street, New York City
Agnew, Andrew Gifford, ... 45 Wall Street, " " "
Aiken, William A., ... 157 Washington Street, Norwich, Conn.
Aitken, John W. . . . . . 873 Broadway, New York City
Albers Julius, ... 27 Grace Court, Brooklyn
Allen, Calvin H., ... 1 W. 72nd Street, New York City
Allen, Elmer A., ... 80 Broadway, " " "
Allen, Franklin, ... 371 Fulton Street, Brooklyn
Alling, Joseph T., ... 400 Oxford Street, Rochester, N. Y.
Alsop, Reese F., ... 127 Remsen Street, Brooklyn
Anderson, Frank E., ... 715 Broadway, New York City
Andrews, Avery D., ... 11 Broadway, " " "
Andrews, J. Sherlock, ... 111 St. Paul Street, Rochester, N. Y.
Appleton, D. F., ... 28 E. 36th Street, New York City
Appleton, R. Ross, ... 146 Joralemon Street, Brooklyn
Arnold, Lemuel H., ... 3 Broad Street, New York City
Arnstein, Eugene, ... 10 Wall Street, " " "
Atterbury, Grosvenor, . . . 18 W. 34th Street, " " "
Avery, Samuel P., Jr., . . . 4 E. 38th Street, " " "

Babbott, Frank L., ... 149 Lincoln Place, Brooklyn
Backus, Truman J., ... Packer Institute, "
Bacon, Gorham, ... 63 W. 54th Street, New York City
Bagley, Valentine N., . . . 641 Washington Street, " " "
Bailey, H. P., ... 312 Broadway, " " "
Baldwin, Elbert F., ... "The Outlook," " " "
Baldwin, Henry de Forest, . . . 49 Wall Street, " " "
Baldwin, William H., Jr., ... 128 Broadway, " " "
Ball, Thomas P., ... 116 Broad Street, " " "
Bangs, Francis S., ... 40 Wall Street, " " "
Bangs, L. Bolton, ... 39 E. 72nd Street, " " "
Bannard, Otto T., ... 30 Broad Street, " " "
Bard, Albert Sprague, ... 25 Broad Street, " " "
Barker, Benjamin, ... 120 Broadway, " " "
Barkley, Charles H., ... 82 Wall Street, " " "
Barlow, Charles L., ... 39 E. 31st Street, " " "
Barney, A. H., (Life) . . . 101 E. 38th Street, " " "
Barney, Danford N., ... Farmington, Conn
Barrett, Frank R., ... Box 616, Portland, Me.
Bartlett, P. G., ... 25 Broad Street, New York City
Batterman, Henry, ... 360 Clinton Avenue, Brooklyn
Baylies, Edmund L., ... 54 Wall Street, New York City

Bayne, Hugh,	40 Wall Street, New York City
Beckers, Alexander,	618 Hudson Street, Hoboken, N. J.
Beebe, William H. H.,	30 E. 64th Street, New York City
Beekman, Gerard,	47 Cedar Street, " " "
Beer, George Lewis,	65 Pine Street, " " "
Beers, Lucius H.,	49 Wall Street, " " "
Behr, Herman,	75 Beekman Street, " " "
Benson Frank Sherman,	214 Columbia Heights, Brooklyn
Biggs, Charles,	13 Astor Place, New York City
Bijur, Nathan,	34 Nassau Street, " " "
Bishop, George R.,	142 E. 18th Street, " " "
Bispham, William,	66 Broadway, " " "
Blagden, George,	18 E. 36th Street, " " "
Blair, John N.,	32 Liberty Street, " " "
Boas, Franz,	123 W. 82d Street, " " "
Bode, Frederick H.,	care Gage Bros., Chicago, Ill.
Boller, Alfred P.,	1 Nassau Street, New York City
Borden, M. C. D.,	Box 1794, " " "
Bowen, C. Winthrop,	5 E. 63rd Street, " " "
Brachhausen, G. A.,	Rahway, N. J.
Brackett, George C.,	50 Remsen Street, Brooklyn
Brewster, Charles O.,	32 Liberty Street, New York City
Briesen, Arthur von, (Life)	49 Wall Street, " " "
Briscoe, S. William,	61 Elm Street, " " "
Brite, James,	111 Fifth Avenue, " " "
Brown, Addison,	45 W. 89th Street, " " "
Brown, Augustus H.,	262 W. 136th Street, " " "
Brown, Edward M.,	235 West Street, " " "
Brown, Edwin H.,	141 Broadway, " " "
Brown, Everit,	56 Pine Street, " " "
Brown, Henry T.,	192 Lincoln Place, Brooklyn
Brown, Roscoe C. E.,	"Tribune Office, New York City
Brown, Thatcher M.,	36 E. 37th Street, " " "
Brownell, William C.,	153 Fifth Avenue, " " "
Brush, W. Franklin,	16 E. 37th Street, " " "
Buckingham, C. L.,	195 Broadway, " " "
Bunnell, James S.	49 Second Street, San Francisco, Cal.
Burlingham, Charles C.,	45 William Street, New York City
Burnett, Henry L.,	P. O. Building, " " "
Burr, Winthrop,	7 Wall Street, " " "
Burt, Silas W.,	30 Broad Street, " " "
Bush, J. Adriance,	110 Broadway, " " "
Butler, Howard R.,	22 E. 91st Street, " " "
Butler, Nicholas Murray,	119 E. 30th Street, " " "
Byrne, James,	30 Broad Street, " " "
Cadwalader, John L.,	40 Wall Street, New York City
Caesar, Henry A.,	20 Green Street, " " "
Cahen, I. J.,	1 Madison Avenue, " " "
Calkins, Leighton,	25 Broad Street, " " "

Canfield, George F.,	49 Wall Street, New York City
Carnegie, Andrew, (Life)	2 E. 91st Street, " " "
Carter, Frederick B.,	61 Church Street, Montclair, N. J.
Carter, George F.,	Fanwood, N. J.
Cary, Clarence,	59 Wall Street, New York City
Cassatt, George M.,	327 Broadway, " " "
Cauldwell, John B.,	Southampton, N. Y.
Chadwick, John White,	626 Carlton Avenue, Brooklyn
Chamberlain, D. H.,	West Brookfield Mass.
Chamberlain, L. T.,	222 W. 23 Street, New York City
Chambers, William,	59 Liberty Street, " " "
Chanute, Octave,	413 East Huron Street, Chicago, Ill.
Chapman, Henry G,	79 Wall Street, New York City
Chase, George,	35 Nassau Street, " " "
Chauncey, Daniel,	129 Joralemon Street, Brooklyn
Cheney, F. W.,	South Manchester, Conn.
Cheney, George L.,	131 E. 57th Street, New York City
Cheny, Louis R.,	Woodland Street, Hartford, Conn.
Cheritree, Theodore,	Niagara, N. Y.
Childs, Edwards H.,	59 Wall Street, New York City
Choate, Joseph H.,	American Embassy, London
Choate, William G.,	40 Wall Street, New York City
Cillis, Hubert,	20 Nassau Street, " " "
Claflin, John,	224 Church Street, " " "
Clarke, Samuel B.,	32 Nassau Street, " " "
Cleveland, Treadwell,	25 Broad Street, " " "
Codington, Perley M.,	32 W. 32nd Street, " " "
Cohen, William N.,	22 William Street, " " "
Collins, Atwood,	Asylum Avenue, Hartford, Conn.
Collins, Stephen W,	69 Wall Street, New York City
Collyer, Robert,	201 W. 55th Street, " " "
Comstock, Albert,	56 Pine Street, " " "
Conger, Clarence R.,	37 Liberty Street, " " "
Conger, Henry C.,	140 W. 82nd Street, " " "
Cook, Walter,	3 W. 29th Street, " " "
Cooley, Alford Warriner,	Westchester, " " "
Cope, Francis R,	1 Walnut Street, Philadelphia, Pa.
Cotton, Joseph P., Jr.,	52 William Street, New York City
Coudert, Frederick R., Jr.,	71 Broadway, " " "
Cowperthwait, J. Howard,	195 Park Row, " " "
Coykendall, S. D.,	33 Coenties Slip, " " "
Crane, Frederick,	Bloomfield, N. J.
Crane, Leroy B.,	237 Broadway, New York City
Cranford, Walter V.,	215 Montague Street, Brooklyn
Cravath, Paul D.,	52 William Street, New York City
Crawford, Gilbert H.,	32 Liberty Street, " " "
Creevey, John J.,	41 Wall Street, " " "
Cromwell, Frederic,	32 Nassau Street, " " "
Cromwell, Lincoln,	1 Greene Street, " " "

Cross, R. T.,	38 Nassau Street, New York City
Croswell, J. G.,	17 W. 44th Street, " " "
Curtis, William E.,	30 Broad Street, " " "
Cushing, William E.,	Society for Savings Bldg., Cleveland, O.
Cutler, Arthur H.,	20 E. 50th Street, New York City
Cutting, R. Bayard,	32 Nassau Street, " " "
Cutting, W. Bayard,	24 E. 72nd Street, " " "
Cuyler, C. C.,	44 Pine Street, " " "
Daboll, Henry E.,	30 Broad Street, New York City
Dana, Charles L.,	50 W. 46th Street, " " "
Davies, Julien T.,	32 Nassau Street, " " "
Davies, William Gilbert,	32 Nassau Street, " " "
Davis, Benjamin P.,	107 Wall Street, " " "
Davis, G. Pierrepont,	Woodland Street, Hartford, Conn.
Davis, Horace A.,	135 Broadway, New York City
Day, Clarence S.,	45 Wall Street, " " "
DeForest, R. W.,	30 Broad Street, " " "
Delano, Warren, Jr.,	1 Broadway, " " "
Deming, Horace E.,	13 William Street, " " "
Denison, Winfred T.,	126 E. 28th Street, " " "
Despard, W. D.,	6 Hanover Street, " " "
Dettmer, Jacob G.,	27 Prospect Park W., Brooklyn
Devine, Thomas J.,	19 Portsmouth Terrace, Rochester, N. Y.
DeWitt, Theodore,	88 Nassau Street, New York City
Dickinson, Robert L.,	168 Clinton Street, Brooklyn
Dittenhoefer, A. J.,	96 Broadway, New York City
Dodge, Cleveland H.,	99 John Street, " " "
Dominick, H. B.,	Broadway and 17th Street, " " "
Dommerich, L. F.,	57 Greene Street, " " "
Donnelly, Samuel B.,	369 Nostrand Avenue, Brooklyn
Doty, Ethan Allen,	726 St. Mark's Place, "
Dougherty, J. Hampden,	27 William Street, New York City
Dows, Tracy,	Room 102, Produce Exchange, " " "
Dulon, Rudolf,	115 Broadway, " " "
Dunham, Edward K.,	338 E. 26th Street, " " "
Dunham, Lawrence,	7 E. 42nd Street, " " "
Dunning, S. Wright,	80 Madison Avenue, " " "
Eastman, A. H.,	363 Grand Avenue, Brooklyn
Eaton, S. Edward,	20 Fulton Street, New York City
Ecaubert, F.,	18 Rose Street, " " "
Elderkin, John,	150 W. 83d Street, " " "
Eliot, Charles W.,	Cambridge, Mass.
Elkins, Stephen B.,	1626 K Street, Washington, D. C.
Ely, Alfred,	31 Nassau Street, New York City
Ely, Arthur H.,	56 Wall Street, " " "
Ely, Moses,	2 Wall Street, " " "
Ely, Robert E.,	23 West 44th Street, " " "
Emmons, Arthur B.,	60 Park Avenue, " " "
Emmons, Samuel F.,	U. S. Geological Survey, Washington, D. C.

Erbslöh, R., ... 364 Broadway, New York City
Everest, Charles M., ... 350 West Avenue, Rochester, N. Y.
Ewart, Richard H., ... 115 Franklin Street, New York City

Fabbri, Alessandro, ... 11 E. 62d Street, New York City
Fabbri, Ernesto G., ... 11 E. 62d Street, " " "
Fahnestock, H. C., ... 2 Wall Street, " " "
Fairchild, Benjamin T., . . . P. O. Box 1120, " " "
Fairchild, Charles S., . . . 46 Wall Street, " " "
Faure, John P., ... 346 Broadway, " " "
Fay, Charles, ... 49 Wall Street, " " "
Fechheimer, M. S., ... 748 Broadway, " " "
Fisher, George H., ... 308 Walnut Street, Philadelphia, Pa.
Fisher, George H., ... 310 Throop Avenue, Brooklyn
Fleitmann, Ewald, ... 484 Broome Street, New York City
Floyd, John G., ... 138 E. 37th Street, " " "
Ford, Worthington C., . Care Library of Congress, Washington, D. C.
Forrest, C. R., ... Asylum Avenue, Hartford, Conn.
Foster, Abbott, ... Box 16, Litchfield, "
Fox, Austen G., (Life), . . . 45 W. 33d Street, New York City
Fraenckel, Richard H., . . 19 and 21 Greene Street, " " "
Frankenheimer, John, . . . 22 Broad Street, " " "
Frissell, H. B., ... Hampton, Va.
Frothingham, Howard P., . . . 2 Wall Street, New York City
Fuller, Frank, ... , . 61 Fifth Avenue, " " "
Fuller, Paul, ... 100 Broadway, " " "
Fullerton, Alexander, (Life), . 5 University Place, " " "
Fullerton, Henry S., ... 71 Broadway, " " "
Fulton, Thomas A., ... 34 Union Square, East, " " "
Funk, T. K., ... 195 Washington Park, Brooklyn

Gaillard, William D., ... 141 Broadway, New York City
Garrison, Wendell P., ... 206 Broadway, " " "
Garver, John A., ... 44 Wall Street, " " "
Gibbs, Theodore K., ... 137 Broadway, " " "
Gibson, William J., ... 26 Liberty Street, " " "
Gitterman, John M., . . . 63 William Street, " " "
Goadby, Clarence, . . . 21 W. 35th Street, " " "
Goddard, George A., . . . 10 Tremont Street, Boston, Mass.
Goldman, Julius, ... 31 Nassau Street, New York City
Goldmark, James, ... 121 Worth Street, " " "
Goodale, John McGregor, . . . 271 Broadway, " " "
Goodnow, Frank J., . . . 49 Riverside Drive, " " "
Goodwin, Elliot H., ... 79 Wall Street, " " "
Goddard, Norton, ... 93 Bleecker Street, " " "
Gottheil, Paul, ... Produce Exchange, " " "
Gould, Elgin R. L., . . . 281 Fourth Avenue, " " "
Grant, De Forest, ... 22 E. 46th Street, " " "
Grant, Percy S., ... 7 W. 10th Street, " " "
Green, George Walton, . . . 30 Broad Street, " " "

Green, Noah, ... 10 E. 130th Street, New York City
Greenbaum, Samuel. . . . . 141 Broadway, " " "
Greene, Francis V., ... 33 E. 30th Street, " " "
Greene, Jacob L.. . . . . Hartford, Conn.
Greene, J. Warren, ... 3 Broad Street, New York City
Greenfield, George J., ... 32 Broadway, " " "
Greenough, John, ... 31 W. 35th Street, " " "
Greer, David H., ... 342 Madison Avenue, " " "
Grinnell, William Morton, . . . 20 Broad Street, " " "
Gross, Charles E., ... Asylum Avenue, Hartford, Conn.
Gulliver, W. C., ... 120 Broadway, New York City
Guthrie, William D., . . . 52 William Street, " " "
Gwynne, Arthur C., ... Rye, N. Y.
Gwynne, John A., ... " "

Hagemeyer, F. E., . . . F 15, Produce Exchange, New York City
Hall, Elial F., ... 108 St. Joseph Street, Mobile, Ala.
Hall, Valentine G., ... 45 Broadway, New York City
Hamilton, E. Luther, ... 146 Broadway, " " "
Hamlin, Frank. H . . . . Canandaigua, N. Y.
Hand, Augustus N., ... 49 Wall Street, New York City
Hand, Learned, ... 49 Wall Street, " " "
Harbeck, Charles T., ... Islip, N. Y.
Harding, Edward,. . . . . 54 Wall Street, New York City
Hardon, Henry Winthrop, . . . 313 W. 71st Street, " " "
Hasslacher, Jacob, ... 100 William Street, " " "
Hastings, Thomas S., ... 27 W. 45th Street, " " "
Hayes, J. Noble, ... 120 Broadway, " " "
Heath, Frank E., ... 95 Liberty Street, " " "
Healy, A. Augustus, ... 198 Columbia Heights, Brooklyn
Henderson, Harold G., ... 128 E. 34th Street, New York City
Hendrick, Ellwood, ... 139 E. 40th Street, " " "
Henriques, C. A., ... 25 W. 49th Street, " " "
Hentz, Henry, ... 769 St. Mark's Avenue, Brooklyn
Hentz, Leonard S., ... 769 St. Mark's Avenue, "
Hessberg, Max, ... 13 William Street, New York City
Hicks, Benjamin D., ... Old Westbury, N. Y.
Higginson, James J., ... 16 E. 41st Street, New York City
Hill, J. E. R., ... 115 High Street, Boston, Mass.
Hill, John Sprunt, ... 37 Liberty Street, New York City
Hinrichs, Frederick W., ... 76 William Street, " " "
Hitchcock, Welcome G., (Life) . . 453 Broome Street, " " "
Hobart, Henry L., ... 120 Front Street, " " "
Hoe, Richard M., . . . Room 102, Produce Exchange, " " "
Hoe, Robert, ... 504 Grand Street, " " "
Holls, Frederick W., ... 120 Broadway, " " "
Holt, George C., ... 34 Pine Street, " " "
Holt, Henry, ... 29 W. 23d Street, " " "
Holt, Roland, ... 711 Madison Avenue, " " "
Hooper, Franklin W., ... 71 St. James Place, Brooklyn

Hoppin, Frederick S., Jr.., ... 131 E. 19th Street, New York City
Hoppin, William W., ... 111 Broadway, " " "
Hornblower, William B., . . . 30 Broad Street, " " "
Howe, Daniel R., ... Asylum Avenue. Hartford, Conn.
Howe, Wirt, ... 27 William Street, New York City
Howland, Charles P., ... 35 Wall Street, " " "
Hoyt, Gerald L., ... 9 W 37th Street, " " "
Hubbard, Thomas H., ... 16 W. 58th Street, " " "
Hubbell, Charles Bulkeley, ... 2 Wall Street, " " "
Hughes, Charles E., ... 96 Broadway, " " "
Hull. Charles A., ... 72 Wall Street, " " "
Huntington, Francis C., . . . 54 William Street, " " "
Huntington, Samuel. . . . . . 146 Broadway, " " "
Huntington, William R., ... 804 Broadway, " " "

Ide, George E., ... 256 Broadway, New York City
Ireland, F. G., ... 61 Elm Street, " " "
Isaacs, Myer S., ... 27 Pine Street. " " "
Ives, Brayton, ... 37 Wall Street, " " "

Jackson, Frederick W., ... Westchester, N. Y.
James, D. Willis, ... 11 Cliff Street, New York City
Jay, Pierre, ... 49 E. 64th Street, " " "
Jay, William, ... 48 Wall Street, " " "
Jefferson. Joseph, ... , , . . Buzzards Bay, Mass.
Jennings, Frederick B., . . . 15 Broad Street, New York City
Jesup, Morris K., ... 195 Madison Avenue, " " "
Johnson. James G., ... 655 Broadway, " " "
Johnson, Willis Fletcher, ... 154 Nassau Street, " " "
Jones, Edward H., . . . Naval Office, Custom House, " " "

Kahn, Otto H.. (Life), . . . 27 Pine Street, New York City
Kane, S. Nicholson, ... 23 W. 47th Street, " " "
Kelsey, Clarence H., ... 146 Broadway, " " "
Kenneson, Thaddeus D., . . . 13 William Street, " " "
Kenyon, Alan D., ... 49 Wall Street, " " "
Kenyon, William Houston. . . . 49 Wall Street, " " "
Keppler, Rudolph, . . . , . 25 Broad Street, " " "
Kernan, John D., ... 37 Liberty Street, " " "
Kick, Ludwig, ... Passaic, N. J.
Kidder, Camillus G., . . . 27 William Street, New York City
Kidder, Edward H., ... 170 Broadway. " " "
Kimball, A. R., ... Orange, N. J.
King, William F., ... 346 Broadway, New York City
Kinnicutt. Francis H., ... 32 Liberty Street, " " "
Kinnicutt, Francis P., ... 42 W. 37th Street, " " "
Kirchhoff, Charles, ... 232 William Street, " " "
Kissell, Gustav E., (Life), . . . 32 Liberty Street, " " "
Kohler, Max J., ... 119 Nassau Street, " " "
Klupfel, Charles, Care North German Lloyd. 5 Broadway, " " "
Knauth, Antonio, ... 233 West 70th Street, " " "

Klein, Isaac H., ... 45 Cedar Street, New York City
Kuhne, Percival, ... 13 William Street, " " "
Kunhardt, Henry R., ... 124 W. 74th Street, " " "

Laimbeer, Francis E., ... 99 Nassau Street, New York City
Lambert, William B., ... Highland Avenue, Cambridge Mass.
Lambert, William S., ... Produce Exchange, New York City
Lansing J. Townsend, ... 82 State Street, Albany, N. Y.
Larocque, Joseph, ... 40 Wall Street, New York City
Larremore, Wilbur, ... 32 Nassau Street, " " "
Lawrence, Cyrus J., ... 15 Wall Street, " " "
Lawrence, Richard H., ... 15 Wall Street, " " "
Lawshe, Jay E., ... 69 Wall Street, " " "
Lea, Henry Charles, . . . 2000 Walnut Street, Philadelphia, Pa.
Leavens, George St. J., . . . 72 Bible House, New York City
Leavitt, J. Brooks, ... 111 Broadway, " " "
Leaycraft, J. Edgar, ... 19 W. 42nd Street, " " "
Lederle, Ernest J., ... Dept. of Health, " " "
Ledoux, Albert R., ... 9 Cliff Street, " " "
Lee, W. H. L., ... 20 Nassau Street, " " "
Le Gendre, William, ... 59 Wall Street, " " "
Lehmaier, Louis A., ... 78 Beekman Street, " " "
Levi, Albert A., ... 108 Exchange Court, " " "
Levi, Joseph C., ... 35 Nassau Street, " " "
Lewis, August, ... 151 Greene Street, " " "
Lewis, Richard V., ... 130 W. 42d Street, " " "
Lindsay, Alexander M., . . . 373 East Avenue, Rochester, N. Y.
Littauer, Lucius N., ... Gloversville, N. Y.
Lockwood, Benoni, ... 56 Irving Place, New York City
Loeb, Morris, ... 118 W. 72d Street, " " "
Logan, Walter S., ... 27 William Street, " " "
Loines, Russell H., ... 26 Garden Place, Brooklyn
Loines, Stephen, ... 26 Garden Place, "
Lord, Franklin B., ... 49 Wall Street, New York City
Lord, F. B., Jr., ... 49 Wall Street, " " "
Lounsbery, Richard P., . . . 15 Broad Street, " " "
Lovell, Joseph J., ... Avondale Place, Woodhaven, N. Y.
Low, C. Adolph, ... 41 Liberty Street, New York City
Lowndes, James, . . . 1505 Pennsylvania Avenue, Washington, D. C.
Ludlow, James B., ... 45 Cedar Street, New York City
Luther, George Martin, . . . 25 Broad Street, " " "
Lyman, Frank, ... 50 Remsen Street, Brooklyn
Lyman, George T., ... Bellport, N. Y.
Lyman, Theodore, ... Woodland Street, Hartford, Conn.
Lynde, Rollin H., ... 31 Pine Street, New York City

Macdonough, A. R., ... 105 E. 15th Street, New York City
Macfarlane, Wallace, ... 32 Liberty Street, " " "
MacVeagh, Charles, ... 15 Broad Street, " " "
Magee, John H., ... Scottsburg, N. Y.
Mallinckrodt, Edward, . . Mallinckrodt Chemical Works, St. Louis, Mo.

Mansfield, Howard, ... 49 Wall Street, New York City
Mapes, Charles V., ... 143 Liberty Street, " " "
Markoe, Francis H., ... 15 E. 49th Street, " " "
Marshall, Charles H., ... 45 William Street, " " "
Marshall, Fielding L., ... 35 Nassau Street, " " "
Marshall, Louis, ... 30 Broad Street, " " "
Marsters, A., A., ... 15 Dey Street, " " "
Martin, John, ... 973 Lexington Avenue, " " "
Martin, Newell, ... 25 Broad Street, " " "
Martin, T. Comerford, ... 120 Liberty Street, " " "
Mason, Alfred Bishop, ... Apartado 130, City of Mexico
Mason, James Weir, ... 82 W. 129th Street, New York City
Mathews, Albert, ... 222 W. 23d Street, " " "
Matthews, Brander, . . . 681 West End Avenue, " " "
Mathews, Robert, ... 135 Spring Street, Rochester, N. Y.
Matthewson, Arthur, ... 139 Montague Street, Brooklyn
Maxwell, William H., ... 121 W. 82nd Street, New York City
Mellen, Chase, ... 45 Cedar Street, " " "
Merck, George, ... 15 University Place, " " "
Merrill, Charles E., ... 43 E. 10th Street, " " "
Merrill, Payson, ... 31 Nassau Street, " " "
Meyer, Jacob, ... 29 E. 63d Street, " " "
Miller, Hoffman, ... 80 Broadway, " " "
Miller, Theodore C., ... 177 Montague Street, Brooklyn
Mitchell, Edward, ... 31 E. 50th Street, New York City
Moffat, George B., ... 1 Nassau Street, " " "
Moffat, R. Burnham, ... 63 Wall Street, " " "
Montgomery, R. M., ... 25 Pine Street, " " "
Moore, W. H. H., ... Box 402, " " "
Morse, Horace J., ... 820 St. Mark's Avenue, Brooklyn
Morse, James H., ... 423 Madison Avenue, New York City
Morse, Richard C., ... 13 W. L.9th Street, " " "
Mortimer, Richard, ... 11 Wall Street, " " "
Mosenthal, P. J., ... 46 Cedar Street, " " "
Mosle, A. Henry, ... 30 Broad Street, " " "
Mott, William F., ... Toms River, N. J.
Munro, J. G., ... 61 Erie County Bank Building, Buffalo, N. Y.
Munro, Willis, ... Criminal Court Building, New York City
Murray, James B., ... 23 Belmont Terrace, Yonkers, N. Y.
Murray, Joseph K., ... 63 Wall Street, New York City
Myers, Nathaniel, ... 25 Broad Street, " " "

McAlpin, George L., ... 9 E. 90th Street, New York City
McCagg, Louis Butler, ... 291 Madison Avenue, " " "
McClain, John F., ... 327 Broadway, " " "
McCook, Philip J., ... 120 Broadway, " " "
McKeen, James, ... 136 Henry Street, Brooklyn
McKeever, J. Lawrence, . . . 164 Lexington Avenue, New York City
McKim, John A., ... 18 Wall Street, " " "
McMahon, Fulton, ... 54 William Street, " " "

Nadal, Charles C., ... 143 E. 35th Street, New York City
Naumberg, Elkan, ... 48 W. 58th Street, " " "
Naumberg. George W., ... 33 Wall Street, " " "
Naumberg, Walter W., ... 33 Wall Street, " " "
Nelson, Henry Loomis, . . Williams.College, Williamstown, Mass.
Nelson, H. W., Jr., ... Marshfield Hills, "
Nevius, John H. C., ... 33 Union Square, New York City
Newton, R. Heber, . . . Leland Stanford Univ., Palo Alto. Cal.
Newton, Virginius, ... Box 906. Richmond, Va.
Nichols, George M., ... 277 Adelphi Street, Brooklyn
Nichols, W. N., ... 353 Clinton Avenue, "
Nicoll, James C., ... 51 W. 10th Street, New York City
North. Thomas M., . . . 160 Central Park South, " " "
Nourse, Charles J., Jr., ... 27 William Street, " " "

Oakes, Charles, ... 9 Pine Street. New York City
O'Connor, John A., ... 12 E. 44th Street. " " "
Olin, Stephen H., ... 32 Nassau Street, " " "
Olyphant, Robert, . . . 21 Cortlandt Street, " " "
Opdyke, William S., ... 20 Nassau Street, " " "
Orr, Alexander E., ... 102 Remsen Street, Brooklyn
Osborn, William Church, ... 71 Broadway, New York City
Osborne, Thomas M., ... Auburn, N. Y.

Packard, Edwin, ... 241 Henry Street, Brooklyn
Page. Walter H., ... 34 Union Square, New York City
Parker, Frederick S., ... 32 Garden Place, Brooklyn
Parrish, Samuel L., ... 44 Broadway, New York City
Parsons, Herbert, ... 111 Broadway, " " "
Parsons, John E., ... 111 Broadway, " " "
Paulding, James Kirk, ... 130 E. 24th Street. " " "
Pauli, H. G., ... 15 S. William Street, " " "
Peck, George G., ... 18 East 65th Street, " " "
Peckham, W. G., ... 54 William Street. " " "
Peckham, Wheeler H., ... 80 Broadway, " " "
Pedesen, James, ... 20 E. 46th Street, " " "
Pell, Frederick A., ... 51 Wall Street, " " "
Pendleton, Francis K., ... 25 Broad Street, " " "
Perkins, Robert P., ... 41 Union Square, " " "
Perrine, William A., ... 23 Park Row, " " "
Phillips, Lee, ... 247 W. 71st Street, " " "
Phoenix, Phillips, ... 68 Broad Street, " " "
Pierce, Franklin, ... 31 Nassau Street, " " "
Pierrepont, Henry E., ... 216 Columbia Heights, Brooklyn
Pierrepont, Robert Low, . . . 216 Columbia Heights, "
Pinchot, Gifford, . . . 1615 Rhode Island Avenue, Washington, D. C.
Pope, A. A., ... Pope Building. Boston, Mass.
Pope, George A., ... 926 St. Paul Street, Baltimore, Md.
Pott, James, ... 119 W. 23d Street, New York City
Potter, Frederick, ... 71 Broadway, " " "

Potter, Henry C., ... 113 W. 40th Street, New York City
Potts, William, ... 65 Essex Avenue, Orange, N. J.
Powell. Wilson M., Jr., . . . 29 Wall Street. New York City
Prentice, William P., ... 52 Broadway, " " "
Pryer, Charles, ... New Rochelle, N. Y.
Pryor, James W., ... 19 W. 34th Street, New York City
Putnam, George Haven, . . . 27 W. 23d Street, " " "
Putnam, George P., ... 160 Fifth Avenue, " " "
Putnam, Harrington, ... 404 Washington Avenue, Brooklyn
Putnam, Irving, ... 27 W. 23rd Street, New York City
Pyne, Moses Taylor, ... 42 W. 53d Street, " " "

Rainsford, W. S., ... 209 E. 16th Street, New York City
Rand, George C., ... 107 Wall Street, " " "
Rand. William H., Jr. . . . Criminal Court Building, " " "
Raven, A. A., ... 51 Wall Street, " " "
Raymond, Charles H., ... 32 Liberty Street, " " "
Raymond, Rossiter W. . . . . 123 Henry Street, Brooklyn
Reichhelm, Edward P., ... 23 John Street, New York City
Reynolds, James B., ... 19 W. 34th Street, " " "
Rice, Edwin T., Jr., ... 59 Wall Street, " " "
Richards, C. A. L., ... 169 Power Street, Providence, R. I.
Rives, George L., ... 14 W. 38th Street. New York City
Robb, J. Hampden, ... 23 Park Avenue, " " "
Robinson, Beverly R., ... 42 W. 37th Street, " " "
Rogers, Henry A. . . . . 19 John Street, " " "
Romaine, Louis Tyson, ... 84 Beaver Street, " " "
Roome, W. Harris, ... 287 Fourth Avenue, " " "
Roosevelt, Theodore, ... Oyster Bay, N. Y.
Root, Elihu, ... War Department, Washington, D. C.
Rose, Arthur P., ... Geneva. N. Y.
Rose, Charles J., ... " "
Rosenbaum, S. D., ... 51 Franklin Street, New York City
Rosenfield, George, . . . 35 South William Street, " " "
Rowe, William V., ... 49 Wall Street, " " "
Rumsey, Dexter P., ... 742 Delaware Street, Buffalo, N. Y.

Saint Gaudens, Augustus, ... Windsor, Vt.
Salomon, William, ... 2 Wall Street, New York City
Sand, Max E., ... Ardsley-on-Hudson, N. Y.
Sanger, William Cary, . . . War Department, Washington. D. C.
Savage, Minot J., . . . 34th Street and Park Avenue, New York City
Sayer, W. Murray, Jr., ... 398 Washington Avenue, Brooklyn
Scharmann, Hermann B., . . . 170 W. 59th Street, New York City
Schieren, Charles A. . . . . 405 Clinton Avenue, Brooklyn
Schnakenberg, D., ... 6 Hanover Street, New York City
Schrader, George H. F., ... 32 Rose Street, " " "
Schumacher, Charles, . . . 41 Exchange Place, " " "
Schurman, George W., . . . 15 W. 57th Street, " " "
Schurman, Jacob Gould, ... Cornell University, Ithaca, N. Y.

Nadal, Charles C.,	143 E. 35th Street, New York City
Naumberg, Elkan,	48 W. 58th Street, " " "
Naumberg, George W.,	33 Wall Street, " " "
Naumberg, Walter W.,	33 Wall Street, " " "
Nelson, Henry Loomis,	Williams College, Williamstown, Mass.
Nelson, H. W., Jr.,	Marshfield Hills, "
Nevius, John H. C.,	33 Union Square, New York City
Newton, R. Heber,	Leland Stanford Univ., Palo Alto, Cal.
Newton, Virginius,	Box 906, Richmond, Va.
Nichols, George M.,	277 Adelphi Street, Brooklyn
Nichols, W. N.,	353 Clinton Avenue, "
Nicoll, James C.,	51 W. 10th Street, New York City
North, Thomas M.,	160 Central Park South, " " "
Nourse, Charles J., Jr.,	27 William Street, " " "
Oakes, Charles,	9 Pine Street, New York City
O'Connor, John A.,	12 E. 44th Street, " " "
Olin, Stephen H.,	32 Nassau Street, " " "
Olyphant, Robert,	21 Cortlandt Street, " " "
Opdyke, William S.,	20 Nassau Street, " " "
Orr, Alexander E.,	102 Remsen Street, Brooklyn
Osborn, William Church,	71 Broadway, New York City
Osborne, Thomas M.,	Auburn, N. Y.
Packard, Edwin,	241 Henry Street, Brooklyn
Page, Walter H.,	34 Union Square, New York City
Parker, Frederick S.,	32 Garden Place, Brooklyn
Parrish, Samuel L.,	44 Broadway, New York City
Parsons, Herbert,	111 Broadway, " " "
Parsons, John E.,	111 Broadway, " " "
Paulding, James Kirk,	130 E. 24th Street, " " "
Pauli, H. G.,	15 S. William Street, " " "
Peck, George G.,	18 East 65th Street, " " "
Peckham, W. G.,	54 William Street, " " "
Peckham, Wheeler H.,	80 Broadway, " " "
Pedersen, James,	20 E. 46th Street, " " "
Pell, Frederick A.,	51 Wall Street, " " "
Pendleton, Francis K.,	25 Broad Street, " " "
Perkins, Robert P.,	41 Union Square, " " "
Perrine, William A.,	23 Park Row, " " "
Phillips, Lee,	247 W. 71st Street, " " "
Phoenix, Phillips,	68 Broad Street, " " "
Pierce, Franklin,	31 Nassau Street, " " "
Pierrepont, Henry E.,	216 Columbia Heights, Brooklyn
Pierrepont, Robert Low,	216 Columbia Heights, "
Pinchot, Gifford,	1615 Rhode Island Avenue, Washington, D. C.
Pope, A. A.,	Pope Building, Boston, Mass.
Pope, George A.,	926 St. Paul Street, Baltimore, Md.
Pott, James,	119 W. 23d Street, New York City
Potter, Frederick,	71 Broadway, " " "

Potter, Henry C., . . . 113 W. 40th Street, New York City
Potts, William, ... 65 Essex Avenue, Orange, N. J.
Powell. Wilson M., Jr., . . 29 Wall Street. New York City
Prentice, William P., . . . 52 Broadway, " " "
Pryer, Charles, ... New Rochelle, N. Y.
Pryor, James W., ... 19 W. 34th Street, New York City
Putnam, George Haven, . . 27 W. 23d Street, " " "
Putnam, George P., . . . 160 Fifth Avenue, " " "
Putnam, Harrington, . . . 404 Washington Avenue, Brooklyn
Putnam, Irving, ... 27 W. 23rd Street, New York City
Pyne, Moses Taylor, . . . 42 W. 53d Street, " " "

Rainsford, W. S., ... 209 E. 16th Street, New York City
Rand, George C., ... 107 Wall Street, " " "
Rand, William H., Jr. . . Criminal Court Building, " " "
Raven, A. A., ... 51 Wall Street, " " "
Raymond, Charles H., . . . 32 Liberty Street, " " "
Raymond, Rossiter W. . . . 123 Henry Street, Brooklyn
Reichhelm, Edward P., . . . 23 John Street, New York City
Reynolds, James B., . . . 19 W. 34th Street, " " "
Rice, Edwin T., Jr., . . . 59 Wall Street, " " "
Richards, C. A. L., . . . 169 Power Street, Providence, R. I.
Rives, George L., ... 14 W. 38th Street. New York City
Robb, J. Hampden, . . . 23 Park Avenue, " " "
Robinson, Beverly R., . . . 42 W. 37th Street, " " "
Rogers, Henry A. . . . . 19 John Street, " " "
Romaine, Louis Tyson, . . . 84 Beaver Street, " " "
Roome, W. Harris, . . . 287 Fourth Avenue, " " "
Roosevelt, Theodore, ... Oyster Bay, N. Y.
Root, Elihu, ... War Department, Washington, D. C.
Rose, Arthur P., ... Geneva. N. Y.
Rose, Charles J., ...
Rosenbaum, S. D., ... 51 Franklin Street, New York City
Rosenfield, George, . . . 35 South William Street, " " "
Rowe, William V., ... 49 Wall Street, " " "
Rumsey, Dexter P., . . . 742 Delaware Street, Buffalo, N. Y.

Saint Gaudens, Augustus, ... Windsor, Vt.
Salomon, William, . . . 2 Wall Street, New York City
Sand, Max E., ... Ardsley-on-Hudson, N. Y.
Sanger, William Cary, . . War Department, Washington, D. C.
Savage, Minot J., . . 34th Street and Park Avenue, New York City
Sayer, W. Murray, Jr., . . . 398 Washington Avenue, Brooklyn
Scharmann, Hermann B., . . 170 W. 59th Street, New York City
Schieren, Charles A. . . . 405 Clinton Avenue, Brooklyn
Schnakenberg, D., . . . 6 Hanover Street, New York City
Schrader, George H. F., . . . 32 Rose Street, " " "
Schumacher, Charles, . . . 41 Exchange Place, " " "
Schurman, George W., . . . 15 W. 57th Street, " " "
Schurman, Jacob Gould, . . . Cornell University, Ithaca, N. Y.

Schurz, Carl,	24 E. 91st Street, New York City
Schurz, Carl Lincoln,	19 William Street, " " "
Scott, J. F.,	349 W. 121st Street, " " "
Scribner, Arthur H.,	153 Fifth Avenue. " " "
Scribner, Charles,	153 Fifth Avenue, " " "
Searle. Arthur,	41 Concord Avenue, Cambridge, Mass.
Seaver, Benjamin F.,	111 Pierrepont Street, Brooklyn
Sedgwick, Arthur G.,	52 William Street, New York City
Sedgwick, Ellery,	143 Fifth Avenue, " " "
Sedgwick, Henry D., Care Mrs. Minturn, 109 E. 21st Street, " " "
Seligman, E. R. A.,	324 W. 86th Street, " " "
Serveu, A. Ralph,	Civil Service Commission, Washington, D. C.
Seward, George F.,	97 Cedar Street, New York City
Sexton, Lawrence E.,	34 Pine Street, " " "
Shainwald, Ralph L.,	100 William Street, " " "
Shaw, Albert,	13 Astor Place, " " "
Sheldon, Edward W.,	45 Wall Street, " " "
Sherman, Arnold W,	265 Henry Street, Brooklyn
Sherman, Frederick T.,	265 Henry Street, "
Shillaber, William Jr.,	1 Broadway, New York City
Siedenberg, Reinhard,	Cotton Exchange, " " "
Simes, William,	Petersham, Mass.
Sinclair, John,	16 E. 66th Street, New York City
Slicer, Thomas R.,	156 E. 38th Street, " " "
Slosson, J. Lawrence,	Geneva, N. Y.
Smillie, James D.,	110 E. 38th Street, New York City
Smith, Adelbert J.,	108 Madison Avenue, " " "
Smith, Bryan H.,	79 Pierrepont Street, Brooklyn
Smith, Charles Robinson,	25 Broad Street, New York City
Smith, Charles Stewart,	25 W. 47th Street, " " "
Smith, Clarence B.,	101 E. 69th Street, " " "
Smith, Frederick J.,	61 Elm Street, " " "
Smith, J. Henry,	10 Wall Street, " " "
Smith, William Alexander,	71 Broadway, " " "
Smyth, Nathan A.,	Criminal Court Building, " " "
Snow, Henry Sanger,	81 Willoughby Street, Brooklyn
Spahr, Charles B.,	Care "The Outlook," New York City
Spaulding, Henry K.,	501 W. 120th Street, " " "
Stapler, H. B. B.,	48 Wall Street, " " "
Stark, Joshua,	Sentinel Building, Milwaukee, Wis.
Stedman, Edmund C.,	Bronxville, New York City
Steers, James R.,	31 Nassau Street, " " "
Steinway, Frederick T.,	53rd Street and Park Avenue, " " "
Sternberger, M. M.,	117 W. 74th Street, " " "
Stewart, William R.,	31 Nassau Street, " " "
Stickney, Joseph,	1 Broadway, " " "
Stimson, Daniel M.,	11 W. 17th Street, " " "
Stoiber, Louis,	722 Broadway, " " "
Stokes, Anson Phelps, Jr., (Life),	Yale University, New Haven, Conn.
Stokes, Harold M. Phelps, (Life),	229 Madison Avenue, New York City

Stokes, I. N. Phelps, (Life),	229 Madison Avenue, New York City
Stokes, James,	49 Cedar Street, " " "
Stokes, J. G. Phelps, (Life),	229 Madison Avenue, " " "
Strauss, Albert,	15 Broad Street, " " "
Strauss, Frederick.	15 Broad Street, " " "
Sturgis, Russell,	307 E. 17th Street, " " "
Strong, George A.,	50 Wall Street, " " "
Strong, Theron G.,	49 Wall Street, " " "
Sturges, S. Perry,	305 Washington Avenue, Brooklyn
Sturgis, Thomas,	138 E. 36th Street, New York City
Stuyvesant, Rutherford,	16 Exchange Place, " " "
Sulzberger, Ferdinand,	45th Street and First Avenue, " " "
Swan, Lyndon M.,	7 Wall Street, " " "
Taft, Henry W.,	40 Wall Street, New York City
Taggard, Rush,	195 Broadway, " " "
Tatham, Charles,	302 Lexington Avenue, " " "
Tatham, Edwin,	82 Beekman Street, " " "
Taussig, Walter M.,	9-15 Murray Street, " " "
Taylor, Henry Ling,	60 W. 55th Street, " " "
Taylor, Walter F.,	54 Wall Street, " " "
Taylor, Thomas Fenton,	31 Nassau Street, " " "
Taylor, William C.,	94 Keap Street, Brooklyn
Terry, Roderick,	169 Madison Avenue, New York City
Terry, Seth Sprague,	126 E. 34th Street, " " "
Thomae, Robert L.	Scotch Plains, N. J.
Thompson, Hugh S.,	346 Broadway, New York City
Thomson, William H.,	23 E. 47th Street, " " "
Thorne, Samuel, Jr.,	55 Liberty Street. " " "
Thurber, Francis B.,	90 West Broadway, " " "
Tiebout, Charles H.,	31 Grand Street, Brooklyn
Tod, J. Kennedy,	45 Wall Street, New York City
Todd, Henry A.,	824 West End Avenue, " " "
Tomkins, Calvin,	120 Liberty Street, " " "
Tompkins, Hamilton B.,	229 Broadway, " " "
Train, Arthur C.,	28 W. 47th Street, " " "
Tuckerman, Alfred,	1123 Broadway, " " "
Turnbull, George R.	33 Mercer Street, " " "
Turner, Herbert B.,	22 William Street, " " "
Uhl, Edward,	P. O. Box 1207, New York City
Unckles, D. S.,	957 St. Mark's Avenue, Brooklyn
Valentine, Henry C., (Life),	57 Broadway, New York City
Valentine, Robert G.,	Mass. Inst. Tech., Boston, Mass.
Vallandingham, Edward N.,	Reform Club, New York City
Van Dusen, Samuel C.,	27 Cliff Street, " " "
Van Iderstine, Robert,	461 Washington Avenue, Brooklyn
Van Ingen, Edward H.,	9 E. 71st Street, New York City
Van Nest, George W.,	20 Broad Street, " " "

Veysey, William F. W.,	P. O. Box 345, New York City
Villard, Harold G.,	10 Wall Street, " " "
Villard, Oswald Garrison, (Life),	206 Broadway, " " "
Warburg, F. M., (Life),	52 William Street, New York City
Wadsworth, James W.,	Geneseo, N. Y.
Walcott, Philip K.,	111 Broadway, New York City
Walker, Hay,	Care of W. & H. Walker, Alleghany City, Pa.
Walker, John,	1231 Western Avenue, " " "
Walker, Samuel C.,	Harbison & Walker, Pittsburg, "
Walker, William,	" " " "
Wallace, Jackson,	26 Liberty Street, New York City
Wallace, William H.,	66 Broadway, " " "
Wallace, W. J.,	201 W. 80th Street, " " "
Ward, Henry Galbreath,	160 Broadway, " " "
Ward, J. H.,	34 Kenyon Bldg., Louisville, Ky.
Ward, J. Q. A.,	119 W. 52nd Street, New York City
Warner, John De Witt,	54 William Street, " " "
Warren, E. Walpole,	823 Madison Avenue, " " "
Warren, Edward H.,	40 Wall Street, " " "
Warren, George A.,	620 I Street, N. W., Washington, D. C.
Warren, H. Langford,	110 Boylston Street, Boston, Mass.
Wasson, James B.,	154 Nassau Street, New York City
Watson, Charles W.,	500 Madison Avenue, " " "
Weed, John W.,	62 William Street, " " "
Weeks, E. R.,	3408 Harrison Street, Kansas City, Mo.
Weeks, Rufus W.,	P. O. Box 1663, New York City
Wohle, Theodore,	59 W. 83d Street, " " "
Welch, Archibald A.,	Woodland Street, Hartford, Conn.
Welling, R. W. G.,	2 Wall Street, New York City
Werdell, Evert J.,	8 E. 38th Street, " " "
Werthein, H. P.,	27 William Street, " " "
Weston, Edward,	P. O. Box 617, Yonkers, N. Y.
Wetmore, Edmund,	34 Pine Street, New York City
Wheeler, A. S.,	511 Sears Bldg., Boston, Mass.
Wheeler, Everett P.,	21 State Street, New York City
Wheeler, James R.,	Columbia College, " " "
White, Alexander M.,	2 Pierrepont Place, Brooklyn
White, Alexander M., Jr.,	158 Columbia Heights, "
White, Andrew D., (Life),	Ithaca, N. Y.
White, George C.,	Glen Ridge, N. J.
White, Harold T.,	1 Nassau Street, New York City
White, Horace,	18 W. 69th Street, " " "
Whitlock, Bache McE.,	59 William Street, " " "
Whitney, Edward B.,	59 Wall Street, " " "
Whitridge, Frederick W.,	59 Wall Street, " " "
Wickersham, George W.,	40 Wall Street, " " "
Wiggin, Frederick H.,	55 W. 36th Street, " " "
Wilcox, Ansley,	295 Main Street, Buffalo, N. Y.
Wilcox, David,	Metropolitan Club, New York City

Wilds, Howard Payson,	University Club, New York City
Williams, L. L., Care E. C Williams,	1910 Seventh Avenue, " " "
Williams, Perry P.,	Produce Exchange, " " "
Wilson, Richard T.,	511 Fifth Avenue, " " "
Wing, Henry T.,	152 Clinton Street, Brooklyn
Winslow, Edward,	P. O. Box 486, New York City
Wise, B. E.,	21 Broad Street, " " "
Wisner, Charles,	Cotton Exchange, " " "
Wisner, H. G.,	18 W. 12th Street, " " "
Wolff, Lewis S.,	12 E. 70th Street, " " "
Woodbridge, Charles E.,	63 Wall Street, " " "
Worcester, Edwin D., Jr.,	35 Nassau Street, " " "
Wright, Jonathan,	73 Remsen Street, Brooklyn
Yates, Arthur G.,	130 So. Fitzhugh Street, Rochester, N.Y.
Yonge, Henry,	Hotel Margaret, Brooklyn
Zabriskie, George,	49 Wall Street, New York City
Zerega, Richard A.,	101 Classon Avenue, Brooklyn

ARTICLES OF INCORPORATION

OF

THE CIVIL SERVICE REFORM ASSOCIATION

[Filed May 11, 1900.]

KNOW ALL MEN BY THESE PRESENTS: That we, the undersigned, being persons of full age and all citizens of the United States, a majority of whom are also citizens of the State of New York, and being now Directors of an incorporated association known as the New York Civil Service Reform Association, and organized for the purposes hereinafter mentioned; being desirous of incorporation for the same purposes under the Membership Corporations Law of the State of New York, do hereby, pursuant to unanimous vote of all the members of the said Association, present and voting at a regularly called meeting thereof, and pursuant to authority given by the said unanimous vote at the said meeting, of which meeting notice of the intention so to incorporate was given personally or by mail to each member of such Association whose residence or Post Office address was known, at least thirty days before said meeting, and at which meeting the corporate name stated in paragraph First was by unanimous vote adopted, do hereby certify as follows:

FIRST.—The name or title by which the Association in which we desire to form ourselves as aforesaid shall be known in law, shall be the Civil Service Reform Association.

SECOND.—The territory in which its operations are to be principally conducted shall be the City of New York.

THIRD.—The city in which its principal office is to be located is the City of New York.

FOURTH.—The objects of the Association shall be to further the establishment of a system of appointment, promotion and removal in the Civil Service, founded upon the principle that public office is a public trust, admission to and retention in which should depend upon proven fitness; and to take such action as may tend to secure the honest and efficient execution of laws and rules relating to the civil service, and to the proper administration thereof.

FIFTH.—The number of its directors shall be twenty-eight.

SIXTH.—The names of the persons to be its directors until its first annual meeting are as follows :

Samuel P. Avery, Truman J. Backus, Henry De Forest Baldwin, Edward Cary, Charles Collins, W. Bayard Cutting, Horace E. Deming, A. S. Frissell, Richard Watson Gilder, Edwin L. Godkin, J. Warren Greene, George McAneny, James McKeen, Jacob F. Miller, Samuel H. Ordway, William A. Perrine, George Foster Peabody, William J. Schieffelin, Carl Schurz, Charles A. Schieren, Thomas R. Slicer, Henry Sanger Snow, Anson Phelps Stokes, S. Perry Sturges, Henry W. Taft, William H. Thomson, Charles W. Watson and Everett P. Wheeler.

In WITNESS WHEREOF we have made, signed, acknowledged and filed this certificate in duplicate.

Dated this Eighth day of May, 1900.

C. SCHURZ,	WILLIAM H. THOMSON,
JACOB F. MILLER,	A. S. FRISSELL,
ANSON PHELPS STOKES,	GEORGE MCANENY,
EVERETT P. WHEELER,	CHARLES A. SCHIEREN,
CHARLES COLLINS,	SAMUEL P. AVERY,
SAMUEL H. ORDWAY,	GEORGE FOSTER PEABODY.
J. WARREN GREENE,	

STATE OF NEW YORK, } ss.
COUNTY OF NEW YORK,

On this eighth day of May, one thousand and nine hundred, before me personally came Carl Schurz, Jacob F. Miller, Anson Phelps Stokes, Everett P. Wheeler, Charles Collins, J. Warren Greene, William H. Thomson, Samuel H. Ordway, A. S. Frissell, George McAneny, Charles A. Schieren, Samuel P. Avery and George Foster Peabody, to me personally known to be the persons described in and who made and signed the foregoing certificate, and severally duly acknowledged to me that they had made, signed and executed the same for the uses and purposes therein set forth.

F. W. HOERSCHGEN,
Notary Public, Kings County. (149)
(Certificate filed in New York County.)

Approved, May 9, 1900.

DAVID LEVINTRITT,
Justice of the Supreme Court of the State of New York.

REPORT

OF THE

Executive Committee

OF THE

New York

Civil Service Reform Association

Read at the Annual Meeting, May 18, 1904.

LIST OF MEMBERS, ETC.

NEW YORK
PUBLISHED FOR THE
CIVIL SERVICE REFORM ASSOCIATION
79 Wall Street
1904

CONTENTS

Annual Report of the Executive Committee.   -   5
Annual Report of the Treasurer,   -   -   -   21
Constitution and By-Laws,   -   -   -   -   23
Roll of Officers and Members,   -   -   -   -   31
Articles of Incorporation,   -   -   -   -   51

ANNUAL REPORT

OF THE

Executive Committee of the New York Civil Service Reform Association.

The Executive Committee, in submitting its report for the past year—the twenty-seventh year of the Association's existence—desires to call attention to the advance which the cause of civil service reform has recently made throughout the country. This is shown not only by the marked increase in interest in the subject in all directions, but also by concrete results. The year has seen the adoption of a charter providing for the introduction of the merit system in Denver, Colorado; there is sure promise for municipal civil service reform in Kansas City, Missouri, within the next few months, and substantial hopes for the adoption of State laws in both Illinois and Colorado at the next session of their respective legislatures. It must be regarded as a very encouraging sign that many organizations other than those formed solely for the purpose of advancing the merit system, have included civil service reform among the measures which they are most actively advocating.

In the Federal service there has been continued without material change the forward policy adopted by President Roosevelt and his first Civil Service Commission. In the State of New York there has been no change in the State government and consequently no marked changes in the administration of the civil service law. The incoming of the new administration in New

York City on January first brought about a complete change in the personnel of the Municipal Civil Service Commission. The city administration has not been considered favorable to the merit system; but it remains a fact that sweeping changes in the service have not been attempted and that such efforts as have been made, through the new Commission, to secure further patronage through additions to the exempt class have been defeated, in most cases, by the State Commission at Albany.

The vacancies in the Executive Committee of the Association caused by the death of William Brookfield, the declination of Theodore L. Miller, and the resignation of Henry W. Taft have been filled through appointment by the President of Nelson S. Spencer, Homer Folks and Roscoe C. E. Brown.

THE FEDERAL SERVICE.

CHANGES IN THE UNITED STATES COMMISSION.

At the time of the last annual meeting there was one vacancy existing in the United States Commission, due to the resignation of James R. Garfield. Shortly afterward, William Dudley Foulke resigned on account of ill health. It was with great regret that the Committee heard of the resignation of these two commissioners, for under Messrs Procter, Foulke and Garfield the Commission had reached its highest point of efficiency. During the summer the vacancies were filled by the appointment of Alford W. Cooley of New York and Henry F. Greene of Minnesota. Both men were well known as sincere advocates of civil service reform. The Association has reason to feel particularly gratified at the appointment of Mr. Cooley, who has for years been one of its members, at one time serving as its counsel, and who, since his appointment, has shown great enthusiasm for the work as well as fitness for the office.

The sudden death of John R. Procter, last December, just after completing ten years of continuous service on the Commission—the greater part of that time as its President—came as a shock to his friends, a large number of whom were counted among the members of the Association. Mr. Procter's unfailing tact and humor had accomplished a great deal in aid of the Commission's work with the departments and with Congress. His experience was almost invaluable. His death has deprived the Commission of an able, earnest and experienced administrator and the cause of civil service reform of one of its most effective advocates. At its January meeting resolutions were adopted by the Executive Committee and publicly printed expressing appreciation of his worth and services.

The vacancy caused by the death of Mr. Procter was filled by the appointment of General John C. Black of Illinois, Commander-in-Chief of the Grand Army, who has also been made President of the Commission. General Black is a veteran of the Civil War, somewhat enfeebled by his wounds. He served as Pension Commissioner under President Cleveland in his first term, and at that time gave little evidence of sympathy with the civil service law. His selection came of necessity as a peculiar disappointment to the friends of civil service reform.

THE WORK OF THE COMMISSION.

There are no extensions of the Federal classified service to record and practically nothing has been done to further the establishment of labor employment boards in cities in accordance with the President's order of March 26, 1903. Before undertaking other lines of work, the Commission wishes to see well established and in good running order the plan for the establishment of fixed examination districts throughout the country, with a central board of examiners in each district. This centralization will simplify the Commission's work and permit the exercise of better supervision and control over examinations held outside of Washington. Gratifying progress has already been made in the introduction of this system.

THE POSTAL SCANDALS.

It was originally attempted by enemies of the merit system to charge to that system the frauds in the Post Office Department which have been agitating the country for over a year; but the results of investigations have, on the contrary, proved the strongest possible argument for the extension of civil service reform. Out of all the officials indicted in connection with these frauds not one came in through the regular channel of competitive examination. The number of those connected with the frauds in any way, up to the present time, who have been dismissed or otherwise punished, and who were regularly appointed through examination has been insignificantly small. This is the most complete answer possible to the charge that the competive system cannot test the moral qualifications of applicants. The merit plan has obviously resulted in producing a higher class of officials, as its advocates promised it would.

THE SUSPENSION OF THE RULES.

Much criticism has been directed at the President as the result of a letter from the Civil Service Commission to Congress, giving the cases of suspension of the civil service rules since 1885. From this letter it appears that President Roosevelt has suspended certain rules sixty times to allow the appointment, certification, transfer, extension of temporary appointment or the acceptance of an application of particular individuals. It has been pointed out that President McKinley made three such suspensions only.

The comparison is meaningless and much of the criticism has been based on an entire misconception of the nature of the particular method of suspension in question. President McKinley, as is well known, took some eight thousand places out of the competitive list. President Roosevelt has increased the scope of competition materially, and has made very few fixed additions to the excepted list. The Civil Service Commission has considered it better policy where, it has been urged that, for one reason or another, a certain vacancy should not be filled by competition, to promulgate a special rule permitting the appointment in that single instance without examination, but leaving the position itself in the competitive class and subject in future cases in all respects to the competitive rule.

Opinions may well differ as to the wisdom of this policy. In general it would seem that where the same reasons for filling a position without examination will apply with each recurring vacancy, the position might better be permanently excepted, and that where there are valid reasons applying only at a particular time, a special exception might be made. But in order to avoid misunderstanding by the public, or the feeling that the rules are being tampered with to favor the appointment or advancement of individuals, we would very strongly urge that in each case of a special exception, the reasons upon which it is granted should be given the utmost publicity at the time it is made.

To form a correct judgment of these sixty cases of special exceptions made by President Roosevelt it would be necessary to know all the reasons governing each case. Under the circumstances, therefore, we can do little more than express surprise at the length of the list and call attention to certain features. It is clear, for instance, that the Department of Commerce and Labor is not deserving of all the praise it has received for not having asked for a single exception, for, while this may be technically true, the list shows that it has been permitted, under special exceptions, to make eleven appointments without compliance with the rules requiring competition. It is known that the Commission has itself recommended several of these special exceptions to the President, and in a number of instances this has been done to provide for cases which have appealed to their sympathies, although the vacancies could undoubtedly have been filled in the regular manner from the eligible lists. The appointment of Joseph Murray without examination to the competitive position of Assistant Commissioner of Immigration at the Port of New York under a special exception, was the subject of criticism by the Executive Committee in its report for 1902. Of the practice in general of making special exceptions to permit the appointment of individuals already selected it may at least be said that it creates a dangerous precedent.

THE FEDERAL OFFICES IN NEW YORK.

But few complaints have been brought to the Association's notice against the administration of the Federal law in New York City. There is a wide-spread belief that abuses have existed in the New York post office under the administration of Postmaster Van Cott, and this belief appears to have been confirmed in some degree by the report recently made to the President as the result of investigations of the office. Until the report itself is published in full we must withhold judgment as to the extent of the abuses existing. If the uncontradicted statements as to its findings which have appeared in the newspapers are to be believed, the report reflects severely on the conduct of Richard Van Cott, the son of the postmaster, and the President has decided on his summary dismissal. Richard Van Cott was appointed to the competitive position of superintendent of delivery without examination on January 24, 1900, under a rule permitting such appointments without examination only in case " the appointing officer . . . . shall certify that in his opinion the position to be filled requires such peculiar qualifications in respect to knowledge and ability, or such scientific or special attainments wholly or in part professional or technical, as are not ordinarily required in the executive service of the United States, and for the reasons set forth the best interest of the public service requires that an examination should be waived in whole or in part." The utter absurdity of applying this rule to the case of Van Cott was pointed out and protested against at the time the appointment was made.

A complaint was made to the Commission in Washington in regard to the number of persons employed temporarily in the New York Custom House, many of whom after their term had expired were re-employed under other titles and again upon temporary certificates. A change in the method of certification for temporary employment will, it is believed, put a stop to this practice and safeguard the rights of appointment of the man on the eligible list.

CONGRESS.

Beyond the fact that the House of Representatives repeated at this session its exhibition of spite against the civil service law, by cutting out the appropriation for the Civil Service Commission in Committee of the Whole —where the ayes and nays are not recorded—by a vote of 78 to 65, and restoring it the next day in the open House by a vote of 172 to 88, there is little to record in connection with the session of Congress just ended. The House Committee on Reform in the Civil Service made an extended investigation into the operations of the law and reported toward the end of the session a bill in favor of a fixed retiring age for all employees. This was presented, however, too late in the session to receive much attention.

NEW YORK STATE.

THE STATE CIVIL SERVICE COMMISSION.

The vacancy in the State Civil Service Commission caused by the resignation of its President, William Miller Collier, was filled by the appointment of Charles F. Milliken of Canandaigua, a newspaper editor and a prominent republican. Commissioner Cuthbert W. Pound of Ithaca, was elected President and has filled the office with marked ability. In its last report the Commission called attention to the poor manner in which the civil service law is working in many of the smaller cities of the State, owing to the ignorance or prejudice of the local commissioners, the small number of competitors and the lack of an aroused public opinion in support of the law. The Executive Committee of the Association has had under consideration suggestions for the remedying of these conditions.

The State Commission has continued its practice of allowing a hearing to representatives of the Association whenever requested, thus giving it an opportunity of presenting its views in regard to proposed changes in the New York City rules and classification, as well as in those of the State. From time to time the Association has protested against further extension of the schedule of exempt positions in the State service. The Executive Committee is strongly of the conviction that before the civil service law can work with entire satisfaction in the State service, the exempt list must be materially reduced, and urges upon the State Commission, in the interest of better service and greater public confidence, the adoption of a more conservative policy in the granting of requests for the exemption of individual positions.

MEASURES IN THE STATE LEGISLATURE.

The legislature, which completed its session on April 15, had before it a large number of bills affecting in one way or another the merit system in the State and cities. An agent was employed by the Executive Committee to send to the office of the Association copies of all bills introduced and to make regular reports on the status of bills. As the bills were received they were scrutinized and sorted into classes. Briefs were filed with the appropriate committees on all measures which the Law Committee determined should be either favored or opposed. If the bills were of sufficient importance to warrant it hearings were requested.

One bill only was introduced expressly on behalf of the Association. This provided that corporation inspectors in New York City should be appointed in accordance with the civil service law. There was a marked reluctance shown by members of the legislature to further in any way the passage of this bill, cutting off as it would the petty patronage of these positions, controlled chiefly by the borough president. Although its passage was urged at hearings before the Cities' Committees of both Houses, it was not reported by either.

Of the bills opposed by the Association but a small number were passed by both Houses, and none of importance have become laws. A representative of the Association appeared at almost all hearings on civil service bills before the mayor, and Mayor McClellan should be given great credit for not having approved a single bill which was opposed by the Association as calculated to injure seriously the merit system. Particularly commendable were his vetoes of the Remsen Retirement Bill and the Police and Fire Departments reinstatement bills. The retirement, or civil pension bill, was opposed by the Association after a careful investigation of its provisions by a special committee, on the grounds that the provision it made for a retiring fund was wholly inadequate and unscientific and that there would be no justification for laying any charge of this nature upon the city. The passage of the bill was advocated by the Association of Civil Employees, which numbers some five thousand in its membership. The reinstatement bills were an ill-advised attempt on the part of the Legislature to get rid of the annoyance to it of passing on bills providing for the retrial and reinstatement of individuals dismissed from the Police and Fire Departments, by giving the power to the Board of Estimate and Apportionment and the heads of the respective departments to act on all such requests. If these bills had become laws it would have made it possible for a new administration to reinstate any or all of those dismissed, for whatever reason, from these two departments under a previous administration.

NEW YORK CITY.

THE NEW RULES.

By far the most important action of the Low Civil Service Board in its last six months in office was the introduction of an entirely new and greatly improved set of rules. The rules as they stood had been badly in need of amendment and a revision had been promised by the Commission as far back as December 1902. At the invitation of the Commission, Mr. George McAneny, the former secretary of the Association, acted with the revision committee in the preparation of its draft.

After the adoption of this, with amendments, by the Commission, in the fall of 1903, but little time was allowed for public discussion, as it was desired by the Commission that the revised rules should be approved by the mayor prior to the city election. The revision was made the subject of very careful consideration by a special committee of the Association, appointed for the purpose. The special committee, while approving the proposed rules as a whole, and recognizing their marked improvement over the old code, took exception to certain important features, and as sufficient time had not been allowed it to present its case before the Commission, requested a hearing from Mayor Low. The hearing was granted and full opportunity given the committee to present its suggestions, both orally and in writing, but the mayor took the view that any amendment requiring further delay so close to election would prejudice the chances of the revision as a whole. He therefore approved the rules as submitted to him. When the revision came before the State Board it was considered better policy by the Executive Committee that the Association should withdraw its suggestions as to details and urge the passage of the rules as they stood. Objections were presented by State Civil Service Commissioner Kraft, but they were, almost without exception, frivolous in character and were overruled. The new rules accordingly went in force on December 4.

It can be stated positively that there was no intention on the part of the Low Commission in establishing these rules to hamper a new administration of different party. The work was decided on and the first draft made many months in advance of the election. It is, however, unfortunate that the rules were not prepared in time to permit of their being operated for an extended period, instead of less than one month, by the Commission that drafted and introduced them.

WORK DURING THE CAMPAIGN.

During the campaign, letters were addressed to the candidates of both parties for city offices, for the Board of Aldermen and for the Assembly, asking each to state his position in regard to the maintenance and enforcement of the civil service law. In most of the replies received the candidates expressed themselves in favor of the merit system; in fact very few declared against the law, but there were many cases of failure to reply. The usual request was also made of heads of departments—and, it is believed, in most cases complied with—that copies of the provisions of the law prohibiting political assessments, should be called to the attention of all employees.

EXEMPTIONS FROM COMPETITION UNDER THE LOW ADMINISTRATION.

During the Low administration, the number of positions exempted from examination was not, as the Association had hoped would be the case, diminished, but, on the contrary, was increased. Notwithstanding the repeated request of the Association for a revision of the exempt schedule, no attempt at systematic revision or reduction was made. A number of hearings were granted the Association on the question of restoring the clerical positions under the Board of Elections to the competitive class, but, so far as known, no action was taken.

THE NEW MUNICIPAL COMMISSION.

Mayor McClellan, on assuming authority, appointed an entirely new commission of six, four democrats and two republicans. Not one of the appointees had ever been known as an advocate of the merit system, nor, aside from John H. McCooey, who was appointed President, at a salary of $6000, had any of them possessed any special knowledge of its workings. Mr.

McCooey has not been supposed to have any sympathy with the law, but he has a very thorough working knowledge of the system, gained by his long service as assistant secretary—to which position he was appointed as a representative of the Brooklyn democratic organisation in 1898—and by previous experience as a member of the local board of federal examiners and assistant postmaster, in the Brooklyn post office. He is a democratic, district leader, and was appointed President of the commission on the recommendation of Senator Patrick H. McCarren, at the time the unquestioned democratic leader in Brooklyn. Almost the first action of the commission was to secure the resignation of S. William Briscoe, who had efficiently and continuously served both the Municipal and State Commissions in various capacities for many years, having been appointed first as labor clerk and then as secretary, under Mayor Strong's administration. In his place as secretary, Henry Berlinger, a Tammany democrat without previous experience in the Commission's work, was appointed.

CHANGES IN THE CITY SERVICE.

In spite of the large number of offices and positions exempted from competition, it must be said that the number of changes occurring in the service generally since the advent of the new administration has, comparatively speaking, not been large. Nor has any attempt been made to subvert the competitive system. The Commission has approved numerous requests for exemptions from competition and has asked for certain changes in the rules, but where these were of a nature calculated to injure the service they have, in most cases, been successfully opposed by the Association before the State Commission at Albany.

THE DEPUTY TAX COMMISSIONERS.

The most important matter which has arisen since the first of the year was the attempt to secure the exemption from competitive examination of the entire body of deputy tax commissioners, who are charged with the assessment of both real and personal property in the first instance. In the fight to prevent the treatment of these offices as political spoils the Association had the aid of the Merchants' Association, the Manufacturers' Association, the Board of Trade and Transportation, the Brooklyn League, the City Club and the Citizens' Union. Hearings were obtained before the Municipal Commission, the Mayor and the State Commission. The resolution of the Municipal Commission exempting the sixty deputies was approved by the Mayor, but was disapproved by the State Commission. Mr. Charles E. Hughes appeared for the Association. For his able presentation of the case before both the Mayor and the State Commission the Association is greatly indebted to him.

APPEALS FOR RE-RATING.

The abuse in the matter of appeals for re-rating of examination papers, referred to in the last report of the Executive Committee, still continues. No substantial change in the method of handling appeals was made in the new rules, which was one of the points in which the Association desired their amendment. The number granted, as compared with other commissions, is excessive and tends to undermine public confidence in the integrity of the system, and experience has abundantly confirmed the original statement of the Association, that the Commission's course invites appeals from the judgment of its examiners.

LITIGATION.

The Law Committee has had charge of no new litigation during the past year. Two important decisions were rendered in May and June, 1903, in the cases of Greene v. Knox, which was instituted by the Association, and People ex. rel. Sims et al. v. Collier, the latter commonly known as the County cases. Both of these actions were described in the Committee's last report. In the Greene case the Association was defeated, the Court of Appeals holding that a tax payer's action could not be used to review a title to office, the proper remedy being by *quo warranto*. In the County cases the result was a substantial victory, although the court merely decided that mandamus to compel the Commissioners to classify positions in a certain way was not the proper procedure, but did not enter at all upon the question of the proper classification of the positions involved.

FINANCES.

The receipts from all sources during the past year amounted to $7,254.50, slightly less than in the previous year, and the disbursements to $7,546.93, somewhat more than in the previous year. The Association ends the year entirely free from debt. In order to carry out the plan for the extension of the work to the smaller cities of the State, a substantial addition to the funds will be required during the coming year.

MEMBERSHIP.

The membership of the Association, owing to the work of the Committee on Membership, has increased during the year from 757 to 803. There are 16 life members, 71 sustaining members and 716 regular members. As recommended last year, efforts should be made to bring the regular membership up to 1000 and the sustaining membership to 100 in order to provide the Association with a regular income more nearly adequate to its needs.

In closing this report the Executive Committee desires to express its appreciation of the work of the Women's Auxiliary and of the assistance they have rendered the Association. It also wishes to thank the members of its standing and special committees for the important work they have each performed.

Respectfully submitted.

JACOB F. MILLER.
Chairman.

ELLIOT H. GOODWIN.
Secretary.

ANNUAL REPORT OF THE TREASURER.

MAY 1, 1904.

Balance on hand, as per report, May 1, 1903..................$485.79

RECEIPTS:

From Annual Dues............................	$3,165.00	
" Sustaining Membership Dues........	1,575.00	
" Subscriptions.......................	1,152.50	
" Women's Auxiliary..................	500.00	
" National League, for rent advanced...	500.00	
" Subscriptions to Annual Dinner......	362.00	7,254.50
		$7,740.29

DISBURSEMENTS:

Salary of Secretary.......................	1,500.00	
" " Assistant Secretary.............	900.00	
" " Clerks	1,208.83	
Rent of Office............................	1,000.00	
Telephone Service........................	150.09	
Printing.................................	135.75	
Postage and Stamped Envelopes...........	203.61	
Stationery...............................	122.84	
Office Expenses	207.11	
Expenses of Litigation...................	735.79	
Traveling Expenses......................	64.80	
Membership Committee Expenses...........	181.90	
Subscription to GOOD GOVERNMENT........	511.21	
Albany Represenative....................	146.50	
Expenses of Annual Dinner...............	478.50	7,546.93
Balance on hand, April 30, 1904.......................		$ 193.36

E. & O. E.

A. S. FRISSELL,
Treasurer.

ORGANIZATION

OF

THE NEW YORK CIVIL SERVICE REFORM ASSOCIATION

CONSTITUTION.

ARTICLE I.

The name of this organization shall be The Civil Service Reform Association.

ARTICLE II.

The object of the Association shall be to establish a system of appointment, promotion, and removal in the Civil Service, founded upon the principle that public office is a public trust, admission to which should depend upon proven fitness. To this end the Association will demand that appointments to subordinate executive offices, with such exceptions as may be expedient, not inconsistent with the principle already mentioned, shall be made from persons whose fitness has been ascertained by competitive examinations open to all applicants properly qualified, and that removals shall be made for legitimate cause only, such as dishonesty, negligence, or inefficiency, but not for political opinion or refusal to render party service; and the Association will advocate all other appropriate measures for securing integrity, intelligence, efficiency, good order, and due discipline in the Civil Service.

ARTICLE III.

The Association will hold meetings, raise funds, publish and circulate appropriate information, correspond and cooperate with associations organized elsewhere for the objects

set forth in this Constitution, and support all executive and legislative action which promote its purposes.

ARTICLE IV.

The conditions of membership shall be wholly independent of party preference. Questions shall not be discussed in the debate or in the publications of the Association upon party grounds. Neither the name nor influence of the Association shall be used on behalf of any party, or for procuring office or promotion for any person. But nothing in this article shall be construed to prevent the Association from opposing any candidate when in its opinion, or in that of three-fourths of the members of the Executive Committee, such course is demanded by the objects of the Association.

ARTICLE V.

There shall be a President, to be elected by the Association at the annual meeting, who shall perform the usual and prescribed duties of that office. He shall be, ex-officio, a member of all committees, with a casting vote only, and he may call special meetings of the Executive Committee whenever he thinks it necessary, and, with the assent of two members of the Executive Committee, special meetings of the Association.

There shall be ten Vice-Presidents, to be annually elected by the Association.

There shall be a Treasurer and Secretary, who shall perform the usual and prescribed duties of such officers. They shall be respectively appointed by the Executive Committee, and may be removed by them. The Treasurer shall be, ex-officio, a member of the Finance Committee of the Association.

There shall be an Executive Committee of twenty-five members, to be elected annually by the Association. Subject to these articles, the Executive Committee shall manage the affairs of the Association, direct and dispose of its funds, and from time to time make and modify by-laws for the Association and for its own action. The Executive Committee shall keep a record of its proceedings, and shall make a report to the

Association at the annual meeting. No appropriation of money by the Executive Committee beyond the amount in the hands of the Treasurer at the time shall bind any member of the Association, excepting those members of the Executive Committee who shall vote for it. Vacancies in the Executive Committee may be filled by the President for the remainder of the term. Other vacancies may be filled by the Executive Committee.

All the officers of the Association and members of the several Standing Committees shall be, ex-officio, members of the Executive Committee.

ARTICLE VI.

Each officer of the Association shall continue to hold office until his successor has been selected and is ready to enter upon the duties of the office.

ARTICLE VII.

There shall be an annual meeting of the Association on the second Wednesday of May, at which officers shall be elected for the ensuing year, and other appropriate business may be transacted; except in the year 1898, when the annual meeting shall be held on the second Wednesday of January.

ARTICLE VIII.

Any person may be proposed in writing for membership by any member of the Association, and shall be admitted upon approval of the Executive Committee. Members failing to pay their dues may be dropped from the roll by the Executive Committee.

ARTICLE IX.

The annual dues of each member shall be $5, payable on the 1st of May, and each member shall receive the annual report and all other publications of the Association. Sustaining members, on payment of twenty-five dollars annually, and Life members, exempt from annual dues on payment of one hundred dollars, may be elected by the Executive Committee at any regular meeting thereof.

Article X.

All provisions of this Constitution, except those relating to the rights of members, and the term of officers, may be suspended or amended by a vote of two-thirds of the Executive Committee, subject to the approval of the Association by a two-thirds vote of the members present either at the annual meeting or at a special meeting duly called. Due notice shall be given before any such annual or special meeting that the approval of the Association will, thereat, be asked for such action of the Executive Committee, and the notice shall clearly state the effect of such suspension or amendment in the text of the Constitution. Any member of the Association may propose amendments to the Constitution, which may be approved under the same conditions.

BY-LAWS.

FOR THE GOVERNMENT OF THE ASSOCIATION AND ITS COMMITTEES.

§ 1. The Annual meeting of the Association shall be held at such hour and place as the Executive Committee shall designate. The election of officers shall be by ballot, but any member not present may declare his vote by letter to the Secretary and it shall be counted.

§ 2. The meetings of each committee, unless otherwise especially provided for, shall be at half-past eight P. M., at which time the chairman shall direct the call of the names of its members and the Secretary shall record the names of those present and others as they appear.

§ 3. The order of business, before each committee shall be:

    1. The reading and correction of the records of the last meeting.

And, thereafter, unless otherwise ordered, as follows:

    2. Any statement due from the Treasurer.
    3. Unfinished business from the last meeting.
    4. Report from the Secretary's office.
    5. Reports of standing committees.
    6. Reports of special committees.
    7. Proposals of new members and their election.
    8. Miscellaneous business.

§ 4. Regular meetings of the Executive Committee shall be held on the second Wednesday of every month except July and August, but if that day be a holiday, then on the third Wednesday. Ten members of the Executive Committee shall constitute a quorum.

§ 5. Neither in the meetings of the Association nor of any committee shall any member speak more than once on any motion nor more than ten minutes at one time, without unanimous consent, nor shall any person, or his actions, be characterized on party grounds.

§ 6. Special meetings of any committee may be called by its chairman or by any three members, and due notice thereof shall be given by the Secretary.

§ 7. All notices to a member shall be sent to his address filed with the Secretary.

§ 8. On the demand of one-fifth of the members present, at any meeting of the Association or of a committee, the ayes and nays shall be called and recorded on any motion.

§ 9. All committees shall be appointed by the chair unless their selection shall be otherwise provided for.

§ 10. At each regular meeting of the Executive Committee, it shall be the duty of the Treasurer to make a statement of the amount of money in the treasury and of the place of its deposit, and, at the annual meeting, he shall state the source of all moneys received and the use made of the same during the past year.

§ 11. The Secretary shall keep a record of the proceedings of the Association and of the Executive Committee, and perform the other duties assigned him.

§ 12. Without the consent of three-fourths of the members present, no vote which will declare or fill a vacancy or elect a member of the Association shall be deemed carried, at the same meeting in which it was first moved.

§ 13. It shall require a vote of two-thirds of the members of the Executive Committee present to pass any vote under which more than $100 will be appropriated or the Association be pledged for more than that amount, and the Executive Committee alone shall have authority to create any charge upon the funds of the Association. But neither said committee nor any officer or officers of the Association shall be authorized to create a personal liability against any members but themselves.

§ 14. There shall be the following Standing Committees, of seven members each, which shall be selected annually by the Executive Committee:

(1) A Law Committee, whose duty it shall be to consider all legislation affecting the civil service, to promote such as may be approved, and to oppose such as may be disapproved by the Executive Committee, and to prepare and recommend

such amendments to the law as in their opinion will advance the purposes of the Association. The Law Committee shall have power to represent the Association in any legal proceedings which may be necessary in order to maintain or enforce the laws affecting the State or Municipal civil service.

(2) A Finance Committee, whose duty it shall be to devise and carry into effect, subject to the direction of the Executive Committee, suitable measures for raising funds, and to supervise and report upon the income and expenditures of the Association. The Finance Committee shall, in advance of each annual meeting of the Association, appoint an Auditing Committee from among its members, whose duty it shall be to examine all vouchers and audit the accounts of the Treasurer, and to report thereon at the annual meeting.

(3) A Publication Committee, whose duty it shall be to prepare and recommend matters suitable for publication by the Association, and to take charge of the printing and distribution of whatever may be ordered printed.

(4) A Committee on Correspondence, whose duty it shall be to promote the objects of the Association through correspondence and co-operation with other organizations.

(5) A Commitee on Examinations, whose duty it shall be to consider and recommend suitable methods of examination for admission to and promotion in the public service, and to investigate and report on the conduct of such examinations.

There shall also be a Standing Committee on Membership of fifteen members, which shall be selected annually by the Executive Committee. Its duties shall be to devise and carry into effect measures for increasing the membership of the Association.

Each Standing Committee shall be competent to fix the number of its own quorum; but such quorum shall in no case be less than three.

§ 15. These By-Laws may be amended, or new By-Laws added, by a four-fifths vote at any meeting of the Executive Committee; or by a two-thirds vote, provided a statement of the proposed change had been entered on the minutes at the last meeting.

§ 16. Amendments proposed under the last clause of the tenth section of the constitution shall be first submitted to the Executive Committee.

OFFICERS—1904-1905.

PRESIDENT:

CARL SCHURZ

VICE-PRESIDENTS:

JAMES C. CARTER	THEODORE ROOSEVELT
D. WILLIS JAMES	ELIHU ROOT
WILLIAM G. LOW	EDWARD M. SHEPARD
LEVI P. MORTON	OSCAR S. STRAUS
ALEXANDER E. ORR	EVERETT P. WHEELER

SECRETARY:

ELLIOT H. GOODWIN

ASSISTANT SECRETARY:

HENRY G. CHAPMAN

TREASURER:

A. S. FRISSELL

EXECUTIVE COMMITTEE:

JACOB F. MILLER, *Chairman.*	J. WARREN GREENE
R. ROSS APPLETON	A. JACOBI
SAMUEL P. AVERY	FRANKLIN B. LORD
HENRY DE FOREST BALDWIN	GEORGE McANENY
ROSCOE C. E. BROWN	SAMUEL H. ORDWAY
CHARLES C. BURLINGHAM	GEORGE FOSTER PEABODY
SILAS W. BURT	WILLIAM JAY SCHIEFFELIN
EDWARD CARY	THOMAS R. SLICER
CHARLES COLLINS	HENRY SANGER SNOW
HORACE E. DEMING	NELSON S. SPENCER
SAMUEL B. DONNELLY	ANSON PHELPS STOKES
HOMER FOLKS	WILLIAM H. THOMPSON

CHARLES W. WATSON

Offices of the Association,
79 WALL STREET, NEW YORK

STANDING COMMITTEES.

LAW:

SAMUEL H. ORDWAY, *Chairman.*
HENRY DE FOREST BALDWIN
CHARLES C. BURLINGHAM
JOSEPH P. COTTON, Jr.
J. WARREN GREENE
HENRY W. HARDON
CHARLES E. HUGHES

FINANCE:

WILLIAM JAY SCHIEFFELIN, *Chairman.*
L. T. CHAMBERLAIN
HENRY G. CHAPMAN
JAMES J. HIGGINSON
JACOB W. MACK
SETH SPRAGUE TERRY
HORACE WHITE

PUBLICATION:

ROB'T UNDERWOOD JOHNSON, *Ch'n.*
GEORGE R. BISHOP
ROSCOE C. E. BROWN
EDWARD CARY
LEARNED HAND
PAUL KENNADAY
ISIDOR LEWI

CORRESPONDENCE:

EVERETT V. ABBOT, *Chairman.*
WIRT HOWE
HERBERT PARSONS
WILLIAM POTTS
WILLIAM H. RAND
CORNELIUS B. SMITH
WALTER U. TAYLOR

EXAMINATIONS:

SILAS W. BURT, *Chairman.*
HENRY G. CHAPMAN
CHARLES COLLINS
GEORGE McANENY
PHILIP J. McCOOK
CLARENCE BISHOP SMITH
NELSON S. SPENCER

MEMBERSHIP:

WINFRED T. DENISON, *Chairman.*
ALBERT S. BARD
ROSCOE C. E. BROWN
EDWARDS S. CHILDS
A. LEO EVERETT
GEORGE J. GREENFIELD
ELLWOOD HENDRICK
FRANCIS H. KINNICUTT
JAY E. LAWSHE
RUSSELL LOINES
CHASE MELLEN
J. H. C. NEVIUS
WILSON M. POWELL, Jr.
CARL L. SCHURZ,
NATHAN A. SMYTH

MEMBERSHIP ROLL.
(May 1, 1904.)

SUSTAINING MEMBERS.

AMEND, BERNARD G.,	205 Third Avenue, New York City
AVERY, SAMUEL P.,	4 E. 38th Street, " " "
BOWKER, R. R.,	298 Broadway, New York City
BREWSTER, WILLIAM,	Broadway and 47th Street, " " "
BULL, WILLIAM LANMAN,	38 Broad Street, " " "
CARTER, JAMES C.,	54 Wall Street, New York City
CARY, EDWARD,	The "Times," " " "
CHAPLIN, DUNCAN D.,	64 Worth Street, " " "
CLYDE, WILLIAM P.,	19 State Street, " " "
COLLINS, CHARLES,	33 E. 17th Street, " " "
CRANE, RICHARD T.,	2541 Michigan Avenue, Chicago, Ill.
CUTTING, R. FULTON,	32 Nassau Street, New York City
DAVISON, CHARLES STEWART,	56 Wall Street, New York City
DE COPPET, E. J.,	30 Broad Street, " " "
DEERING, JAMES,	Fullerton and Clybourne Avenues, Chicago, Ill.
DEMUTH, WILLIAM,	524 Fifth Avenue, New York City
DENISON, WINFRED T.,	126 E. 28th Street, " " "
DIMOCK, HENRY F.,	Pier 11, N. R., " " "
FRISSELL, A. S.,	530 Fifth Avenue, New York City
GILDER, RICHARD WATSON,	33 E. 17th Street, New York City
GOODWIN, J. J.,	11 W. 54th Street, " " "
HARRIOT, S. CARMAN,	57 W. 39th Street, New York City
HEMENWAY, AUGUSTUS,	10 Tremont Street, Boston, Mass.
HUBER, JACQUES,	472 Broome Street, New York City
JACOBI, A.,	19 E. 47th Street, New York City
JOHNSON, ROBERT UNDERWOOD,	33 E. 17th Street, " " "
KENNEDY, JOHN S.,	31 Nassau Street, New York City
LOEB, JAMES,	52 William Street, New York City
LOW, SETH,	30 E. 64th Street, " " "
LOW, WILLIAM G.,	58 Remsen Street, Brooklyn
MACK, JACOB W.,	92 Liberty Street, New York City

MACY, V. EVERIT,	68 Broad Street, New York City
MAITLAND, ALEXANDER,	14 E. 55th Street, " " "
MAXWELL, ROBERT,	62 Worth Street, " " "
MILLER, JACOB F.,	120 Broadway, " " "
MINTURN, ROBERT SHAW,	109 E. 21st Street, " " "
MORTON, LEVI P.,	38 Nassau Street, " " "
MOSLE, GEORGE R.,	16-18 Exchange Place, " " "
McANENY, GEORGE,	19 E. 47th Street, New York City
OGDEN, ROBERT C.	784 Broadway, New York City
ORDWAY, SAMUEL H.,	27 William Street, " " "
PAGE, EDWARD D.,	60 Worth Street, New York City
PAGE, WILLIAM H., Jr.,	32 Liberty Street, " " "
PAGENSTECHER, A.,	P. O. Box 683, " " "
PEABODY, GEORGE FOSTER,	54 William Street, " " "
PHIPP, HENRY,	6 E. 87th Street, " " "
PINCHOT, JAMES W.,	1615 Rhode Island Avenue, Washington, D. C.
POWERS, NATHANIEL B.,	Lansingburg, N. Y.
RANDOLPH, STUART F.,	31 Nassau Street, New York City
RUSSELL, CHARLES H.,	15 Broad Street, " " "
SANDS, B. AYMAR,	31 Nassau Street, New York City
SCHEFER, CARL,	476 Broome Street, " " "
SCHIEFFELIN, WILLIAM JAY,	5 E. 66th Street, " " "
SCHIFF, JACOB H.,	P. O. Box 1198, " " "
SCHWAB, GUSTAV H.,	5 Broadway, " " "
SCRYMSER, JAMES A.,	107 E. 21st Street, " " "
SELIGMAN, ISAAC N.,	15 Broad Street, " " "
SHEPARD, EDWARD M.,	26 Liberty Street, " " "
SMITH, CORNELIUS B.,	101 E. 69th Street, " " "
SPENCER, NELSON S.,	27 William Street, " " "
SPEYER, JAMES,	257 Madison Avenue, " " "
STETSON, FRANCIS LYNDE,	15 Broad Street, " " "
STOKES, ANSON PHELPS,	100 William Street, " " "
STRAUS, OSCAR S.,	44 Warren Street, " " "
TRASK, SPENCER,	54 William Street, New York City
VOSS, F. G.,	100 William Street, New York City
WARE, WILLIAM R.,	Milton, Mass.
WHITE, ALFRED T.,	130 Water Street, New York City
WHITE, WILLIAM A.,	130 Water Street, " " "
WUNDERLICH, F. W.,	165 Remsen Street, Brooklyn

Abbot, Everett V.,	45 Cedar Street, New York City
Abbott, Lawrence F.,	" The Outlook," " " "
Abbott, Lyman,	287 Fourth Avenue, " " "
Achelis, John,	68 Leonard Street, " " "
Adams, Edward D.,	71 Broadway, " " "
Adams, Joseph,	Union Stock Yards, Chicago, Ill.
Adams, Thatcher M.,	36 Wall Street, New York City
Adler, Felix,	1524 Park Avenue. " " "
Affeld, Francis O.,	873 President Street, Brooklyn
Agar. John G.,	31 Nassau Street. New York City
Agnew, Andrew Gifford,	45 Wall Street, " " "
Aiken, William A.,	157 Washington Street, Norwich, Conn.
Aitken, John W.	873 Broadway, New York City
Allen, Calvin H.,	1 W. 72nd Street, " " "
Allen, Elmer A.,	80 Broadway, " " "
Allen. Franklin,	371 Fulton Street, Brooklyn
Alling, Joseph T.,	400 Oxford Street, Rochester, N. Y.
Alsop, Reese F.,	96 Remsen Street, Brooklyn
Anderson. Frank E.,	486 Broadway, New York City
Andrews, J. Sherlock,	111 St. Paul Street, Rochester, N. Y.
Appleton, R. Ross,	146 Joralemon Street, Brooklyn
Arend F. J.,	133 W. 92nd Street, New York City
Arnold, Lemuel H.,	8 Broad Street, " " "
Arnstein, Eugene,	10 Wall Street, " " "
Atterbury, Grosvenor,	20 W. 43rd Street, " " "
Avery, Samuel P., Jr.,	4 E. 38th Street, " " "
Babbott, Frank L.,	149 Lincoln Place, Brooklyn
Bacon, Gorham,	63 W. 54th Street, New York City
Bagley, Valentine N.,	641 Washington Street, " " "
Bailey. H. P.,	312 Broadway, " " "
Baldwin, Elbert F.,	" The Outlook," " " "
Baldwin, Henry de Forest,	49 Wall Street, " " "
Baldwin, William H., Jr.,	128 Broadway, " " "
Ball, Thomas P.,	116 Broad Street, " " "
Bangs, Francis S.,	40 Wall Street, " " "
Bangs, L. Bolton,	39 E. 72nd Street, " " "
Bannard, Otto T.,	26 Broad Street, " " "
Banta, Theodore M,	348 Broadway, " " "
Bard, Albert Sprague,	25 Broad Street, " " "
Barker, Benjamin,	56 Pine Street. " " "
Barkley, Charles H.,	82 Wall Street, " " "
Barney, A. H., (Life)	101 E. 38th Street, " " "
Barney, Danford N.,	Farmington, Conn
Barrett, Frank R.,	Box 616, Portland, Me.
Bartlett, P. G.,	25 Broad Street, New York City
Batterman, Henry,	360 Clinton Avenue, Brooklyn
Bausch, Edward,	Rochester, N. Y.
Baylies, Edmund L.,	54 Wall Street, New York City

Bayne, Hugh,	40 Wall Street, New York City
Beckers, Alexander,	618 Hudson Street, Hoboken, N. J.
Beebe, William H. H.,	30 E. 64th Street, New York City
Beekman, Gerard,	47 Cedar Street, " " "
Beer, George Lewis,	65 Pine Street, " " "
Beers, Lucius H.,	49 Wall Street, " " "
Behr, Herman,	75 Beekman Street, " " "
Bell, Gordon Knox,	22 William Street, " " "
Benedict, Elliot S.,	76 William Street, " " "
Benson, Frank Sherman,	214 Columbia Heights, Brooklyn
Biggs, Charles,	13 Astor Place, New York City
Bijur, Nathan,	34 Nassau Street, " " "
Bishop, George R ,	142 E. 18th Street, " " "
Bispham, William,	66 Broadway, " " "
Blagden, George,	18 E. 36th Street, " " "
Blair, John N.,	26 Liberty Street, " " "
Boas, Franz,	123 W. 82d Street, " " "
Bode, Frederick H.,	care Gage Bros., Chicago, Ill.
Boller, Alfred P.,	1 Nassau Street, New York City
Borden, M. C. D.,	Box 1794, " " "
Bowen, C. Winthrop,	5 E. 63rd Street, " " "
Brachhausen, G. A.,	Rahway. N. J.
Brackett, George C.,	50 Remsen Street, Brooklyn
Brewster, Charles O.,	32 Liberty Street, New York City
Briesen, Arthur von, (Life)	49 Wall Street, " " "
Briscoe, S. William,	20 Sanford Avenue. Flushing. N Y.
Brite, James,	111 Fifth Avenue. New York City
Brown, Addison,	45 W. 89th Street, " " "
Brown, Augustus H.,	262 W. 136th Street, " " "
Brown, Edwin H.,	141 Broadway. " " "
Brown, Everit,	56 Pine Street, " " "
Brown, Henry T.,	192 Lincoln Place, Brooklyn
Brown, Roscoe C. E.,	" Tribune " Office, New York City
Brown, Thatcher M.,	36 E. 37th Street, " " "
Browne, Thomas Q , Jr.,	Morristown, N J.
Brownell, William C.,	153 Fifth Avenue, New York City
Brush, W. Franklin,	16 E. 37th Street, " " "
Buckingham, C. L.,	38 Park Row, " " "
Bunnell, James S.,	49 Second Street, San Francisco. Cal.
Burlingham, Charles C ,	45 William Street, New York City
Burnett, Henry L.,	P. O. Building, " " "
Burr, Winthrop,	7 Wall Street, " " "
Burt, Silas W.,	30 Broad Street, " " "
Bush, J. Adriance,	110 Broadway. " " "
Butler, Howard R.,	22 E. 91st Street, " " "
Butler, Nicholas Murray,	119 E. 30th Street, " " "
Buttfield, William J ,	96 Wall S reet, " " "
Byrne, James,	24 Broad Street, " " "

Cadwalader, John L.,	40 Wall Street, New York City
Cahen, I. J.,	1 Madison Avenue, " " "
Calkins, Leighton,	25 Broad Street, " " "
Canfield, George F.,	49 Wall Street, " " "
Carnegie, Andrew, (Life)	2 E. 91st Street, " " "
Carter, Frederick B.,	61 Church Street, Montclair, N. J.
Carter, George F.,	Fanwood, N. J.
Cary, Clarence,	59 Wall Street, New York City
Cassatt, George M.,	327 Broadway, " " "
Cauldwell, John B.,	Southampton, N. Y.
Chadwick, John White,	626 Carlton Avenue, Brooklyn
Chaffee, J. Irwin,	Sedgwick Avenue, Fordham Heights, New York City
Chamberlain, D. H.,	West Brookfield Mass.
Chamberlain, L. T.,	222 W. 23 Street, New York City
Chambers, William P.,	55 Liberty Street, " " "
Chanute, Octave,	413 East Huron Street, Chicago, Ill.
Chapman, Henry G.,	79 Wall Street, New York City
Chase, George,	35 Nassau Street, " " "
Chauncey, Daniel,	129 Joralemon Street, Brooklyn
Cheney, F. W.,	South Manchester, Conn.
Cheney, George L.,	131 E. 57th Street, New York City
Cheny, Louis R.,	Woodland Street, Hartford, Conn.
Childs, Edwards H.,	59 Wall Street, New York City
Choate, Joseph H.,	American Embassy, London
Choate, William G.,	40 Wall Street, New York City
Cillis, Hubert,	20 Nassau Street, " " "
Claflin, John,	224 Church Street, " " "
Clarke, Samuel B.,	32 Nassau Street, " " "
Cleveland, Treadwell,	27 William Street, " " "
Codington, Perley M.,	32 W. 32nd Street, " " "
Cohen, William N.,	122 William Street, " " "
Collins, Atwood,	Asylum Avenue, Hartford, Conn.
Collins, Stephen W.,	69 Wall Street, New York City
Collyer, Robert,	201 W. 55th Street, " " "
Comstock, Albert,	56 Pine Street, " " "
Conger, Clarence R.,	37 Liberty Street, " " "
Conger, Henry C.,	140 W. 82nd Street, " " "
Cook, Walter,	3 W. 29th Street, " " "
Cooley, Alford Warriner,	Civil Service Commission, Washington, D C.
Cope, Francis R.,	1 Walnut Street, Philadelphia, Pa.
Corrigan, Joseph E.,	District Attorney's Office, New York City
Corthell, Elmer L,	1 Nassau Street, " " "
Cotton, Joseph P., Jr.,	52 William Street, " " "
Coudert, Frederick R., Jr.,	71 Broadway, " " "
Cowperthwait, J. Howard,	195 Park Row, " " "
Coykendall, S. D.,	33 Coenties Slip, " " "
Crane, Frederick,	Bloomfield, N. J.
Crane, Leroy B.,	237 Broadway, New York City
Cranford, Walter V.,	215 Montague Street, Brooklyn
Cravath, Paul D.,	52 William Street, New York City

Crawford, Gilbert H.,	32 Liberty Street, New York City
Creevey, John J.,	41 Wall Street, " " "
Cromwell, Frederic,	32 Nassau Street, " " "
Cromwell, Lincoln,	1 Greene Street, " " "
Croswell, J. G.,	17 W 44th Street, " . " "
Curtis, William E.,	30 Broad Street, " " "
Cushing, William E.,	Society for Savings Bldg., Cleveland, O.
Cutler, Arthur H.,	20 E. 50th Street, New York City
Cutting, R. Bayard,	32 Nassau Street, " " "
Cutting, W Bayard,	24 E. 72nd Street, " " "
Cuyler, C. C.,	44 Pine Street, " " "
Daboll, Henry E.,	Plainfield, N. J.
Dale, Alfred G.,	7 E. 42nd Street, New York City
Dana, Charles L.,	50 W. 46th Street, " " "
Davies, Julien T.,	32 Nassau Street, " " "
Davies, William Gilbert,	32 Nassau Street, " " "
Davis, Benjamin P.,	107 Wall Street, " " "
Davis, Charles Henry,	25 Broad Street, " " "
Davis, G. Pierrepont,	Woodland Street, Hartford, Conn.
Davis, Horace A.,	135 Broadway, New York City
Day Clarence S.,	45 Wall Street, " " "
DeForest, R. W	30 Broad Street, " " "
Delano, Warren, Jr.,	1 Broadway, " " "
Deming, Horace E.,	13 William Street, " " "
Despard, W D.,	6 Hanover Street, " " "
Dettmer, Jacob G.,	27 Prospect Park W., Brooklyn
Devine, Thomas J	19 Portsmouth Terrace, Rochester, N. Y.
DeWitt, Theodore,	88 Nassau Street, New York City
Dickinson, Robert L.,	166 Clinton Street, Brooklyn
Dittenhoefer, A. J.	96 Broadway, New York City
Dodge, Cleveland H.,	99 John Street, " " "
Dominick, H. B.	Broadway and 17th Street, " " "
Dommerich, L. F	57 Greene Street, " " "
Donnelly, Samuel B.,	360 Putnam Avenue, Brooklyn
Doty Ethan Allen,	726 St. Mark's Place, "
Dougherty, J. Hampden,	27 William Street, New York City
Dows, Tracy,	Room 102, Produce Exchange, " " "
Dulon, Rudolf,	115 Broadway, " " "
Dunham, Edward K.,	338 E 26th Street, " " "
Dunham, Lawrence,	7 E. 42nd Street, " " "
Dunning, S. Wright,	80 Madison Avenue, " " "
Eastman, A. H,	363 Grand Avenue, Brooklyn
Eastman, George,	400 East Avenue, Rochester, N. Y.
Eaton, Henry W.,	45 William Street, New York City
Eaton, S. Edward,	660 Hudson Street, " " "
Ecaubert, F.,	18 Rose Street, " " "
Elderkin, John,	150 W. 83d Street, " " "

Eliot, Charles W., ... Cambridge, Mass.
Elkins, Stephen B., ... 1626 K Street, Washington, D. C.
Ely, Alfred, ... 31 Nassau Street, New York City
Ely, Arthur H., ... 56 Wall Street, " " "
Ely, Moses, ... 2 Wall Street, " " "
Ely, Robert E., ... 23 West 44th Street, " " "
Emmons, Arthur B., ... 60 Park Avenue, " " "
Emmons, Samuel F., . . U. S. Geological Survey, Washington, D. C
Eppinger, Isaac, ... 66 Broad Street, New York City
Erbslöh, R., ... 364 Broadway, " " "
Everest, Charles M., ... 506 West Avenue, Rochester, N. Y.
Everett, A. Leo, ... 49 Wall Street, New York City
Ewart, Richard H., ... 115 Franklin Street, " " "

Fabbri, Alessandro, ... 11 E. 62d Street, New York City
Fabbri, Ernesto G., ... 11 E. 62d Street, " " "
Fahnestock, H. C., ... 2 Wall Street, " " "
Fairchild, Benjamin T., ... P. O. Box 1120, " " "
Fairchild, Charles S., ... 46 Wall Street, " " "
Faure, John P., ... 346 Broadway, " " "
Fay, Charles J., ... 49 Wall Street, " " "
Finch, Edward R., . . . 53 Washington Square, " " "
Fisher, George H., ... 308 Walnut Street, Philadelphia, Pa.
Fisher, George H., ... 278 Sterling Place, Brooklyn
Fleitmann, Ewald, ... 484 Broome Street, New York City
Folks, Homer, ... 105 E. 22nd Street, " " "
Ford, Worthington C., . Care Library of Congress, Washington, D. C.
Forrest, C. R., ... Asylum Avenue, Hartford, Conn.
Fox, Austen G., (Life), . . . 45 W. 33d Street, New York City
Fraenckel, Richard H., . . 19 and 21 Greene Street, " " "
Frankenheimer, John, ... 22 Broad Street, " " "
Frissell, H. B., ... Hampton, Va.
Frothingham, Howard P., ... 2 Wall Street, New York City
Fuller, Frank, ... 61 Fifth Avenue, " " "
Fuller, Paul, ... 100 Broadway, " " "
Fullerton, Alexander, (Life), . . 7 W. 8th Street, " " "
Fullerton, Henry S., ... 71 Broadway, " " "
Funk, T. K., ... 195 Washington Park, Brooklyn

Gaillard, William D., ... 141 Broadway, New York City
Garrison, Wendell P., ... 206 Broadway, " " "
Garver, John A., ... 44 Wall Street, " " "
Gibney, V. P., ... 16 Park Avenue, " " "
Gibson, William J., ... 26 Liberty Street, " " "
Gitterman, John M., ... 63 William Street, " " "
Goadby, Clarence, ... 21 W. 35th Street, " " "
Goddard, George A., ... 10 Tremont Street, Boston, Mass.
Goldman, Julius, ... 31 Nassau Street, New York City
Goldmark, James, ... 121 Worth Street, " " "

Goodale, John McGregor,	42 Broadway, New York City
Goodnow, Frank J.,	49 Riverside Drive, " " "
Goodwin, Elliot H.,	79 Wall Street, " " "
Goddard, Norton,	98 Bleecker Street, " " "
Gottheil, Paul,	Produce Exchange, " " "
Gottsberger, Francis,	156 Broadway, " " "
Gould, Elgin R. L.,	281 Fourth Avenue, " " "
Grant, De Forest,	22 E. 46th Street, " " "
Grant Percy S.,	7 W. 10th Street, " " "
Gray, Henry G,	135 Madison Avenue, " " "
Green, Noah,	478 Central Park, West, " " "
Greenbaum, Samuel.	141 Broadway, " " "
Greene, Francis V.,	884 Ellicott Square, Buffalo, N. Y.
Greene, Jacob L..	Hartford, Conn.
Greene, J. Warren,	3 Broad Street, New York City
Greenfield, George J.,	32 Broadway, " " "
Greenough, John,	31 W. 35th Street, " " "
Greer, David H.,	342 Madison Avenue. " " "
Grinnell, William Morton,	20 Broad Street, " " "
Gross, Charles E.,	Asylum Avenue, Hartford, Conn.
Gulliver, W. C.,	120 Broadway, New York City
Guthrie, William D.,	52 William Street, " " "
Gwynne, Arthur C.,	Rye, N. Y.
Gwynne, John A.,	" "
Hagemeyer, F. E.,	F 15, Produce Exchange, New York City
Haines, Henry F.,	2 Wall Street, " " "
Hall, Elial F.,	East 4th Street, Jamestown, N. Y.
Hall, Valentine G.,	45 Broadway, New York City
Hamilton, E. Luther,	146 Broadway, " " "
Hamlin, Frank, H.,	Canandaigua, N. Y.
Hand, Learned,	2 Wall Street, New York City
Harbeck, Charles T.,	Islip, N. Y.
Harding, Edward,	Chestnut Hill, Philadelphia, Pa
Hardon, Henry Winthrop,	313 W. 71st Street, New York City
Hasslacher, Jacob,	100 William Street, " " "
Hastings, Thomas S.,	27 W. 46th Street, " " "
Hayes, J. Noble,	120 Broadway, " " "
Heath, Frank E.,	95 Liberty Street, " " "
Healy, A. Augustus,	198 Columbia Heights, Brooklyn
Henderson, Harold G..	128 E. 34th Street, New York City
Hendrick, Ellwood,	139 E. 40th Street, " " "
Henriques, C. A.,	25 W. 49th Street, " " "
Hentz, Henry,	769 St. Mark's Avenue, Brooklyn
Hentz, Leonard S.,	769 St. Mark's Avenue, "
Hess, Henry E.,	32 Nassau Street, New York City
Hessberg, Max,	13 William Street, " " "
Hicks, Benjamin D.,	Old Westbury, N. Y.
Higginson, James J.,	16 E. 41st Street, New York City

Hinrichs, Frederick W., ... 76 William Street, New York City
Hitchcock, Welcome G., (Life) . . . 453 Broome Street, " " "
Hobart, Henry L., ... 120 Front Street, " " "
Hodges, Harrison B., ... 16 Gramercy Park, " " "
Hodgman, George F., ... 806 Broadway, " " "
Hoe, Richard M., . . . Room 102, Produce Exchange, " " "
Hoe, Robert, ... 504 Grand Street, " " "
Holt, Henry, ... 29 W. 23d Street, " " "
Holt, Roland, ... 711 Madison Avenue, " " "
Hoppin, Frederick S., Jr., . . . 131 E. 19th Street, " " "
Hoppin, William W., ... 54 William Street, " " "
Hornblower, William B., . . . 24 Broad Street, " " "
Howe, Daniel R., ... Asylum Avenue, Hartford, Conn.
Howe, Wirt, ... 27 William Street, New York City
Howland, Charles P., ... 35 Wall Street, " " "
Hoyt, Gerald L., ... 9 W. 37th Street, " " "
Hubbard, Thomas H., ... 16 W. 58th Street, " " "
Hubbell, Charles Bulkeley, . . . 35 Nassau Street, " " "
Hughes, Charles E., ... 96 Broadway, " " "
Hull, Charles A., ... 72 Wall Street, " " "
Huntington, Francis C., . . . 54 William Street, " " "
Huntington, Samuel, ... 146 Broadway, " " "
Huntington, William R., . . . 804 Broadway, " " "
Huyler, John S., ... 64 Irving Place, " " "

Ide, George E., ... 256 Broadway, New York City
Ireland, F. G., ... 61 Elm Street, " " "
Ives, Brayton, ... 37 Wall Street, " " "

Jackson, Frederick W., ... Westchester, N. Y.
James, D. Willis, ... 99 John Street, New York City
Jay, Pierre, ... 5 Exeter Street, Boston, Mass.
Jay, William, ... 48 Wall Street, New York City
Jefferson, Joseph, ... , , . . Buzzards Bay, Mass.
Jellenix, Felix, ... 17 William Street, New York City
Jennings, Frederick B., ... 15 Broad Street, " " "
Jesup, Morris K., ... 195 Madison Avenue, " " "
Johnsón, James G., ... 655 Broadway, " " "
Johnson, Willis Fletcher, . . . 154 Nassau Street, " " "

Kahn, Otto H., (Life), ... 54 William Street, New York City
Kane, S. Nicholson, ... 23 W. 47th Street, " " "
Kelsey, Clarence H., ... 146 Broadway, " " "
Kennaday, Paul, ... 88 Grove Street, " " "
Kenneson, Thaddeus D., . . . 13 William Street, " " "
Kenyon, Alan D., ... 49 Wall Street, " " "
Kenyon, William Houston, . . . 49 Wall Street, " " "
Keppler, Rudolph, ... , 25 Broad Street, " " "
Kernan, John D., ... 37 Liberty Street, " " "

Kidder, Camillus G.,	27 William Street,	New York City
Kidder, Edward H.,	170 Broadway,	" " "
Kimball, A. R.,		Orange, N. J.
King, William F.,	410 Broadway,	New York City
Kinnicutt, Francis H.,	35 Wall Street,	" " "
Kinnicutt, Francis P.,	42 W. 37th Street,	" " "
Kirchhoff, Charles,	232 William Street,	" " "
Kissell, Gustav E., (Life),	32 Liberty Street,	" " "
Kissel, Rudolph H.,	32 Nassau Street,	" " "
Klein, Isaac H.,	45 Cedar Street,	" " "
Klupfel, Charles, Care North German Lloyd, 5 Broadway,		" " "
Knapp, Shepherd,	206 Lexington Avenue,	" " "
Knauth, Antonio,	233 West 70th Street,	" " "
Knox, Herbert H.,	45 Broadway,	" " "
Kohler, Max J.,	119 Nassau Street,	" " "
Kuhne, Percival,	13 William Street,	" " "
Kunhardt, Henry R.,	124 W. 74th Street,	" " "
Kunhardt, William B.,	1 Broadway,	" " "
Laimbeer, Francis E.,	99 Nassau Street,	New York City
Lambert, William B.,	Highland Street,	Cambridge Mass.
Lambert, William S.,	Produce Exchange,	New York City
Lansing J. Townsend,	82 State Street,	Albany, N. Y.
Larocque, Joseph,	40 Wall Street,	New York City
Larremore, Wilbur,	32 Nassau Street,	" " "
Lawrence, Cyrus J.,	15 Wall Street,	" " "
Lawrence, Richard H.,	15 Wall Street,	" " "
Lawrence, Walter B.,	35 Wall Street,	" " "
Lawshe, Jay E.,	69 Wall Street,	" " "
Lea, Henry Charles,	2000 Walnut Street,	Philadelphia, Pa.
Leavens, George St. J.,	72 Bible House,	New York City
Leavitt, John Brooks,	115 Broadway,	" " "
Leaycraft, J. Edgar,	19 W. 42nd Street,	" " "
Lederle, Ernest J.,	471 W. 143d Street,	" " "
Ledoux, Albert R.,	9 Cliff Street,	" " "
Lee, W. H. L.,	20 Nassau Street,	" " "
Le Gendre, William,	59 Wall Street,	" " "
Lehmaier, Louis A.,	78 Beekman Street,	" " "
Levi, Albert A.,	108 Exchange Court,	" " "
Lewi, Isidore,	3 E. 81st Street,	" " "
Lewis, August,	151 Greene Street,	" " "
Lewis, Richard V.,	130 W. 42d Street,	" " "
Lindsay, Alexander M.,	373 East Avenue,	Rochester, N. Y.
Littauer, Lucius N.,		Gloversville, N. Y.
Livingston, Goodhue,	38 E. 65th Street,	New York City
Livingston, Julius I.,	52 Broadway,	" " "
Lockwood, Benoni,	56 Irving Place,	" " "
Loeb, Morris,	273 Madison Avenue,	" " "
Logan, Walter S.,	27 William Street,	" " "

Loines, Russell H.,	27 W. 11th Street, New York City
Loines, Stephen,	26 Garden Place, Brook·yn
Lord, Franklin B.,	49 Wall Street, New York City
Lord, F. B., Jr..	49 Wall Street, " " "
Lounsbery, Richard P.,	15 Broad Street, " " "
Lovell, Joseph J.,	Avondale Place, Woodhaven, N. Y.
Low, C. Adolph,	41 Liberty Street, New York City
Lowndes, James,	1505 Pennsylvania Avenue, Washington, D. C.
Ludlow, James B.,	45 Cedar Street, New York City
Luther, George Martin,	25 Broad Street, " " "
Lyman, Frank,	34 Remsen Street, Brooklyn
Lyman, George T.,	Bellport, N. Y.
Lyman, Theodore,	Woodland Street, Hartford, Conn.
Lynde, Rollin H.,	31 Pine Street, New York City
Macdonough, A. R.,	105 E. 15th Street, New York City
Macfarlane, Wallace,	32 Liberty Street, " " "
MacVeagh, Charles,	15 Broad Street, " " "
Magee, John H.,	Scottsburg, N. Y.
Mallinckrodt, Edward,	Mallinckrodt Chemical Works. St. Louis, Mo.
Mansfield, Howard,	49 Wall Street, New York City
Mapes, Charles V.,	143 Liberty Street, " " "
Marling, Alfred E.,	21 Liberty Street, " " "
Markoe, Francis H.,	15 E. 49th Street, " " "
Marshall, Charles H.,	45 William Street, " " "
Marshall, Fielding L.,	35 Nassau Street, " " "
Marshall, Louis,	30 Broad Street, " " "
Marsters, A., A.,	15 Dey Street, " " "
Martin, John,	Grymes Hill, Staten Island, N. Y.
Martin, Newell,	25 Broad Street, New York City
Martin, T. Comerford,	120 Liberty Street, " " "
Mason, Alexander T.,	13 William Street, " " "
Mason, Alfred Bishop.	Apartado 130, City of Mexico
Mason, James Weir,	32 W. 129th Street, New York City
Matthews, Brander,	681 West End Avenue, " " "
Mathews, Robert,	135 Spring Street, Rochester, N. Y.
Matthewson, Arthur,	139 Montague Street, Brooklyn
Maxwell, William H.,	121 W. 82nd Street, New York City
Mellen, Chase,	52 William Street, " " "
Merck, George,	15 University Place, " " "
Merrill, Charles E.,	43 E. 10th Street, " " "
Merrill, Payson,	31 Nassau Street, " " "
Meyer, Jacob,	29 E. 63d Street, " " "
Milburn, John G.,	54 William Street, " " "
Miller, Hoffman,	80 Broadway, " " "
Miller, Theodore C.,	177 Montague Street, Brooklyn
Mills, L. H.,	473 Broome Street, New York City
Mitchell, Edward,	44 Wall Street, " " "
Moffat, George B.,	1 Nassau Street, " " "

Moffat, R. Burnham,	63 Wall Street, New York City
Montgomery, R. M.,	25 Pine Street, " " "
Moore, W. H. H.,	Box 402, " " "
Morse, Horace J.,	820 St. Mark's Avenue, Brooklyn
Morse, Richard C.,	35 Sidney Place, "
Mortimer, Richard,	11 Wall Street, New York City
Mosenthal, P. J.,	46 Cedar Street, " " "
Mosle, A. Henry,	30 Broad Street, " " "
Mott, William F.,	Toms River, N. J.
Moulton, Franklin W.,	59 Wall Street, New York City
Munro, J. G.,	61 Erie County Bank Building, Buffalo, N. Y.
Munro, Willis,	5 Nassau Street, New York City
Murray, James B.,	23 Belmont Terrace, Yonkers, N. Y.
Murray, Joseph K.,	106 Wall Street, New York City
Myers, Nathaniel,	25 Broad Street, " " "
McAlpin, George L.,	9 E. 90th Street, New York City
McCagg, Louis Butler,	18 E. 84th Street, " " "
McClain, John F.,	327 Broadway, " " "
McCook, Philip J.,	15 William Street, " " "
McIntosh, James H.,	346 Broadway, " " "
McKeen, James,	136 Henry Street, Brooklyn
McKeever, J. Lawrence,	164 Lexington Avenue, New York City
McKim, John A.,	6 E. 74th Street, " " "
McMahon, Fulton,	54 William Street, " " "
Nadal, Charles C.,	142 E. 35th Street, New York City
Naumberg, Elkan,	48 W. 58th Street, " " "
Naumberg, George W.,	33 Wall Street, " " "
Naumberg, Walter W.,	33 Wall Street, " " "
Nelson, Henry Loomis,	Williams College, Williamstown, Mass.
Nelson, H. W., Jr.,	Marshfield Hills, "
Nevius, John H. C.,	33 Union Square, New York City
Newton, R. Heber,	East Hampton, N. Y.
Newton, Virginius,	Box 906, Richmond, Va.
Nichols, George L.,	66 E. 56th Street, New York City
Nichols, George M.,	277 Adelphi Street, Brooklyn
Nichols, W. N.,	353 Clinton Avenue, "
Nicoll, James C.,	51 W. 10th Street, New York City
North, Thomas M.,	160 Central Park South, " " "
Nourse, Charles J., Jr.,	27 William Street, " " "
Oakes, Charles,	9 Pine Street, New York City
O'Connor, John A.,	12 E. 44th Street, " " "
Ogden, Rollo,	206 Broadway, " " "
Olin, Stephen H.,	32 Nassau Street, " " "
Olyphant, Robert,	21 Cortlandt Street, " " "
Opdyke, William S.,	20 Nassau Street, " " "
Oppenheimer, Henry S.,	16 E. 32nd Street, " " "
Ordway, Edward W.,	1093 Dean Street, Brooklyn

Orr, Alexander E., ... 102 Remsen Street, Brooklyn
Osborn, William Church, ... 71 Broadway, New York City
Osborne, Thomas M., ... Auburn, N. Y.

Packard, Edwin, ... 241 Henry Street, Brooklyn
Page, Walter H., ... 34 Union Square, New York City
Parker, Frederick S., ... 32 Garden Place, Brooklyn
Parks, J. Waring, . . . , . 49 Wall Street, New York City
Parrish, Samuel L., ... 25 Broad Street, " " "
Parsons, Herbert, ... 52 William Street, " " "
Parsons, John E., ... 52 William Street, " " "
Paulding, James Kirk, . . . 130 E. 24th Street, " " "
Pauli, H. G., ... 15 S. William Street, " " "
Peck, George G., ... 18 East 65th Street, " " "
Peckham, Wheeler H., ... 80 Broadway, " " "
Pedersen, James, . , . . . 20 E. 46th Street, " " "
Pell, Frederick A., ... Lakewood, N J.
Pendleton, Francis K., ... 25 Broad Street, New York City
Perkins, Robert P., ... 41 Union Square, " "
Perrine, William A., . . . 2440 N. Marshall Street, Philadelphia, Pa.
Phillips, Lee, ... 247 W. 71st Street, New York City
Phoenix, Phillips, ... 68 Broad Street, " ' "
Pierce, Franklin, ... 31 Nassau Street, " " "
Pierrepont, Henry E., ... 216 Columbia Heights, Brooklyn
Pierrepont, Robert Low, ... 12 Pierrepont Street, "
Pinchot, Gifford, . . . 1615 Rhode Island Avenue, Washington, D. C.
Pope, A. A., ... Pope Building, Boston, Mass.
Pope, George A., ... 926 St. Paul Street, Baltimore, Md.
Pott, James, ... 119 W. 23d Street, New York City
Potter, Frederick, ... 71 Broadway, " " "
Potter, Henry C., ... 113 W. 40th Street, " " "
Potts, William, ... 65 Essex Avenue, Orange, N. J.
Powell, Wilson M., Jr., ... 29 Wall Street, New York City
Prentice, William P., ... 52 Broadway, " " "
Pryer, Charles, ... New Rochelle, N. Y.
Pryor, James W., ... 55 W. 44th Street, New York City
Putnam, George Haven, . . . 27 W. 23d Street, " " "
Putnam, George P., ... 160 Fifth Avenue, " " "
Putnam, Harrington, . . . 404 Washington Avenue, Brooklyn
Putnam, Irving, ... 27 W. 23rd Street, New York City
Pyne, Moses Taylor, . . . 263 Madison Avenue, " " "

Rainsford, W. S., ... 209 E. 16th Street, New York City
Rand, George C., ... 107 Wall Street, " " "
Rand, William H., Jr., . . Criminal Court Building, " " "
Raven, A. A., ... 51 Wall Street, " " "
Raymond, Charles H., ... 32 Liberty Street, " " "
Raymond, Rossiter W., ... 123 Henry Street, Brooklyn

Reichhelm, Edward P., ... 23 John Street, New York City
Reynolds, James B., ... 55 W. 44th Street,   "   "   "
Rice, Edwin T., Jr., ... 59 Wall Street,   "   "   "
Richards, C. A. L., ... 169 Power Street, Providence, R. I.
Rickerson, Charles L., ... 212 West Street, New York City
Rives, George L., ... 14 W. 38th Street.   "   "   "
Robb, J. Hampden, ... 23 Park Avenue,   "   "   "
Robinson, Beverly R., ... 42 W. 37th Street,   "   "   "
Rogers, Henry A. . . . . . 19 John Street,   "   "   "
Romaine, Louis Tyson, . . . 84 Beaver Street,   "   "   "
Roome, W. Harris, ... 287 Fourth Avenue,   "   "   "
Roosevelt, Theodore, ... Oyster Bay, N. Y.
Root, Elihu. . . . . . 32 Nassau Street, New York City
Rose, Arthur P, ... Geneva. N. Y.
Rose, Charles J., ...   "   "
Rosenbaum, S. D., ... 51 Franklin Street, New York City
Rosenfield, George, . . . 35 South William Street,   "   "   "
Rowe, William V., ... 49 Wall Street,   "   "   "
Rumsey, Dexter P., ... 742 Delaware Street, Buffalo, N. Y.

Saint Gaudens, Augustus, ... Windsor, Vt.
Salomon, William, ... 25 Broad Street, New York City
Sand, Henry A. L., ... , 32 Liberty Street,   "   "   "
Sand, Max E., ... Ardsley-on-Hudson, N. Y.
Sanger, William Cary, ... Sangerfield, N. Y.
Savage, Minot J., . . . 34th Street and Park Avenue, New York City
Sayer, W. Murray, Jr., . . . 398 Washington Avenue, Brooklyn
Scharmann, Hermann B., . . . 170 W. 59th Street, New York City
Schieren, Charles A. . . . . . 405 Clinton Avenue, Brooklyn
Schnakenberg, D., . . . 6 Hanover Street, New York City
Schrader, George H. F., ... 32 Rose Street,   "   "   "
Schumacher, Charles, . . . 41 Exchange Place,   "   "   "
Schurman, George W., . . . 15 W. 57th Street,   "   "   "
Schurman, Jacob Gould, ... Cornell University, Ithaca, N. Y.
Schurz, Carl. . . . . . . 24 E. 91st Street, New York City
Schurz, Carl Lincoln, . . . 19 William Street,   "   "   "
Scott, J. F., ... 349 W. 121st Street,   "   "   "
Scott, William, ... 25 Duane Street,   "   "   "
Scribner, Arthur H., ... 153 Fifth Avenue,   "   "   "
Scribner, Charles, ... 153 Fifth Avenue,   "   "   "
Seaman, Louis L., ... 247 Fifth Avenue,   "   "   "
Searle. Arthur, ... 41 Concord Avenue, Cambridge, Mass.
Seaver, Benjamin F., ... 111 Pierrepont Street, Brooklyn
Sedgwick, Arthur G., ... 52 William Street, New York City
Sedgwick, Ellery, ... 143 Fifth Avenue,   "   "   "
Sedgwick, Henry D., Care Mrs. Minturn, 109 E. 21st Street,   "   "   "
Seligman, E. R. A., ... 324 W. 86th Street,   "   "   "
Serven, A. Ralph, . . . 1419 "F" Street, N. W.. Washington, D. C.
Seward, George F , ... 97 Cedar Street, New York City

Sexton, Lawrence E.,	34 Pine Street,	New York City
Shainwald, Ralph L.,	100 William Street,	" " "
Shaw, Albert,	13 Astor Place,	" " "
Sheldon, Edward W.,	45 Wall Street,	" " "
Sherman, Arnold W,	265 Henry Street,	Brooklyn
Sherman, Frederick T.,	265 Henry Street,	"
Shillaber, William Jr.,	1 Broadway,	New York City
Shortt, W. A.,	32 Broadway,	" " "
Siedenberg, Reinhard,	Cotton Exchange,	" " "
Simes, William,		Petersham, Mass.
Sinclair, John,	16 E. 66th Street,	New York City
Slade, Francis Louis,	49 Cedar Street,	" " "
Slicer, Thomas R.,	156 E. 38th Street,	" " "
Smillie, James D.,	110 E. 38th Street,	" " "
Smith, Adelbert J.,	374 Central Park, West,	" " "
Smith, Bryan H.,	79 Pierrepont Street,	Brooklyn
Smith, Charles Robinson,	25 Broad Street,	New York City
Smith, Charles Stewart,	25 W. 47th Street,	" " "
Smith, Clarence B.,	71 E. 87th Street,	" " "
Smith, Frederick J.,	278 Mulberry Street,	" " "
Smith, Graham,	Reform Club,	" " "
Smith, J. Henry,	10 Wall Street,	" " "
Smith, William Alexander,	412 Madison Avenue,	" " "
Smyth, Nathan A.,	Criminal Court Building,	" " "
Snow, Henry Sanger,	81 Willoughby Street,	Brooklyn
Spahr, Charles B.,	Care "The Outlook,"	New York City
Spaulding, Henry K.,	501 W. 120th Street,	" " "
St. John, William M.,	Union League Club,	" " "
Stapler, H. B. B.,	48 Wall Street,	" " "
Stark, Joshua,	1206 Welles Building,	Milwaukee, Wis.
Stedman, Edmund C.,	Bronxville,	New York City
Steers, James R.,	31 Nassau Street,	" " "
Steinway, Frederick T.,	53rd Street and Park Avenue,	" " "
Stern, Benjamin,	32 W. 23rd Street,	" " "
Stewart, William R.,	31 Nassau Street,	" " "
Stimson, Daniel M.,	11 W. 17th Street,	" " "
Stokes, Anson Phelps, Jr., (Life),	Yale University,	New Haven, Conn.
Stokes, Harold M. Phelps, (Life),	229 Madison Avenue,	New York City
Stokes, I. N. Phelps, (Life),	229 Madison Avenue,	" " "
Stokes, James,	49 Cedar Street,	" " "
Stokes, J. G. Phelps, (Life),	229 Madison Avenue,	" " "
Strauss, Albert,	15 Broad Street,	" " "
Strauss, Frederick,	15 Broad Street,	" " "
Sturgis, Russell,	307 E. 17th Street,	" " "
Strong, George A.,	50 Wall Street,	" " "
Strong, Theron G.,	49 Wall Street,	" " "
Sturges, S. Perry,	305 Washington Avenue,	Brooklyn
Stuyvesant, Rutherford,	16 Exchange Place,	New York City
Sulzberger, Ferdinand,	45th Street and First Avenue,	" " "
Swan, Lyndon M.,	7 Wall Street,	" " "

Taft, Henry W., ... 40 Wall Street, New York City
Taggard, Rush, ... 195 Broadway, " " "
Tatham, Charles, ... 465 W. 23rd Street, " " "
Tatham, Edwin, ... 82 Beekman Street, " " "
Taussig, Walter M., ... 9-15 Murray Street, " " '
Taylor, Henry Ling, ... 60 W. 55th Street, " " '
Taylor, Stevenson, ... 123 W. 85th Street, " " "
Taylor, Walter F., ... 54 Wall Street, " " "
Taylor, William C., ... 94 Keap Street, Brooklyn
Terry, Roderick, ... 169 Madison Avenue, New York City
Terry, Seth Sprague, ... 126 E. 34th Street, " " "
Thacher, George O., ... 2 E. 86th Street, " " "
Thomae, Robert L. . . . . Scotch Plains, N. J.
Thompson, Hugh S., ... 346 Broadway, New York City
Thomson, William H., ... 23 E. 47th Street, " " "
Thorne, Samuel, Jr., ... 55 Liberty Street. " " "
Thornton, William, ... 117 Prince Street, " " "
Thurber, Francis B., ... 90 West Broadway, " " "
Tiebout, Charles H., ... 31 Grand Street, Brooklyn
Tod, J. Kennedy, ... 45 Wall Street, New York City
Todd, Henry A., ... 824 West End Avenue, " " "
Tomkins, Calvin, ... 17 Battery Place, " " "
Tompkins, Hamilton B., ... 229 Broadway, " " "
Train, Arthur C., ... 28 W. 47th Street, " " "
Trotter, William, ... 29 W. 35th Street, " " "
Tuckerman, Alfred, ... 1123 Broadway, " " "
Turnbull, George R.. . . . . . 33 Mercer Street, " " "

Uhl, Edward, ... P. O. Box 1207, New York City
Unckles, D. S., ... 957 St. Mark's Avenue, Brooklyn

Vail, Charles D., ... Geneva, N. Y.
Valentine, Henry C., (Life), ... 257 Broadway, New York City
Valentine, Robert G., . . Farmers Loan and Trust Co., " " "
Vallandingham, Edward N., ... Reform Club, " " "
Van Dusen, Samuel C., ... 27 Cliff Street, " " "
Van Iderstine, Robert, . . . 461 Washington Avenue, Brooklyn
Van Ingen, Edward H., ... 9 E. 71st Street, New York City
Van Nest, George W., ... 20 Broad Street, " " "
Villard, Harold G. . . . -. . 43 Cedar Street, " " "
Villard, Oswald Garrison, (Life), . . 206 Broadway, " " "

Warburg, F. M., (Life), . . . 52 William Street, New York City
Wadsworth, James W., ... Geneseo, N. Y.
Walcott, Philip K., ... 111 Broadway, New York City
Walker, Hay, ... Care of W. & H. Walker, Pittsburg, Pa.
Walker, John, ... 1231 Western Avenue, Alleghany City, "
Walker, Samuel C., ... Harbison & Walker, Pittsburg, "
Walker, William, ... " " " " "

Wallace, Jackson,	5 Liberty Street, New York City
Wallace, William H.,	6 Broadway, " "
Wallace, W. J.,	25 W 8th Street, " "
Walting, William English,	154 Eldridge Street, " "
Ward, Henry Galbreath,	7 Wall Street, " "
Ward, J. H.,	8 Kenyon Bldg., Louisville, Ky
Ward, J. Q. A.,	119 W 82nd Street, New York City
Warner, John De Witt,	54 William Street, " "
Warren, Edward H.,	4 Wall Street, " "
Warren, George A.,	630 I Street, N W, Washington, D C
Warren, H. Langford,	120 Boylston Street, Boston, Mass
Wasson, James B.,	154 Nassau Street, New York City
Watson, Charles W.,	50 Madison Avenue, " "
Webb, Willoughby L.,	63 Wall Street, " "
Weed, John W.,	62 William Street, " "
Weeks, E. R.,	346 Harrison Street, Kansas City, Mo
Weeks, Rufus W.,	P O Box 1683, New York City
Wehle, Theodore,	30 W. 83d Street, " "
Welch, Archibald A.,	Woodland Street, Hartford, Conn
Weld, Francis M.,	36 Nassau Street, New York City
Welling, R. W. G.,	2 Wall Street, " "
Wendell, Evert J.,	8 E. 38th Street, " "
Werthein, H. P.,	27 William Street, " "
Wetmore, Edmund,	34 Pine Street, " "
Wheeler, A. S.,	511 Sears Bldg., Boston, Mass
Wheeler, Everett P.,	21 State Street, New York City
Wheeler, James R.,	Columbia College, " "
Wheelock, George G.,	75 Park Avenue, " "
White, Alexander M.,	2 Pierrepont Place, Brooklyn
White, Alexander M., Jr.,	158 Columbia Heights, " "
White, Andrew D., (Life),	Ithaca, N Y
White, George C.,	Glen Ridge, N J
White, Harold T.,	1 Nassau Street, New York City
White, Horace,	18 W. 69th Street, " "
Whitlock, Bache McE.,	50 William Street, " "
Whitney, Edward B.,	50 Wall Street, " "
Whitridge, Frederick W.,	50 Wall Street, " "
Wickersham, George W.,	40 Wall Street, " "
Wiggin, Frederick H.,	55 W. 38th Street, " "
Wilcox, Ansley,	395 Main Street, Buffalo, N Y
Wilcox, David,	Metropolitan Club, New York City
Wilds, Howard Payson,	University Club, " "
Williams, L. L.,	Care E. C. Williams, 1010 7th Ave, " "
Williams, Perry P.,	Produce Exchange, " "
Williams, Richard H.,	1 Broadway, " "
Willis, Albert L.,	W. 183rd St., near Sedgwick Ave, " "
Wilson, Richard T.,	511 Fifth Avenue, " "
Wing, Henry T.,	162 Clinton Street, Brooklyn
Wise, B. E.,	21 Broad Street, New York City

Taft, Henry W.,	40 Wall Street, New York City
Taggard, Rush,	195 Broadway, " " "
Tatham, Charles,	465 W. 23rd Street, " " "
Tatham, Edwin,	82 Beekman Street, " " "
Taussig, Walter M,	9-15 Murray Street, " " "
Taylor, Henry Ling,	60 W. 55th Street, " " "
Taylor, Stevenson,	123 W. 85th Street, " " "
Taylor, Walter F.,	54 Wall Street, " " "
Taylor, William C.,	94 Keap Street, Brooklyn
Terry, Roderick,	169 Madison Avenue, New York City
Terry, Seth Sprague,	126 E. 34th Street, " " "
Thacher, George O.,	2 E. 86th Street, " " "
Thomae, Robert L.	Scotch Plains, N. J.
Thompson, Hugh S.,	346 Broadway, New York City
Thomson, William H.,	23 E. 47th Street, " " "
Thorne, Samuel, Jr.,	55 Liberty Street. " " "
Thornton, William,	117 Prince Street, " " "
Thurber, Francis B.,	90 West Broadway, " " "
Tiebout, Charles H.,	31 Grand Street, Brooklyn
Tod, J. Kennedy,	45 Wall Street, New York City
Todd, Henry A.,	824 West End Avenue, " " "
Tomkins, Calvin,	17 Battery Place, " " "
Tompkins, Hamilton B.,	229 Broadway, " " "
Train, Arthur C.,	28 W. 47th Street, " " "
Trotter, William,	29 W. 35th Street, " " "
Tuckerman, Alfred,	1123 Broadway, " " "
Turnbull, George R..	33 Mercer Street, " " "
Uhl, Edward,	P. O. Box 1207, New York City
Unckles, D. S.,	957 St. Mark's Avenue, Brooklyn
Vail, Charles D.,	Geneva, N. Y.
Valentine, Henry C., (Life),	257 Broadway, New York City
Valentine, Robert G.,	Farmers Loan and Trust Co., " " "
Vallandingham, Edward N.,	Reform Club, " " "
Van Dusen, Samuel C.,	27 Cliff Street, " " "
Van Iderstine, Robert,	461 Washington Avenue, Brooklyn
Van Ingen, Edward H.,	9 E. 71st Street, New York City
Van Nest, George W.,	20 Broad Street, " " "
Villard, Harold G.	43 Cedar Street, " " "
Villard, Oswald Garrison, (Life),	206 Broadway, " " "
Warburg, F. M., (Life),	52 William Street, New York City
Wadsworth, James W.,	Geneseo, N. Y.
Walcott, Philip K.,	111 Broadway, New York City
Walker, Hay,	Care of W. & H. Walker, Pittsburg, Pa.
Walker, John,	1231 Western Avenue, Alleghany City, "
Walker, Samuel C.,	Harbison & Walker, Pittsburg, "
Walker, William,	" " " " "

Wallace, Jackson,	26 Liberty Street, New York City
Wallace, William H.,	66 Broadway. " " "
Wallace, W. J.,	203 W. 80th Street, " " "
Walling, William English,	184 Eldridge Street, " " "
Ward, Henry Galbreath,	79 Wall Street, " " "
Ward, J. H.,	34 Kenyon Bldg., Louisville, Ky.
Ward, J. Q. A.,	119 W. 52nd Street, New York City
Warner, John De Witt,	54 William Street, " " "
Warren, Edward H.,	40 Wall Street, " " "
Warren, George A.,	620 I Street, N. W., Washington, D. C.
Warren, H. Langford,	120 Boylston Street, Boston, Mass.
Wasson, James B.,	154 Nassau Street, New York City
Watson, Charles W.,	500 Madison Avenue, " " "
Webb, Willoughby L.,	63 Wall Street, " " "
Weed, John W.,	62 William Street, " " "
Weeks, E. R.,	3408 Harrison Street, Kansas City, Mo.
Weeks, Rufus W.,	P. O. Box 1663, New York City
Wehle, Theodore,	59 W. 83d Street, " " "
Welch, Archibald A.,	Woodland Street, Hartford, Conn.
Weld, Francis M.,	36 Nassau Street, New York City
Welling, R. W. G.,	2 Wall Street, " " "
Wendell, Evert J.,	8 E. 38th Street, " " "
Werthein, H. P.,	27 William Street, " " "
Wetmore, Edmund,	34 Pine Street, " " "
Wheeler, A. S.,	511 Sears Bldg., Boston, Mass.
Wheeler, Everett P.,	21 State Street, New York City
Wheeler, James R.,	Columbia College, " " "
Wheelock, George G.,	75 Park Avenue, " " "
White, Alexander M.,	2 Pierrepont Place, Brooklyn
White, Alexander M., Jr.,	158 Columbia Heights, "
White, Andrew D., (Life).	Ithaca, N. Y.
White, George C.,	Glen Ridge, N. J.
White, Harold T.,	1 Nassau Street, New York City
White, Horace,	18 W. 69th Street, " " "
Whitlock, Bache McE.,	59 William Street, " " "
Whitney, Edward B.,	59 Wall Street, " " "
Whitridge, Frederick W.,	59 Wall Street, " " "
Wickersham, George W.,	40 Wall Street, " " "
Wiggin, Frederick H.,	55 W. 36th Street, " " "
Wilcox, Ansley,	295 Main Street, Buffalo, N. Y.
Wilcox, David,	Metropolitan Club, New York City
Wilds, Howard Payson,	University Club, " " "
Williams, L. L.,	Care E. C. Williams, 1910 7th Ave., " " "
Williams, Perry P.,	Produce Exchange, " " "
Williams, Richard H.,	1 Broadway. " " "
Willis, Albert L.,	W. 183rd St., near Sedgwick Ave., " " "
Wilson, Richard T.,	511 Fifth Avenue, " " "
Wing, Henry T.,	152 Clinton Street, Brooklyn
Wise, B. E.,	21 Broad Street, New York City

Wisner, Charles, ... Cotton Exchange, New York City
Wisner, H. G., ... 18 W. 12th Street, " " "
Witherbee. F. S., ... 71 Broadway, " " "
Wolff, Lewis S., ... 12 E. 70th Street, " " "
Woodbridge, Charles E., ... 63 Wall Street, " " "
Worcester, Edwin D., Jr., ... 35 Nassau Street, " " "
Wright, Jonathan, ... 73 Remsen Street, Brooklyn

Yates, Arthur G., . . . 130 So. Fitzhugh Street, Rochester, N.Y.
Yonge, Henry, ... Hotel Margaret, Brooklyn

Zabriskie, George, ... 49 Wall Street, New York City
Zerega, Richard A., ... 101 Classon Avenue, Brooklyn

ARTICLES OF INCORPORATION

OF

THE NEW YORK CIVIL SERVICE REFORM ASSOCIATION

[Filed May 11, 1900.]

KNOW ALL MEN BY THESE PRESENTS: That we, the undersigned, being persons of full age and all citizens of the United States, a majority of whom are also citizens of the State of New York, and being now Directors of an unincorporated association known as the New York Civil Service Reform Association, and organized for the purposes hereinafter mentioned ; being desirious of incorporation for the same purposes under the Membership Corporations Law of the State of New York, do hereby, pursuant to unanimous vote of all the members of the said Association, present and voting at a regularly called meeting thereof, and pursuant to authority given by the said unanimous vote at the said meeting, of which meeting notice of the intention so to incorporate was given personally or by mail to each member of such Association whose residence or Post Office address was known, at least thirty days before said meeting, and at which meeting the corporate name stated in paragraph First was by unanimous vote adopted, do hereby certify as follows :

FIRST.—The name or title by which the Association in which we desire to form ourselves as aforesaid shall be known in law, shall be the Civil Service Reform Association.

SECOND.—The territory in which its operations are to be principally conducted shall be the City of New York.

THIRD.—The city in which its principal office is to be located is the City of New York.

FOURTH.—The objects of the Association shall be to further the establishment of a system of appointment, promotion and removal in the Civil Service, founded upon the principle that public office is a public trust, admission to and retention in which should depend upon proven fitness ; and to take such action as may tend to secure the honest and efficient execution of laws and rules relating to the civil service, and to the proper administration thereof.

FIFTH.—The number of its directors shall be twenty-eight.

SIXTH.—The names of the persons to be its directors until its first annual meeting are as follows:

Samuel P. Avery, Truman J. Backus, Henry De Forest Baldwin, Edward Cary, Charles Collins, W. Bayard Cutting, Horace E. Deming, A. S. Frissell, Richard Watson Gilder, Edwin L. Godkin, J. Warren Greene, George McAneny, James McKeen, Jacob F. Miller, Samuel H. Ordway, William A. Perrine, George Foster Peabody, William J. Schieffelin, Carl Schurz, Charles A. Schieren, Thomas R. Slicer, Henry Sanger Snow, Anson Phelps Stokes, S. Perry Sturges, Henry W. Taft, William H. Thomson, Charles W. Watson and Everett P. Wheeler.

In WITNESS WHEREOF we have made, signed, acknowledged and filed this certificate in duplicate.

Dated this Eighth day of May, 1900.

C. SCHURZ,	WILLIAM H. THOMSON,
JACOB F. MILLER,	A. S. FRISSELL,
ANSON PHELPS STOKES,	GEORGE MCANENY,
EVERETT P. WHEELER,	CHARLES A. SCHIEREN,
CHARLES COLLINS,	SAMUEL P. AVERY,
SAMUEL H. ORDWAY,	GEORGE FOSTER PEABODY.
J. WARREN GREENE,	

STATE OF NEW YORK, } ss.
COUNTY OF NEW YORK, }

On this eighth day of May, one thousand and nine hundred, before me personally came Carl Schurz, Jacob F. Miller, Anson Phelps Stokes, Everett P. Wheeler, Charles Collins, J. Warren Greene, William H. Thomson, Samuel H. Ordway, A. S. Frissell, George McAneny, Charles A. Schieren, Samuel P. Avery and George Foster Peabody, to me personally known to be the persons described in and who made and signed the foregoing certificate, and severally duly acknowledged to me that they had made, signed and executed the same for the uses and purposes therein set forth.

F. W. HOERSCHGEN,
Notary Public, Kings County. (149)
(Certificate filed in New York County.)

Approved, May 9, 1900.

DAVID LEVINTRITT,
Justice of the Supreme Court of the State of New York

REPORT

OF THE

Executive Committee

OF THE

New York

Civil Service Reform Association

READ AT THE ANNUAL MEETING, MAY 10, 1905.

LIST OF MEMBERS, ETC.

NEW YORK
PUBLISHED FOR THE
CIVIL SERVICE REFORM ASSOCIATION
79 WALL STREET
1905

CONTENTS

Annual Report of the Executive Committee, - 5

Annual Report of the Treasurer, - - - 17

Constitution and By-Laws, - - - - 19

Roll of Officers and Members, - - - - 27

Articles of Incorporation, - - - - - 47

ANNUAL REPORT

OF THE

Executive Committee of the Civil Service Reform Association.

The twenty-eighth year of the Association has covered events of peculiar interest. In the Federal service, the competitive classification has been extended by President Roosevelt to additional branches until a very limited number of positions subject to classification, outside the seventy thousand fourth class postmasterships, remain unclassified. The system of labor registration has been extended to the Federal offices in four of the largest cities, and both in Washington and in these cities has been placed directly under the supervision and control of the Civil Service Commission. Throughout the country, interest in civil service reform is more marked than ever before. Even where defeat has followed the efforts to secure State or city laws, as in Colorado and Kansas City, we are assured that there will be no lessening of effort when the opportunity for again presenting the question occurs. In Wisconsin, a bill to cover the State service, supported by the strong recommendations of Governor LaFollette, has passed one house of the Legislature. Illinois is expected this year to pass a law applying the merit system to the State charitable institutions. In New Jersey, a law has already been enacted applying the examination system to the police and fire departments of Newark and Jersey City.

The New York State Commission, by instituting a system of thorough and periodical investigations of the work of municipal commisssions, has increased the respect for the civil service law and impressed on local authorities the necessity for its enforcement. Its action in removing from office the Troy Commissioners will have a particularly salutary effect. In the same way, the prompt action of Mayor McClellan in removing from office a Park Commissioner and an inefficient Board of Civil Service Commissioners for violation of the civil service rules, was an effective reminder to those who believed that under a Tammany administration the rules existed only to be broken. It is, however, to be regretted that the moral effect of this action has to a great degree been dissipated by the failure of the present commission to grasp the situation and to adopt administrative measures to cope with abuses which are known to exist. Its attitude of *laissez faire*, its condoning of lesser infractions, have led the patronage brokers, after a brief pause, to resume operations on the same scale as before. The Committee is so firmly convinced that the law and rules are being evaded by the heads of some departments, without real hindrance from the Municipal Commission, that it has felt it necessary, with considerable reluctance, to ask the State Commission to extend its investigations to New York City.

With a sense of the great loss the Association has sustained, we note here the deaths during the past year of James C. Carter and Samuel P. Avery. Mr. Carter had been a Vice-President for many years, and Mr. Avery had served long and faithfully as a member of the Executive Committee The Committee has placed upon its records and published resolutions expressing its appreciation of their long and valued services.

THE FEDERAL SERVICE.

It is not our purpose to do more in this report than briefly to refer to the important changes in the Federal service since the meeting of the National League in December last. By a series of orders the President has placed in the competitive service the Forest Reserve

Corps, numbering 538 ; the Finance Clerks in the post offices, numbering about 360, and, in addition, a number of positions of Inspectors and Special Agents in the Interior Department, and of persons employed in the Immigration service in foreign territory contiguous to the United States. The system of labor registration was put in operation in the Federal offices in New York on February 15th. This should effectually end the practice of placing these positions at the disposition of political leaders and should lead to a practical improvement in in the service.

The Committee has received few complaints in regard to the Federal offices in New York during the year. Some attempts were made in the course of the campaign to levy political assessments, with what success we are unable to say; but under the present administration a competitive employee at least may safely afford to disregard these requests, and undoubtedly many do. We take this opportunity to thank Collector Stranahan for his co-operation in defeating one of these attempts brought directly to his atttention.

THE STATE SERVICE.

CHANGES IN THE STATE CIVIL SERVICE COMMISSION.

At the end of 1904, Cuthbert W. Pound resigned from the State Commission to become legal adviser to Governor Higgins. The Committee cannot pass this by without an expression of appreciation of the important services rendered by Mr. Pound as an active and conscientious member of the board and later as its able presiding officer. His thorough knowledge of the civil service law, coupled with a sincere belief in the soundness of the principle upon which it is based, gave to his service as commissioner a peculiar value.

The vacancy has been filled by the appointment of Roscoe C. E. Brown, of New York City. Mr. Brown has been for a number of years a member of the Executive Committee of the Association, taking a deep and ing, removed the entire board from office and appointed as their successors a commission of three, two Democrats and one Republican. This action was not only fully justified, but, indeed, called for by the circumstances. There was no abuse of power, no attempt made to gain a partisan advantage. The wise, thorough and conservative policy of the State Commission in this case won general approbation and established a most important precedent.

INVESTIGATION OF THE NEW YORK COUNTY CLERK'S OFFICE.

Another important investigation was undertaken upon the complaint of the Association in regard to violations of law by Thomas L. Hamilton, County Clerk of New York County. It was alleged that he had made use of the many exempt and non-competitive positions in his office for political purposes and had distributed them among the Republican district leaders. Further, that the assent of the State Commission to certain transfers had been obtained, but that afterwards the transfers had not been carried out in good faith. The complaint originated in the case of one man who had been very unjustly treated. and who, as a result of this investigation, has been restored to his original position. Further action has been postponed to a later meeting.

NEED FOR A REVISION OF THE EXEMPT SCHEDULE.

The evidence laid before the State Commission in the case just referred to showed very clearly the abuses which exist in connection with exempt positions. In its last report the Committee urged a material reduction of the exempt list in the State service and we now renew this recommendation, in the belief that it is a matter of great importance, and should have the early consideration of the Commission

We express our appreciation of the uniform curtesy shown by the State Commission in granting hearings upon all matters in which the Association is interested and in furthering the investigations which the Association has desired to make through the records in its office.

MEASURES IN THE STATE LEGISLATURE.

The Association has watched the course of all bills in the legislature affecting directly or indirectly the merit system. Every bill introduced was carefully scrutinized and all those of importance were considered by the Law Committee. Through an arrangement with the Legislative Bureau of the City Club we received reports of the changes in status of the bills on our list a day after the changes were made. Briefs were filed with the appropriate committees, and, when necessary, hearing were requested. In all 152 bills were watched, of which 98 were opposed.

A large number of these bills provided for the payment of salary to persons retained in the City service in 1899 and 1900 in violation of the provisions of the civil service law. Still another large class of bills provided that the Police and Fire Commissioners might, after a re-hearing of the charges, reinstate policemen and firemen who had been dismissed after trial and had been out of the service for a number of years. Far more important were the bills amending the civil service law, and those providing pensions for civil employees.

Of the bills to amend the civil service law, only two secured passage by the legislature. One of these provided for the restoration of the salaries of veterans, which were reduced under the so-called "sweep bills" passed during the first year of Mayor Low's administration. The bill was particularly objectionable in that it attempted to accomplish this object by an amendment to the general civil service law. The other was an attempt to make it mandatory for the Civil Service Commission to admit to examination persons who had been guilty of crime before the age of fourteen, where now it is discretionary with the Commission.

The most important measure opposed by the Association was the Yale Bill, providing for the pensioning of

CONTENTS

Annual Report of the Executive Committee, - 5
Annual Report of the Treasurer, - - - 17
Constitution and By-Laws, - - - - 19
Roll of Officers and Members, - - - - 27
Articles of Incorporation, - - - - - 47

ATTITUDE OF THE MAYOR TOWARD THE CIVIL SERVICE LAW.

The Association publicly commended the action of the Mayor in removing an inefficient Commission and in appointing a new Commission with a reduced membership. It pledged its cordial co-operation at all times and in all efforts tending toward the enforcement of the civil service statute and rules. It felt that it had further ground for encouragement and congratulation when Mayor McClellan, in his annual message, called attention to the importance of the work of the Commission, spoke of the merit system as having been "accepted as a permanent part of our public policy," and characterized the principle of competition as essentially democratic. The appointment as President of the Commission of a man without experience in the working of the law, and who had not been known as interested in its purposes, was the more regretted; but the Association hopes that Mr. Baker will overcome this handicap and that his administration will show a decided advance in efficiency.

APPROPRIATION OF SALARIES FOR THE COMMISSIONERS.

One of the first matters agitated by the Commission appointed in October was the question of the salaries of the commissioners. Until May, 1902, all of the commissioners had served without compensation. At that time a salary of $6,000 was attached to the office of President, with the understanding that he should take executive control of the office. The contention of the new Commission, that the two associate members should receive some compensation for services rendered, appealed to many members of the Executive Committee as a fair proposition. When it was stated, however, that it was planned to give all three commissioners salaries of $6,000 the Secretary was instructed to communicate to the Mayor and to President Coler, that it was the sense of this Committee that to make the civil service commissionerships highly salaried offices would be dangerous to the merit system, in that it would tend to bring it into disrepute with the public. Nevertheless the Board of Estimate and Apportionment, against the protest of Comptroller Grout, fixed the salaries of the two Commissioners, other than the President, at $5,000 each and this action received the approval of the Mayor.

THE GENERAL CONDITION OF THE CITY SERVICE.

The many complaints received at the Association's office, which, on examination, proved to be well founded, and the results of the investigations which the Committee conducted into different branches of the city service, have led us to believe that the civil service law and rules are being violated by heads of departments to a very considerable degree, and that the present condition of the service is far from satisfactory. The Committee has believed, therefore, as we have stated above, that the good of the service would be promoted if the State Commission might hold its next investigation, under its general powers, here. It has asked that such an investigation be undertaken and this request has been granted. Among the specific matters presented to the State Commission were the charges against the Secretary of the Municipal Commission of misconduct in office; the general misuse of exempt positions to further partisan ends, as shown by the careful examination made by a special committee of appointments to exempt positions in the Finance Department; the employment without examination of examiners at ten dollars per day to mark ordinary examination papers; the large number of temporary appointments made without competitive examination; the frequent and continued violations of the labor rules and the use of labor positions for partisan purposes; the failure to keep efficiency records in accordance with the provisions of the rules, and, in addition, a number of individual cases arising in the competitive class.

WORK OF THE STANDING COMMITTEES.

The Standing Committees on Law, Examinations and Membership have held frequent meetings during the past year. No litigation has been undertaken by the Association, but the Law Committee has followed with interest the suits which are now pending, which are expected to test the question whether a classification duly established by the Civil Service Commission can be reviewed by means of a writ of certiorari. The Committee on Examinations has conducted a series of investigations into the administration of the law, the results of which have been embodied in the presentment to the State Commission. The Committee on Correspondence is now engaged in organizing correspondence committees throughout the State.

The receipts of the Treasury from all sources during the past year amounted to $6,588, an increase of $196.50 over the previous year, and the disbursements to $6,095.79. The membership has increased from 803 to 821. Of these, 17 are life members, 79 sustaining members and 725 regular members.

The Executive Committee wishes, in closing, to bear testimony to the importance of the work, particularly along educational lines, accomplished by the Women's Auxiliary, and cordially thanks them for the valuable assistance they have rendered to the Association.

Respectfully submitted,

JACOB F. MILLER,
Chairman.

ELLIOT H. GOODWIN,
Secretary.

ANNUAL REPORT OF THE TREASURER.

MAY 1, 1905.

Balance on hand, as per report, May 1, 1904..................$193.36

RECEIPTS :

From Annual Dues......................	$3,085.00		
" Sustaining Membership Dues........	1,640.00		
" Life Membership Dues..............	100.00		
" Subscriptions.......................	1,563.00		
" Women's Auxiliary..................	200.00	6,588.00	
		$6,781.36	

DISBURSEMENTS :

Salary of Secretary.......................	1,412.50		
" " Assistant Secretary.	637.50		
" " Editor of GOOD GOVERNMENT.....	625.00		
" " Clerks.........................	1,197.00		
Rent of Office...........................	500.00		
Telephone Service.......................	187.60		
Printing................................	162.72		
Postage and Stamped Envelopes...........	216.79		
Stationery..............................	144.99		
Office Expenses	166.16		
Expenses of Litigation...................	31.91		
Traveling Expenses	81.25		
Membership Committee Expenses..........	26.52		
Subscription to GOOD GOVERNMENT.......	532.65		
Expenses of Annual Dinner...............	173.20	6,095.79	

Balance on hand, April 30, 1905........................ $ 685.57

E. & O. E.

A. S. FRISSELL,
Treasurer.

set forth in this Constitution, and support all executive and legislative action which promote its purposes.

Article IV.

The conditions of membership shall be wholly independent of party preference. Questions shall not be discussed in the debate or in the publications of the Association upon party grounds. Neither the name nor influence of the Association shall be used on behalf of any party, or for procuring office or promotion for any person. But nothing in this article shall be construed to prevent the Association from opposing any candidate when in its opinion, or in that of three-fourths of the members of the Executive Committee, such course is demanded by the objects of the Association.

Article V.

There shall be a President, to be elected by the Association at the annual meeting, who shall perform the usual and prescribed duties of that office. He shall be, ex-officio, a member of all committees, with a casting vote only, and he may call special meetings of the Executive Committee whenever he thinks it necessary, and, with the assent of two members of the Executive Committee, special meetings of the Association.

There shall be ten Vice-Presidents, to be annually elected by the Association.

There shall be a Treasurer and Secretary, who shall perform the usual and prescribed duties of such officers. They shall be respectively appointed by the Executive Committee, and may be removed by them. The Treasurer shall be, ex-officio, a member of the Finance Committee of the Association.

There shall be an Executive Committee of twenty-five members, to be elected annually by the Association. Subject to these articles, the Executive Committee shall manage the affairs of the Association, direct and dispose of its funds, and from time to time make and modify by-laws for the Association and for its own action. The Executive Committee shall keep a record of its proceedings, and shall make a report to the

Association at the annual meeting. No appropriation of money by the Executive Committee beyond the amount in the hands of the Treasurer at the time shall bind any member of the Association, excepting those members of the Executive Committee who shall vote for it. Vacancies in the Executive Committee may be filled by the President for the remainder of the term. Other vacancies may be filled by the Executive Committee.

All the officers of the Association and members of the several Standing Committees shall be, ex-officio, members of the Executive Committee.

Article VI.

Each officer of the Association shall continue to hold office until his successor has been selected and is ready to enter upon the duties of the office.

Article VII.

There shall be an annual meeting of the Association on the second Wednesday of May, at which officers shall be elected for the ensuing year, and other appropriate business may be transacted; except in the year 1898, when the annual meeting shall be held on the second Wednesday of January.

Article VIII.

Any person may be proposed in writing for membership by any member of the Association, and shall be admitted upon approval of the Executive Committee. Members failing to pay their dues may be dropped from the roll by the Executive Committee.

Article IX.

The annual dues of each member shall be $5, payable on the 1st of May, and each member shall receive the annual report and all other publications of the Association. Sustaining members, on payment of twenty-five dollars annually, and Life members, exempt from annual dues on payment of one hundred dollars, may be elected by the Executive Committee at any regular meeting thereof.

Article X.

All provisions of this Constitution, except those relating to the rights of members, and the term of officers, may be suspended or amended by a vote of two-thirds of the Executive Committee, subject to the approval of the Association by a two-thirds vote of the members present either at the annual meeting or at a special meeting duly called. Due notice shall be given before any such annual or special meeting that the approval of the Association will, thereat, be asked for such action of the Executive Committee, and the notice shall clearly state the effect of such suspension or amendment in the text of the Constitution. Any member of the Association may propose amendments to the Constitution, which may be approved under the same conditions.

BY-LAWS.

FOR THE GOVERNMENT OF THE ASSOCIATION AND ITS COMMITTEES.

§ 1. The Annual meeting of the Association shall be held at such hour and place as the Executive Committee shall designate. The election of officers shall be by ballot, but any member not present may declare his vote by letter to the Secretary and it shall be counted.

§ 2. The meetings of each committee, unless otherwise especially provided for, shall be at half-past eight P. M., at which time the chairman shall direct the call of the names of its members and the Secretary shall record the names of those present and others as they appear.

§ 3. The order of business, before each committee shall be:
1. The reading and correction of the records of the last meeting.

And, thereafter, unless otherwise ordered, as follows:
2. Any statement due from the Treasurer.
3. Unfinished business from the last meeting.
4. Report from the Secretary's office.
5. Reports of standing committees.
6. Reports of special committees.
7. Proposals of new members and their election.
8. Miscellaneous business.

§ 4. Regular meetings of the Executive Committee shall be held on the second Wednesday of every month except July and August, but if that day be a holiday, then on the third Wednesday. Ten members of the Executive Committee shall constitute a quorum.

§ 5. Neither in the meetings of the Association nor of any committee shall any member speak more than once on any motion nor more than ten minutes at one time, without unanimous consent, nor shall any person, or his actions, be characterized on party grounds.

§ 6. Special meetings of any committee may be called by its chairman or by any three members, and due notice thereof shall be given by the Secretary.

Article X.

All provisions of this Constitution, except those relating to the rights of members, and the term of officers, may be suspended or amended by a vote of two-thirds of the Executive Committee, subject to the approval of the Association by a two-thirds vote of the members present either at the annual meeting or at a special meeting duly called. Due notice shall be given before any such annual or special meeting that the approval of the Association will, thereat, be asked for such action of the Executive Committee, and the notice shall clearly state the effect of such suspension or amendment in the text of the Constitution. Any member of the Association may propose amendments to the Constitution, which may be approved under the same conditions.

BY-LAWS.

FOR THE GOVERNMENT OF THE ASSOCIATION AND ITS COMMITTEES.

§ 1. The Annual meeting of the Association shall be held at such hour and place as the Executive Committee shall designate. The election of officers shall be by ballot, but any member not present may declare his vote by letter to the Secretary and it shall be counted.

§ 2. The meetings of each committee, unless otherwise especially provided for, shall be at half-past eight P. M., at which time the chairman shall direct the call of the names of its members and the Secretary shall record the names of those present and others as they appear.

§ 3. The order of business, before each committee shall be:
    1. The reading and correction of the records of the last meeting.

And, thereafter, unless otherwise ordered, as follows:
    2. Any statement due from the Treasurer.
    3. Unfinished business from the last meeting.
    4. Report from the Secretary's office.
    5. Reports of standing committees.
    6. Reports of special committees.
    7. Proposals of new members and their election.
    8. Miscellaneous business.

§ 4. Regular meetings of the Executive Committee shall be held on the second Wednesday of every month except July and August, but if that day be a holiday, then on the third Wednesday. Ten members of the Executive Committee shall constitute a quorum.

§ 5. Neither in the meetings of the Association nor of any committee shall any member speak more than once on any motion nor more than ten minutes at one time, without unanimous consent, nor shall any person, or his actions, be characterized on party grounds.

§ 6. Special meetings of any committee may be called by its chairman or by any three members, and due notice thereof shall be given by the Secretary.

§ 7. All notices to a member shall be sent to his address filed with the Secretary.

§ 8. On the demand of one-fifth of the members present, at any meeting of the Association or of a committee, the ayes and nays shall be called and recorded on any motion.

§ 9. All committees shall be appointed by the chair unless their selection shall be otherwise provided for.

§ 10. At each regular meeting of the Executive Committee, it shall be the duty of the Treasurer to make a statement of the amount of money in the treasury and of the place of its deposit, and, at the annual meeting, he shall state the source of all moneys received and the use made of the same during the past year.

§ 11. The Secretary shall keep a record of the proceedings of the Association and of the Executive Committee, and perform the other duties assigned him.

§ 12. Without the consent of three-fourths of the members present, no vote which will declare or fill a vacancy or elect a member of the Association shall be deemed carried, at the same meeting in which it was first moved.

§ 13. It shall require a vote of two-thirds of the members of the Executive Committee present to pass any vote under which more than $100 will be appropriated or the Association be pledged for more than that amount, and the Executive Committee alone shall have authority to create any charge upon the funds of the Association. But neither said committee nor any officer or officers of the Association shall be authorized to create a personal liability against any members but themselves.

§ 14. There shall be the following Standing Committees, of seven members each, which shall be selected annually by the Executive Committee:

(1) A Finance Committee, whose duty it shall be to devise and carry into effect, subject to the direction of the Executive Committee, suitable measures for raising funds, and to supervise and report upon the income and expenditures of the Associaton. The Finance Committee shall, in advance of each annual meeting of the Association, appoint an Auditing Committee from among its members, whose duty

it shall be to examine all vouchers and audit the accounts of the Treasurer, and to report thereon at the annual meeting.

(2) A Publication Committee, whose duty it shall be to prepare and recommend matters suitable for publication by the Association, and to take charge of the printing and distribution of whatever may be ordered printed.

(3) A Committee on Correspondence, whose duty it shall be to promote the objects of the Association through correspondence and co-operation with other organizations.

(4) A Committee on Administration, whose duty it shall be to investigate and report upon the administration of the civil service law and rules and to consider and recommend suitable methods of examination for admission to and promotion in the public service, and suitable procedure tending to make the system more efficient.

There shall also be a Standing Committee on Law of nine members, which shall be selected annually by the Executive Committee. Its duty shall be to consider all legislation affecting the civil service, to promote such as may be approved, and to oppose such as may be disapproved by the Executive Committee, and to prepare and recommend such amendments to the law as in their opinion will advance the purposes of the Association. The Law Committee shall have power to represent the Association in any legal proceedings which may be necessary in order to maintain or enforce the laws affecting the State or Municipal civil service.

There shall also be a Standing Committee on Membership of fifteen members, which shall be selected annually by the Executive Committee. Its duties shall be to devise and carry into effect measures for increasing the membership of the Association.

Each Standing Committee shall be competent to fix the number of its own quorum; but such quorum shall in no case be less than three.

§ 15. These By-Laws may be amended, or new By-Laws added, by a four-fifths vote at any meeting of the Executive Committee; or by a two-thirds vote, provided a statement of the proposed change had been entered on the minutes at the last meeting.

§ 16. Amendments proposed under the last clause of the tenth section of the constitution shall be first submitted to the Executive Committee.

OFFICERS—1905-1906.

PRESIDENT:

CARL SCHURZ

VICE-PRESIDENTS:

SILAS W. BURT
D. WILLIS JAMES
WILLIAM G. LOW
LEVI P. MORTON
ALEXANDER E. ORR

THEODORE ROOSEVELT
ELIHU ROOT
EDWARD M. SHEPARD
OSCAR S. STRAUS
EVERETT P. WHEELER

SECRETARY:
ELLIOT H. GOODWIN

ASSISTANT SECRETARY:
ALBERT DE ROODE

TREASURER:

A. S. FRISSELL

EXECUTIVE COMMITTEE:

JACOB F. MILLER, *Chairman.*
R. ROSS APPLETON
HENRY De FOREST BALDWIN
THEODORE M. BANTA
CHARLES C. BURLINGHAM
EDWARD CARY
CHARLES COLLINS
HORACE E. DEMING
SAMUEL B. DONNELLY
HOMER FOLKS
J. WARREN GREENE
GEORGE J. GREENFIELD

A. JACOBI
FRANKLIN B. LORD
GEORGE McANENY
JOHN G. MILBURN
SAMUEL H. ORDWAY
GEORGE FOSTER PEABODY
WILLIAM JAY SCHIEFFELIN
THOMAS R. SLICER
HENRY SANGER SNOW
NELSON S. SPENCER
ANSON PHELPS STOKES
WILLIAM H. THOMSON

CHARLES W. WATSON

STANDING COMMITTEES.

FINANCE:
WILLIAM JAY SCHIEFFELIN, *Chairman.*   ISAAC N. SELIGMAN
L. T. CHAMBERLAIN   JACOB W. MACK
HENRY G. CHAPMAN   SETH SPRAGUE TERRY
HORACE WHITE

PUBLICATION:
EDWARD CARY, *Chairman.*   ROB'T UNDERWOOD JOHNSON
GROSVENOR H. BACKUS   ISIDOR LEWI
GEORGE R. BISHOP   HERBERT PARSONS
WILSON M. POWELL, Jr.

CORRESPONDENCE:
EVERETT V. ABBOT, *Chairman.*   LEARNED HAND
ALBERT S. BARD   WILLIAM POTTS
EDWARDS H. CHILDS   CORNELIUS B. SMITH
WALTER U. TAYLOR

ADMINISTRATION:
SILAS W. BURT, *Chairman.*   GEORGE McANENY
HENRY G. CHAPMAN   PHILIP J. McCOOK
CHARLES COLLINS   CLARENCE BISHOP SMITH
NELSON S. SPENCER

LAW:
SAMUEL H. ORDWAY, *Chairman.*   WINFRED T. DENISON
HENRY De FOREST BALDWIN   A. LEO EVERETT
CHARLES C. BURLINGHAM   J. WARREN GREENE
JOSEPH P. COTTON, Jr.   HENRY W. HARDON
CHARLES E. HUGHES

MEMBERSHIP:
NATHAN A. SMYTH, *Chairman,*   CHARLES P. HOWLAND
ALBERT DE ROODE   FRANCIS H. KINNICUTT
CHARLES J. FAY   JAY E. LAWSHE
ROY C. GASSER   RUSSELL LOINES
GEORGE J. GREENFIELD   CHARLES W. McCANDLESS
ELLWOOD HENDRICK   CARL L. SCHURZ
ALFRED TUCKERMAN

MEMBERSHIP ROLL.
(May 1, 1905.)

SUSTAINING MEMBERS.

AMEND, BERNARD G.,	205 Third Avenue, New York City
BEHR, HERMAN,	75 Beekman Street, New York City
BREWSTER, WILLIAM,	Broadway and 47th Street, " " "
BULL, WILLIAM LANMAN,	38 Broad Street, " " "
BURLINGHAM, CHARLES C.,	27 William Street, " " "
CARY, EDWARD,	The "Times," New York City
CHAPLIN, DUNCAN D.,	64 Worth Street, " " "
CLYDE, WILLIAM P.,	19 State Street, " " "
COLLINS, CHARLES,	33 E. 17th Street, " " "
CRANE, RICHARD T.,	2541 Michigan Avenue, Chicago, Ill.
CUTTING, R. FULTON,	32 Nassau Street, New York City
DE COPPET, E. J.,	30 Broad Street, New York City
DEERING, JAMES,	Fullerton and Clybourne Avenues, Chicago, Ill.
DELANO, WARREN Jr.,	1 Broadway, New York City
DEMUTH, WILLIAM,	524 Fifth Avenue, " " "
DENISON, WINFRED T.,	126 E. 28th Street, " " "
DIMOCK, HENRY F.,	Pier 11, N. R., " " "
FRISSELL, A. S.,	530 Fifth Avenue, New York City
GILDER, RICHARD WATSON,	33 E. 17th Street, New York City
GOODWIN, J. J.,	11 W. 54th Street, " " "
GREENE, J. WARREN,	3 Broad Street, " " "
GREENFIELD, GEORGE J.,	32 Broadway, " " "
HARRIOT, S. CARMAN,	57 W. 39th Street, New York City
HEMENWAY, AUGUSTUS,	10 Tremont Street, Boston, Mass.
HENTZ, HENRY,	760 St. Mark's Avenue, Brooklyn
HUBER, JACQUES,	472 Broome Street, New York City
JACOBI, A.,	19 E. 47th Street, New York City
JOHNSON, ROBERT UNDERWOOD,	33 E. 17th Street, " " "
KENNEDY, JOHN S.,	31 Nassau Street, New York City
LOEB, JAMES,	52 William Street, New York City
LOEB, MORRIS,	273 Madison Avenue, " " "
LOINES, STEPHEN,	26 Garden Place, Brooklyn
LORD, FRANKLIN B.,	49 Wall Street, New York City
LOW, SETH,	30 E. 64th Street, " " "
LOW, WILLIAM G.,	58 Remsen Street, Brooklyn
MACK, JACOB W.,	92 Liberty Street, New York City

MACY, V. EVERIT,	68 Broad Street, New York City
MAITLAND, ALEXANDER,	14 E. 55th Street, " " "
MAXWELL, ROBERT.	62 Worth Street, " " "
MEYER, JACOB,	29 E. 63d Street, " " "
MILLER, JACOB F.,	120 Broadway, " " "
MINTURN, ROBERT SHAW,	109 E. 21st Street, " " "
MORTON, LEVI P.,	38 Nassau Street, " " "
MOSLE, GEORGE R.,	16–18 Exchange Place, " " "
McANENY, GEORGE,	19 E. 47th Street, New York City
McKIM, JOHN A.,	6 E. 74th Street, " " "
ORDWAY, SAMUEL H.,	27 William Street, New York City
OSBORN, WILLIAM CHURCH,	71 Broadway, " " "
PAGE, EDWARD D.,	60 Worth Street, New York City
PAGE, WILLIAM H., Jr.,	32 Liberty Street, " " "
PAGENSTECHER, A.,	P. O. Box 683, " " "
PEABODY, GEORGE FOSTER,	54 William Street, " " "
PHIPP, HENRY,	6 E. 87th Street, " " "
PINCHOT, JAMES W.,	1615 Rhode Island Avenue, Washington, D. C.
POWERS, NATHANIEL B.,	Lansingburg, N. Y.
RANDOLPH, STUART F.,	31 Nassau Street, New York City
RUSSELL, CHARLES H.,	15 Broad Street, " " "
SANDS, B. AYMAR,	31 Nassau Street, New York City
SCHEFER, CARL,	476 Broome Street, " " "
SCHIEFFELIN, WILLIAM JAY,	5 E. 66th Street, " " "
SCHIFF, JACOB H.,	P. O. Box 1193, " " "
SCHWAB, GUSTAV H.,	5 Broadway, " " "
SCRYMSER, JAMES A.,	107 E. 21st Street, " " "
SELIGMAN, ISAAC N.,	15 Broad Street, " " "
SHEPARD, EDWARD M.,	26 Liberty Street, " " "
SMITH, CORNELIUS B.,	101 E. 69th Street, " " "
SPENCER, NELSON S.,	27 William Street, " " "
SPEYER, JAMES,	257 Madison Avenue, " " "
STETSON, FRANCIS LYNDE,	15 Broad Street, " " "
STOKES, ANSON PHELPS,	100 William Street, " " "
STRAUS, OSCAR S.,	44 Warren Street, " " "
TAGGART, RUSH,	195 Broadway, New York City
THOMSON, WILLIAM H.,	23 E. 47th Street. " " "
TRASK, SPENCER,	54 William Street, " " "
VOSS, F. G.,	40 Wall Street, New York City
WARE, WILLIAM R.,	Milton, Mass.
WHITE, ALFRED T.,	130 Water Street, New York City
WHITE, HORACE,	18 W. 69th Street, " " "
WHITE, WILLIAM A.,	130 Water Street, " " "
WUNDERLICH, F. W.,	165 Remsen Street, Brooklyn

Abbot, Everett V., ... 45 Cedar Street, New York City
Abbott, Lawrence F., ... "The Outlook," " " "
Abbott, Lyman, ... 287 Fourth Avenue, " " "
Achelis, John, ... 68 Leonard Street, " " "
Adams, Edward D., ... 71 Broadway, " " "
Adams, Joseph, ... Union Stock Yards, Chicago, Ill.
Adams, Thatcher M., ... 36 Wall Street, New York City
Adler, Felix, ... 123 E. 60th Street, " " "
Affeld, Francis O., ... 873 President Street, Brooklyn
Agar, John G., ... 31 Nassau Street, New York City
Agnew, Andrew Gifford, . . . 22 William Street, " " "
Aiken, William A., . . . 157 Washington Street, Norwich, Conn.
Aitken, John W. . . . . . . 873 Broadway, New York City
Allen, Calvin H., ... 1 W. 72nd Street, " " "
Allen, Elmer A., ... 141 Broadway, " " "
Allen, Franklin, ... 371 Fulton Street, Brooklyn
Allert, Rudolf, . . 108th Street and Columbus Avenue, New York City
Alling, Joseph T., ... 400 Oxford Street, Rochester, N. Y.
Alsop, Reese F., ... 96 Remsen Street, Brooklyn
Anderson, Frank E., ... 486 Broadway, New York City
Andrews, J. Sherlock, . . . 111 St. Paul Street, Rochester, N. Y.
Appleton, Herbert . . . . 16 Exchange Place, New York City
Appleton, R. Ross, ... 146 Joralemon Street, Brooklyn
Arend F. J., ... 32 W. 73rd Street, New York City
Arnold, Lemuel H., ... 8 Broad Street, " " "
Arnstein, Eugene, ... 10 Wall Street, " " "
Atterbury, Grosvenor, . . . 20 W. 43rd Street, " " "
Avery, Samuel P., ... 4 E. 38th Street, " " "

Babbott, Frank L., ... 149 Lincoln Place, Brooklyn
Backus, Grosvenor H , ... 32 Liberty Street, New York City
Bacon, Gorham, ... 47 W. 54th Street, " " "
Bagley, Valentine N., ... 641 Washington Street, " " "
Bailey, H. P., ... 312 Broadway, " " "
Baldwin, Elbert F., ... "The Outlook," " " "
Baldwin, Henry de Forest, . . 49 Wall Street, " " "
Ball, Thomas P., ... 116 Broad Street, " " "
Bangs, Francis S , ... 40 Wall Street, " " "
Bangs, L. Bolton, ... 39 E. 72nd Street, " " "
Bannard, Otto T., ... 26 Broad Street, " " "
Banta, Theodore M , ... 348 Broadway, " " "
Bard, Albert Sprague, ... 25 Broad Street, " " "
Barker, Benjamin, ... 56 Pine Street, " " "
Barkley, Charles H., ... 82 Wall Street, " " "
Barney, A. H., (Life) . . . . 101 E. 38th Street, " " "
Barney, Danford N., ... Farmington, Conn
Barrett, Frank R., ... Box 105, Portland, Me.
Barrett, John D. . . . . . 49 Wall Street, New York City
Bartlett, P. G., ... 25 Broad Street, " " "

Batterman, Henry,	21 Clinton Street, Brooklyn
Bausch, Edward,	Rochester, N. Y.
Baylies, Edmund L.,	54 Wall Street, New York City
Bayne, Hugh,	40 Wall Street, " " "
Beckers, Alexander,	618 Hudson Street, Hoboken, N. J.
Beebe, William H. H.,	30 E. 64th Street, New York City
Beekman, Gerard,	47 Cedar Street, " " "
Beer, George Lewis,	329 W. 71st Street, " " "
Beers, Lucius H.,	49 Wall Street, " " "
Bell, Gordon Knox,	22 William Street, " " "
Benedict, Elliot S.,	76 William Street, " " "
Benson, Frank Sherman,	214 Columbia Heights, Brooklyn
Biggs, Charles,	13 Astor Place, New York City
Bijur, Nathan,	34 Nassau Street, " " "
Bishop, George R.,	142 E. 18th Street, " " "
Bispham, William,	66 Broadway, " " "
Blair, John N.,	26 Liberty Street, " " "
Boas, Franz,	123 W. 82d Street, " " "
Bode, Frederick H.,	care Gage Bros., Chicago, Ill.
Boller, Alfred P.,	1 Nassau Street, New York City
Borden, M. C. D.,	Box 1794, " " "
Bowen, C. Winthrop,	5 E. 63rd Street, " " "
Bowker, R. R.,	298 Broadway, " " "
Brachhausen, G. A.,	Rahway, N. J.
Brackett, George C.,	50 Remsen Street, Brooklyn
Bradt, Herbert S.,	120 Broadway, New York City
Brewer, Calvert,	55 Cedar Street, " " "
Brewster, Charles O.,	32 Liberty Street, " " "
Briesen, Arthur von, (Life)	49 Wall Street, " " "
Briscoe, S. William,	20 Sanford Avenue, Flushing, N. Y.
Brite, James,	111 Fifth Avenue, New York City
Brown, Addison,	45 W. 89th Street, " " "
Brown, Augustus H.,	262 W. 136th Street, " " "
Brown, Edwin H.,	141 Broadway, " " "
Brown, Everit,	27 William Street, " " "
Brown, Henry T.,	16 St. Paul's Place, Brooklyn
Brown, Roscoe C. E.,	" Tribune " Office, New York City
Brown, Thatcher M.,	36 E. 37th Street, " " "
Browne, Thomas Q., Jr.,	Morristown, N. J.
Brownell, William C.,	153 Fifth Avenue, New York City
Brush, W. Franklin,	16 E. 37th Street, " " "
Buckingham, C. L.,	38 Park Row, " " "
Bunnell, James S.,	51 Broadway, " " "
Burnett, Henry L.,	P. O. Building, " " "
Burr, Winthrop,	7 Wall Street, " " "
Burt, Silas W.,	30 Broad Street, " " "
Bush, J. Adriance,	100 Broadway, " " "
Butler, Howard R.,	22 E. 91st Street, " " "

Butler, Nicholas Murray, ... 119 E. 30th Street, New York City
Buttfield. William J., ... 96 Wall Street, " " "
Byrne, James, ... 24 Broad Street, " " "

Cadwalader, John L., ... 40 Wall Street, New York City
Cahen, I. J., ... 1 Madison Avenue, " " "
Calkins, Leighton, ... 25 Broad Street, " " "
Canfield, George F., ... 49 Wall Street, " " "
Carnegie, Andrew, (Life) . . . . 2 E. 91st Street, " " "
Carter, Frederick B., ... 61 Church Street, Montclair, N. J.
Carter, George F., ... Fanwood, N. J.
Cary, Clarence, ... 59 Wall Street, New York City
Cassatt, George M., ... 327 Broadway, " " "
Cauldwell, C. M., ... 16 W. 54th Street, " " "
Cauldwell, S. Millbank, ... Pelham Manor, N. Y.
Chaffee, J. Irwin, . Sedgwick Avenue, Fordham Heights, New York City
Chamberlain, D. H., ... West Brookfield, Mass.
Chamberlain, L. T., ... 222 W. 23 Street, New York City
Chambers, William P., ... 55 Liberty Street, " " "
Chanute, Octave, ... 413 East Huron Street, Chicago, Ill.
Chapman, George, ... 2717 Broadway, New York City
Chapman, Henry G., ... 79 Wall Street, " " "
Chase, George, ... 35 Nassau Street, " " "
Chauncey, Daniel, ... 129 Joralemon Street, Brooklyn
Cheney, F. W., ... South Manchester, Conn.
Cheney, George L., ... 131 E. 57th Street, New York City
Cheney, Louis R., ... Woodland Street, Hartford, Conn.
Childs, Edwards H., ... 59 Wall Street, New York City
Choate, Joseph H., ... 40 Wall Street, " " "
Choate, Joseph H. Jr., ... 40 Wall Street, " " "
Choate, William G., ... 40 Wall Street, " " "
Cillis, Hubert, ... 20 Nassau Street, " " "
Claflin, John, ... 224 Church Street, " " "
Clarke, Samuel B., ... 32 Nassau Street, " " "
Cleveland, Treadwell, ... 27 William Street, " " "
Codington, Perley M., ... 1487 Broadway, " " "
Coffin, E. R., ... 62 Cedar Street, " " "
Cohen, William N., ... 22 William Street, " " "
Collins, Atwood, ... Asylum Avenue, Hartford, Conn.
Collins, Stephen W., ... 69 Wall Street, New York City
Collyer, Robert, ... 201 W. 55th Street, " " "
Comstock, Albert, ... 56 Pine Street, " " "
Conant, Charles A., ... 38 Nassau, Street, " " "
Conger, Clarence R., ... 37 Liberty Street, " " "
Conger, Henry C., ... 140 W. 82nd Street, " " "
Conger, Henry Rutgers, ... 40 Wall Street, " " "
Cook, Walter, ... 3 W. 29th Street, " " "
Cooley, Alford Warriner, . Civil Service Commission. Washington, D C.
Cope, Francis R., ... Aubury, Germantown, Pa.

Corrigan, Joseph E.,	District Attorney's Office, New York City
Cotton, Joseph P., Jr.,	52 William Street, " " "
Coudert, Frederick R., Jr.,	71 Broadway, " " "
Cowperthwait, J. Howard,	195 Park Row, " " "
C ykendall, S. D.,	33 Coenties Slip, " " "
Crane, Frederick,	Bloomfield, N. J.
Crane, Leroy B.,	277 Broadway, New York City
Cranford, Walter V.,	215 Montague Street, Brooklyn
Cravath, Paul D.,	52 William Street, New York City
Crawford, Gilbert H.,	32 Liberty Street, " " "
Creevey, John J.,	41 Wall Street, " " "
Croly, Herbert D.,	14 Vesey Street, " " "
Cromwell, Frederic,	32 Nassau Street, " " "
Cromwell, Lincoln,	1 Greene Street, " " "
Croswell, J. G.,	17 W. 44th Street, " " "
Curtis, William E.,	30 Broad Street, " " "
Cushing, William E.,	Society for Savings Bldg., Cleveland, O.
Cutler, Arthur H.,	20 E. 50th Street, New York City
Cutting, R. Bayard,	32 Nassau Street, " " "
Cutting, W. Bayard,	24 E. 72nd Street, " " "
Cuyler, C. C.,	44 Pine Street, " " "
Daboll, Henry E.,	Plainfield, N. J.
Dale, Alfred G.,	Ozone Park, N. Y.
Dana, Charles L.,	53 W. 53rd Street, New York City
Davidge, William H.,	49 Wall Street, " " "
Davies, Julien T.,	32 Nassau Street, " " "
Davies, William Gilbert,	32 Nassau Street, " " "
Davis, Benjamin P.,	107 Wall Street, " " "
Davis, Charles Henry,	25 Broad Street, " " "
Davis, G. Pierrepont,	Woodland Street, Hartford, Conn.
Davis, Horace A.,	135 Broadway, New York City
Davison, Charles Stewart,	56 Wall Street, " " "
Day, Clarence S.,	45 Wall Street, " " "
DeForest, R. W.,	30 Broad Street, " " "
Deming, Horace E.,	13 William Street, " " "
de Roode, Albert,	79 Wall Street, " " "
Despard, W. D.,	6 Hanover Street, " " "
Dettmer, Jacob G.,	27 Prospect Park W., Brooklyn
Devine, Thomas J.,	19 Portsmouth Terrace, Rochester, N. Y.
DeWitt, Theodore,	88 Nassau Street, New York City
Dickinson, Robert L.,	168 Clinton Street, Brooklyn
Dickson, James B.,	49 Wall Street, New York City
Dittenhoefer, A. J.,	96 Broadway, " " "
Dix, John A.,	Care L. Thomson & Co., Albany, N. Y.
Dodge, Cleveland H.,	99 John Street, New York City
Dominick, H. B.,	3 W. 29th Street, " " "
Dommerich, L. F.,	57 Greene Street, " " "

Donnelly, Samuel B.,	360 Putnam Avenue, Brooklyn
Doty, Ethan Allen,	726 St. Mark's Avenue, "
Dougherty, J. Hampden,	27 William Street, New York City
Dows, Tracy,	Room 102, Produce Exchange, " " "
Dulon, Rudolf,	115 Broadway, " " "
Dunham, Edward K.,	338 E 26th Street, " " "
Dunning, S. Wright,	80 Madison Avenue, " " "
Eastman, A. H.,	363 Grand Avenue, Brooklyn
Eastman, George,	400 East Avenue. Rochester, N. Y.
Eaton, Henry W.,	45 William Street, New York City
Eaton, S. Edward,	660 Hudson Street, " " "
Ecaubert, F.,	18 Rose Street, " " "
Elderkin, John.	Lotos Club, 558 Fifth Avenue, " " "
Eliot, Charles W.,	Cambridge, Mass.
Elkins, Stephen B.,	1626 K Street, Washington, D. C.
Ely, Alfred,	31 Nassau Street, New York City
Ely, Arthur H.,	56 Wall Street, " " "
Ely, Moses,	2 Wall Street, " " "
Ely, Robert E.,	23 West 44th Street, " " "
Emmons, Arthur B.,	60 Park Avenue, " " "
Emmons, Samuel F.,	U. S. Geological Survey, Washington, D. C.
Erbslöh, R.,	364 Broadway, New York City
Everest, Charles M.,	506 West Avenue, Rochester, N. Y.
Everett, A. Leo,	49 Wall Street, New York City
Ewart, Richard H.,	115 Franklin Street, " " "
Ewing, Thomas,	67 Wall Street, " " "
Fabbri, Alessandro,	11 E. 62d Street, New York City
Fabbri, Ernesto G.,	11 E. 62d Street, " " "
Fahnestock, H. C.,	2 Wall Street, " " "
Fairchild, Benjamin T.,	P. O. Box 1120, " " "
Fairchild, Charles S.,	46 Wall Street, " " "
Faure, John P.,	346 Broadway, " " "
Fay, Charles J.,	49 Wall Street, " " "
Field, Hamilton E.,	106 Columbia Heights, Brooklyn
Finch, Edward R.,	53 Washington Square, New York City
Fisher, George H.,	308 Walnut Street, Philadelphia, Pa.
Fisher, George H.,	278 Sterling Place, Brooklyn
Fleitmann, Ewald,	484 Broome Street, New York City
Folks, Homer,	105 E. 22nd Street, " " "
Ford, Worthington C.,	Care Library of Congress, Washington, D. C.
Forrest, C. R.,	Asylum Avenue, Hartford, Conn.
Fox, Austen G., (Life),	45 W. 33d Street, New York City
Fraenckel, Richard H.,	19 and 21 Greene Street, " " "
Frankenheimer, John,	25 Broad Street, " " "
Frissell, H. B.,	Hampton, Va.
Frothingham, Howard P.,	2 Wall Street, New York City
Fuller, Frank,	61 Fifth Avenue, " " "

Fuller, Paul,	71 Broadway, New York City
Fullerton, Alexander, (Life),	7 W. 8th Street, " " "
Fullerton, Henry S.,	71 Broadway, " " "
Funk, I. K.,	195 Washington Park, Brooklyn
Gaillard, William D.,	141 Broadway, New York City
Garrison, Wendell P.,	206 Broadway, " " "
Garver, John A.,	44 Wall Street, " " "
Gasser, Roy C.,	35 Wall Street, " " "
Gibney, V. P.,	16 Park Avenue, " " "
Gibson, William J.,	26 Liberty Street, " " "
Gitterman, John M.,	1317 F Street, N. W., Washington, D C.
Goadby, Clarence,	21 W. 35th Street, New York City
Goddard, George A.,	10 Tremont Street, Boston, Mass.
Goldman, Julius,	31 Nassau Street, New York City
Goldmark, James,	67 Cortlandt Street, " " "
Goodale, John McGregor,	42 Broadway, " " "
Goodnow, Frank J.,	49 Riverside Drive, " " "
Goodwin, Elliot H.,	79 Wall Street, " " "
Gottheil, Paul,	Produce Exchange, " " "
Gottsberger, Francis,	156 Broadway, " " "
Gould, Elgin R. L.,	281 Fourth Avenue, " " "
Grant, De Forest,	22 E. 46th Street, " " "
Grant Percy S.,	7 W. 10th Street, " " "
Gray, Henry G ,	161 Madison Avenue, " " "
Green, Noah,	478 Central Park, West, " " "
Greenbaum, Samuel,	141 Broadway, " " "
Greene, Francis V.,	816 Fidelity Building, Buffalo, N. Y.
Greenough, John,	31 W. 35th Street, New York City
Greer, David H.,	7 Gramercy Park, " " "
Grinnell, William Morton,	40 Wall Street, " " "
Gross, Charles E.,	Asylum Avenue, Hartford, Conn.
Gulliver, W. C.,	120 Broadway, New York City
Guthrie, William D.,	52 William Street, " " "
Gwynne, Arthur C.,	Rye, N. Y.
Gwynne, John A.,	" "
Hagemeyer, F. E.,	F 15, Produce Exchange, New York City
Haines, C. G ,	138 W. 109th Street, " " "
Haines, Henry F.,	2 Wall Street, " " "
Hall, Elial F., (Life)	East 4th Street, Jamestown, N. Y.
Hall, Valentine G.,	45 Broadway, New York City
Hamilton, E. Luther,	146 Broadway, " " "
Hamlin, Frank, H ,	Canandaigua, N. Y.
Hand, Learned,	2 Wall Street, New York City
Harbeck, Charles T.,	Islip, N. Y.
Harding, Edward,	Chestnut Hill, Philadelphia, Pa.
Hardon, Henry Winthrop,	313 W. 71st Street, New York City
Harrison, Robert L.,	59 Wall Street, " " "

Hart, John Wilson, . . District Attorney's Office, New York City
Hasslacher, Jacob, . . . 100 William Street, " " "
Hastings, Thomas S., ... 27 W. 43th Street, " " "
Hayes, J. Noble, ... 68 William, " " "
Heath, Frank E., ... 95 Liberty Street, " " "
Healy, A. Augustus, ... 198 Columbia Heights, Brooklyn
Heinze, Arthur P., ... 31 Nassau Street, New York City
Henderson, Harold G.. . . . . 128 E. 34th Street, " " "
Hendrick, Ellwood, ... 139 E. 40th Street, " " "
Henriques, C. A., ... 25 W. 49th Street, " " "
Hentz, Leonard S., ... 769 St. Mark's Avenue, Brooklyn
Hess, Henry E., ... 32 Nassau Street, New York City
Hessberg, Max, ... 13 William Street, " " "
Hicks, Benjamin D., ... Old Westbury, N. Y.
Higginson, James J., ... 16 E. 41st Street, New York City
Hinkley, Samuel Neilson, . . . Apthorpe Hall Cambridge, Mass.
Hinrichs, Frederick W., . . . 76 William Street, New York City
Hitchcock, Welcome G., (Life) . . 453 Broome Street, " " "
Hobart, Henry L., ... 120 Front Street, " " "
Hodges, Harrison B., ... 16 Gramercy Park, " " "
Hodgman, George F., ... 806 Broadway, " " "
Hoe, Richard M., . . . Room 102, Produce Exchange, " " "
Hoe, Robert, ... 504 Grand Street, " " "
Holt, Henry, ... 29 W. 23d Street, " " "
Holt, Roland, ... 711 Madison Avenue, " " "
Hoppin, Frederick S., Jr.. . . 131 E. 19th Street, " " "
Hoppin, William W., ... 54 William Street, " " "
Hornblower, William B., . . . 24 Broad Street, " " "
Howe, Daniel R., ... Asylum Avenue, Hartford, Conn.
Howe, Horace J., ... 25 Gold Street, Yonkers, N. Y.
Howe, Wirt, ... 135 Broadway, New York City
Howland, Charles P., ... 35 Wall Street, " " "
Hoyt, Gerald L., ... 311 Fifth Avenue, " " "
Hubbard, Thomas H., . . . 16 W. 58th Street, " " "
Hubbell, Charles Bulkeley, . . . 35 Nassau Street, " " "
Hughes, Charles E., ... 96 Broadway, " " "
Hull, Charles A., ... 72 Wall Street, " " "
Huntington, Francis C., . . . 54 William Street, " " "
Huntington, Samuel, ... 146 Broadway, " " "
Huntington, William R., . . . 804 Broadway, " " "
Huyler, John S., ... 64 Irving Place, " " "

Ireland, F. G., ... 61 Elm Street, New York City
Isham, Samuel, . . . 6th Avenue and 40th Street, " " "
Ives, Brayton, ... 37 Wall Street, " " "

Jackson, Frederick W., ... Westchester, N. Y.
Jackson, John G., ... 35 Wall Street, New York City
James, D. Willis, ... 99 John Street, " " "

Jaretzki, Alfred, ... 49 Wall Street, New York City
Jay, Pierre, ... 5 Exeter Street, Boston, Mass.
Jay, William, ... 48 Wall Street, New York City
Jellenix, Felix, ... 17 William Street, " " "
Jennings, Frederick B., ... 15 Broad Street, " " "
Jesup, Morris K., ... 195 Madison Avenue, " " "
Johnson, James G., ... 655 Broadway, " " "
Johnson, Willis Fletcher, . . . 154 Nassau Street, " " "
Josephthal, Sidney L., ... 350 Broadway, " " "

Kahn, Otto H., (Life), ... 54 William Street, New York City
Kane, S. Nicholson, ... 23 W. 47th Street, " " "
Kellogg, Francis B , ... 328 Douglas Bldg, Los Angeles, Cal.
Kelsey, Clarence H., ... 146 Broadway, New York City
Kennaday, Paul, ... 88 Grove Street, " " "
Kennedy, Edward G., ... 220 Fifth Avenue, " " "
Kenneson, Thaddeus D., . . . 13 William Street, " " "
Kenyon, Alan D., ... 49 Wall Street, " " "
Kenyon, William Houston. . . . 49 Wall Street, " " "
Keppler, Rudolph, ... 25 Broad Street, " " "
Kernan, John D., ... 37 Liberty Street, " " "
Kidder, Camillus G., ... 27 William Street, " " "
Kidder, Edward H., ... 170 Broadway. " " "
Kilmer, Alfred G., ... 80 Broadway, " " "
Kimball, A. R., ... Orange, N. J.
King, Delcevare, ... 126 Summer Street, Boston, Mass.
King, William F., ... 410 Broadway, New York City
Kinnicutt, Francis H., ... 35 Wall Street, " " "
Kinnicutt, Francis P., ... 42 W. 37th Street, " " "
Kirchhoff, Charles, ... 232 William Street, " " "
Kissell, Gustav E., (Life), . . . 32 Liberty Street, " " "
Kissel, Rudolph H., ... 32 Nassau Street, " " "
Klein, Isaac H., ... 45 Cedar Street, " " "
Klupfel, Charles, Care North German Lloyd, 5 Broadway, " " "
Knapp, Shepherd, ... 266 Lexington Avenue, " " "
Knauth, Antonio, ... 233 West 70th Street, " " "
Knox, Herbert H., ... 45 Broadway, " " "
Kohler, Max J., ... 119 Nassau Street, " " "
Kuhne, Percival, ... 13 William Street, " " "
Kunhardt, Henry R., ... 124 W. 74th Street, " " "
Kunhardt, William B., ... 1 Broadway, " " "

Laimbeer, Francis E., ... 99 Nassau Street, New York City
Lambert, William B., ... Highland Street, Cambridge Mass.
Lansing, J. Townsend, ... 82 State Street, Albany, N. Y.
Larocque, Joseph, ... 40 Wall Street, New York City
Larremore, Wilbur, ... 32 Nassau Street. " " "
Lawrence, Cyrus J., ... 15 Wall Street, " " "
Lawrence, Walter B., ... 35 Wall Street, " " "

Lawshe, Jay E., ... 69 Wall Street, New York City
Lea, Henry Charles, ... 2000 Walnut Street, Philadelphia, Pa.
Leavens, George St. J.. . . . 72 Bible House, New York City
Leavitt, John Brooks, ... 30 Broad Street. " " "
Leaycraft, J. Edgar, ... 19 W. 42nd Street, " " "
Lederle, Ernest J., ... 471 W. 143d Street, " " "
Ledoux, Albert R., ... 9 Cliff Street, " " "
Lee, W. H. L., ... 25 Pine Street, " " "
Le Gendre, William, ... 59 Wall Street, " " "
Lehmaier, Louis A., ... 78 Beekman Street, " " "
Lethbridge, R. P., ... 49 Wall Street, " " "
Levi, Albert A., ... 108 Exchange Court, " " "
Lewi, Isidore, ... 3 E. 81st Street, " " "
Lewis, August, ... 151 Greene Street, " " "
Lewis, Richard V., ... 130 W. 42d Street, " " "
Lindsay, Alexander M., . . . 373 East Avenue, Rochester, N. Y.
Littauer, Lucius N., ... Gloversville, N. Y.
Livingston, Goodhue, . . . 38 E. 65th Street, New York City
Livingston, Julius I., ... 52 Broadway, " " "
Lockwood, Benoni, ... 56 Irving Place, " " "
Lockwood, Charles D., . . District Attorney's Office, " " "
Logan, Walter S., ... 27 William Street, " " "
Loines, Russell H., ... 27 W. 11th Street, " " "
Lord, F. B., Jr.. . . . . . 49 Wall Street, " " "
Lounsbery, Richard P., . . . 15 Broad Street, " " "
Lovell, Joseph J., ... Avondale Place, Woodhaven, N. Y.
Low, C. Adolph, ... 41 Liberty Street, New York City
Lowe, William E., ... 49 Wall Street, " " "
Lowndes, James, . . . 1505 Pennsylvania Avenue, Washington, D. C.
Ludlow, James B., ... 45 Cedar Street, New York City
Luther, George Martin, . . . 25 Broad Street, " " "
Lyman, Frank, ... 34 Remsen Street, Brooklyn
Lyman, George T., ... Bellport, N. Y.
Lyman, Theodore, ... Woodland Street, Hartford, Conn.
Lynde, Rollin H., ... 82 Beaver Street, New York City

Macdonough, A. R., ... 105 E. 15th Street, New York City
Macfarlane, Wallace, ... 32 Liberty Street, " " "
MacMullen, C. W., ... 20 Broad Street, " " "
MacVeagh, Charles, . . . 15 Broad Street, " " "
Mallinckrodt, Edward, . Mallinckrodt Chemical Works, St. Louis, Mo.
Mansfield, Howard, ... 49 Wall Street, New York City
Mapes, Charles V., ... 143 Liberty Street, " " "
Marling, Alfred E., ... 21 Liberty Street, " " "
Markoe, Francis H., ... 15 E. 49th Street, " " "
Marshall, Charles H., ... 45 William Street, " " "
Marshall, Fielding L., ... 32 Nassau Street, " " "
Marshall, Louis, ... 30 Broad Street, " " "
Marsters, A., A., ... 15 Dey Street, " " "

Martin, John, ... Grymes Hill, Staten Island, N. Y.
Martin, T. Comerford, ... 114 Liberty Street, New York City
Mason, Alexander T., ... 13 William Street, " " "
Mason, Alfred Bishop, ... Apartado 130, City of Mexico
Matthews, Brander, . . . 681 West End Avenue, New York City
Mathews, Robert, ... 135 Spring Street, Rochester, N. Y
Matthewson, Arthur, ... 139 Montague Street, Brooklyn
Maxwell, William H., ... 121 W. 82nd Street, New York City
Mellen, Chase, ... 52 William Street, " " "
Merck, George, ... 15 University Place, " " "
Merrill, Charles E., ... 44 E. 23d Street, " " "
Merrill, Payson, ... 31 Nassau Street, " " "
Messervy, George P., ... 7 Wall Street, " " "
Milburn, John G., ... 54 Wall Street, " " "
Miller, George Douglas, . . . 125 State Street, Albany, N. Y.
Miller, Hoffman, ...' 80 Broadway, New York City
Miller, Theodore C., ... 177 Montague Street, Brooklyn
Mills, L. H., ... 473 Broome Street, New York City
Mitchell, Edward, ... 44 Wall Street, " " "
Moffat, George B., ... 5 Nassau Street, " " "
Moffat, R. Burnham, ... 63 Wall Street, " " "
Montgomery, R. M., ... 27 Pine Street, " " "
Moore, W. H. H., ... Box 402, " " "
Morse, Horace J., ... 820 St. Mark's Avenue, Brooklyn
Morse, Richard C., ... 35 Sidney Place, "
Mortimer, Richard, ... 11 Wall Street, New York City
Mosenthal, P. J., ... 46 Cedar Street, " " "
Mosle, A. Henry, ... 30 Broad Street, " " "
Mott, William F., ... Toms River, N. J.
Moulton, Franklin W., ... 59 Wall Street, New York City
Munro, J. G., ... 61 Erie County Bank Building, Buffalo, N. Y.
Munro, Willis, . . 61 Erie County Bank Building, " "
Murray, James B., ... 23 Belmont Terrace, Yonkers, "
Murray, Joseph K., ... 90 Wall Street, New York City
Myers, Nathaniel, ... 25 Broad Street, " " "

McAlpin, George L., ... 9 E. 90th Street, New York City
McCagg, Louis Butler, ... 18 E. 84th Street, " " "
McCandless, Charles W., ... 90 Nassau Street, " " "
McCook, Philip J., ... 15 William Street, " " "
McIntosh, James H., ... 346 Broadway, " " "
McKeen, James, ... 136 Henry Street, Brooklyn
McKeever, J. Lawrence, . . . 164 Lexington Avenue, New York City
McMahon, Fulton, ... 54 William Street, " " "

Nadal, Charles C., ... 142 E. 35th Street, New York City
Naumberg, Elkan, ... 48 W. 58th Street, " " "
Naumberg, George W., ... 33 Wall Street, " " "
Naumberg, Walter W., ... 33 Wall Street, " " " .

Nelson, Henry Loomis,	Williams College, Williamstown, Mass.
Nelson, H. W., Jr.,	Marshfield Hills, "
Nevius, John H. C.,	33 Union Square, New York City
Newton, R. Heber,	East Hampton, N. Y.
Nichols, George L.,	66 E. 56th Street, New York City
Nichols, George M.,	277 Adelphi Street, Brooklyn
Nichols, W. N.,	353 Clinton Avenue, "
Nicoll, James C.,	51 W. 10th Street, New York City
North, Thomas M.,	160 Central Park South, " " "
Nourse, Charles J., Jr.,	82 Beaver Street, " " "
Oakes, Charles,	9 Pine Street, New York City
O'Connor, John A.,	12 E. 44th Street. " " "
Ogden, Rollo,	206 Broadway, " " "
Olin, Stephen H.,	32 Nassau Street, " " "
Olyphant, Robert,	21 Cortlandt Street, " " "
Opdyke, William S.,	20 Nassau Street, " " "
Oppenheimer, Henry S.,	741 Madison Avenue. " " "
Ordway, Edward W.,	1093 Dean Street, Brooklyn
Orr, Alexander E.,	102 Remsen Street, "
Osborne, Thomas M.,	Auburn, N. Y.
Packard, Edwin,	241 Henry Street, Brooklyn
Page, Walter H.,	34 Union Square, New York City
Parker, Frederick S.,	32 Garden Place, Brooklyn
Parks, J. Waring,	49 Wall Street, New York City
Parrish, Samuel L.,	25 Broad Street, " " "
Parsons, Herbert,	52 William Street, " " "
Parsons, John E.,	52 William Street, " " "
Paulding, James Kirk,	130 E. 24th Street. " " "
Pauli, H. G.,	15 S. William Street, " " "
Peck, George G.,	18 East 65th Street, " " "
Peckham, Wheeler H.,	80 Broadway, " " "
Pedersen, James,	20 E. 46th Street, " " "
Pell, Frederick A.,	Lakewood, N. J.
Pendleton, Francis K.,	25 Broad Street, New York City
Perkins, Robert P.,	41 Union Square, " " "
Perrine, William A.,	2440 N. Marshall Street, Philadelphia, Pa.
Phillips, Lee,	247 W. 71st Street, New York City
Phoenix, Phillips,	568 Broad Street, " " "
Pierce, Franklin,	31 Nassau Street, " " "
Pierce, Henry H.,	120 Broadway, " " "
Pierrepont, Henry E.,	216 Columbia Heights, Brooklyn
Pierrepont, Robert Low,	Box 449, Bay Shore, N. Y.
Pinchot, Gifford,	1615 Rhode Island Avenue, Washington, D. C.
Pope, A. A.,	Hartford, Conn.
Pope, George A.,	926 St. Paul Street, Baltimore, Md.
Potter, Frederick,	71 Broadway, New York City
Potter, Henry C.,	113 W. 40th Street, " " "

Potts, William,	65 Essex Avenue, Orange, N. J.
Powell, Wilson M., Jr.,	29 Wall Street, New York City
Prentice, William P.,	52 Broadway, " " "
Price, Joseph M.,	158 West Broadway, " " "
Pryer, Charles,	New Rochelle, N. Y.
Pryor, James W.,	65 Wall Street, New York City
Putnam, George Haven,	27 W. 23d Street, " " "
Putnam, George P.,	160 Fifth Avenue, " " "
Putnam, Harrington,	404 Washington Avenue, Brooklyn
Putnam, Irving,	27 W. 23rd Street, New York City
Pyne, Moses Taylor,	263 Madison Avenue, " " "
Rainsford, W. S.,	209 E. 16th Street, New York City
Rand, George C.,	107 Wall Street, " " "
Rand, William H., Jr.	Criminal Court Building, " " "
Raven, A. A.,	51 Wall Street, " " "
Raymond, Charles H.,	26 Liberty Street, " " "
Raymond, Rossiter W.	123 Henry Street, Brooklyn
Reichhelm, Edward P.,	23 John Street, New York City
Reynolds, James B.,	55 W. 44th Street, " " "
Rice, Edwin T., Jr.,	59 Wall Street, " " "
Richards, C. A. L.,	169 Power Street, Providence, R. I.
Rives, George L.,	14 W. 38th Street, New York City
Robb, J. Hampden,	23 Park Avenue, " " "
Robinson, Beverly R.,	42 W. 37th Street, " " "
Robinson, Moncure,	7 E. 42d Street, " " "
Rogers, John S.,	31 Nassau Street, " " "
Romaine, Louis Tyson,	84 Beaver Street, " " "
Roome, W. Harris,	287 Fourth Avenue, " " "
Roosevelt, Theodore,	Oyster Bay, N. Y.
Root, Elihu,	32 Nassau Street, New York City
Rose, Arthur P.,	Geneva, N. Y.
Rose, Charles J.,	" "
Rosenbaum, S. D.,	51 Franklin Street, New York City
Rosendale, Simon L.,	57 State Street, Albany, N. Y.
Rosenfeld, George,	35 South William Street, New York City
Rowe, William V.,	49 Wall Street, " " "
Rublee, George,	15 Broad Street, " " "
Rumsey, Dexter P.,	742 Delaware Street, Buffalo, N. Y.
Saint Gaudens, Augustus,	Windsor, Vt.
Salomon, William,	25 Broad Street, New York City
Sand, Henry A. L.,	32 Liberty Street, " " "
Sand, Max E.,	Ardsley-on-Hudson, N. Y.
Sanger, William Cary,	Sangerfield, "
Savage, Minot J.,	34th Street and Park Avenue, New York City
Sayer, W. Murray, Jr.,	398 Washington Avenue, Brooklyn
Scharmann, Hermann B.,	170 W. 59th Street, New York City
Schieren, Charles A.	405 Clinton Avenue, Brooklyn

Schnakenberg, D.,	6 Hanover Street, New York City
Schrader, George H. F.,	32 Rose Street, " " "
Schumacher, Charles,	41 Exchange Place, " " "
Schurman, George W.,	15 W. 57th Street, " " "
Schurz, Carl.	24 E. 91st Street, " " "
Schurz, Carl Lincoln,	19 William Street, " " "
Scott, J. F.,	349 W. 121st Street, " " "
Scott, William,	25 Duane Street, " " "
Scribner, Arthur H,	153 Fifth Avenue. " " "
Scribner, Charles,	153 Fifth Avenue, " " "
Seaman, Louis L.,	247 Fifth Avenue. " " "
Searle, Arthur,	41 Concord Avenue, Cambridge, Mass.
Seaver, Benjamin F.,	111 Pierrepont Street, Brooklyn
Sedgwick, Arthur G.,	52 William Street, New York City
Sedgwick, Ellery,	143 Fifth Avenue, " " "
Sedgwick, Henry D.,	120 E. 22d Street, " " "
Seligman, E. R. A.,	324 W. 86th Street, " " "
Serveu, A. Ralph,	1419 "F" Street; N. W., Washington, D. C.
Seward, George F.,	97 Cedar Street, New York City
Sexton, Lawrence E.,	34 Pine Street, " " "
Seymour, Origen S.,	35 Wall Street, " " "
Shainwald, Ralph L.,	100 William Street, " " "
Shaw, Albert.	13 Astor Place, " " "
Sheldon, Edward W.,	45 Wall Street, " " "
Sherman, Arnold W,	265 Henry Street, Brooklyn
Shillaber. William Jr.,	1 Broadway, New York City
Shortt, W. A.,	32 Broadway, " " "
Siedenberg, Reinhard,	Cotton Exchange, " " "
Simes, William,	Petersham, Mass.
Sinclair, John,	16 E 66th Street, New York City
Slade, Francis Louis,	49 Cedar Street, " " "
Slicer, Thomas R.,	156 E. 38th Street, " " "
Smillie, James D.,	110 E. 38th Street, " " "
Smith, Adelbert J.,	35 Nassau Street, " " "
Smith, Charles Robinson,	25 Broad Street, " " "
Smith, Charles Stewart,	25 W. 47th Street, " " "
Smith, Clarence B.,	71 E. 87th Street, " " "
Smith, F. Hopkinson,	150 E. 34th Street, " " "
Smith, Frederick J.,	278 Mulborry Street, " " "
Smith, Graham,	Harvard Club, " " "
Smith, J. Henry,	10 Wall Street, " " "
Smith, William Alexander,	412 Madison Avenue, " " "
Smyth, Nathan A.,	Criminal Court Building, " " "
Snow, Henry Sanger,	81 Willoughby Street, Brooklyn
Spaulding, Henry K.,	501 W. 120th Street, New York City
St. John, William M.,	Union League Club, " " "
Stapler, H. B. B.,	32 Liberty Street, " " "
Stark, Joshua,	1206 Welles Building, Milwaukee, Wis.
Stedman, Edmund C.,	Bronxville, New York City

Steers, James R.,	31 Nassau Street, New York City
Steinway, Frederick T.,	53rd Street and Park Avenue, " " "
Stern, Benjamin,	32 W. 23rd Street, " " "
Stewart, William R.,	31 Nassau Street, " " "
Stimson, Daniel M.,	11 W. 17th Street, " " "
Stokes, Anson Phelps, Jr., (Life),	Yale University, New Haven, Conn.
Stokes, Harold M. Phelps, (Life),	229 Madison Avenue, New York City
Stokes, I. N. Phelps, (Life),	229 Madison Avenue, " " "
Stokes, James,	49 Cedar Street, " " "
Stokes, J. G. Phelps, (Life),	229 Madison Avenue, " " "
Strauss, Albert,	15 Broad Street, " " "
Strauss, Frederick,	15 Broad Street, " " "
Strong, George A.,	50 Wall Street, " " "
Strong, Theron G.,	49 Wall Street, " " "
Sturges, S. Perry,	305 Washington Avenue, Brooklyn
Sturgis, Russell,	307 E. 17th Street, New York City
Stuyvesant, Rutherford,	16 Exchange Place, " " "
Sulzberger, Ferdinand,	45th Street and First Avenue, " " "
Taft, Henry W.,	40 Wall Street, New York City
Tatham, Charles,	465 W. 23rd Street, " " "
Tatham, Edwin,	82 Beekman Street, " " "
Taussig, Walter M.,	9-15 Murray Street, " " "
Taylor, Stevenson,	123 W. 85th Street, " " "
Taylor, Walter F.,	54 Wall Street, " " "
Taylor, William C.,	25 So. Portland Avenue, Brooklyn
Terry, Roderick,	169 Madison Avenue, New York City
Terry, Seth Sprague,	126 E. 34th Street, " " "
Thacher, George O.,	2 E. 86th Street, " " "
Thomae, Robert L.	Scotch Plains, N. J.
Thorne, Samuel, Jr.,	Criminal Court Building, New York City
Thornton, William,	117 Prince Street, " " "
Thurber, Francis B.,	90 West Broadway, " " "
Tiebout, Charles H.,	31 Grand Street, Brooklyn
Tison, Alexander,	11 William Street, New York City
Tod, J. Kennedy,	45 Wall Street, " " "
Todd, Henry A.,	824 West End Avenue, " " "
Tomkins, Calvin,	17 Battery Place, " " "
Tompkins, Hamilton B.,	229 Broadway, " " "
Train, Arthur C.,	28 W. 47th Street, " " "
Trotter, William,	124 E. 30th Street, " " "
Tuckerman, Alfred,	1123 Broadway, " " "
Tuckerman, Eliot,	44 Pine Street, " " "
Turnbull, George R.,	33 Mercer Street, " " "
Uhl, Edward,	P. O. Box 1207, New York City
Unckles, D. S.,	957 St. Mark's Avenue, Brooklyn
Vail, Charles D.,	Geneva, N. Y.

Valentine, Charles A.,	1 E. 27th Street, New York City
Valentine, Henry C., (Life),	257 Broadway, " " "
Valentine, Robert G.,	112 E. Capitol Street, Washington, D. C.
Vallandingham, Edward N.,	Reform Club, New York City
Van Dusen, Samuel C.,	27 Cliff Street, " " "
Van Iderstine, Robert,	43 Cedar Street, " " "
Van Ingen, Edward H.,	9 E. 71st Street, " " "
Van Nest, George W.,	20 Broad Street, " " "
Villard, Harold G.	43 Cedar Street, " " "
Villard, Oswald Garrison, (Life),	206 Broadway, " " "
Warburg, F. M., (Life),	52 William Street, New York City
Wadsworth, James W.,	Geneseo, N. Y.
Walcott, Philip K.,	111 Broadway, New York City
Walker, Hay,	Care of W. & H. Walker, Pittsburg, Pa.
Walker, John,	1231 Western Avenue, Alleghany City, "
Walker, Samuel C.,	Harbison & Walker, Pittsburg, "
Walker, William,	" " " " "
Wallace, Jackson,	26 Liberty Street, New York City
Wallace, William H.,	66 Broadway, " " "
Wallace, W. J.,	203 W. 80th Street, " " "
Walling, William English,	184 Eldridge Street, " " "
Ward, Henry Galbreath,	79 Wall Street, " " "
Ward, J. H.,	34 Kenyon Bldg., Louisville, Ky.
Ward, J. Q. A.,	119 W. 52nd Street, New York City
Warner, John De Witt,	54 William Street, " " "
Warren, George A.,	308 V Street, N. E., Washington, D. C.
Warren, H. Langford,	120 Boylston Street, Boston, Mass.
Wasson, James B.,	154 Nassau Street, New York City
Watson, Charles W.,	500 Madison Avenue, " " "
Webb, Willoughby L.,	63 Wall Street, " " "
Weed, John W.,	62 William Street, " " "
Weeks, E. R.,	3408 Harrison Street, Kansas City, Mo.
Weeks, Rufus W.,	P. O. Box 1663, New York City
Welch, Archibald A.,	Woodland Street, Hartford, Conn.
Weld, Francis M.,	5 Nassau Street, New York City
Welling, R. W. G.,	2 Wall Street, " " "
Wendell, Evert J.,	8 E. 38th Street, " " "
Werthein, H. P.,	27 William Street, " " "
Wetmore, Edmund,	34 Pine Street, " " "
Wheeler, A. S.,	511 Sears Bldg., Boston, Mass.
Wheeler, Everett P.,	21 State Street, New York City
Wheeler, James R.,	Columbia College, " " "
Wheelock, George G.,	75 Park Avenue, " " "
White, Alexander M.,	2 Pierrepont Place, Brooklyn
White, Alexander M., Jr.,	158 Columbia Heights, "
White, Andrew D., (Life).	Ithaca, N. Y.
White, George C.,	Glen Ridge, N. J.
White, Harold T.,	1 Nassau Street, New York City

Whitlock, Bache McE.,	59 William Street, New York City
Whitney, Edward B.,	49 Wall Street, " " "
Whitridge, Frederick W.,	59 Wall Street, " " "
Wickersham, George W.,	40 Wall Street. " " "
Wilcox, Ansley,	295 Main Street, Buffalo, N. Y.
Wilcox, David,	Metropolitan Club, New York City
Wilds. Howard Payson,	University Club, " " "
Williams, L. L.,	Care E. C. Williams, 135 Broadway, " " "
Williams, Norman A.,	42 E. 41st Street, " " "
Williams, Perry P.,	Produce Exchange, " " "
Williams, Richard H.,	1 Broadway. " " "
Williams, Stephen G.,	953 Madison Avenue, " " "
Willis, Albert L.,	W. 183rd St., near Sedgwick Ave., " " "
Wilson, Richard T.,	511 Fifth Avenue, " " "
Wing, Henry T.,	152 Clinton Street, Brooklyn
Wise, B. E.,	21 Broad Street, New York City
Wisner, Charles,	Cotton Exchange, " " "
Wisner, H. G.,	18 W. 12th Street, " " "
Witherbee F. S.,	71 Broadway, " " "
Wolff, Lewis S.,	12 E. 70th Street, " " "
Woodbridge, Charles E.,	63 Wall Street, " " "
Worcester, Edwin D., Jr.,	35 Nassau Street, " " "
Wright, Jonathan,	44 W. 49th Street, " " "
Yates, Arthur G.,	130 So. Fitzhugh Street, Rochester, N.Y.
Yonge, Henry,	Hotel Margaret, Brooklyn
Zabriskie, George,	49 Wall Street, New York City
Zerega, Richard A.,	101 Classon Avenue, Brooklyn

ARTICLES OF INCORPORATION

OF

THE NEW YORK CIVIL SERVICE REFORM ASSOCIATION

[Filed May 11, 1900.]

KNOW ALL MEN BY THESE PRESENTS: That we, the undersigned, being persons of full age and all citizens of the United States, a majority of whom are also citizens of the State of New York, and being now Directors of an unincorporated association known as the New York Civil Service Reform Association, and organized for the purposes hereinafter mentioned; being desirious of incorporation for the same purposes under the Membership Corporations Law of the State of New York, do hereby, pursuant to unanimous vote of all the members of the said Association, present and voting at a regularly called meeting thereof, and pursuant to authority given by the said unanimous vote at the said meeting, of which meeting notice of the intention so to incorporate was given personally or by mail to each member of such Association whose residence or Post Office address was known, at least thirty days before said meeting, and at which meeting the corporate name stated in paragraph First was by unanimous vote adopted, do hereby certify as follows:

FIRST.—The name or title by which the Association in which we desire to form ourselves as aforesaid shall be known in law, shall be the Civil Service Reform Association.

SECOND.—The territory in which its operations are to be principally conducted shall be the City of New York.

THIRD.—The city in which its principal office is to be located is the City of New York.

FOURTH.—The objects of the Association shall be to further the establishment of a system of appointment, promotion and removal in the civil service, founded upon the principle that public office is a public trust, admission to and retention in which should depend upon proven fitness; and to take such action as may tend to secure the honest and efficient execution of laws and rules relating to the civil service, and to the proper administration thereof.

FIFTH.—The number of its directors shall be twenty-eight.

SIXTH.—The names of the persons to be its directors until its first annual meeting are as follows :

Samuel P. Avery, Truman J. Backus, Henry De Forest Baldwin, Edward Cary, Charles Collins, W. Bayard Cutting, Horace E. Deming, A. S. Frissell, Richard Watson Gilder, Edwin L. Godkin, J. Warren Greene, George McAneny, James McKeen, Jacob F. Miller, Samuel H. Ordway, William A. Perrine, George Foster Peabody, William J. Schieffelin, Carl Schurz, Charles A. Schieren, Thomas R. Slicer, Henry Sanger Snow, Anson Phelps Stokes, S. Perry Sturges, Henry W. Taft, William H. Thomson, Charles W. Watson and Everett P. Wheeler.

In WITNESS WHEREOF we have made, signed, acknowledged and filed this certificate in duplicate.

Dated this Eighth day of May, 1900.

C. SCHURZ,	WILLIAM H. THOMSON,
JACOB F. MILLER,	A. S. FRISSELL,
ANSON PHELPS STOKES,	GEORGE MCANENY,
EVERETT P. WHEELER,	CHARLES A. SCHIEREN,
CHARLES COLLINS,	SAMUEL P. AVERY,
SAMUEL H. ORDWAY,	GEORGE FOSTER PEABODY.
J. WARREN GREENE,	

STATE OF NEW YORK, } ss.
COUNTY OF NEW YORK,

On this eighth day of May, one thousand and nine hundred, before me personally came Carl Schurz, Jacob F. Miller, Anson Phelps Stokes, Everett P. Wheeler, Charles Collins, J. Warren Greene, William H. Thomson, Samuel H. Ordway, A. S. Frissell, George McAneny, Charles A. Schieren, Samuel P. Avery and George Foster Peabody, to me personally known to be the persons described in and who made and signed the foregoing certificate, and severally duly acknowledged to me that they had made, signed and executed the same for the uses and purposes therein set forth.

F. W. HOERSCHGEN,
Notary Public, Kings County. (149)
(Certificate filed in New York County.)

Approved, May 9, 1900.

DAVID LEVINTRITT,
Justice of the Supreme Court of the State of New York.

REPORT

OF THE

Executive Committee

OF THE

New York

Civil Service Reform Association

Read at the Annual Meeting, May 9, 1906.

LIST OF MEMBERS, ETC.

NEW YORK
PUBLISHED FOR THE
CIVIL SERVICE REFORM ASSOCIATION
79 WALL STREET
1906

CONTENTS

Annual Report of the Executive Committee,
Annual Report of the Treasurer,
Constitution and By-Laws,
Roll of Officers and Members,
Articles of Incorporation,

ANNUAL REPORT

OF THE

Executive Committee of the Civil Service Reform Association.

The year just passed—the twenty-ninth of the Association's existence—has been a year of continued progress for civil service reform both in the country at large and locally in New York State and City. In the last few years, in fact since Theodore Roosevelt became President, and unquestionably to a large extent on account of his well known attitude toward this cause, there has been a marked revival of interest and activity, shown strikingly in the introduction of civil service reform laws for states and cities. The two bills mentioned in our last report, one applying to the state service of Wisconsin, and the other to the state charitable institutions of Illinois, both became laws which are now being intelligently and efficiently enforced by commissioners thoroughly in sympathy with their purpose. This year the special session of the Pennsylvania legislature, after refusing to pass the state civil service law called for by the Governor's message, at the urgent request of Mayor Weaver, strongly seconded by the efforts of the Pennsylvania Civil Service Reform Association, has passed an act applying to Philadelphia under which an excellent commission has been appointed. The introduction of state civil service bills in Ohio and New Jersey, as well as in Pennsylvania, while they failed of passage this year, is further evidence of the increased interest in the movement.

The New York State Commission has conducted a number of important investigations which have resulted in materially strengthening the service locally. In addition, it has taken a more conservative stand in the matter of granting exemptions from competitive examination, has restored to the competitive class a number of positions in the county service, and, pursuant to Governor Higgins' recommendation, has brought four additional counties within the classified service. In spite of the Governor's ambiguous policy in retaining in office for nine months Harry H. Bender, the Fiscal Supervisor of State Charities, accused of levying political assessments in violation of the civil service law and permitting him, without hindrance, to evade investigation by the State Civil Service Commission through a court proceeding, brought on technical grounds to test the Commission's powers, we believe that, in the end, this case will be fully aired and that the Governor may be counted on to take final action which will go far toward putting an end to the despicable practice of extorting money from employees for political purposes, under an implied threat of depriving them of their means of livelihood.

The administration of the New York City service began to show an improvement after the completion of the investigation by the State Commission, which has become marked since the re-election of Mayor McClellan. In view of our former criticism of the Municipal Commission, we are particularly glad to bear testimony to this improvement and promise them our assistance in continuing it.

The Association has gained in numbers during the year and has added to its influence by the formation of correspondence committees in various cities of the state. These committees will prove of great assistance in watching the enforcement of the law and in preventing the passage of hostile legislation.

Through the death, on October 12th, of Elial F. Hall, the Association has lost one of its original members and strongest friends. Although recently Mr. Hall had been compelled by ill health to live elsewhere, he never lost touch with, or interest in, the work in which the Association was engaged and has been a generous contributor toward its support. By his will he has left a bequest to the Association of sixteen shares of stock in the Title Guarantee and Trust Company of New York, which, by resolution of the committee, will be set apart as a special fund to be known as the Elial F. Hall fund.

The two most important matters in which the Association has been engaged during the year have been the investigations by the State Commission of the New York City service and of the collection of political contributions in the office of the Fiscal Supervisor of State Charities in Albany, both undertaken at the instance of the Association.

INVESTIGATION OF THE NEW YORK CITY SERVICE.

At the last annual meeting the Executive Committee reported that at the Association's request, the State Commission had decided upon an investigation of the city service. The investigation began with the examination of witnesses on May 18 and 19. The Association's Committee on Administration tendered to the State Commission the services of Mr. Philip J. McCook as counsel. For the time and labor which he gave to this work the Association is much indebted to him. On May 19, the Commission adjourned to June 22, when the examination of witnesses was concluded. In the interim, its Secretary and Chief Examiner conducted a comprehensive examination of the records.

The inquiry followed closely the line of the Association's presentment, although the Commission did not feel able to take up and examine into certain of its specifications. Two reports were made public by the State Commission after its meeting on September 28. Commissioner Kraft, in his minority report, could find no fault with any of the acts of the Municipal Commission.

The majority report is a painstaking review of the evidence. The charges against the former secretary,

Henry Berlinger, are carefully analyzed and his conduct in a number of instances—particularly in regard to his political activity—is characterized as improper and as reflecting on his fitness to fill the position of secretary. The report suggests that the Municipal Commission "inquire into the fitness of its secretary and other subordinates and into the efficiency of the organization of the examining department with a view to replacing incapable or unworthy public servants and of introducing improved methods."

The employment without examination of so-called "expert examiners" to do work which could be as well done by appointees from the eligible lists, the selection of monitors to serve at examinations by favor rather than in accordance with the rules, the arbitrary re-rating of examination papers after the name of the candidate has become known, are all strongly censured and the Municipal Commission cautioned that further disregard of the rules in these respects "would warrant the inference that opportunity is designedly given for the exercise of political or personal favoritism and would deserve the severest condemnation." The delay in holding and rating examinations after temporary appointments in the absence of lists had been authorized, is held to be inexcusable and the examinations held for provisional appointments are criticised. The Municipal Commission is called upon to correct abuses in the granting of transfers and in the appointment of laborers under special titles unauthorized by the law or rules and attention is called to the unfairness in permitting men to register as foremen simply to get employment as laborers ahead of applicants higher up on the lists. The records of efficiency, as kept in the Municipal Commission itself and as filed by most of the departments, are pronounced farcical. The report concludes with a recognition of the difficulties confronting the Municipal Commission and appreciation of their efforts to correct abuses for which their predecessors were responsible.

The results of this investigation have been much more far-reaching and important for the city service than has been popularly supposed. On January 1, Secretary Berlinger, who had been kept in his position by strong political influence, but of whose shortcomings as secretary the Commission had been fully convinced, was removed and a competent man appointed in his place. Under practically every head dealt with in the report improvements have been made. These can better be dealt with when we come to treat of the city service as a whole.

THE BENDER POLITICAL ASSESSMENT CASE.

The Civil Service Law, Section 24, contains a number of provisions to protect civil employees against the extortion of political contributions. One of the great results which the law has accomplished in the Federal Service and in some States and cities where it is in force, has been the abatement of this practice. However effective a check the civil service law may have been elsewhere, in New York State and City it seems rather to have led to the adoption of more surreptitious methods of collection.

In years past, the newspapers have reported the collection of a fixed percentage on salaries from employees in the state service in Albany for the coffers of the dominant party. Our investigations lead us to believe that these reports have undoubtedly been true. The employees of some departments have been exempt from this annual tax, but they have been the exceptions. The assessments have varied from 1½ per cent. for municipal campaigns to 3 per cent. for state campaigns. Despite the boldness with which this practice was carried on, and the indignation of the employees concerning it, until recently, none has been willing to come forward and give evidence, on account of the general, and well founded, belief in the power of the political leaders to punish them for so doing.

The most prominent officeholder connected with this

business has been Harry H. Bender, the present Fiscal Supervisor of State Charities. For years he held the position of treasurer of the Albany City and County Republican Committees, which he has only recently resigned, and secured an unenviable reputation for his success in collecting campaign funds. He formerly held the office of State Superintendent of Buildings and during his incumbency the employees of the Capitol building were regularly assessed. Governor Odell transferred him to his present office in June, 1902. Assessments were collected from the employees in his new office in the Fall of 1902 and 1904.

In both years the bookkeeper in the department, Edwin A. Doty, a veteran of the Civil War, refused to contribute. In the Spring of 1905, he was suspended by Bender on charges. Doty was convinced that this was a punishment for failure to contribute. The Grand Army became interested, the newspapers took up the case and the Association was appealed to. On the day before the date set for the trial the charges were withdrawn and Doty was transferred to another department.

Mr. Doty felt that he had been wronged and was not willing to drop the matter with his transfer. He gave the secretary of the Association a full account of the manner in which the assessment had been collected in the Fiscal Supervisor's office, and supported his statement by an affidavit. Both Bender and the secretary, Herbert F. Prescott, Bender's personal appointee, were implicated.

The affidavit was formally presented to the State Commission accompanied by a request for an investigation. On July 14, most of the employees of the Fiscal Supervisor's office were examined under oath. The request for payment of the assessment, made by Prescott, was clearly brought out. Many of the witnesses produced checks and receipts. The payment of three per cent. had been general, except in the case of Doty and one page, under the voting age. Even women and Democrats had been called upon to contribute. The testimony was sent to Messrs. Bender and Prescott with a request that they should state when they would be ready to appear. On the ground that some of their witnesses were absent from the city on vacation, they requested a postponement until September, which was granted. The Commission met to continue the investigation on September 14. Neither Bender nor Prescott appeared, but were represented by counsel, who objected to further proceedings, claiming that the Commission had not the power to conduct such an investigation. The point was referred to the Attorney General, the legal adviser of both the Fiscal Supervisor and the State Commission, who gave an opinion on September 28, upholding the power of the State Commission. Upon the Commission's attempting to proceed, counsel for Bender and Prescott served the Commissioners, the Secretary of the Association and Mr. Doty with writs of prohibition.

By agreement of counsel the writs were quashed and an appeal taken to the Appellate Division. At this stage, in view of the obvious attempt to avoid answering the charges and the implied confession that went with it, the Association appealed to the Governor to take up the case. It was pointed out to him in a letter dated November 11, 1905, that the suit Mr. Bender had brought in no wise affected the question of whether or not he had been guilty of violating the civil service law, that by this means he was enabled to avoid answering serious charges, supported by sworn evidence, that the Governor had the power both of appointment and removal, and that no one could question his power to investigate the alleged misconduct of his subordinate. To this letter no reply was given beyond a formal acknowledgement of its receipt.

In January, the Appellate Division handed down a decision upholding the power of the State Commission to make the investigation. Mr. Bender then appealed to the Court of Appeals. Another request to the Governor to interfere was made by the Association on March 5. This brought a reply from his counsel, Hon. Cuthbert W. Pound, in which he stated that the Governor had no doubt of the outcome of the case in court, and as the charges involved a violation of the civil service law he thought it better that the Civil Service Commission should investigate. No justification was offered for the continuance in office of Mr. Bender for eight months without being required, during the period, to answer charges of violating the law.

On April 24 the Court of Appeals finally handed down a decision affirming the decision of the Appellate Division, with costs. The State Commission will meet in a few days and will be asked to set an early date for continuing the investigation.

The conduct of this case for the Association has been in the hands of Hon. Nelson S. Spencer, of the Executive Committee, who has appeared at hearings before the Commission and has taken a large share in the argument before the Appellate Division and the Court of Appeals. The Committee believes the matter could not have been in better hands. For this service, gratuitously given, and involving a very considerable sacrifice of time, Mr. Spencer deserves the thanks of the Association.

THE FEDERAL SERVICE.

Since the meeting of the National Civil Service Reform League, last December, nothing of special note has taken place in the Federal Service. The United States Civil Service Commission has called a meeting in Washington for May 15 and 16, to which all commissions throughout the country have been invited to send representatives, to discuss methods of administration and examination. This is the first meeting of the kind ever called, and should be productive of beneficial results.

The Consular Reform Bill has met its usual fate at the hands of Congress. All the civil service reform features of the bill have been struck out. Some improvement in the service may be expected to result from the enactment of the provisions of the bill, requiring that fees shall, in future, be covered into the United States Treasury, and calling for the appointment of inspectors of consulates.

Early in the year the President let it be known that he intended to reappoint Collector Stranahan and Surveyor Clarkson. The former has shown himself friendly to the civil service law and the latter, in spite of his outspoken enmity in the past, has made no recent attempts, so far as we are aware, to evade it. As the result of an investigation by Civil Service Commissioner Cooley of complaints in regard to political discrimination between candidates for promotion in the Naval Office, Robert A. Sharkey, who during his incumbency retained his position as a district leader, was denied reappointment, and F. J. H. Kracke, of Brooklyn, was appointed in his stead.

THE STATE SERVICE.

There have been no changes in the personnel of the State Commission during the year, and the Committee is glad to report the continuance of those cordial relations which have made it possible for the Commission and the Association to work in harmony for the betterment of the service throughout the state. The service has unquestionably been strengthened, and careful attention is being given to the all-important matter of making the examinations thoroughly practical tests. The greatest drawback to successful administration is still the very large number of exempt positions, a matter which we hope the present Commission will see its way clear to take up and correct.

The most important matters which have arisen in the State service during the year, the classification of the four additional counties of Albany, Monroe, Onondaga and Westchester, completing the classification of all the larger counties of the State, the restoration of a number of county positions to the competitive class, the continuance of the policy of investigating the administration of the law in cities, the investigation of the New York City service, and the investigation of the violation of the political assessment provisions of the law in Albany have already been referred to.

MEASURES IN THE STATE LEGISLATURE.

During the session of the Legislature which closed May 3, a large number of bills affecting the merit system were introduced. As in former years, copies of all the bills were received and examined at the office of the Association, and all those which appeared to require action were referred to the Law Committee. Besides the familiar classes of bills providing for the reinstatement of policemen and firemen who had been discharged after trial in previous years, and for the payment of the salary claims of persons appointed or retained in the service in violation of the law, there were 22 bills to amend the civil service law and a number of joint resolutions to amend or repeal the civil service section of the Constitution. Twenty bills were introduced providing amendments to the New York City charter, calculated to weaken the operation of the merit system. In all, 169 bills were placed on special file and their progress regularly reported by our Albany representative.

The approval or opposition of the Association has been expressed through memoranda filed with the committees to which the bills were referred. Whenever it was thought advisable, hearings were requested. Of the 91 bills thus opposed, seventeen have passed the Legislature, but none has yet become law. Opposition will be continued before the Mayor in the case of city bills and before the Governor.

The most important attacks on the system this year were the attempts to secure further privileges for veterans and volunteer firemen in appointment and removal. Such preferences as now exist are a hindrance to good administration, and further extension would be a very serious blunder. It is, therefore, gratifying to be able to report that none of these measures passed the Legislature. Of the bills to amend the civil service law only two have reached the Governor; one permitting the city legislatures to pay pensions to civil employees who are veterans of the civil war, who have reached the age of 65 and who have served for at least fifteen years, the other making it mandatory to admit to examination persons who have been guilty of crime before the age of fourteen instead of leaving it to the discretion of the Commission.

Two bills were introduced on behalf of the Association. A bill to require the appointment through competitive examination of corporation inspectors in New York City met the opposition of the spoilsmen in both parties, and failed to pass the Assembly, in which it was introduced. Through the other bill, the Association, acting with the City Club, sought to do away with the restriction on the removal from the service of persons who had served as members of a volunteer fire department. During the summer of 1905, more than a thousand New York City employees registered themselves as members of volunteer fire companies about to be disbanded in the Boroughs of Queens and Richmond, in order to secure these privileges in the matter of removal. The best way to meet this obvious fraud appeared to be by an amendment to the civil service law, but this, although it passed the Assembly, failed of passage by the Senate.

NEW YORK CITY.

THE RE-ELECTION OF MAYOR MC CLELLAN.

In the city campaign which took place last Fall the administration of the civil service played a small part. Some reference was made in campaign speeches to the abuses in the city service uncovered by the investigation by the State Commission, but in general the condition of the civil service was lost sight of in the face of more prominent issues.

The usual notice of the provisions of the civil service law in regard to political assessments was sent to all heads of departments with a request that they should be posted in advance of the campaign. The effectiveness of this action is, however, very doubtful, as the contributions from employees are collected with impunity through the medium of the political clubs.

Mayor McClellan, on entering upon the duties of his office for the four year term, made no public announcement of a change of policy in the administration of the civil service law. The personnel of the Commission remained the same. The Commission has, however, owing to changed political conditions, apparently been freed from the pressure which had so seriously hampered it in the enforcement of the law during the previous year, and has started out on a new course, in which it feels it has the support of the Mayor.

The seemingly simple request of the Mayor, that he should be consulted by the heads of departments in regard to the choice of deputies, has been given a sinister significance by some of the appointments which he is credited with dictating. It has been charged by some of his critics that he is attempting to build up a new machine, and that he is using the patronage of the subordinate exempt positions to this end. It is certain, at least, that appointments to and removals from these positions have been dictated by political considerations, regardless of constitutional requirements. We cite particularly the appointment, at the behest of the Mayor, of Michael C. Padden, one of the political workers of the Sullivan faction, to the important position of Water Register in charge of the collection of water rates, displacing an employee whose services were satisfactory to the commissioner. Equally open to criticism was the appointment by the Civil Service Commission, apparently under pressure, of John F. Skelly, as Assistant Secretary. Mr. Skelly had just been forced out of the position of Deputy Commissioner of the Tenement House Department by Commissioner Butler, and was in no wise well fitted for the position under the Civil Service Commission. We suggest to the Commission the advisability of classifying this position as competitive and filling it by the promotion of an experienced employee.

The Mayor has not been the only offender in this misuse of exempt positions. Among the appointments made by Comptroller Metz to help the McCarren faction, we call particular attention to the designation as Deputy Comptroller of John H. McCooey, the former President of the Civil Service Commission, who was removed by Mayor McClellan on charges of dereliction of duty.

THE WORK OF THE MUNICIPAL COMMISSION.

Since the investigation by the State Commission, and more particularly since January first, the Municipal Commission has undertaken many important reforms. In its own office, Mr. Frank A. Spencer, who for years has been in charge of the Labor Bureau, has been made Secretary, and divisions have been established under responsible chiefs who are charged with reporting the efficiency of all employees under them. The non-competitive examinations for temporary employment have been strengthened and the employment without examination of expert examiners to do regular work, together with the assignment of work to monitors through favoritism, have been, to a considerable extent, done away with.

The Commission has ruled that it will not entertain requests for the classification of positions until such positions have been created and appropriated for by the Board of Estimate and Apportionment and the Board of Aldermen. Promotion examinations will in future be held only twice a year, in the months of May and December, and departments have been notified that these examinations are conditioned on the filing of proper efficiency records. The Chief Examiner, in his report, has recommended that graduated fees should be charged for examinations, a change which would go far toward making the work of the Commission self-supporting, but which cannot be carried out without new legislation.

Most important of all, the general practice of rerating examination papers after the name of the candidate had become known, which the Municipal Commission, in its last report, properly characterizes as "the greatest abuse that had crept into the administration of the civil service law in this city," has been reduced to a minimum and strictly regulated.

THE LABOR SERVICE.

We do not regard the changes made in the labor regulations as in any degree adequate to remedy the abuses known to exist and feel that the Municipal Commission would have done well to have undertaken the investigation of the labor service which the State Commission recommended. The discharge of laborers improperly appointed, as the result of such investigation, and an order to the departments to assign laborers to work appropriate to the titles under which they were appointed, would give notice that this part of the law is to be strictly enforced. The transfer of all positions of foreman of laborers to the competitive class, which the Association has repeatedly recommended, would end the favoritism, political and personal, which now exists in the assignments to these positions.

THE EXPENSE OF THE COMMISSION.

In view of the improvements that have been made in the service it may appear somewhat captious to criticise the expense of running the Commission, but any extravagance in this regard will be used as an argument against the system. The President of the Commission, who gives his entire time to the supervision of the work, and who receives a salary of $6,000, is not in any sense overpaid; but it is unfortunate that salaries have been established for the other two Commissioners which will be regarded as larger than are called for properly to compensate them for their services, and which make the places fall within the category of desirable political "plums." It has not proved necessary for these two Commissioners to attend meetings practically every day, as was urged at the time the appropriation was pending, and, in fact, the minutes show that meetings have been held on an average of less than twice a week. Under these circumstances the fixing of their salaries at so large a sum as $5,000 was, in our opinion, a mistake.

THE EXAMINING DIVISION.

Too little heed has been given to the building up of the examination division of the office and providing it with an adequate force so that departments shall not be hampered by delay in securing eligible lists from which to make needed appointments. The retention of certain favored "experts" to do regular work, instead of making appointments from the lists, although this abuse has been reduced, is still open to criticism. The recent resignation of one of the examiners, after he had been called upon to explain apparent frauds in the papers assigned to him, of sufficient importance to cause the cancellation of the entire examination, calls attention to the need for abolishing the class of examiners who are allowed to do their work at home and are paid at the rate of $10 per session, and appointing a sufficient regular force to do all ordinary work at the office of the Commission, under the supervision of the Chief Examiner.

EXEMPTIONS FROM COMPETITIVE EXAMINATION.

The Commission is, in our opinion, much too lax in granting the requests by heads of departments for the exemption of positions and thus adding to the class of places which can in practice be treated as political spoils. This class now numbers over 700. Each request is treated separately with the result that there are glaring inconsistencies in the classification of the different departments. The banner department is the Department of Street Cleaning, in which only two exempt places exist—those of the Deputy Commissioner and Private Secretary.

The most important request of this character which

was made during the year was that of the City Magistrates for the exemption of the position of Probation Officer on the grounds that no examination could adequately test the qualifications necessary for the position, and that these officers held a strictly confidential relation to the judges. The Association, after careful consideration of the question and study of the precedents, conbatted both these contentions. The State Probation Commission appointed by Governor Higgins, has reported in favor of a trial of the system of appointment through competitive examination. The Municipal Commission originally granted the exemption, but their resolution was returned without approval by the State Board and a competitive examination has been held, the success of which cannot as yet be determined. In this matter the Association has had the effective assistance of the Women's Auxiliary, which submitted an extremely important report upon the results of its investigation of the service of the probation officers then holding positions.

In conclusion, the Executive Committee desires to thank the chairmen and members of its active standing and special committees for the work that they have carried on during the year. The entire matter of the investigation of the city service by the State Commission, so far as it concerned the Association, was in charge of the Committee on Administration. The Law Committee has held regular meetings every two weeks during the session of the legislature to consider action upon the bills introduced and in addition has held a number of special meetings. Under the instructions of the Correspondence Committee the Assistant Secretary visited the cities of Binghamton, Elmira, Ithaca, Auburn, Geneva and Rochester, with the result that a correspondence committee was organized in each place. This important work of organizing civil service reform committees in the cities throughout the State will be continued in the near future. As the result of the work of the Membership Committee, the total membership of the Association now amounts to

862, an increase of 41 over last year. Of these, 16 are life members, 80 sustaining members, and 766 regular members. The committee wishes also to express its appreciation of the work for civil service reform carried on independently by the Women's Auxiliary, and to thank them at the same time for the assistance and support they have given to the Association in its work.

        Respectfully submitted,

                JACOB F. MILLER,
                        Chairman.

                ELLIOT H. GOODWIN,
                        Secretary.

ANNUAL REPORT OF THE TREASURER.

MAY 1, 1906.

Balance on hand, as per report, May 1, 1905..................$685.57

RECEIPTS:

From Annual Dues..........................	$3,305.00	
" Sustaining Membership Dues.........	1,850.00	
" Subscriptions........................	1,365.00	
" Women's Auxiliary...................	200.00	6,720.00
		$7,405.57

DISBURSEMENTS:

Salary of Secretary.......................	1,350.00	
" " Assistant Secretary.	662.50	
" " Editor of GOOD GOVERNMENT.....	750.00	
" " Clerks...........................	1,154.30	
Rent of Office............................	500.00	
Telephone Service........................	150.05	
Printing.................................	217.67	
Postage and Stamped Envelopes...........	270.95	
Stationery...............................	155.80	
Office Expenses	206.21	
Expenses of Litigation...................	93.07	
Traveling Expenses.......................	147.78	
Services of Albany Representative.........	150.00	
Subscription to GOOD GOVERNMENT.......	545.38	
Expenses, Committee on Administration....	295.47	
" Committee on Correspondence....	52.22	
Expenses of Annual Dinner..............	79.02	6,780.42

Balance on hand, April 30, 1906........................ $ 625.15

E. & O. E.

A. S. FRISSELL,
Treasurer.

ORGANIZATION

OF

THE NEW YORK CIVIL SERVICE REFORM ASSOCIATION

CONSTITUTION.

ARTICLE I.

The name of this organization shall be The Civil Service Reform Association.

ARTICLE II.

The object of the Association shall be to establish a system of appointment, promotion, and removal in the civil service, founded upon the principle that public office is a public trust, admission to which should depend upon proven fitness. To this end the Association will demand that appointments to subordinate executive offices, with such exceptions as may be expedient, not inconsistent with the principle already mentioned, shall be made from persons whose fitness has been ascertained by competitive examinations open to all applicants properly qualified, and that removals shall be made for legitimate cause only, such as dishonesty, negligence, or inefficiency, but not for political opinion or refusal to render party service; and the Association will advocate all other appropriate measures for securing integrity, intelligence, efficiency, good order, and due discipline in the civil service.

ARTICLE III.

The Association will hold meetings, raise funds, publish and circulate appropriate information, correspond and co-operate with associations organized elsewhere for the objects

set forth in this Constitution, and support all executive and legislative action which promote its purposes.

Article IV.

The conditions of membership shall be wholly independent of party preference. Questions shall not be discussed in the debate or in the publications of the Association upon party grounds. Neither the name nor influence of the Association shall be used on behalf of any party, or for procuring office or promotion for any person. But nothing in this article shall be construed to prevent the Association from opposing any candidate when in its opinion, or in that of three-fourths of the members of the Executive Committee, such course is demanded by the objects of the Association.

Article V.

There shall be a President, to be elected by the Association at the annual meeting, who shall perform the usual and prescribed duties of that office. He shall be, ex-officio, a member of all committees, with a casting vote only, and he may call special meetings of the Executive Committee whenever he thinks it necessary, and, with the assent of two members of the Executive Committee, special meetings of the Association.

There shall be ten Vice-Presidents, to be annually elected by the Association.

There shall be a Treasurer and Secretary, who shall perform the usual and prescribed duties of such officers. They shall be respectively appointed by the Executive Committee, and may be removed by them. The Treasurer shall be, ex-officio, a member of the Finance Committee of the Association.

There shall be an Executive Committee of twenty-five members, to be elected annually by the Association. Subject to these articles, the Executive Committee shall manage the affairs of the Association, direct and dispose of its funds, and from time to time make and modify by-laws for the Association and for its own action. The Executive Committee shall keep a record of its proceedings, and shall make a report to the

Association at the annual meeting. No appropriation of money by the Executive Committee beyond the amount in the hands of the Treasurer at the time shall bind any member of the Association, excepting those members of the Executive Committee who shall vote for it. Vacancies in the Executive Committee may be filled by the President for the remainder of the term. Other vacancies may be filled by the Executive Committee.

All the officers of the Association and members of the several Standing Committees shall be, ex-officio, members of the Executive Committee.

Article VI.

Each officer of the Association shall continue to hold office until his successor has been selected and is ready to enter upon the duties of the office.

Article VII.

There shall be an annual meeting of the Association on the second Wednesday of May, at which officers shall be elected for the ensuing year, and other appropriate business may be transacted; except in the year 1898, when the annual meeting shall be held on the second Wednesday of January.

Article VIII.

Any person may be proposed in writing for membership by any member of the Association, and shall be admitted upon approval of the Executive Committee. Members failing to pay their dues may be dropped from the roll by the Executive Committee.

Article IX.

The annual dues of each member shall be $5, payable on the 1st of May, and each member shall receive the annual report and all other publications of the Association. Sustaining members, on payment of twenty-five dollars annually, and Life members, exempt from annual dues on payment of one hundred dollars, may be elected by the Executive Committee at any regular meeting thereof.

Article X.

All provisions of this Constitution, except those relating to the rights of members, and the term of officers, may be suspended or amended by a vote of two-thirds of the Executive Committee, subject to the approval of the Association by a two-thirds vote of the members present either at the annual meeting or at a special meeting duly called. Due notice shall be given before any such annual or special meeting that the approval of the Association will, thereat, be asked for such action of the Executive Committee, and the notice shall clearly state the effect of such suspension or amendment in the text of the Constitution. Any member of the Association may propose amendments to the Constitution, which may be approved under the same conditions.

BY-LAWS.

FOR THE GOVERNMENT OF THE ASSOCIATION AND ITS COMMITTEES.

§ 1. The Annual meeting of the Association shall be held at such hour and place as the Executive Committee shall designate. The election of officers shall be by ballot, but any member not present may declare his vote by letter to the Secretary and it shall be counted.

§ 2. The meetings of each committee, unless otherwise especially provided for, shall be at half-past eight P. M., at which time the chairman shall direct the call of the names of its members and the Secretary shall record the names of those present and others as they appear.

§ 3. The order of business, before each committee shall be:
    1. The reading and correction of the records of the last meeting.

And, thereafter, unless otherwise ordered, as follows:
    2. Any statement due from the Treasurer.
    3. Unfinished business from the last meeting.
    4. Report from the Secretary's office.
    5. Reports of standing committees.
    6. Reports of special committees.
    7. Proposals of new members and their election.
    8. Miscellaneous business.

§ 4. Regular meetings of the Executive Committee shall be held on the second Wednesday of every month except July and August, but if that day be a holiday, then on the third Wednesday. Ten members of the Executive Committee shall constitute a quorum.

§ 5. Neither in the meetings of the Association nor of any committee shall any member speak more than once on any motion nor more than ten minutes at one time, without unanimous consent, nor shall any person, or his actions, be characterized on party grounds.

§ 6. Special meetings of any committee may be called by its chairman or by any three members, and due notice thereof shall be given by the Secretary.

§ 7. All notices to a member shall be sent to his address filed with the Secretary.

§ 8. On the demand of one-fifth of the members present, at any meeting of the Association or of a committee, the ayes and nays shall be called and recorded on any motion.

§ 9. All committees shall be appointed by the chair unless their selection shall be otherwise provided for.

§ 10. At each regular meeting of the Executive Committee, it shall be the duty of the Treasurer to make a statement of the amount of money in the treasury and of the place of its deposit, and, at the annual meeting, he shall state the source of all moneys received and the use made of the same during the past year.

§ 11. The Secretary shall keep a record of the proceedings of the Association and of the Executive Committee, and perform the other duties assigned him.

§ 12. Without the consent of three-fourths of the members present, no vote which will declare or fill a vacancy or elect a member of the Association shall be deemed carried, at the same meeting in which it was first moved.

§ 13. It shall require a vote of two-thirds of the members of the Executive Committee present to pass any vote under which more than $100 will be appropriated or the Association be pledged for more than that amount, and the Executive Committee alone shall have authority to create any charge upon the funds of the Association. But neither said committee nor any officer or officers of the Association shall be authorized to create a personal liability against any members but themselves.

§ 14. There shall be the following Standing Committees, of seven members each, which shall be selected annually by the Executive Committee:

(1) A Finance Committee, whose duty it shall be to devise and carry into effect, subject to the direction of the Executive Committee, suitable measures for raising funds, and to supervise and report upon the income and expenditures of the Associaton. The Finance Committee shall, in advance of each annual meeting of the Association, appoint an Auditing Committee from among its members, whose duty

it shall be to examine all vouchers and audit the accounts of the Treasurer, and to report thereon at the annual meeting.

(2) A Publication Committee, whose duty it shall be to prepare and recommend matters suitable for publication by the Association, and to take charge of the printing and distribution of whatever may be ordered printed.

(3) A Committee on Correspondence, whose duty it shall be to promote the objects of the Association through correspondence and co-operation with other organizations.

(4) A Committee on Administration, whose duty it shall be to investigate and report upon the administration of the civil service law and rules and to consider and recommend suitable methods of examination for admission to and promotion in the public service, and suitable procedure tending to make the system more efficient.

There shall also be a Standing Committee on Law of nine members, which shall be selected annually by the Executive Committee. Its duty shall be to consider all legislation affecting the civil service, to promote such as may be approved, and to oppose such as may be disapproved by the Executive Committee, and to prepare and recommend such amendments to the law as in their opinion will advance the purposes of the Association. The Law Committee shall have power to represent the Association in any legal proceedings which may be necessary in order to maintain or enforce the laws affecting the State or Municipal civil service.

There shall also be a Standing Committee on Membership of fifteen members, which shall be selected annually by the Executive Committee. Its duties shall be to devise and carry into effect measures for increasing the membership of the Association.

Each Standing Committee shall be competent to fix the number of its own quorum; but such quorum shall in no case be less than three.

§ 15. These By-Laws may be amended, or new By-Laws added, by a four-fifths vote at any meeting of the Executive Committee; or by a two-thirds vote, provided a statement of the proposed change had been entered on the minutes at the last meeting.

§ 16. Amendments proposed under the last clause of the tenth section of the constitution shall be first submitted to the Executive Committee.

OFFICERS—1906-1907.

PRESIDENT:

CARL SCHURZ

VICE-PRESIDENTS:

SILAS W. BURT	THEODORE ROOSEVELT
D. WILLIS JAMES	ELIHU ROOT
WILLIAM G. LOW	EDWARD M. SHEPARD
LEVI P. MORTON	OSCAR S. STRAUS
ALEXANDER E. ORR	EVERETT P. WHEELER

SECRETARY:	*ASSISTANT SECRETARY:*
ELLIOT H. GOODWIN	ALBERT DE ROODE

TREASURER:

A. S. FRISSELL

EXECUTIVE COMMITTEE:

JACOB F. MILLER, *Chairman.*	A. JACOBI
R. ROSS APPLETON	FRANKLIN B. LORD
HENRY De FOREST BALDWIN	GEORGE McANENY
THEODORE M. BANTA	JOHN G. MILBURN
CHARLES C. BURLINGHAM	SAMUEL H. ORDWAY
EDWARD CARY	GEORGE FOSTER PEABODY
CHARLES COLLINS	WILLIAM JAY SCHIEFFELIN
HORACE E. DEMING	THOMAS R. SLICER
SAMUEL B. DONNELLY	HENRY SANGER SNOW
HOMER FOLKS	NELSON S. SPENCER
J. WARREN GREENE	ANSON PHELPS STOKES
GEORGE J. GREENFIELD	WILLIAM H. THOMSON

CHARLES W. WATSON

STANDING COMMITTEES.

FINANCE:

WILLIAM JAY SCHIEFFELIN, *Chairman.* ISAAC N. SELIGMAN
L. T. CHAMBERLAIN   JACOB W. MACK
HENRY G. CHAPMAN   HORACE WHITE

PUBLICATION:

EDWARD CARY, *Chairman.*   ROB'T UNDERWOOD JOHNSON
GROSVENOR H. BACKUS   HERBERT PARSONS
GEORGE R. BISHOP   WILSON M. POWELL, Jr.

CORRESPONDENCE:

EVERETT V. ABBOT, *Chairman.*   LEARNED HAND
ALBERT S. BARD   WILLIAM POTTS
MACGRANE COXE   CORNELIUS B. SMITH
WALTER U. TAYLOR

ADMINISTRATION:

SILAS W. BURT, *Chairman.*   GEORGE McANENY
HENRY G. CHAPMAN   PHILIP J. McCOOK
CHARLES COLLINS   CLARENCE BISHOP SMITH
NELSON S. SPENCER

LAW:

SAMUEL H. ORDWAY, *Chairman.*   WINFRED T. DENISON
HENRY De FOREST BALDWIN   A. LEO EVERETT
CHARLES C. BURLINGHAM   J. WARREN GREENE
JOSEPH P. COTTON, Jr.   HENRY W. HARDON
CHARLES E. HUGHES

MEMBERSHIP:

NATHAN A. SMYTH, *Chairman.*   SAMUEL N. HINCKLEY
ALBERT DE ROODE   WILLIAM C. LANGDON
CHARLES J. FAY   CHARLES P. HOWLAND
ROY C. GASSER   FRANCIS H. KINNICUTT
GEORGE J. GREENFIELD   JAY E. LAWSHE
ELLWOOD HENDRICK   RUSSELL LOINES
CHARLES W. McCANDLESS   CARL L. SCHURZ

MEMBERSHIP ROLL.
(May 1, 1906.)

SUSTAINING MEMBERS.

AMEND, BERNARD G.,	205 Third Avenue, New York City
BEHR, HERMAN,	75 Beekman Street, New York City
BREWSTER, WILLIAM,	Broadway and 47th Street, " " "
BULL, WILLIAM LANMAN,	38 Broad Street, " " "
BURLINGHAM, CHARLES C.,	27 William Street, " " "
CARY, EDWARD,	The "Times," New York City
CHAPLIN, DUNCAN D.,	64 Worth Street, " " "
CLYDE, WILLIAM P.,	19 State Street, " " "
COLLINS, CHARLES,	33 E. 17th Street, " " "
CONNOR, W. E.,	31 Nassau Street, " " "
CRANE, RICHARD T.,	2541 Michigan Avenue, Chicago, Ill.
CUTTING, R. FULTON,	32 Nassau Street, New York City
DE COPPET, E. J.,	42 Broadway, New York City
DEERING, JAMES,	Fullerton and Clybourne Avenues, Chicago, Ill.
DELANO, WARREN Jr,	1 Broadway, New York City
DEMUTH, WILLIAM,	524 Fifth Avenue, " " "
DENISON, WINFRED T.,	15 Broad Street, " " "
DIMOCK, HENRY F.,	Pier 11, N. R., " " "
FRISSELL, A. S.,	530 Fifth Avenue, New York City
GILDER, RICHARD WATSON,	33 E. 17th Street, New York City
GOODWIN, J. J.,	11 W. 54th Street, " " "
GREENE, J. WARREN,	3 Broad Street, " " "
GREENFIELD, GEORGE J.,	32 Broadway, " " "
HARRIOT, S. CARMAN,	57 W. 39th Street, New York City
HEMENWAY, AUGUSTUS,	10 Tremont Street, Boston, Mass.
HENTZ, HENRY,	769 St. Mark's Avenue, Brooklyn
HOPKINS, GEORGE B.,	52 Broadway, New York City
HUBER, JACQUES,	472 Broome Street, " " "
JACOBI, A.,	19 E. 47th Street, New York City
JAMES, DARWIN R.,	266 Gates Avenue, Brooklyn, N. Y.
JOHNSON, ROBERT UNDERWOOD,	33 E. 17th Street, New York City
KENNEDY, JOHN S.,	31 Nassau Street, New York City
LOEB, JAMES,	52 William Street, New York City
LOEB, MORRIS,	273 Madison Avenue, " " "
LOINES, STEPHEN,	26 Garden Place, Brooklyn
LORD, FRANKLIN B.,	49 Wall Street, New York City

LOW, SETH,	30 E. 64th Street, New York City
LOW, WILLIAM G.,	58 Remsen Street, Brooklyn
MACK, JACOB W.,	92 Liberty Street, New York City
MACY, V. EVERIT,	68 Broad Street, " " "
MAITLAND, ALEXANDER,	45 Broadway, " " "
MAXWELL, ROBERT.	62 Worth Street, " " "
MEYER, JACOB,	29 E 63d Street, " " "
MILLER, JACOB F.,	120 Broadway, " " "
MINTURN, ROBERT SHAW,	109 E. 21st Street, " " "
MORTON, LEVI P.,	38 Nassau Street, " " "
MOSLE, GEORGE R.,	16–18 Exchange Place, " " "
McANENY, GEORGE,	19 E. 47th Street, New York City
McKIM, JOHN A.,	6 E. 74th Street, " " "
ORDWAY, SAMUEL H.,	27 William Street, New York City
OSBORN, WILLIAM CHURCH,	71 Broadway, " " "
PAGE, EDWARD D.,	60 Worth Street, New York City
PAGE, WILLIAM H., Jr.,	32 Liberty Street, " " "
PAGENSTECHER, A.,	P. O. Box 683, " " "
PEABODY, GEORGE FOSTER,	54 William Street, " " "
PHIPP, HENRY,	6 E. 87th Street, " " "
PINCHOT, JAMES W.,	1615 Rhode Island Avenue, Washington, D. C.
RANDOLPH, STUART F,	31 Nassau Street, New York City
RUSSELL, CHARLES H.,	15 Broad Street, " " "
SANDS, B. AYMAR,	31 Nassau Street, New York City
SCHEFER, CARL,	476 Broome Street, " " "
SCHIEFFELIN, WILLIAM JAY,	5 E. 66th Street, " " "
SCHIFF, JACOB H.,	P. O. Box 1193, " " "
SCHWAB, GUSTAV H.,	5 Broadway, " " "
SELIGMAN, ISAAC N.,	15 Broad Street, " " "
SHEPARD, EDWARD M.,	128 Broadway, " " "
SMITH, CORNELIUS B.,	101 E. 69th Street, " " "
SPENCER, NELSON S.,	27 William Street, " " "
SPEYER, JAMES,	257 Madison Avenue, " " "
STETSON, FRANCIS LYNDE,	15 Broad Street, " " "
STOKES, ANSON PHELPS,	100 William Street, " " "
STRAUS, OSCAR S.,	44 Warren Street, " " "
THOMSON, WILLIAM H.,	23 E 47th Street. New York City
TRASK, SPENCER,	54 William Street, " " "
VOSS, F. G,	40 Wall Street, New York City
WARE, WILLIAM R.,	Milton, Mass.
WHITE, ALFRED T.,	130 Water Street, New York City
WHITE, HORACE,	18 W. 69th Street, " " "
WHITE, WILLIAM A.,	130 Water Street, " " "
WUNDERLICH, F. W.,	165 Remsen Street, Brooklyn

Abbot, Everett V., ... 45 Cedar Street, New York City
Abbott, Lawrence F., ... "The Outlook," " " "
Abbott, Lyman, ... 287 Fourth Avenue, " " "
Achelis, John, ... 68 Leonard Street, " " "
Adams, Edward D., ... 71 Broadway, " " "
Adams, Joseph, ... Union Stock Yards, Chicago, Ill.
Adams, Thatcher M., ... 36 Wall Street, New York City
Adler, Felix, ... 152 W. 77th Street, " " "
Affeld, Francis O., ... 873 President Street, Brooklyn
Agar, John G., ... 31 Nassau Street, New York City
Agnew, Andrew Gifford, . . . 22 William Street, " " "
Aitken, John W. . . . . . 873 Broadway, New York City
Allen, Calvin H., ... 1 W. 72nd Street, " " "
Allen, Elmer A., ... 42 Broadway, " " "
Allen, Franklin, ... 371 Fulton Street, Brooklyn
Allert, Rudolf, . . 108th Street and Columbus Avenue, New York City
Alling, Joseph T., ... 400 Oxford Street, Rochester, N. Y.
Alsop, Reese F., ... 96 Remsen Street, Brooklyn
Anderson, Frank E., ... 486 Broadway, New York City
Andrews, J. Sherlock, . . . 111 St. Paul Street, Rochester, N. Y.
Appleton, Herbert . . . . 16 Exchange Place, New York City
Appleton, R. Ross, ... 146 Joralemon Street, Brooklyn
Arend, F. J., ... 32 W. 73rd Street, New York City
Arnold, Lemuel H., ... 3 Broad Street, " " "
Arnstein, Eugene, ... 10 Wall Street, " " "
Atterbury, Grosvenor, . . . 20 W. 43rd Street, " " "
Auchincloss, John, ... 35 Nassau Street, " " "
Avery, Samuel P., ... 4 E. 38th Street, " " "

Babbott, Frank L., ... 149 Lincoln Place, Brooklyn
Backus, Grosvenor H., . . . 32 Liberty Street, New York City
Bacon, Gorham, ... 47 W. 54th Street, " " "
Bagley, Valentine N., . . . 641 Washington Street, " " "
Bailey, H. P., ... 312 Broadway, " " "
Baldwin, Elbert F., ... "The Outlook," " " "
Baldwin, Henry de Forest, . . 49 Wall Street, " " "
Ball, Thomas P., ... 116 Broad Street, " " "
Bangs, Francis S., ... 40 Wall Street, " " "
Bangs, L. Bolton, ... 39 E. 72nd Street, " " "
Bannard, Otto T., ... 24 Broad Street, " " "
Banta, Theodore M, ... 348 Broadway, " " "
Bard, Albert Sprague, . . . 25 Broad Street, " " "
Barker, Benjamin, ... 56 Pine Street, " " "
Barkley, Charles H., . . . 82 Wall Street, " " "
Barney, A. H., (Life) . . . 101 E. 38th Street, " " "
Barney, Danford N., ... Farmington, Conn.
Barrett, Frank R., ... Box 105, Portland, Me.
Barrett, John D. . . . . . 49 Wall Street, New York City

Bartlett, P. G., ... 25 Broad Street, New York City
Baruch, Bernard M., ... 111 Broadway, New York City
Batterman, Henry, ... 21 Clinton Street, Brooklyn
Bausch, Edward, ... Rochester, N. Y.
Baylies, Edmund L., ... 54 Wall Street, New York City
Bayne, Hugh, ... 40 Wall Street, " " "
Beckers, Alexander, ... 618 Hudson Street, Hoboken, N. J.
Beekman, Gerard, ... 7 E: 42d Street, New York City
Beer, George Lewis, . . . 329 W. 71st Street, " " "
Beers, E. Le Grand, . . 131 Remsen Street, Brooklyn, " " "
Beers, Lucius H., ... 49 Wall Street, " " "
Bell, Gordon Knox, ... 22 William Street, " " "
Bellamy, Frederick P., . 204 Montague Street, Brooklyn. " " "
Benedict, Elliot S., ... 76 William Street, " " "
Benson, Frank Sherman, ... 214 Columbia Heights, Brooklyn
Bijur, Nathan, ... 34 Nassau Street, New York City
Bishop, George R., ... 142 E. 18th Street, " " "
Bispham, William, ... 66 Broadway, " " "
Boas, Franz, ... 123 W. 82d Street, " " "
Bode, Frederick H., ... care Gage Bros., Chicago, Ill.
Boller, Alfred P., ... 1 Nassau Street, New York City
Borden, M. C. D., ... Box 1794, " " "
Bowen, C. Winthrop, ... 5 E. 63rd Street, " " "
Bowker, R. R., ... 298 Broadway, " " "
Brachhausen, G. A., ... Rahway, N. J.
Brackett, George C., ... 50 Remsen Street, Brooklyn
Bradt, Herbert S., ... 120 Broadway, New York City
Brand, John, ... Elmira, N. Y.
Brewster, Charles O., ... 32 Liberty Street, New York City
Briesen, Arthur von, (Life) . . 49 Wall Street, " " "
Briscoe, S. William, ... 20 Sanford Avenue, Flushing, N. Y.
Brite, James, ... 111 Fifth Avenue, New York City
Brown, Addison, ... 45 W. 89th Street, " " "
Brown, Augustus H., . . . 262 W. 136th Street, " " "
Brown, Edwin H., ... 141 Broadway. " " "
Brown, Everit, ... 27 William Street, " " "
Brown, Henry T., ... 76 St. Paul's Place, Brooklyn
Brown, Roscoe C. E., ... "Tribune" Office, New York City
Brown, Thatcher M., ... 36 E. 37th Street, " " "
Brownell, William C., . . . 153 Fifth Avenue, " " "
Brush, W. Franklin, ... 16 E. 37th Street, " " "
Buckingham, C. L., ... 38 Park Row, " " "
Burnett, Henry L., ... P. O. Building, " " "
Burr, Winthrop, ... 7 Wall Street, " " "
Burt, Silas W., ... 30 Broad Street, " " "
Butler, Howard R., ... 22 E. 91st Street, " " "
Butler, Nicholas Murray, . . . 119 E. 30th Street, " " "

Buttfield, William J., ... 96 Wall Street, New York City
Byrne, James, ... 26 Broad Street, " " "

Cadwalader, John L., ... 40 Wall Street, New York City
Cahen, L J., ... 1 Madison Avenue, " " "
Calkins, Leighton, ... 25 Broad Street, " " "
Canfield, George F., ... 49 Wall Street, " " "
Carnegie, Andrew, (Life) . . . . 2 E. 91st Street, " " "
Carter, Frederick B., ... 61 Church Street, Montclair, N. J.
Cary, Clarence, ... 59 Wall Street, New York City
Case, L. Barton, ... 35 Nassau Street, " " "
Cassatt, George M., ... 327 Broadway, " " "
Cauldwell, S. Millbank, ... Pelham Manor, N. Y.
Chaffee, J. Irwin, . Sedgwick Avenue, Fordham Heights, New York City
Chamberlain, D. H., ... West Brookfield, Mass.
Chamberlain, L. T., ... 222 W. 23 Street, New York City
Chambers, William P., ... 55 Liberty Street, " " "
Chandler, Walter, M., ... 35 Nassau Street, " " "
Chanute, Octave, ... 413 East Huron Street, Chicago, Ill.
Chapman, George, ... 2717 Broadway, New York City
Chapman, Henry G., ... 79 Wall Street, " " "
Chapman, J. W., ... 35 Nassau Street, " " "
Chase, George, ... 35 Nassau Street, " " "
Chauncey, Daniel, ... 129 Joralemon Street, Brooklyn
Cheney, F. W., ... South Manchester, Conn.
Cheney, George L., ... 131 E. 57th Street, New York City
Cheney, Louis R., ... Woodland Street, Hartford, Conn.
Childs, Edwards H., ... 59 Wall Street, New York City
Choate, Joseph H., ... 60 Wall Street, " " "
Choate, Joseph H. Jr., ... 60 Wall Street, " " "
Choate, William G., ... 40 Wall Street, " ' "
Cillis, Hubert, ... 20 Nassau Street, " " "
Claflin, John, ... 224 Church Street, " " "
Clarke, Samuel B., ... 32 Nassau Street, " " "
Cleveland, Treadwell, ... 27 William Street, " " "
Codington, Perley M., ... 1487 Broadway, " " "
Coffin, E. R., ... 62 Cedar Street, " " "
Coffin, I. Sherwood, ... 30 Cliff Street, " " "
Cohen, William N., ... 22 William Street, " " "
Collins, Atwood, ... Asylum Avenue, Hartford, Conn.
Collins, Stephen W., ... 69 Wall Street, New York City
Collyer, Robert, ... 201 W. 55th Street, " " "
Conant, Charles A., ... 38 Nassau, Street, " " "
Conger, Clarence R., ... 37 Liberty Street, " " "
Conger, Henry C., ... 140 W. 82nd Street, " " "
Conger, Henry Rutgers, ... 40 Wall Street, " " "
Cook, Walter, ... 3 W. 29th Street, " " "
Cooley, Alford Warriner, . Civil Service Commission, Washington, D C.

Cope, Francis R., ... Aubury, Germantown, Pa.
Corrigan, Joseph E., . . . District Attorney's Office, New York City
Cotton, Joseph P., Jr., ... 52 William Street, " " "
Coudert, Frederick R., Jr., ... 71 Broadway, " " "
Cowdin, Wintrop, The Algonquin Company, ... Passaic, N. J.
Cowperthwait, J. Howard, . . . 195 Park Row, New York City
Coxe, Macgrane, ... 63 Wall Street, " " "
Coykendall, S. D., ... Rondout, N. Y.
Crane, Frederick, ... Bloomfield, N. J.
Crane, Leroy B., ... 277 Broadway, New York City
Cranford, Walter V., ... 215 Montague Street, Brooklyn
Cravath, Paul D., ... 52 William Street, New York City
Crawford, Gilbert H., ... 32 Liberty Street, " " "
Creevey, John J., ... 41 Wall Street, " " "
Croly, Herbert D., ... 14 Vesey Street, " " "
Cromwell, Frederic, ... 32 Nassau Street, " " "
Cromwell, Lincoln, ... 1 Greene Street, " " "
Croswell, J. G., ... 17 W. 44th Street, " " "
Cummings, G. F., ... 20 Broad Street, " " "
Curtis, William E., ... 30 Broad Street, " " "
Cushing, William E., . . . Society for Savings Bldg., Cleveland, O.
Cutler, Arthur H., ... 20 E. 50th Street, New York City
Cutting, R. Bayard, ... 32 Nassau Street, " " "
Cutting, W. Bayard, ... 24 E. 72nd Street, " " "
Cuyler, C. C., ... 44 Pine Street, " " "

Daboll, Henry E., ... Plainfield, N. J.
Dana, Charles L., ... 53 W. 53rd Street, New York City
Davidge, William H., ... 49 Wall Street, " " "
Davies, Julien T., ... 32 Nassau Street, " " "
Davies, William Gilbert, ... 32 Nassau Street, " " "
Davis, Charles Henry, ... 25 Broad Street, " " "
Davis, G. Pierrepont, ... Woodland Street, Hartford, Conn.
Davis, Horace A., ... 135 Broadway, New York City
Davis John, H., ... , . 10 Wall Street, " " "
Davison, Charles Stewart, . . . 60 Wall Street, " " "
Day, Clarence S., ... 45 Wall Street, " " "
DeForest, R. W., ... 30 Broad Street, " " "
Deming, Horace E., ... 13 William Street, " " "
de Roode, Albert, ... 79 Wall Street, " " "
Despard, W. D., ... 6 Hanover Street, " " "
Dettmer, Jacob G., ... 27 Prospect Park W., Brooklyn
Devine, Thomas J., . . . 19 Portsmouth Terrace, Rochester, N. Y.
DeWitt, Theodore, ... 88 Nassau Street, New York City
Dickinson, Robert L., ... 168 Clinton Street, Brooklyn
Dickson, James B., ... 49 Wall Street, New York City
Dittenhoefer, A. J., ... 96 Broadway, " " "
Dix, John A., ... Care L. Thomson & Co., Albany, N. Y.

Dodge, Cleveland H.,	99 John Street, New York City
Dominick, H. B.,	3 W. 29th Street, " " "
Dommerich, L. F.,	57 Greene Street, " " "
Donnelly, Samuel B.,	360 Putnam Avenue, Brooklyn
Dougherty, J. Hampden,	27 William Street, New York City
Dows, Tracy,	Room 102, Produce Exchange, " " "
Dreier, H. E.,	152-154 West 34th Street, " " "
Dunham, Edward K.,	338 E 26th Street, " " "
Dunning, S. Wright,	80 Madison Avenue, " " "
Eastman, A. H.,	363 Grand Avenue, Brooklyn
Eastman, George,	400 East Avenue, Rochester, N. Y.
Eaton, Henry W.,	45 William Street, New York City
Ecaubert, F.,	18 Rose Street, " " "
Elderkin, John,	Lotos Club, 558 Fifth Avenue, " " "
Eliot, Charles W.,	Cambridge, Mass.
Elkins, Stephen B.,	1626 K Street, Washington, D. C.
Ely, Alfred,	31 Nassau Street, New York City
Ely, Arthur H.,	56 Wall Street, " " "
Ely, Moses,	2 Wall Street, " " "
Ely, Robert E.,	23 West 44th Street, " " "
Emmons, Arthur B.,	60 Park Avenue, " " "
Emmons, Samuel F.,	U. S. Geological Survey, Washington, D. C.
Erbslöh, R.,	364 Broadway, New York City
Everest, Charles M.,	506 West Avenue, Rochester, N. Y.
Everett, A. Leo,	49 Wall Street, New York City
Ewart, Richard H.,	115 Franklin Street, " " "
Ewing, Thomas,	67 Wall Street, " " "
Fabbri, Alessandro,	11 E. 62d Street, New York City
Fabbri, Ernesto G.,	11 E. 62d Street, " " "
Fahnestock, Gates D.,	214 Hicks Street, Brooklyn, N. Y.
Fahnestock, H. C.,	2 Wall Street, New York City
Fairchild, Benjamin T.,	P. O. Box 1120, " " "
Fairchild, Charles S.,	10 West 8th Street, " " "
Faure, John P.,	346 Broadway, " " "
Fay, Charles J.,	49 Wall Street, " " "
Field, Hamilton E.,	106 Columbia Heights, Brooklyn
Finch, Edward R.,	53 Washington Square, New York City
Fisher, George H.,	278 Sterling Place, Brooklyn
Fleitmann, Ewald,	484 Broome Street, New York City
Folks, Homer,	105 E 22nd Street, " " "
Ford, Worthington C.,	Care Library of Congress, Washington, D. C.
Forrest, C. R.,	Asylum Avenue, Hartford, Conn.
Fox, Austen G., (Life),	45 W. 33d Street, New York City
Frankenheimer, John,	25 Broad Street, " " "

Frissell, H. B., ... Hampton, Va.
Frothingham, Howard P., ... 2 Wall Street, New York City
Fuller, Frank, ... 61 Fifth Avenue, " " "
Fuller, Paul, ... 71 Broadway. " " "
Fullerton. Alexander, (Life), . . 7 W. 8th Street, " " "
Fullerton, Henry S., ... 71 Broadway, " " "
Funk, I. K., ... 195 Washington Park, Brooklyn

Gaillard, William D., ... 141 Broadway, New York City
Garrison, Wendell P., ... 206 Broadway, " " "
Garver, John A., ... 44 Wall Street, " ' "
Gasser, Roy C., ... 35 Wall Street, " " "
Germond, H. S., ... 7 Wall Street, " " "
Gibson, William J., ... 26 Liberty Street, " " "
Gitterman, John M., . . . 1317 F Street, N. W., Washington, D C.
Goadby, Clarence, ... 21 W. 35th Street, New York City
Goddard, George A., ... 10 Tremont Street, Boston, Mass.
Goldman, Julius, ... 31 Nassau Street, New York City
Goldmark, James, ... 67 Cortlandt Street, " " "
Goodale, John McGregor, . . . 42 Broadway, " " "
Goodnow, Frank J., ... 49 Riverside Drive, " " "
Goodwin, Elliot H., ... 79 Wall Street, " " "
Gottheil, Paul, ... Produce Exchange, " " "
Gottsberger, Francis, ... 156 Broadway, " " "
Gould, Elgin R. L., ... 281 Fourth Avenue, " " "
Grant, De Forest, ... 22 E. 45th Street, " " "
Grant Percy S., ... 7 W. 10th Street, " " "
Gray, Henry G , ... 161 Madison Avenue, " " "
Green, Noah, ... 478 Central Park, West, " " "
Greenbaum, Samuel. . . . . 141 Broadway, " " "
Greene, Francis V., ... 816 Fidelity Building, Buffalo, N. Y.
Greenough, John, . . . 38 E. 63rd Street, New York City
Greer, David H., ... 7 Gramercy Park, " " "
Gulliver, W. C., ... 120 Broadway, " " "
Guthrie, William D., ... 52 William Street, " " "
Gwynne, Arthur C., ... Rye, N. Y.

Hagemeyer, F. E., . . . F 15, Produce Exchange, New York City
Haines, C. G , ... Ursinus College, Collegeville, Pa.
Haines, Henry F., ... 2 Wall Street, New York City
Hall, Valentine G., ... Tivoli, Duchess Co., N. Y.
Halsted, John F., . . . 93 Remsen Street, Brooklyn, N. Y.
Hamilton, E. Luther, ... 146 Broadway, New York City
Hamlin, Frank H., ... Canandaigua, N. Y.
Hand, Learned, ... 2 Wall Street, New York City
Harbeck, Charles T., ... Islip, N. Y.
Harding, Edward, ... Chestnut Hill, Philadelphia, Pa.

Hardon, Henry Winthrop,	815 W. 71st Street,	New York City
Harrison, Robert L.,	59 Wall Street,	" " "
Hart, John Wilson,	District Attorney's Office,	" " "
Haskin, William H.,	42 East 41st Street,	" " "
Hasslacher, Jacob,	100 William Street,	" " "
Hastings, Thomas S.,	27 W. 46th Street,	" " "
Hayes, J. Noble,	68 William,	" " "
Heath, Frank E.,	95 Liberty Street,	" " "
Healy, A. Augustus,	198 Columbia Heights, Brooklyn
Heinze, Arthur P.,	81 Nassau Street,	New York City
Henderson, Harold G..	80 Irving Place,,	" " "
Hendrick, Ellwood,	139 E. 40th Street,	" " "
Hentz, Leonard S.,	769 St. Mark's Avenue, Brooklyn
Herbert, William,	11 Pine Street,	New York City
Hess, Henry E.,	32 Nassau Street,	" " "
Hessberg, Max,	13 William Street,	" " "
Hicks, Benjamin D.,	Old Westbury, N. Y.
Higginson, James J.,	16 E. 41st Street,	New York City
Hill, William B,	68 William Street,	" " "
Hinkley, Samuel Neilson,	166 E. 61st Street,	" " "
Hinrichs, Frederick W.,	76 William Street,	New York City
Hitchcock, Welcome G., (Life)	453 Broome Street,	" " "
Hobart, Henry L.,	120 Front Street,	" " "
Hodges, Harrison B.,	16 Gramercy Park,	" " "
Hodgman, George F.,	806 Broadway,	" " "
Hoe, Richard M.,	Room 102, Produce Exchange,	" " "
Hoe, Robert,	504 Grand Street,	" " "
Holsapple, F. B,	Hotel St. Andrew, B'way & 72d Street,	" " "
Holt, Henry,	29 W. 23d Street,	" " "
Holt, Roland,	711 Madison Avenue,	" " "
Hopkins, J. A. H,	51 West 11th Street,	" " "
Hoppin, Frederick S., Jr..	131 E. 19th Street,	" " "
Hoppin, William W.,	54 William Street,	" " "
Hornblower, William B.,	24 Broad Street,	" " "
Howe, Daniel R.,	Asylum Avenue, Hartford, Conn.
Howe, Horace J.,	25 Gold Street, Yonkers, N. Y
Howe, Wirt,	135 Broadway, New York City
Howland, Charles P.,	35 Wall Street,	" " "
Hoyt, Gerald L,	311 Fifth Avenue,	" " "
Hubbard, Thomas H.,	16 W. 58th Street,	" " "
Hubbell, Charles Bulkeley,	35 Nassau Street,	" " "
Hughes, Charles E.,	96 Broadway,	" " "
Hull, Charles A.,	72 Wall Street,	" " "
Huntington, Francis C.,	54 William Street,	" " "
Huntington, Samuel,	146 Broadway,	" " "
Huntington, William R.,	804 Broadway,	" " "
Huyler, John S.,	64 Irving Place,	" " "

Ide, Robert L.,	7 Nassau Street, New York City
Ireland, F. G.,	299 Broadway, " " "
Isham, Samuel.	6th Avenue and 40th Street, " " "
Jackson, Frederick W.,	Westchester, N. Y.
Jackson, John G.,	35 Wall Street, New York City
Jacob, Lawrence.	52 Broadway, " " "
James, D. Willis,	99 John Street, " " "
Jaretzki, Alfred.	49 Wall Street, " " "
Jay, Pierre,	Hyde Park, Mass.
Jay, William,	48 Wall Street, New York City
Jellenix, Felix,	17 William Street, " " "
Jennings, Frederick B.,	15 Broad Street, " " "
Jesup, Morris K.,	195 Madison Avenue, " " "
Johnson, James G.,	655 Broadway, " " "
Johnson, Willis Fletcher,	154 Nassau Street, " " "
Joline, Adrian, H ,	54 Wall Street, " " "
Josephthal, Sidney L.,	350 Broadway, " " "
Kahn, Otto H., (Life),	54 William Street, New York City
Kane, S. Nicholson,	23 W. 47th Street, " " "
Kellogg, Francis B.,	328 Douglas Bldg, Los Angeles, Cal.
Kelsey, Clarence H.,	146 Broadway, New York City
Kennaday, Paul,	88 Grove Street, " " "
Kennedy, Edward G.,	220 Fifth Avenue, " " "
Kennedy, Elija R.,	29 & 31 Liberty Street, " " "
Kenneson, Thaddeus D.,	18 William Street, " " "
Kenyon, Alan D.,	49 Wall Street, " " "
Kenyon, William Houston.	49 Wall Street, " " "
Keppler, Rudolph,	25 Broad Street, " " "
Kernan, John D.,	37 Liberty Street, " " "
Kidder, Camillus G.,	27 William Street, " " "
Kidder, Edward H.,	170 Broadway. " " "
Kilmer, Alfred G.,	80 Broadway, " " "
Kimball, A. R.,	Orange, N. J.
King, Delcevare,	126 Summer Street, Boston, Mass.
King, William F.,	410 Broadway, New York City
Kinnicutt. Francis H.,	35 Wall Street, " " "
Kinnicutt, Francis P.,	42 W. 37th Street, " " "
Kinnicutt, G Herman,	39 E 35th Street, " " "
Kirchhoff, Charles,	14 & 16 Park Place, " " "
Kissell, Gustav E., (Life),	1 Nassau Street, " " "
Klein, Isaac H.,	45 Cedar Street, " " "
Klupfel, Charles,	Care North German Lloyd, 5 Broadway, " " "
Knapp, Shepherd,	2 6 Lexington Avenue, " " "
Knauth, Antonio,	233 West 70th Street, " " "
Knox, Herbert H ,	45 Broadway, " " "
Kohler, Max J.,	42 Broadway, " " "
Kuhne, Percival,	13 William Street, " " "

Kunhardt, Henry R., ... 124 W. 74th Street, New York City
Kunhardt, William B., ... 1 Broadway, " " "

Laimbeer, Francis E., ... 99 Nassau Street, New York City
Lambert, William B., ... Highland Street, Cambridge Mass.
Langdon, William Chauncy, . . 636 West 138th Street, New York City
Lansing, J. Townsend, ... 82 State Street, Albany, N. Y.
Larocque, Joseph, ... 40 Wall Street, New York City
Larremore, Wilbur, ... 32 Nassau Street, " " "
Lawrence, Walter B., ... 35 Wall Street, " " "
Lawshe, Jay E., ... 60 Wall Street, " " "
Lea, Henry Charles, ... 2000 Walnut Street, Philadelphia, Pa.
Leavens, George St. J., . . . 72 Bible House, New York City
Leavitt, John Brooks, ... 115 Broadway, " " "
Leaycraft, J. Edgar, ... 19 W. 42nd Street, " " "
Lederle, Ernest J., ... 471 W. 143d Street, " " "
Ledoux, Albert R., ... 9 Cliff Street, " " "
Lee, W. H. L., ... 25 Pine Street, " " "
Lefferts, Marsnall C., ... 30 Washington Place, " " "
Le Gendre, William, ... 59 Wall Street, " " "
Lehmaier, Louis A., ... 78 Beekman Street, " " "
Lethbridge, R. P., ... 49 Wall Street, " " "
Levi, Albert A., ... 108 Exchange Court, " " "
Lewi, Isidore, ... 3 E. 81st Street, " " "
Lewis, August, ... 151 Greene Street, " " "
Lewis, Richard V., ... 130 W. 42d Street, " " "
Lindenthal, Gustav, ... 45 Cedar Street, " " "
Lindsay, Alexander M., . . . 373 East Avenue, Rochester, N. Y.
Littauer, Lucius N., ... Gloversville, N. Y.
Livingston, Goodhue, ... 38 E. 65th Street, New York City
Livingston, Julius I., ... 52 Broadway, " " "
Lockwood, Benoni, ... 56 Irving Place, " " "
Lockwood, Charles D., . . . District Attorney's Office, " " "
Logan, Walter S., ... 27 William Street, " " "
Loines, Russell H., ... 27 W. 11th Street, " " "
Lord, F. B., Jr., ... 49 Wall Street, " " "
Lounsbery, Richard P., . . . 15 Broad Street, " " "
Lovell, Joseph J., ... Avondale Place, Woodhaven, N. Y.
Low, C. Adolph, ... 41 Liberty Street, New York City
Lowe, William E., ... 49 Wall Street, " " "
Lowndes, James, . . . 1515 Massachusetts Avenue, Washington, D. C.
Ludlow, James B., ... 45 Cedar Street, New York City
Luther, George Martin, . . . 25 Broad Street, " " "
Lyall, Arthur V., ... 25 Pine Street, " " "
Lyman, Frank, ... 34 Remsen Street, Brooklyn
Lyman, George T., ... Bellport, N. Y.
Lyman, Theodore, ... Woodland Street, Hartford, Conn.
Lynde, Rollin H., ... 82 Beaver Street, New York City

Macdonough, A. R.,	105 E. 15th Street, New York City
Macfarlane, Wallace,	82 Liberty Street, " " "
MacMullen, C. W.,	20 Broad Street, " " "
MacVeagh, Charles,	15 Broad Street, " " "
Mallet-Prevost, Severo,	30 Broad Street, " " "
Mallinckrodt, Edward,	Mallinckrodt Chemical Works. St. Louis, Mo.
Mansfield, Howard,	49 Wall Street, New York City
Mapes, Charles V.,	143 Liberty Street, " " "
Markoe, Francis H.,	15 E. 49th Street, " " "
Marling, Alfred E.,	21 Liberty Street, " " "
Marshall, Charles H.,	45 William Street, " " "
Marshall, Fielding L.,	35 Nassau Street, " " "
Marshall, Harford,	District Attorney's Office, " " "
Marshall, Louis,	30 Broad Street, " " "
Marsters, A., A.,	125 Milk Street, Boston, Mass.
Martin, John,	Grymes Hill, Staten Island, N. Y.
Martin, Newell,	25 Broad Street, New York City
Martin, T. Comerford,	114 Liberty Street, " " "
Mason, Alexander T.,	13 William Street, " " "
Mason, Alfred Bishop.	Apartado 130, City of Mexico
Masten, Arthur H.,	49 Wall Street, New York City
Mathews W. K.,	36 Wall Street, " " "
Mathews, Robert,	135 Spring Street, Rochester, N. Y.
Matthews, Brander,	681 West End Avenue, New York City
Matthewson, Arthur,	139 Montague Street, Brooklyn
Maxwell, William H.,	500 Park Avenue, New York City
Mellen, Chase,	52 William Street, " " "
Merck, George,	15 University Place, " " "
Merrill, Charles E.,	44 E. 23d Street, " " "
Merrill, Payson,	31 Nassau Street, " " "
Messervy, George P.,	7 Wall Street, " " "
Milburn, John G.,	54 Wall Street, " " "
Miller, Clifford L.,	62 West 89th Street, " " "
Miller, George Douglas,	125 State Street, Albany, N. Y.
Miller, Hoffman,	80 Broadway, New York City
Miller, Theodore C.,	177 Montague Street, Brooklyn
Mills, L. H.,	473 Broome Street, New York City
Mills, Philip O.,	36 Wall Street, " " "
Mitchell, Edward,	44 Wall Street, " " "
Moffat, George B.,	1 Nassau Street, " " "
Moffat, R. Burnham,	63 Wall Street, " " "
Montgomery, R. M.,	27 Pine Street, " " "
Moore, W. H. H.,	Box 402, " " "
Morris, Ray,	81 Fulton Street, " " "
Morrow, Dwight,	Englewood, N. J.
Morse, Horace J.,	820 St. Mark's Avenue, Brooklyn
Morse, Richard C.,	35 Sidney Place, "
Mortimer, Richard,	11 Wall Street, New York City

Mosenthal, P. J., ... 95 William Street, New York City
Mosle, A. Henry, ... 30 Broad Street, " " "
Mott, William F., ... Toms River, N. J.
Munro, J. G., ... 61 Erie County Bank Building, Buffalo, N. Y.
Munro, John R., ... 132 Remsen Street, Brooklyn, N. Y.
Munro, Willis, ... 1088 Trinity Building, New York City
Munroe, Vernon, ... 45 William Street, " " "
Murray, James B., ... 23 Belmont Terrace, Yonkers, "
Murray, Joseph K., ... 90 Wall Street, New York City
Myers, Nathaniel, ... 25 Broad Street, " " "
McAlpin, George L., ... 9 E. 90th Street, " " "
McCagg, Louis Butler, ... 18 E. 84th Street, " " "
McCandless, Charles W., . . . 60 Wall Street, " " "
McCook, Philip J., ... 15 William Street, " " "
McGinness, Remsen, ... 42 East 41st Street, " " "
McIntosh, James H., ... 346 Broadway, " " "
McKeen, James, ... 136 Henry Street, Brooklyn
McKeever, J. Lawrence, . . . 164 Lexington Avenue, New York City
McMahon, Fulton, ... 54 William Street, " " "

Nadal, Charles C., ... 142 E. 35th Street, New York City
Nash, Francis Philip, ... Geneva, N. Y.
Naumberg, Elkan, ... 48 W. 58th Street, New York City
Naumberg, George W., . . . 33 Wall Street, " " "
Naumberg, Walter W., . . . 33 Wall Street, " " "
Nelson, Henry Loomis, . . . Williams College, Williamstown, Mass.
Nelson, H. W., Jr., ... Marshfield Hills, "
Nevius, John H. C., ... 33 Union Square, New York City
Newton Albro J , ... 528 Union Street, Brooklyn, N. Y.
Newton, R. Heber, ... East Hampton, N. Y.
Nichols, George L., ... 66 E. 56th Street, New York City
Nichols, W. N., ... 353 Clinton Avenue, Brooklyn
Nicoll, James C., ... 51 W. 10th Street, New York City
North, Thomas M., . . . 160 Central Park South, " " "
Notman, George, ... 99 John Street, " " "
Nourse, Charles J., Jr., ... 82 Beaver Street, " " "

Oakes, Charles, ... 9 Pine Street, New York City
O'Connor, John A., ... 12 E. 44th Street, " " "
Ogden, Rollo, ... 206 Broadway, " " "
Olin, Stephen H., ... 32 Nassau Street, " " "
Oltman, H. H., ... 20 Broad Street, " " "
Olyphant, Robert, ... 21 Cortlandt Street, " " "
Opdyke, William S., ... 20 Nassau Street, " " "
Oppenheim, Edward L., . . . 30 Broad Street, " " "
Oppenheimer, Henry S., . . . 741 Madison Avenue, " " "
Orcutt C Blake, ... Hudson River Day Line, " " "

Ordway, Edward W., ... 1098 Dean Street, Brooklyn
Orr, Alexander E., ... 102 Remsen Street, "
Osborne, Thomas M., ... Auburn, N. Y.

Packard, Edwin, ... 241 Henry Street, Brooklyn
Page, Walter H., ... 34 Union Square, New York City
Parker, Frederick S., ... 32 Garden Place, Brooklyn
Parks, J. Waring, . . . , . 49 Wall Street, New York City
Parrish, Samuel L., ... 25 Broad Street, " " "
Parsons, Herbert, ... 52 William Street, " " "
Parsons, John E., ... 52 William Street, " " "
Paulding, James Kirk, ... 130 E. 24th Street, " " "
Pauli, H. G., ... 15 S. William Street, " " "
Peck, George G., ... 18 East 65th Street, " " "
Pedersen, James, ... 20 E. 46th Street, " " "
Pell, Frederick A., ... Lakewood, N. J.
Pendleton, Francis K., . . . 25 Broad Street, New York City
Perrine, William A., . . . 2440 N. Marshall Street, Philadelphia, Pa.
Phillips, Lee, ... 438 W. 116th Street, New York City
Phoenix, Phillips, ... 68 Broad Street, " " "
Pierce, Franklin, ... 31 Nassau Street, " " "
Pierce, Henry H., ... 120 Broadway, " " "
Pierrepont, Henry E., ... 216 Columbia Heights, Brooklyn
Pierrepont, John J., ... 66 & 68 Broad Street, New York City
Pierrepont, Robert Low, ... Box 449, Bay Shore, N. Y.
Pinchot, Gifford, . . . 1615 Rhode Island Avenue, Washington, D. C.
Pope, A. A., ... Box 11, Jerusalem Road, Cohasset, Mass.
Pope, George A., ... 926 St. Paul Street, Baltimore, Md.
Potter, Frederick, ... 71 Broadway, New York City
Potter, Henry C., ... 113 W. 40th Street, " " "
Potts, William, ... 7 W. 43rd Street, " " "
Powell, Wilson M., Jr., . . . 29 Wall Street, " " "
Prentice, William P., ... 52 Broadway, " " "
Prentiss, George H., ... 108 Pierrepont Street, Brooklyn, N Y.
Price, Joseph M., ... 158 West Broadway, New York City
Pryer, Charles, ... New Rochelle, N. Y.
Pryor, James W., ... 65 Wall Street, New York City
Putnam, George Haven, . . . 27 W. 23d Street, " " "
Putnam, George P., ... 160 Fifth Avenue, " " "
Putnam, Harrington, ... 404 Washington Avenue, Brooklyn
Putnam, Irving, ... 27 W. 23rd Street, New York City
Pyne, Moses Taylor, ... 263 Madison Avenue, " " "

Rainsford, W. S., ... 209 E. 16th Street, New York City
Rand, George C., ... 107 Wall Street, " " "
Rand, William H., Jr. . . . Criminal Court Building, " " "
Raven, A. A., ... 51 Wall Street, " " "
Raymond, Charles H., ... 26 Liberty Street, " " "

Raymond, Rossiter W. . . . . . 123 Henry Street, Brooklyn
Reichhelm, Edward P., . . . 90 West 34th Street, Bayonne, N. J.
Reynolds, James B., ... 55 W. 44th Street, New York City
Rice, Edwin T., Jr., ... 59 Wall Street, " " "
Richards, C. A. L., ... 169 Power Street, Providence, R. I.
Rives, George L., ... 14 W. 38th Street, New York City
Robb, J. Hampden, ... 23 Park Avenue, " " "
Robinson, Beverly R., ... 42 W. 37th Street, " " "
Robinson, Moncure, ... 7 E. 42d Street, " " "
Romaine, Louis Tyson, . . . 84 Beaver Street, " " "
Roome, W. Harris, ... 287 Fourth Avenue, " " "
Roosevelt, Theodore, ... Oyster Bay, N. Y.
Root, Elihu, ... State Department, Washington, D. C.
Rose, Arthur P , ... Geneva, N. Y.
Rose, Charles J., ... " "
Rosenbaum, S. D., ... 201 Wooster Street, New York City
Rosendale, Simon L., ... 57 State Street, Albany, N. Y.
Rosenfeld, George, . . . 35 South William Street, New York City
Rowe, William V., ... 50 Wall Street, " " "
Rublee, George, . . , . . 15 Broad Street, " " "

Sackett, Henry W., ... 154 Nassau Street, New York City
Saint Gaudens, Augustus, ... Windsor, Vt.
Salomon, William, ... 25 Broad Street, New York City
Sand, Henry A. L., . . . , 32 Liberty Street, " " "
Sand, Max E., ... Ardsley-on-Hudson, N. Y.
Sanger, William Cary, ... Sangerfield, "
Savage, Minot J., . . 34th Street and Park Avenue, New York City
Sayer, W. Murray, Jr., ... 398 Washington Avenue, Brooklyn
Schafer, Samuel M., ... 35 Wall Street, New York City
Scharmann, Hermann B., . . . 170 W. 59th Street, " " "
Schieren, Charles A. . . . . . 405 Clinton Avenue, Brooklyn
Schnakenberg, D., ... 6 Hanover Street, New York City
Schrader, George H. F., ... 32 Rose Street, " "
Schumacher, Charles, . . . 41 Exchange Place, " " "
Schurman, George W., . . . 15 W. 57th Street, " " "
Schurz, Carl Lincoln, ... 19 William Street, " " "
Scott, J. F., ... , . 349 W. 121st Street, " " "
Scott, William, ... 25 Duane Street, " " "
Scribner, Arthur H., ... 153 Fifth Avenue, " " "
Scribner, Charles, ... 153 Fifth Avenue, " " "
Seaman, Louis L., ... 247 Fifth Avenue, " " "
Searle, Arthur, ... 41 Concord Avenue, Cambridge, Mass.
Seaver, Benjamin F., ... 111 Pierrepont Street, Brooklyn
Sedgwick, Arthur G., . . . 52 William Street, New York City
Sedgwick, Ellery, ... 143 Fifth Avenue, " " "
Sedgwick, Henry D., ... 120 E. 22d Street, " " "
Seligman, E. R. A., ... 324 W. 86th Street, " " "

Seligman, Jefferson,	15 Broad Street, New York City
Serveu, A. Ralph,	1419 "F" Street, N. W., Washington, D. C.
Seward, George F.,	97 Cedar Street, New York City
Sexton, Lawrence E.,	34 Pine Street, " " "
Seymour, Origen S.,	54 William Street, " " "
Shainwald, Ralph L.,	100 William Street, " " "
Shaw, Albert,	13 Astor Place, " " "
Sheldon, Edward W.,	45 Wall Street, " " "
Sheppard, John S., Jr.,	26 Liberty Street, " " "
Sherman, Arnold W,	265 Henry Street, Brooklyn
Shillaber, William Jr.,	1 Broadway, New York City
Shortt, W. A.,	32 Broadway, " " "
Siedenberg, Reinhard,	Cotton Exchange, " " "
Simes, William,	Petersham, Mass.
Sinclair, John,	16 E. 66th Street, New York City
Skillin, Augustus H.,	34 Pine Street, " " "
Slade, Francis Louis,	49 Cedar Street, " " "
Slicer, Thomas R.,	156 E. 38th Street, " " "
Smillie, James D.,	9 E. 39th Street, " " "
Smith, Adelbert J.,	35 Nassau Street, " " "
Smith, Bryan H.,	Brooklyn Savings Bank, Brooklyn, N. Y.
Smith, Charles Robinson,	25 Broad Street, New York City
Smith, Charles Stewart,	25 W. 47th Street, " " "
Smith, Clarence B.,	71 E. 87th Street, " " "
Smith, F. Hopkinson,	150 E. 34th Street, " " "
Smith, Frederick J.,	278 Mulborry Street, " " "
Smith, Graham,	Harvard Club, " " "
Smith, Howard M,	Brevoort Savings Bank. Brooklyn, N. Y.
Smith, J. Henry,	10 Wall Street, New York City
Smith, William Alexander,	412 Madison Avenue, " " "
Smyth, Nathan A.,	Criminal Court Building, " " "
Snow, Henry Sanger,	81 Willoughby Street, Brooklyn
Southard, George H., Jr.,	164 Montague Street, Brooklyn, N. Y.
Spaulding, Henry K.,	501 W. 120th Street, New York City
St. John, William M.,	Union League Club, " " "
Stanton, George, A,	45 Cedar Street, " " "
Stapler, H. B. B.,	32 Liberty Street, " " "
Stark, Joshua,	176 Martin Street, Milwaukee, Wis.
Stedman, Edmund C.,	2643 Broadway, New York City
Steers, James R.,	31 Nassau Street, " " "
Steinway, Frederick T.,	53rd Street and Park Avenue, " " "
Stern, Benjamin,	32 W. 23rd Street, " " "
Stewart, William R.,	31 Nassau Street, " " "
Stimson, Daniel M.,	11 W. 17th Street, " " "
Stokes, Anson Phelps, Jr., (Life),	Yale University, New Haven, Conn.
Stokes, Harold M. Phelps, (Life),	229 Madison Avenue, New York City
Stokes, I. N. Phelps, (Life),	229 Madison Avenue, " " "
Stokes. James,	49 Cedar Street, " " "

Stokes, J. G. Phelps, (Life), . . 229 Madison Avenue, New York City
Strauss, Albert, ... 15 Broad Street, " " "
Strauss, Frederick, ... 15 Broad Street, " " "
Strong, George A., ... 50 Wall Street, " " "
Strong, Theron G., ... 49 Wall Street, " " "
Sturges, S. Perry, . . . 305 Washington Avenue, Brooklyn
Sturgis, F. K., ... 36 Broad Street, New York City
Sturgis, Russell, ... 307 E. 17th Street, " " "
Stuyvesant, Rutherford, . . . 16 Exchange Place, " " "
Sulzberger, Ferdinand, . 45th Street and First Avenue, " " "

Taft, Henry W., ... 40 Wall Street, New York City
Taggart, Rush, ... 195 Broadway, " " "
Tatham, Charles, ... 465 W. 23rd Street, " " "
Tatham, Edwin, ... 82 Beekman Street, " " "
Taussig, Walter M., . . . 9-15 Murray Street, " " "
Taylor, E. P., Jr., ... 25 Pine Street, " " "
Taylor, Stevenson, . . . 123 W. 85th Street, " " "
Taylor, Walter F., ... 54 Wall Street, " " "
Taylor, William C., . . . 25 So. Portland Avenue, Brooklyn
Terry, Roderick, . . . 169 Madison Avenue, New York City
Terry, Seth Sprague, . . . 126 E. 34th Street, " " "
Thacher, George O., . . . 2 E 86th Street, " " "
Thomae, Robert L. . . . . . Scotch Plains, N. J.
Thorne, Samuel, Jr., . . . 54 Wall Street, New York City
Thornton, William, . . . 117 Prince Street, " " "
Thurber, Francis B., . . . 90 West Broadway, " " "
Tiebout, Charles H., . . . 31 Grand Street, Brooklyn
Tinkham, Julian R., . . . 42 Broadway, New York City
Tison, Alexander, . . . 11 William Street, " " "
Tod, J. Kennedy, ... 45 Wall Street, " " "
Todd, Henry A., ... 824 West End Avenue, " " "
Tomkins, Calvin, ... 17 Battery Place, " " "
Tompkins, Hamilton B., . . 229 Broadway, " " "
Train, Arthur C., ... 28 W. 47th Street, " " "
Trotter, William, ... 124 E. 30th Street, " " "
Tuckerman, Alfred, . . . 1123 Broadway, " " "
Tuckerman, Eliot, ... 44 Pine Street, " " "
Turnbull, George R.. . . . 33 Mercer Street, " " "

Uhl, Edward, ... P. O. Box 1207, New York City
Unckles, D. S., ... 957 St. Mark's Avenue, Brooklyn

Vail, Charles D., ... Geneva, N. Y.
Valentine, Charles A., . . . 1 E. 27th Street, New York City
Valentine, Henry C., (Life), . . . 257 Broadway, " " "
Valentine, Robert G. . . 112 East Capitol St., Washington, D. C.
Vallandingham, Edward N., . . . Reform Club, New York City

Vandiver, Almuth C.,	District Attorney's Office, New York City
Van Dusen, Samuel C.,	27 Cliff Street, " " "
Van Ingen, Edward H.,	9 E. 71st Street, " " "
Van Nest, George W.,	20 Broad Street, " " "
Villard, Harold G.,	43 Cedar Street, " " "
Villard, Oswald Garrison, (Life),	206 Broadway, " " "
Wadsworth, James W.,	Geneseo, N. Y.
Walcott, Philip K.,	111 Broadway, New York City
Walker, John,	1231 Western Avenue, Alleghany City, Pa.
Walker, Samuel C.,	Harbison & Walker, Pittsburg, "
Walker, William,	" " " " "
Wallace, Jackson,	26 Liberty Street, New York City
Wallace, William H.,	66 Broadway, " " "
Wallace, W. J.,	209 W. 81st Street, " " "
Walling, William English,	184 Eldridge Street, " " "
Warburg, F. M., (Life),	52 William Street, " " "
Ward, Henry Galbreath,	79 Wall Street, " " "
Ward, J. H.,	34 Kenyon Bldg., Louisville, Ky.
Ward, J. Q. A.,	119 W. 52nd Street, New York City
Warner, John De Witt,	54 William Street, " " "
Warren, George A.,	1118 20th Street, N. W., Washington, D. C.
Warren, H. Langford,	120 Boylston Street, Boston, Mass.
Wasson, James B.,	154 Nassau Street, New York City
Watson, Charles W.,	500 Madison Avenue, " " "
Webb, Willoughby L.,	63 Wall Street, " " "
Weed, John W.,	62 William Street, " " "
Weeks, E. R.,	3408 Harrison Street, Kansas City, Mo.
Weeks, Rufus W.,	P. O. Box 1663, New York City
Welch, Archibald A.,	Woodland Street, Hartford, Conn.
Weld, Francis M.,	5 Nassau Street, New York City
Welling, R. W. G.,	2 Wall Street, " " "
Wendell, Evert J.,	8 E. 38th Street, " " "
Werthein, H. P.,	27 William Street, " " "
Wetmore, Edmund,	34 Pine Street, " " "
Wheeler, A. S.,	511 Sears Bldg., Boston, Mass.
Wheeler, Everett P.,	21 State Street, New York City
Wheeler, James R.,	Columbia College, " " "
Wheelock, George G.,	75 Park Avenue, " " "
White, Alexander M.,	2 Pierrepont Place, Brooklyn
White, Alexander M., Jr.,	52 Remsen Street, "
White, Andrew D., (Life),	Ithaca, N. Y.
White, George C.,	Glen Ridge, N. J.
Whiteside, George W,	District Attorney's Office, New York City
Whitney, Edward B.,	26 Liberty Street, " " "
Whitridge, Frederick W.,	59 Wall Street, " " "
Wickersham, George W.,	40 Wall Street. " " "
Wilcox, Ansley,	295 Main Street, Buffalo, N. Y.

Wilcox, David,	Metropolitan Club, New York City
Wilds, Howard Payson,	University Club, " " "
Williams, L. L.,	Care E. C. Williams, 135 Broadway, " " "
Williams, Norman A.,	42 E. 41st Street, " " "
Williams, Perry P.,	Produce Exchange, " " "
Williams, Richard H.,	1 Broadway, " " "
Williams, Stephen G.,	953 Madison Avenue, " " "
Williams, William,	35 Wall Street, " " "
Willis, Albert L.,	124 W. 183rd St., " " "
Wilson, Richard T.,	511 Fifth Avenue, " " "
Wilson, Theodore,	Orange, N. J.
Wing, Henry T.,	152 Clinton Street, Brooklyn
Wise, B. E.,	21 Broad Street, New York City
Wisner, Charles,	Cotton Exchange, " " "
Wisner, H. G.,	18 W. 12th Street, " " "
Witherbee F. S.,	71 Broadway, " " "
Wolff, Lewis S.,	12 E. 70th Street, " " "
Woodbridge, Charles E.,	8 Bridge Street, " " "
Worcester, Edwin D., Jr.,	35 Nassau Street, " " "
Wright, Jonathan,	44 W. 49th Street, " " "
Yates, Arthur G.,	130 So. Fitzhugh Street, Rochester, N.Y.
Yonge, Henry,	Hotel Margaret, Brooklyn
Zabriskie, George,	49 Wall Street, New York City
Zerega, Richard A.,	101 Classon Avenue, Brooklyn

ARTICLES OF INCORPORATION

OF

THE NEW YORK CIVIL SERVICE REFORM ASSOCIATION

[Filed May 11, 1900.]

KNOW ALL MEN BY THESE PRESENTS: That we, the undersigned, being persons of full age and all citizens of the United States, a majority of whom are also citizens of the State of New York, and being now Directors of an unincorporated association known as the New York Civil Service Reform Association, and organized for the purposes hereinafter mentioned; being desirious of incorporation for the same purposes under the Membership Corporations Law of the State of New York, do hereby, pursuant to unanimous vote of all the members of the said Association, present and voting at a regularly called meeting thereof, and pursuant to authority given by the said unanimous vote at the said meeting, of which meeting notice of the intention so to incorporate was given personally or by mail to each member of such Association whose residence or Post Office address was known, at least thirty days before said meeting, and at which meeting the corporate name stated in paragraph First was by unanimous vote adopted, do hereby certify as follows

FIRST.—The name or title by which the Association in which we desire to form ourselves as aforesaid shall be known in law, shall be the Civil Service Reform Association.

SECOND.—The territory in which its operations are to be principally conducted shall be the City of New York.

THIRD.—The city in which its principal office is to be located is the City of New York.

FOURTH.—The objects of the Association shall be to further the establishment of a system of appointment, promotion and removal in the civil service, founded upon the principle that public office is a public trust, admission to and retention in which should depend upon proven fitness; and to take such action as may tend to secure the honest and efficient execution of laws and rules relating to the civil service, and to the proper administration thereof.

FIFTH.—The number of its directors shall be twenty-eight.

SIXTH.—The names of the persons to be its directors until its first annual meeting are as follows:

Samuel P. Avery, Truman J. Backus, Henry De Forest Baldwin, Edward Cary, Charles Collins, W. Bayard Cutting, Horace E. Deming, A. S. Frissell, Richard Watson Gilder, Edwin L Godkin, J. Warren Greene, George McAneny, James McKeen, Jacob F. Miller, Samuel H. Ordway, William A. Perrine, George Foster Peabody, William J. Schieffelin, Carl Schurz, Charles A. Schieren, Thomas R. Slicer, Henry Sanger Snow, Anson Phelps Stokes, S. Perry Sturges, Henry W. Taft, William H. Thomson, Charles W. Watson and Everett P. Wheeler.

In WITNESS WHEREOF we have made, signed, acknowledged and filed this certificate in duplicate.

Dated this Eighth day of May, 1900.

C. SCHURZ,	WILLIAM H. THOMSON,
JACOB F. MILLER,	A. S. FRISSELL,
ANSON PHELPS STOKES,	GEORGE MCANENY,
EVERETT P. WHEELER,	CHARLES A. SCHIEREN,
CHARLES COLLINS,	SAMUEL P. AVERY,
SAMUEL H. ORDWAY,	GEORGE FOSTER PEABODY.
J. WARREN GREENE,	

STATE OF NEW YORK, } ss.
COUNTY OF NEW YORK, }

On this eighth day of May, one thousand and nine hundred, before me personally came Carl Schurz, Jacob F. Miller, Anson Phelps Stokes, Everett P. Wheeler, Charles Collins, J. Warren Greene, William H. Thomson, Samuel H. Ordway, A. S. Frissell, George McAneny, Charles A. Schieren, Samuel P. Avery and George Foster Peabody, to me personally known to be the persons described in and who made and signed the foregoing certificate, and severally duly acknowledged to me that they had made, signed and executed the same for the uses and purposes therein set forth.

F. W. HOERSCHGEN,
Notary Public, Kings County. (149)
(Certificate filed in New York County.)

Approved, May 9, 1900.

DAVID LEVINTRITT,
Justice of the Supreme Court of the State of New York.

REPORT

OF THE

Executive Committee

OF THE

New York

Civil Service Reform Association

READ AT THE ANNUAL MEETING, MAY 8, 1907.

LIST OF MEMBERS, ETC.

NEW YORK
PUBLISHED FOR THE
CIVIL SERVICE REFORM ASSOCIATION
79 WALL STREET
1907

CONTENTS

Annual Report of the Executive Committee -	5
Annual Report of the Treasurer - - -	21
Constitution and By Laws - - - .	23
Roll of Officers and Members - - - -	31
Articles of Incorporation - - - - -	53

ANNUAL REPORT

OF THE

Executive Committee of the Civil Service Reform Association.

It is the sad duty of the Executive Committee to report the death, during the past year, of two of the leaders and pioneers in the civil service reform movement, who as members and officers of the New York Association from its early years, by wise counsel and disinterested service have contributed in large measure to the success of its work. Carl Schurz, who succeeded George William Curtis as President of the Association in 1893, died May 14. Jacob F. Miller, the Chairman of the Executive Committee since 1897, died December 11. At meetings held May 16 and December 12 the following minutes were unanimously adopted by the Executive Committee:

MINUTE IN MEMORY OF HON. CARL SCHURZ.

Great in intellect, pure in life, tender in heart, noble of purpose, courageous in word and deed, courteous in address, sincere in thought, large of vision, gifted with incisive and rarely persuasive eloquence, loyal in friendship, loving much and much beloved—Carl Schurz died on Monday, the fourteenth day of May, 1906, in his seventy-seventh year, leader in the contest for freedom in two continents in each of which he had wrought mightily to uplift his fellow men.

We, his friends and associates in the New York Civil Service Reform Association, are deprived of his wise leadership and constant co-operation, but the great cause for which we labor will find an ever increasing support from those to whom the lofty ideals, unselfish patriotism and splendid achievements of his long life devoted to the public good will appeal with compelling force.

MINUTE IN MEMORY OF HON. JACOB F. MILLER.

In the death of Jacob F. Miller, December 11, 1906, in his seventieth year, the cause of Civil Service Reform has lost one of its most faithful friends. Especially severe is the loss to the New York Civil Service Reform Association, and to its Executive Committee of which, for nine years, he had been chairman. To that chairmanship Mr. Miller brought a fine, unvarying courtesy, an excellent knowledge of parliamentary law, and an unusual efficiency in the transaction of business. To all members of the Committee, one distinct attraction of the recurring sessions was the pleasure of meeting their loved and honored presiding officer.

Mr. Miller's services to Civil Service Reform began at an early date. When a candidate for state assemblyman in 1882, he publicly declared his conviction of the need of a Civil Service Reform Law and after his election he introduced in the legislature a civil service bill the provisions of which were afterwards incorporated in the Civil Service Law enacted in 1883. The adoption of the present civil service system in New York, which is based upon this original act of 1883, is due in no small part to his efforts.

Mr. Miller has been an active member of the New York Civil Service Reform Association since 1883. In 1884, he was elected a member of its Executive Committee. In 1887, he was transferred to the Standing Committee on Affiliated Societies, and became chairman of that committee in 1888. In 1891, he was re-elected to the Executive Committee, and served as its chairman from 1897 until his death. One month before his death he was chosen a member of the Council of the National League, to fill the vacancy caused by the death of Carl Schurz.

In Mr. Miller were combined in high degree the qualities of a cultured and useful citizen. A graduate of Williams College; a sound, trusted lawyer; a fair-minded, independent member of his political party; trustee of various worthy institutions; and the light and joy of his own home; he embodied a rare union of Christian virtues both private and public.

The Executive Committee of the New York Civil Service Reform Association, in its own behalf and in behalf of the Association it represents, hereby places on record its high appreciation of Mr. Miller's worth, and its keen sense of affliction by reason of his death.

At a meeting of the Executive Committee on January 9, Vice-President Silas W. Burt was elected President of the Association and Samuel H. Ordway, Chairman of the Law Committee, was elected Chairman of the Executive Committee.

The Association has been notified of a bequest of $1,000 by the will of Jacob Meyer of New York, which will become available, however, only in the future.

THE FEDERAL SERVICE.

It is the province of the National Civil Service Reform League to report on everything that concerns the Federal civil service. This report will, therefore, refer to such important matters only as have taken place since the meeting of that body in November last and to such other matters as affect the administration of the law in Federal offices within New York State.

INCREASE IN SALARIES OF CIVIL SERVICE COMMISSIONERS.

The appropriation bill passed by the last Congress carried an item for the increase of the salaries of the Federal Civil Service Commissioners from $3,500 to $4,000. Even with this increase the salaries remain inadequate, when it is considered that the Commissioners are obliged to live in Washington and to devote all of their time to the work. The absurd practice that obtained for many years of voting down the entire appropriation for the Commission in Committee of the Whole, only to restore it when the votes were recorded, has been discontinued, but Congress has not yet reached the point of appraising at its full value the work of the Commission for efficiency and economy in the public service.

EXAMINATION FOR THE CONSULAR SERVICE.

Recently was held the first examination for the consular service under the President's order of June 27, 1906. The examination was of high standard and the candidates who succeeded in passing should be exceptionally well qualified for service. Entrance to the consular service has by no means been placed on an open competitive basis; only those nominated by the President are admitted, but if the standard set in this examination is maintained under future administrations, it will unquestionably result in a material increase in the efficiency of the service.

PERNICIOUS POLITICAL ACTIVITY CASES IN NEW YORK.

Last Summer, Collin H. Woodward, who then held the competitive position of Deputy Surveyor of the Port, announced himself as a candidate for the position of Republican leader of the 23rd Assembly district and proceeded to take an active part in the campaign. Although, by so doing he violated no specific provision of the civil service law, he was clearly guilty of flagrant violation of the Executive Order in regard to the political activity of officeholders and his continuance in office led Federal employees in New York City to believe that this regulation had been permitted to lapse. The matter was called to the President's attention by the Association in December and a reply was received that Woodward had resigned. A place was found for him in the State service —in which there is no prohibition against political activity—as Deputy Superintendent of Elections. It is interesting to note that the man whom he succeeded in this position—another district leader—failed to secure appointment from Governor Hughes as Superintendent of Elections and has just been provided with a position in the Federal service as secretary to the Naval Officer who is himself a Republican district leader. The "pernicious activity order" has been enforced also in the case of Philip Leininger, the Deputy Collector of Customs at Buffalo. Mr. Leininger was a Republican general committeeman and took an active part in a contest for the chairmanship of that committee. As he held a competitive position the Treasury Department required his resignation.

REMOVAL OF COLLECTOR SANDERS.

The press has heralded the recent removal of a Collector of Internal Revenue in Rochester as indicating an intention on the part of President Roosevelt to use the Federal patronage for political purposes and in support of Governor Hughes. That support gained by such questionable methods would not be welcomed or approved by the Governor can be confidently asserted in view of his well known principles in regard to the public service. President Roosevelt has placed himself on record squarely against such practices. In 1895, he said "Removals for political reasons in places where the duties are wholly non-political cannot be defended by any man who looks at public affairs from the proper standpoint." He has done so much to carry out the principles of civil service reform, that we should regret to be compelled to accept the view of the press as stated above.

NEW STATE AND CITY CIVIL SERVICE LAWS.

New civil service laws have been enacted this year in Porto Rico and Colorado. The Colorado law applies to the state institutions, but contains a clause permitting cities to adopt its provisions by popular vote. Indiana has passed a law requiring non-competitive examinations for appointment to positions in all state institutions. Since the last annual meeting, the cities of Norfolk, Va., Wheeling, W. Va., and Springfield, Ill., have voted to adopt the merit system. Civil service bills are still pending in the legislatures of Pennsylvania, Michigan and Illinois. The civil service bill in New Jersey was defeated in the Assembly on the last day of the session after passing the Senate with only three negative votes. This record marks a year of progress in civil service reform.

THE BENDER CASE.

Considerable space in the last report was devoted to the case of Harry H. Bender, Fiscal Supervisor of State Charities, who was accused in evidence presented by the Association, and substantiated by the testimony of his employees, of violating the provisions of the civil s law prohibiting the collection of political assessments. At the time that report was made, a decisive halt had been called in the dilatory tactics so long successfully employed by Mr. Bender to prevent the continuance of the investigation, by the decision of the Court of Appeals maintaining the power of the State Civil Service Commission to conduct investigations. The subsequent history of the case commanded such general popular interest and was so fully covered in the public press that it calls for but short comment here. In the face of a unanimous report by the State Commission, after completing the examination of witnesses, that Bender had clearly violated the civil service law and "that Mr. Bender and Mr. Prescott, acting with a common purpose and understanding, sat at the receipt of custom for the collection of political contributions from the employees in the office," Governor Higgins dismissed the charges and administered a reprimand to Mr. Bender.

The entire inconsistency of such a conclusion in view of the evidence against Bender aroused practically universal criticism from the press in all parts of the State. As the Governor, however, refused to reopen the case or to reconsider his decision, the Association was forced to regard the case as closed and on September 19 the following resolution was adopted by the Executive Committee:

> Resolved, That in the opinion of this Committee the practice of levying campaign contributions upon public employees is a method of extortion, corrupting the political health and calculated to deprive the people's servants of their right of free choice in election. The failure of the Governor of the State of New York to uphold the State Civil Service Commission in the findings of their report on the violation of the Civil Service Law by Fiscal Supervisor Harry H. Bender, and Secretary Herbert F. Prescott, and his dismissal of the charges with merely an impotent reprimand in the face of the evidence and of the Commission's report was a sacrifice of the interests of good government as established by legislative enactment and a check to the movement for the abolition of corrupt practices in elections.

The Association has been subjected to some criticism for not requesting Governor Hughes, immediately upon assuming office, to remove Mr. Bender. Your Committee has, however, felt it would not be justified in so doing in the absence of any new charges against Mr. Bender and in view of the fact that Governor Higgins had made a final decision in the case after considering all the evidence. Mr. Bender's term of office will expire in June and we are confident—without having received or asked for any assurance from the Governor—that in view of his civil service record he will not be reappointed.

THE EXEMPT CLASS.

A civil service law has been on the statute books of this State for twenty-four years and has unquestionably won the support of public opinion. The Constitution of the State provides for it. An attempt to repeal it could not receive serious consideration. Under these circumstances the only danger by which the system can be threatened is the lack of thorough and intelligent enforcement of the law.

The Constitution provides that appointments and promotions shall be made for merit and fitness "to be ascertained, so far as practicable, by examinations which, so far as practicable, shall be competitive." The greatest difficulty has been met in establishing a satisfactory test of practicability and the greatest menace to proper enforcement lies in the inflated and ever growing list of positions which are exempt from competitive examination on the dictum of the commissioners that competitive examination is impracticable.

This applies to both the State service and the Municipal service. The classification has never been drawn with a view to adhering strictly to the letter of the Constitution in the matter of practicability. Other considerations have entered into the determination since the law was first put in force and each position exempted from competition has served as a precedent for the exemption of other positions of the same general character. The exempt class has consequently, and inevitably, been been steadily increasing.

The Constitution requires that *all* appointments must be made for merit and fitness and the civil service law forbids appointments in any class for political considerations, but it is notorious that these provisions are violated almost every day in appointments to the exempt class. Positions are exempted because of their confidential character, because of personal responsibility of the head of the department for the acts of his subordinates, because they involve the handling of large sums of money, and then are treated, in a majority of cases, as mere party spoils. The recent use—or rather misuse—of exempt positions in a factional political contest in New York City, to which reference will be made later, gives added emphasis to the need for revision of the classification.

The figures showing the increase in the exempt class since the passage of the White Law in 1899 have been carefully compiled. While the increase in the total number of exempt positions is due, to some extent, to the creation of new offices and commissions, such as, for instance, the Boards of Water Supply which require a number of expert engineers who cannot be secured through competition, yet glaring inconsistencies now exist in the classification which are due to action by the Commissioners on each individual request for exemption without regard to any general rule or standard. All the data are being brought together in the belief that this is a favorable time to request the state and city commissions **to** undertake a complete revision of the exempt class with a view to its material reduction and the establishment of certain definite precedents by which future requests for exemption can be judged.

The Executive Committee of the Association has suggested to the State Commission the desirability of making a record of its reasons for denying requests for exemptions, in the hope that a line of precedents may thus be established which will to some extent govern and control the action of the Commission on future applications of this character.

THE STATE SERVICE.

THE ELECTION OF GOVERNOR HUGHES.

The election of one of its own members as Governor, last Fall, was a source of satisfaction and encouragement to the Association. Although Mr. Hughes' views were well known, as he had served for some years as a member of the Association's law committee, the usual custom was followed of addressing letters to each candidate asking him to place on record his attitude toward civil service reform. Mr. Hughes' reply was strictly to the point:

"As a member of your Association who has served upon its Law Committee I am deeply interested in its work. I believe in the principles of civil service reform and shall do all in my power to see that the Civil Service Law is maintained and enforced."

No reply was received from Mr. Hearst, the Democratic candidate, nor are his views on the subject known to the Association.

The party platforms contained no reference to the merit system and it was not in any sense an issue in the campaign. The usual precaution of sending copies of the section of the law prohibiting political assessments to all heads of departments was followed and, in view of the Bender case, we believe these provisions were more strictly observed than has been customary in the past. We are particularly indebted to Comptroller Metz for his prompt action in suppressing circulars asking for contributions from employees which were issued over the printed signatures of certain officials in his department.

THE STATE CIVIL SERVICE COMMISSION.

Governor Hughes has made no change in the personnel of the State Civil Service Commission, and it has, consequently, pursued the same conservative policy and maintained the same standard as in past years. Its last annual report shows that the work of the Commission has materially increased and that it constantly demands more and more of the time and labor of the Commissioners, all of whom are prominent newspaper editors in cities situated at considerable distances from Albany. When it is taken into account that a municipal commission can make no changes in its rules or classification without the approval of the State Commission, and that the State Commission is expected to conduct investigations into the administration of the law throughout the State, the question arises whether the time has not come when more frequent meetings of the board have become necessary and whether it might not be good policy to provide for a president resident in Albany to supervise and direct the executive work.

The Commission has continued the policy of sending out its Secretary and Chief Examiner to investigate and report on the work of municipal commissions, with excellent results. Local commissions err far more often through ignorance of proper methods than through intent to defeat the purpose of the law and these periodical investigations by trained officials will do a great deal to bring about higher standards of administration, as well as to correct abuses. The Commission is also steadily making progress in successfully applying competitive examinations to the higher positions in the State service, thus proving the practicability of transferring many of these positions from the exempt to the competitive class.

CONFERENCE OF REPRESENTATIVES OF COMMISSIONS.

One of the most interesting and encouraging events of the year was the conference of representatives of civil service commissions held, at the invitation of the State Commission, in Albany on October 11 and 12, at which many important and difficult problems of administration were discussed. Such an interchange of ideas among persons charged with the responsibility of administering the law cannot fail to have good results. It is hoped that meetings of this character will be held at frequent intervals in the future.

Before adjourning, the conference adopted two resolutions. One favored an amendment to the civil service law to require that an employee should be furnished with the reasons for his removal and be allowed an opportunity to make an explanation before removal is made; the other recommended that the requirement that laborers in cities should be appointed from registration lists, should be made optional in the case of the smaller cities.

MEASURES IN THE STATE LEGISLATURE.

THE STATE COMMISSION'S BILLS.

The State Commission has drawn up and introduced in both houses of the legislature three bills amending the civil service law. Two of these carry out the purpose of the resolutions passed by the conference just referred to. The third provides for an annual statement by each civil employee of all contributions made by him, directly or indirectly, for any political purpose. All three bills have received the approval of the Association's law committee, which assisted in drafting them, and its representatives have appeared before committees of the legislature to urge their passage. The bill making labor registration optional in third class cities, which also provides that the State Commission may establish competitive registration of laborers in institutions and offices in the State service, has been favorably reported in the Assembly. Owing to the selfish and ill-advised action of the organizations of county employees in New York and Kings County, in seeking from the legislature a limited court review by writ of certiorari in the case of removal of county employees in those counties only, the State Commission's conservative removal bill for all competitive employees has not been reported in the Assembly.

BILLS INTRODUCED BY THE ASSOCIATION.

The Association has also had three bills introduced. Assemblyman O'Brian of Erie, a member of the Executive Committee of the Civil Service Reform Association of Buffalo, introduced a bill to prohibit employees in the competitive class from serving as members of political conventions or committees. This is in line with the Executive Order restricting the political activity of officeholders in the Federal service, the Shern Law passed last year for Philadelphia and the Burrage Ordinance which has been in force in Boston since 1892. It stands, however, little chance of passage at the hands of the present legislature. Senator Agnew and Assemblyman Prentice introduced a bill to do away with the particular restriction on the removal of persons who had served as members of a volunteer fire department. This bill, in view of the opposition it aroused among organizations of exempt volunteer firemen, has been materially modified, and in its modified form has been favorably reported in the Assembly. Senator Saxe and the late Assemblyman Stanley introduced a bill to require that the so-called corporation inspectors, who inspect on behalf of the City the work done by corporations in making street openings, should be in fact City employees, paid by the City and appointed through competitive examination.

The Assembly Cities Committee has failed to report Mr. Stanley's bill although urged to do so. In place of Senator Saxe's bill the Senate Cities Committee, with the approval of the Law Committee of the Association, reported a bill introduced by Senator Fuller to accomplish the same purpose, which was somewhat more specific in its provisions. This bill was defeated in the Senate on April 25 by a vote of 26 to 19, all the Democrats, except Senator Fuller, and a number of up-State Republicans voting against it. This must be regarded as a victory for the spoilsmen.

The work of keeping watch of bills affecting the

merit system has been particularly onerous this year in view of their large number. Briefs have been filed and representatives sent before committees wherever such action was in the opinion of the law committee called for. As the legislature will not adjourn for some weeks it is too early yet to report on the results of these efforts.

NEW YORK CITY.

THE WORK OF THE MUNICIPAL COMMISSION.

The administration of the civil service law by the Municipal Commission has continued steadily to improve and its work is now carried on with both efficiency and despatch. The relations existing between the Commission and the Association have been cordial and this has made it possible to work together for improvements in the system. The amendments to the rules proposed by the Commission have all been made in the interest of greater simplicity and practicability or to put a stop to existing abuses. Among the more important changes have been the adoption of a reasonable and practical system for keeping a record of the efficiency of employees; an amendment to the rules to prevent discrimination between persons of the same grade in making promotions and the adoption of an improved system of numbering examination papers in order completely to conceal the identity of the candidate from the examiners. The Commission has also regulated the examinations for promotion so that it may hold them for all departments once a year and has adopted a form of application in which each candidate for promotion is required to state in full the facts in regard to his previous service. The practice of employing "expert examiners" without examination to do routine work has been discontinued and a competitive examination for civil service examiner has recently been held.

EMPLOYMENT BY SPECIAL CONTRACT.

Each year many persons are employed without examination to perform services for the City by means of special contracts for services. While the Corporation Counsel has rendered an opinion that, under certain circumstances, such employment is legal and not an infringement of the civil service law, there is no question that this practice has been extensively resorted to in order to avoid the necessity of making appointments from the eligible lists. The Commission has been helpless in the matter, and indeed has had no means of ascertaining how far the abuse has been carried, as the bills rendered for these services have been sent directly to the Comptroller and paid by him without a certificate from the Civil Service Commission. This state of facts led the Association to make an investigation of the vouchers in the Comptroller's office and, in view of the result, to suggest a compromise to the Comptroller and the Commission by which all bills for services should be sent to the Civil Service Commission, who would certify, whenever the facts warranted it, that, in accordance with the opinion of the Corporation Counsel, the employment did not properly come under the provisions of the civil service law. Comptroller Metz desired to put an end to the abuse and to facilitate the keeping of a record of all persons employed by special contract. The plan suggested by the Association has been accepted and is, we understand, working satisfactorily.

USE OF THE PATRONAGE IN THE M^CCLELLAN-MURPHY FUED.

The Commission is entitled to the greater credit for the improvements made in its methods in view of the fact that there has been an undoubted tendency on the part of the City administration to draw the civil service into politics and to use the patronage of the unclassified and exempt positions as weapons in the factional war for the control of Tammany Hall between Mayor McClellan and Charles F. Murphy. Immediately on his return from Europe last Summer, Mayor McClellan removed the

Commissioner of Parks for the Borough of the Bronx and put in one of his own adherents, and from that time on there have been a series of removals of heads of departments, deputies, secretaries, cashiers and superintendents. The Tammany boss has not been without means of retaliation, as he retained control of the patronage of certain departments, and places have been made for his removed adherents under the Board of Coroners, the City Clerk and others.

Street Cleaning Commissioner Woodbury, who conducted his department on the strictest civil service lines, resigned because, as he stated in his letter of resignation, the Mayor was "so insistent on the injection of politics" into his department. His successor, Commissioner Craven, has obtained the exemption of two Deputy Commissionerships, which Major Woodbury, in his desire to keep his department clear of politics, refused to ask for, one of which has been filled by the appointment of a McCarren district leader.

That under such disturbing conditions the work of the Commission should have progressed is remarkable; but a peculiar combination of political circumstances has given them a freer hand than ever before to institute improvements for the competitive and labor services and to hold the departments to stricter accountability. The work on these lines is not open to criticism, but we regret the readiness of the Commission to accede to requests for exemption from competition, upon which the more conservative policy of the State Commission has served as a wholesome check. It would take too much space to enumerate all the instances of this, but one example may be cited. Twice the Municipal Commission has granted requests for large increases in the number of exempt positions in the Law Department, and in both cases, after careful examination into the organization of the department, the State Commission has refused its approval on the ground that such additional exemptions were unnecessary.

COMMISSION ON SALARIES AND GRADES.

Last May, Mayor McClellan made the frequent increases in salary of city employees, and the consequent growth of the expenses of maintaining the civil service, the subject of a special message. Subsequently, the Board of Estimate and Apportionment appointed a commission, composed of representatives of the Board, the Borough Presidents, the Civil Service Commission, the Commissioners of Accounts and the Corporation Counsel to revise the classification of titles of positions and grades of salary. The Commission has completed its work for positions in the clerical and engineering services. If its plan is adopted it will not only result in greater economy but also will provide a much more satisfactory basis than in the past for conducting competitive examinations for promotion from grade to grade as required by law. Their work has been closely followed by the Association's Committee on Administration, which has from time to time submitted suggestions that have received courteous consideration.

In closing, the Executive Committee expresses its thanks to the chairmen and members of its standing committees, for the attention they have given to the details of the Association's work. Through the efforts of the Assistant Secretary, correspondence committees have been formed in several new places, to aid in the work of securing proper enforcement of the civil service law. The total membership of the Association numbers 886, an increase of 24 over last year. Of these, 16 are life members, 78 sustaining members and 792 regular members. The Committee thanks the Women's Auxiliary for their assistance and support and takes this opportunity to express its appreciation of the great value of the educational work they have carried on.

SAMUEL H. ORDWAY,
Chairman.
ELLIOT H. GOODWIN,
Secretary.

ANNUAL REPORT OF THE TREASURER.

MAY 1, 1907.

Balance on hand, as per report May 1, 1906		$ 625.15
RECEIPTS:		
From Annual Dues	$3,270.00	
" Sustaining Membership Dues	1,900.00	
" Subscriptions	1,061.00	
" Women's Auxiliary	200.00	6,431.00
		$7,056.15
DISBURSEMENTS:		
Salary of Secretary	$1,475.00	
" " Assistant Secretary	812.50	
" " Editor of GOOD GOVERNMENT	437.50	
" " Charles W. McCandless "of Counsel"	90.00	
" " Clerks	1,179.47	
Rent of Office	500.00	
Telephone Service	125.35	
Office Expenses	238.92	
Expenses of Litigation	33.37	
Expenses of Annual Dinner	142.15	
Traveling Expenses	205.75	
Subscription to GOOD GOVERNMENT	540.02	
Expenses of Membership Committee	108.79	
Legislative Information	185.00	
Stationery	111.85	
Printing	209.36	
Postage and Stamped Envelopes	341.70	
Subscription to National League	70.00	6,806.73
Balance on hand, April 30, 1907		$ 249.42

E. & O. E.   A. S. FRISSELL, *Treasurer.*

Account examined and found correct, May 7, 1907,

        ALFRED B. MEACHAM, } *Auditing Committee.*
        GEORGE R. BISHOP,

REPORT OF THE TREASURER ON THE ELIAL F. HALL FUND.

MAY 1, 1907.

Held as a special deposit at the Fifth Avenue Bank, certificate No. 5844 for sixteen shares Title Guarantee & Trust Company stock.

There has thus far been paid in dividends as follows;

Received from the executor of the Hall estate	$320.00
April 1, 1907, dividend	64.00
	$384.00

This $384.00 is deposited in the Greenwich Savings Bank, and the savings bank book is being held at the Fifth Avenue Bank as a special deposit.

The above stock pays dividends of 16% per annum, namely, $256.

ORGANIZATION

OF

THE NEW YORK CIVIL SERVICE REFORM ASSOCIATION

CONSTITUTION.

ARTICLE I.

The name of this organization shall be The Civil Service Reform Association.

ARTICLE II.

The object of the Association shall be to establish a system of appointment, promotion, and removal in the civil service, founded upon the principle that public office is a public trust, admission to which should depend upon proven fitness. To this end the Association will demand that appointments to subordinate executive offices, with such exceptions as may be expedient, not inconsistent with the principle already mentioned, shall be made from persons whose fitness has been ascertained by competitive examinations open to all applicants properly qualified, and that removals shall be made for legitimate cause only, such as dishonesty, negligence, or inefficiency, but not for political opinion or refusal to render party service; and the Association will advocate all other appropriate measures for securing integrity, intelligence, efficiency, good order, and due discipline in the civil service.

ARTICLE III.

The Association will hold meetings, raise funds, publish and circulate appropriate information, correspond and co-operate with associations organized elsewhere for the objects

set forth in this Constitution, and support all executive and legislative action which promote its purposes.

Article IV.

The conditions of membership shall be wholly independent of party preference. Questions shall not be discussed in the debate or in the publications of the Association upon party grounds. Neither the name nor influence of the Association shall be used on behalf of any party, or for procuring office or promotion for any person. But nothing in this article shall be construed to prevent the Association from opposing any candidate when in its opinion, or in that of three-fourths of the members of the Executive Committee, such course is demanded by the objects of the Association.

Article V.

There shall be a President, to be elected by the Association at the annual meeting, who shall perform the usual and prescribed duties of that office. He shall be, ex-officio, a member of all committees, with a casting vote only, and he may call special meetings of the Executive Committee whenever he thinks it necessary, and, with the assent of two members of the Executive Committee, special meetings of the Association.

There shall be ten Vice-Presidents, to be annually elected by the Association.

There shall be a Treasurer and Secretary, who shall perform the usual and prescribed duties of such officers. They shall be respectively appointed by the Executive Committee, and may be removed by them. The Treasurer shall be, ex-officio, a member of the Finance Committee of the Association.

There shall be an Executive Committee of twenty-five members, to be elected annually by the Association. Subject to these articles, the Executive Committee shall manage the affairs of the Association, direct and dispose of its funds, and from time to time make and modify by-laws for the Association and for its own action. The Executive Committee shall keep a record of its proceedings, and shall make a report to the

Association at the annual meeting. No appropriation of money by the Executive Committee beyond the amount in the hands of the Treasurer at the time shall bind any member of the Association, excepting those members of the Executive Committee who shall vote for it. Vacancies in the Executive Committee may be filled by the President for the remainder of the term. Other vacancies may be filled by the Executive Committee.

All the officers of the Association and members of the several Standing Committees shall be, ex-officio, members of the Executive Committee.

Article VI.

Each officer of the Association shall continue to hold office until his successor has been selected and is ready to enter upon the duties of the office.

Article VII.

There shall be an annual meeting of the Association on the second Wednesday of May, at which officers shall be elected for the ensuing year, and other appropriate business may be transacted; except in the year 1898, when the annual meeting shall be held on the second Wednesday of January.

Article VIII.

Any person may be proposed in writing for membership by any member of the Association, and shall be admitted upon approval of the Executive Committee. Members failing to pay their dues may be dropped from the roll by the Executive Committee.

Article IX.

The annual dues of each member shall be $5, payable on the 1st of May, and each member shall receive the annual report and all other publications of the Association. Sustaining members, on payment of twenty-five dollars annually, and Life members, exempt from annual dues on payment of one hundred dollars, may be elected by the Executive Committee at any regular meeting thereof.

Article X.

All provisions of this Constitution, except those relating to the rights of members, and the term of officers, may be suspended or amended by a vote of two-thirds of the Executive Committee, subject to the approval of the Association by a two-thirds vote of the members present either at the annual meeting or at a special meeting duly called. Due notice shall be given before any such annual or special meeting that the approval of the Association will, thereat, be asked for such action of the Executive Committee, and the notice shall clearly state the effect of such suspension or amendment in the text of the Constitution. Any member of the Association may propose amendments to the Constitution, which may be approved under the same conditions.

BY-LAWS.

FOR THE GOVERNMENT OF THE ASSOCIATION AND ITS COMMITTEES.

§ 1. The Annual meeting of the Association shall be held at such hour and place as the Executive Committee shall designate. The election of officers shall be by ballot, but any member not present may declare his vote by letter to the Secretary and it shall be counted.

§ 2. The meetings of each committee, unless otherwise especially provided for, shall be at half-past eight P. M., at which time the chairman shall direct the call of the names of its members and the Secretary shall record the names of those present and others as they appear.

§ 3. The order of business, before each committee shall be:
1. The reading and correction of the records of the last meeting.

And, thereafter, unless otherwise ordered, as follows:
2. Any statement due from the Treasurer.
3. Unfinished business from the last meeting.
4. Report from the Secretary's office.
5. Reports of standing committees.
6. Reports of special committees.
7. Proposals of new members and their election.
8. Miscellaneous business.

§ 4. Regular meetings of the Executive Committee shall be held on the second Wednesday of every month except July and August, but if that day be a holiday, then on the third Wednesday. Ten members of the Executive Committee shall constitute a quorum.

§ 5. Neither in the meetings of the Association nor of any committee shall any member speak more than once on any motion nor more than ten minutes at one time, without unanimous consent, nor shall any person, or his actions, be characterized on party grounds.

§ 6. Special meetings of any committee may be called by its chairman or by any three members, and due notice thereof by the Secretary.

§ 7. All notices to a member shall be sent to his address filed with the Secretary.

§ 8. On the demand of one-fifth of the members present, at any meeting of the Association or of a committee, the ayes and nays shall be called and recorded on any motion.

§ 9. All committees shall be appointed by the chair unless their selection shall be otherwise provided for.

§ 10. At each regular meeting of the Executive Committee, it shall be the duty of the Treasurer to make a statement of the amount of money in the treasury and of the place of its deposit, and, at the annual meeting, he shall state the source of all moneys received and the use made of the same during the past year.

§ 11. The Secretary shall keep a record of the proceedings of the Association and of the Executive Committee, and perform the other duties assigned him.

§ 12. Without the consent of three-fourths of the members present, no vote which will declare or fill a vacancy or elect a member of the Association shall be deemed carried, at the same meeting in which it was first moved.

§ 13. It shall require a vote of two-thirds of the members of the Executive Committee present to pass any vote under which more than $100 will be appropriated or the Association be pledged for more than that amount, and the Executive Committee alone shall have authority to create any charge upon the funds of the Association. But neither said committee nor any officer or officers of the Association shall be authorized to create a personal liability against any members but themselves.

§ 14. There shall be the following Standing Committees, of seven members each, which shall be selected annually by the Executive Committee:

(1) A Finance Committee, whose duty it shall be to devise and carry into effect, subject to the direction of the Executive Committee, suitable measures for raising funds, and to supervise and report upon the income and expenditures of the Association. The Chairman of the Executive Committee shall, in advance of each annual meeting of the Association, appoint an Auditing Committee from among the members of the Association, whose duty it shall be to examine all vouchers

and audit the accounts of the Treasurer, and to report thereon at the annual meeting.

(2) A Publication Committee, whose duty it shall be to prepare and recommend matters suitable for publication by the Association, and to take charge of the printing and distribution of whatever may be ordered printed.

(3) A Committee on Correspondence, whose duty it shall be to promote the objects of the Association through correspondence and co-operation with other organizations.

(4) A Committee on Administration, whose duty it shall be to investigate and report upon the administration of the civil service law and rules and to consider and recommend suitable methods of examination for admission to and promotion in the public service, and suitable procedure tending to make the system more efficient.

There shall also be a Standing Committee on Law of nine members, which shall be selected annually by the Executive Committee. Its duty shall be to consider all legislation affecting the civil service, to promote such as may be approved, and to oppose such as may be disapproved by the Executive Committee, and to prepare and recommend such amendments to the law as in their opinion will advance the purposes of the Association. The Law Committee shall have power to represent the Association in any legal proceedings which may be necessary in order to maintain or enforce the laws affecting the State or Municipal civil service.

There shall also be a Standing Committee on Membership of fifteen members, which shall be selected annually by the Executive Committee. Its duties shall be to devise and carry into effect measures for increasing the membership of the Association.

Each Standing Committee shall be competent to fix the number of its own quorum; but such quorum shall in no case be less than three.

§ 15. These By-Laws may be amended, or new By-Laws added, by a four-fifths vote at any meeting of the Executive Committee; or by a two-thirds vote, provided a statement of the proposed change had been entered on the minutes at the last meeting.

§ 16. Amendments proposed under the last clause of the tenth section of the constitution shall be first submitted to the Executive Committee.

OFFICERS—1907-1908.

PRESIDENT:

SILAS W. BURT

VICE-PRESIDENTS:

D. WILLIS JAMES
WILLIAM G. LOW
LEVI P. MORTON
ALEXANDER E. ORR
THEODORE ROOSEVELT

ELIHU ROOT
EDWARD M. SHEPARD
ANSON PHELPS STOKES
OSCAR S. STRAUS
EVERETT P. WHEELER

SECRETARY:

ELLIOT H. GOODWIN

ASSISTANT SECRETARY:

ALBERT DE ROODE

TREASURER:

A. S. FRISSELL

EXECUTIVE COMMITTEE:

SAMUEL H. ORDWAY, *Chairman.*
R. ROSS APPLETON
HENRY De FOREST BALDWIN
THEODORE M. BANTA
GEORGE R. BISHOP
CHARLES C. BURLINGHAM
EDWARD CARY
LEANDER T. CHAMBERLAIN
CHARLES COLLINS
HORACE E. DEMING
SAMUEL B. DONNELLY
HOMER FOLKS

J. WARREN GREENE
GEORGE J. GREENFIELD
ABRAHAM JACOBI
JACOB W. MACK
GEORGE McANENY
JOHN G. MILBURN
GEORGE FOSTER PEABODY
WILLIAM JAY SCHIEFFELIN
HENRY SANGER SNOW
NELSON S. SPENCER
WILLIAM H. THOMSON
CHARLES W. WATSON

STANDING COMMITTEES.

FINANCE:

L. T. CHAMBERLAIN, *Chairman.* ISAAC N. SELIGMAN
HENRY G. CHAPMAN JACOB W. MACK
A. S. FRISSELL, *ex-officio* HORACE WHITE

PUBLICATION:

EDWARD CARY, *Chairman.* ROB'T UNDERWOOD JOHNSON
GROSVENOR H. BACKUS WILSON M. POWELL, Jr.
GEORGE R. BISHOP CARL L. SCHURZ
JOHN A. SLEICHER

CORRESPONDENCE:

EVERETT V. ABBOT, *Chairman.* LEARNED HAND
ALBERT S. BARD WILLIAM POTTS
MACGRANE COXE CORNELIUS B. SMITH
WALTER U. TAYLOR

ADMINISTRATION:

SILAS W. BURT, *Chairman.* PHILIP J. McCOOK
CHARLES COLLINS CLARENCE BISHOP SMITH
GEORGE McANENY NATHAN A. SMYTH
NELSON S. SPENCER

LAW:

SAMUEL H. ORDWAY, *Chairman.* WINFRED T. DENISON
HENRY De FOREST BALDWIN A. LEO EVERETT
CHARLES C. BURLINGHAM J. WARREN GREENE
JOSEPH P. COTTON, Jr. HENRY W. HARDON
CHARLES P. HOWLAND

MEMBERSHIP:

FRANCIS H KINNICUTT, *Chairman,* CHARLES W. McCANDLESS
FRANCIS W. BIRD SAMUEL N. HINCKLEY
ALBERT DE ROODE WILLIAM C. LANGDON
CHARLES J. FAY JAY E. LAWSHE
ROY C. GASSER RUSSELL LOINES
GEORGE J. GREENFIELD ALFRED B. MEACHAM
ELLWOOD HENDRICK GEORGE W. SCHURMAN
EDWARD L. TINKER

MEMBERSHIP ROLL.
(May 1, 1907.)

SUSTAINING MEMBERS.

AMEND, BERNARD G., ... 205 Third Avenue, New York City
APPLETON, R. ROSS, . . 146 Joralemon Street, Brooklyn, N. Y.

BEHR, HERMAN, . , . . 75 Beekman Street, New York City
BREWSTER, WILLIAM, . Broadway and 47th Street, " " "
BURLINGHAM, CHARLES C., . . 27 William Street, " " "

CARY, EDWARD, ... The "Times," New York City
CHAPLIN, DUNCAN D., ... 64 Worth Street, " " "
CLYDE, WILLIAM P., ... 19 State Street, " " "
COLLINS, CHARLES, ... 33 E. 17th Street, " " "
CONNOR, W. E., ... 31 Nassau Street, " " "
CRANE, RICHARD T., . . . 2541 Michigan Avenue, Chicago, Ill.
CURTIS, W. J., ... 49 Wall Street, New York City
CUTTING, R. FULTON, ... 32 Nassau Street, " " "

DAY, WILLIAM S., . . . 337 W. 87th Street, New York City
DE COPPET, E. J., ... 42 Broadway, " " "
DEERING, JAMES, . Fullerton and Clybourne Avenues, Chicago, Ill.
DELANO, WARREN Jr., . . . 1 Broadway, New York City
DEMUTH, WILLIAM, . . . 524 Fifth Avenue, " " "
DENISON, WINFRED T., . Room 50, Post Office Building, " " "
DIMOCK, HENRY F., ... Pier 11, N. R., " " "

FRISSELL, A. S., ... 530 Fifth Avenue, New York City

GILDER, RICHARD WATSON, . . 33 E. 17th Street, New York City
GOODWIN, J. J., ... 11 W. 54th Street, " " "
GREENE, J. WARREN, . . . 3 Broad Street, " " "
GREENFIELD, GEORGE J., . . . 32 Broadway, " " "

HARRIOT, S. CARMAN, . . . 212 Broadway, New York City
HEMENWAY, AUGUSTUS, . . . 10 Tremont Street, Boston, Mass.
HENTZ, HENRY, ... 769 St. Mark's Avenue, Brooklyn
HOPKINS, GEORGE B., ... 52 Broadway, New York City
HUBER, JACQUES, ... 472 Broome Street, " " "

JACOBI, A., ... 19 E. 47th Street, New York City
JAMES, DARWIN R., . . . 266 Gates Avenue, Brooklyn, N. Y.
JOHNSON, ROBERT UNDERWOOD, . 33 E. 17th Street, New York City

KENNEDY, JOHN S., . . . 31 Nassau Street, New York City

LOEB, JAMES,	52 William Street, New York City
LOEB, MORRIS,	273 Madison Avenue, " " "
LOINES, STEPHEN,	152 Columbia Heights, Brooklyn
LORD, FRANKLIN B.,	49 Wall Street, New York City
LOW, SETH,	30 E. 64th Street, " " "
LOW, WILLIAM G.,	58 Remsen Street, Brooklyn
MACK, JACOB W.,	92 Liberty Street, New York City
MACY, V. EVERIT,	68 Broad Street, " " "
MAITLAND, ALEXANDER,	45 Broadway, " " "
MINTURN, ROBERT SHAW,	116 E. 22d Street, " " "
MORTON, LEVI P.,	38 Nassau Street, " " "
MOSLE, GEORGE R.,	16-18 Exchange Place, " " "
McANENY, GEORGE,	19 E. 47th Street, New York City
McKIM, JOHN A.,	6 E. 74th Street, " " "
ORDWAY, SAMUEL H.,	27 William Street, New York City
OSBORN, WILLIAM CHURCH,	71 Broadway, " " "
PAGE, EDWARD D.,	60 Worth Street, New York City
PAGE, WILLIAM H., Jr.,	32 Liberty Street, " " "
PAGENSTECHER, A.,	P. O. Box 683, " " "
PHIPP, HENRY,	6 E. 87th Street, " " "
PINCHOT, JAMES W.,	1615 Rhode Island Avenue, Washington, D. C.
RANDOLPH, STUART F.,	31 Nassau Street, New York City
RUSSELL, CHARLES H.,	15 Broad Street, " " "
SANDS, B. AYMAR,	31 Nassau Street, New York City
SCHEFER, CARL,	476 Broome Street, " " "
SCHIEFFELIN, WILLIAM JAY,	5 E. 66th Street, " " "
SCHIFF, JACOB H.,	P. O. Box 1198, " " "
SCHWAB, GUSTAV H.,	5 Broadway, " " "
SELIGMAN, ISAAC N.,	15 Broad Street, " " "
SHEPARD, EDWARD M.,	128 Broadway, " " "
SMITH, CORNELIUS B.,	101 E. 69th Street, " " "
SPENCER, NELSON S.,	27 William Street, " " "
SPEYER, JAMES,	257 Madison Avenue, " " "
STETSON, FRANCIS LYNDE,	15 Broad Street, " " "
STOKES, ANSON PHELPS,	100 William Street, " " "
STRAUS, OSCAR S.,	Dep't of Commerce and Labor, Washington, D. C.
THOMSON, WILLIAM H.,	23 E. 47th Street, New York City
TRASK, SPENCER,	54 William Street, " " "
VOSS, F. G.,	40 Wall Street, New York City
WARE, WILLIAM R.,	Milton, Mass.
WHITE, ALFRED T.,	130 Water Street, New York City
WHITE, HORACE,	18 W. 69th Street, " " "
WUNDERLICH, F. W.,	165 Remsen Street, Brooklyn

Abbot, Everett V.,	45 Cedar Street, New York City
Abbott, Lawrence F.,	"The Outlook," " " "
Abbott, Lyman,	287 Fourth Avenue, " " "
Achelis, John,	68 Leonard Street, " " "
Adams, Edward D.,	71 Broadway, " " "
Adams, Elbridge L.,	299 Broadway, " " "
Adams, Joseph,	Union Stock Yards, Chicago, Ill.
Adams, Thatcher M.,	36 Wall Street, New York City
Adler, Felix,	152 W. 77th Street, " " "
Affeld, Francis O.,	873 President Street, Brooklyn
Agar, John G.,	31 Nassau Street, New York City
Agnew, Andrew Gifford,	22 William Street, " " "
Aitken, John W.	873 Broadway, " " "
Allen, Calvin H.,	1 W. 72nd Street, " " "
Allen, Elmer A.,	42 Broadway, " " "
Allen, Franklin,	371 Fulton Street, Brooklyn
Allert, Rudolf,	108th Street and Columbus Avenue, New York City
Alling, Joseph T.,	400 Oxford Street, Rochester, N. Y.
Allison, Charles R.,	60 Wall Street, New York City
Alsop, Reese F.,	96 Remsen Street, Brooklyn
Anderson, Frank E.,	486 Broadway, New York City
Andrews, J. Sherlock,	111 St. Paul Street, Rochester, N. Y.
Appleton, Herbert	16 Exchange Place, New York City
Arend, F. J.,	32 W. 73rd Street, " " "
Armstrong, James,	71 Nassau Street, " " "
Arnold, Lemuel H.,	3 Broad Street, " " "
Arnstein, Eugene,	10 Wall Street, " " "
Atterbury, Grosvenor,	20 W. 43rd Street, " " "
Auchincloss, John,	27 Pine Street, " " "
Avery, Samuel P.,	4 E. 38th Street, " " "
Babbott, Frank L.,	149 Lincoln Place, Brooklyn
Backus, Grosvenor H,	32 Liberty Street, New York City
Bacon, Gorham,	47 W. 54th Street, " " "
Bagley, Valentine N.,	641 Washington Street, " " "
Bailey, H. P.,	312 Broadway, " " "
Baldwin, Elbert F.,	"The Outlook," " " "
Baldwin, Henry de Forest,	49 Wall Street, " " "
Bangs, Francis S.,	65 Wall Street, " " "
Bangs, L. Bolton,	39 E. 72nd Street, " " "
Bannard, Otto T.,	24 Broad Street, " " "
Banta, Theodore M.,	348 Broadway, " " "
Bard, Albert Sprague,	25 Broad Street, " " "
Barker, Benjamin,	56 Pine Street, " " "
Barkley, Charles H.,	82 Wall Street, " " "
Barney, A. H., (Life)	101 E. 38th Street, " " "
Barney, Danford N.,	Farmington, Conn.
Barrett, Frank R.,	Box 105, Portland, Me.

Barrett, John D.	49 Wall Street, New York City
Bartlett, P. G.,	25 Broad Street, " " "
Baruch, Bernard M.,	111 Broadway, " " "
Batterman, Henry,	21 Clinton Street, Brooklyn
Bausch, Edward,	Rochester, N. Y.
Bausch, Henry,	746 St. Paul Street, " "
Bausch, J. J.,	13 Hyde Park, " "
Bausch, William,	745 St. Paul Street, " "
Baylies, Edmund L.,	54 Wall Street, New York City
Bayne, Hugh,	40 Wall Street, " " "
Beckers, Alexander,	618 Hudson Street, Hoboken, N. J.
Beekman, Gerard,	7 E: 42d Street, New York City
Beer, George Lewis,	329 W. 71st Street, " " "
Beers, E. Le Grand,	131 Remsen Street, Brooklyn
Beers, Lucius H.,	49 Wall Street, New York City
Bell, Gordon Knox,	22 William Street, " " "
Bellamy, Frederick P.,	204 Montague Street, Brooklyn
Benedict, Elliot S.,	60 Wall Street, New York City
Bernard. William.	206 Broadway, " " "
Bijur, Nathan,	34 Nassau Street, " " "
Bird, Francis W.,	40 W. 59th Street, " " "
Bisbee, Ralph,	63 Wall Street, " " "
Bishop, George R.,	142 E. 18th Street, " " "
Bispham, William,	66 Broadway, " " "
Blagden, Arthur C,	Dunster Hall, Cambridge, Mass.
Boas, Franz,	123 W. 82d Street, New York City
Bode, Frederick H.,	care Gage Bros., Chicago, Ill.
Bogert, Eugene T.,	66 Broadway, New York City
Borden, M. C. D.,	Box 1794, " " "
Bowen, C. Winthrop,	5 E. 63rd Street, " " "
Bowker, R. R.,	298 Broadway, " " "
Brachhausen, G. A.,	Rahway, N. J.
Brackett, George C.,	50 Remsen Street, Brooklyn
Bradt, Herbert S.,	120 Broadway, New York City
Brady, William H.,	17 Battery Place, " " "
Brand, John,	Elmira, N. Y.
Brewster, Charles O.,	32 Liberty Street, New York City
Briesen, Arthur von, (Life)	49 Wall Street, " " "
Briscoe, S. William,	20 Sanford Avenue, Flushing, N Y.
Brite, James,	111 Fifth Avenue, New York City
Brown, Addison,	45 W. 89th Street, " " "
Brown, Augustus H.,	262 W. 136th Street, " " "
Brown, Edwin H.,	141 Broadway. " " "
Brown, Everit,	27 William Street, " " "
Brown, Roscoe C. E.,	" Tribune " Office, " " "
Brown, Thatcher M.,	36 E. 37th Street, " " "
Brownell, William C.,	153 Fifth Avenue, " "

Brush, W. Franklin,	16 E. 37th Street, New York City
Buckingham, C. L.,	38 Park Row, " " "
Bulkley, Edwin M.,	54 William Street, " " "
Burr, Winthrop,	7 Wall Street, " " "
Burt, Silas W.,	30 Broad Street, " " "
Butler, Howard R.,	22 E. 91st Street, " " "
Butler, Nicholas Murray,	119 E. 30th Street, " " "
Buttfield. William J.,	96 Wall Street, " " "
Byrne, James,	26 Broad Street, " " "
Cadwalader, John L.,	40 Wall Street, New York City
Cahen, I. J.,	1 Madison Avenue, " " "
Calkins, Leighton,	25 Broad Street, " " "
Canfield, George F.,	49 Wall Street, " " "
Carnegie, Andrew, (Life)	2 E. 91st Street, " " "
Cary, Clarence,	59 Wall Street, " " "
Cassatt, George M.,	327 Broadway, " " "
Cauldwell, S. Millbank,	Pelham Manor, N. Y.
Chadbourne, William M.,	24 Broad Street, New York City
Chaffee, J. Irwin,	Sedgwick Avenue, Fordham Heights, " " "
Chamberlain, L. T.,	222 W. 23 Street, " " "
Chambers, William P.,	55 Liberty Street, " " "
Chandler, Walter, M.,	35 Nassau Street, " " "
Chapman, George,	2717 Broadway, " " "
Chapman, Henry G.,	135 Madison Avenue, " " "
Chapman, J. W.,	35 Nassau Street, " " "
Chase, George,	35 Nassau Street, " " "
Chauncey, Daniel,	129 Joralemon Street, Brooklyn
Cheney, F. W.,	South Manchester, Conn.
Cheney, George L.,	131 E. 57th Street, New York City
Cheney, Louis R.,	Woodland Street, Hartford, Conn.
Childs, Edwards H.,	59 Wall Street, New York City
Choate, Joseph H.,	60 Wall Street, " " "
Choate, Joseph H. Jr.,	60 Wall Street, " " "
Choate, William G.,	40 Wall Street, " " "
Cillis, Hubert,	20 Nassau Street, " " "
Claflin, John,	224 Church Street, " " "
Clarke, Samuel B.,	32 Nassau Street, " " "
Cleveland, Treadwell,	27 William Street, " " "
Codington, Perley M.,	1487 Broadway, " " "
Coffin, E. R.,	62 Cedar Street, " " "
Coffin, I. Sherwood,	30 Cliff Street, " " "
Cohen, William N.,	22 William Street, " " "
Collins, Atwood,	Asylum Avenue, Hartford, Conn.
Collins, Minturn Past,	1 W. 34th Street, New York City
Collins, Stephen W.,	69 Wall Street, " " "
Collyer, Robert,	201 W. 55th Street, " " "
Conant, Charles A.,	38 Nassau, Street, " " "

Conger, Clarence R.,	87 Liberty Street, New York City
Conger, Henry Rutgers,	40 Wall Street, " " "
Cook, Walter,	3 W. 29th Street, " " "
Cooley, Alford Warriner,	Department of Justice, Washington, D. C.
Cope, Francis R.,	Aubury, Germantown, Pa.
Corbett, George J.,	54 Wall Street, New York City
Corrigan, Joseph E.,	District Attorney's Office, " " "
Cotton, Joseph P., Jr.,	52 William Street, " " "
Coudert, Frederick R., Jr.,	71 Broadway, " " "
Cowdin, Wintrop, The Algonquin Company,	Passaic, N. J.
Cowperthwait, J. Howard,	195 Park Row, New York City
Coxe, Macgrane,	63 Wall Street, " " "
Coykendall, S. D.,	Rondout, N. Y.
Crane, Frederick,	Bloomfield, N. J.
Crane, Leroy B.,	277 Broadway, New York City
Cranford, Walter V.,	215 Montague Street, Brooklyn
Cravath, Paul D.,	52 William Street, New York City
Crawford, Gilbert H.,	32 Liberty Street, " " "
Creevey, John J.,	41 Wall Street, " " "
Croly, Herbert D.,	19 E. 24th Street, " " "
Cromwell, Frederic,	32 Nassau Street, " " "
Cromwell, Lincoln,	1 Greene Street, " " "
Croswell, J. G.,	17 W. 44th Street, " " "
Cummings, G. F.,	20 Broad Street, " " "
Curtis, William E.,	30 Broad Street, " " "
Cushing, H. A,	43 Cedar Street, " ' "
Cushing, William E.,	Society for Savings Bldg., Cleveland, O.
Cutler, Arthur H.,	20 E. 50th Street, New York City
Cutting, R. Bayard,	32 Nassau Street, " " "
Cutting, W. Bayard,	24 E. 72nd Street, " " "
Cuyler, C. C.,	44 Pine Street, L " " "
Daboll, Henry E.,	Plainfield, N. J.
Dana, Charles A.,	40 Wall Street, New York City
Dana, Charles L.,	53 W. 53rd Street, " " "
Davidge, William H.,	49 Wall Street, " " "
Davies, Julien T.,	32 Nassau Street, " " "
Davies, William Gilbert,	32 Nassau Street, " " "
Davis, G. Pierrepont,	Woodland Street, Hartford, Conn,
Davis, Horace A.,	135 Broadway, New York City
Davis John, H.,	10 Wall Street, " " "
Davison, Charles Stewart,	60 Wall Street, " " "
Day, Clarence S.,	45 Wall Street, " " "
DeForest, R. W.,	30 Broad Street, " " "
Deming, Horace E.,	13 William Street, " " "
Demorest, William C.,	60 Liberty Street, " " "
de Roode, Albert,	79 Wall Street, " " "
Despard, W. D.,	6 Hanover Street, " " "

Devine, Thomas J.,	19 Portsmouth Terrace, Rochester, N. Y.
DeWitt, Theodore,	88 Nassau Street, New York City
Dickinson, A. Lowes,	54 William Street, " " "
Dickinson, Robert L.,	168 Clinton Street, Brooklyn
Dickson, James B.,	49 Wall Street, New York City
Dittenhoefer, A. J.,	96 Broadway, " " "
Dix, John A.,	Care L. Thomson & Co., Albany, N. Y.
Dodge, Cleveland H.,	99 John Street, New York City
Dominick, H. B.,	3 W. 29th Street, " " "
Dommerich, L. F.,	57 Greene Street, " " "
Donnelly, Samuel B.,	360 Putnam Avenue, Brooklyn
Dougherty, J. Hampden,	27 William Street, New York City
Dows, Tracy,	Room 102, Produce Exchange, " " "
Dreier, H. E.,	152-154 West 34th Street, " " "
Drescher, William,	715 St. Paul Street, Rochester, N. Y.
Driggs, Laurence,	41 Park Row, New York City
Dunham, Edward K.,	338 E. 26th Street, " " "
Dunning, S. Wright,	80 Madison Avenue, " " "
Dutton, George D.,	40 W. 59th Street, " " "
Eastman, George,	400 East Avenue, Rochester, N. Y.
Eaton, Henry W.,	45 William Street, New York City
Ecaubert, F.,	18 Rose Street, " " "
Elderkin, John,	Lotos Club, 558 Fifth Avenue, " " "
Eliot, Charles W.,	Cambridge, Mass.
Elkins, Stephen B.,	1626 K Street, Washington, D. C.
Ely, Arthur H.,	56 Wall Street, New York City
Ely, Moses,	2 Wall Street, " " "
Ely, Robert E.,	23 West 44th Street, " " "
Emmons, Arthur B.,	60 Park Avenue, " " "
Emmons, Samuel F.,	U. S. Geological Survey, Washington, D. C.
Erbe, Gustav,	344 St. Paul Street, Rochester, N. Y.
Erbslöh, R.,	364 Broadway, New York City
Everest, Charles M.,	506 West Avenue, Rochester, N. Y.
Everett, A. Leo,	49 Wall Street, New York City
Ewart, Richard H.,	115 Franklin Street, " " "
Ewing, Thomas, Jr.,	67 Wall Street, " " "
Faburi, Alessandro,	11 E. 62d Street, New York City
Fabbri, Ernesto G.,	11 E. 62d Street, " " "
Fahnestock, Gates D.,	214 Hicks Street, Brooklyn, N. Y.
Fahnestock, H. C.,	2 Wall Street, New York City
Fairchild, Benjamin T.,	P. O. Box 1120, " " "
Fairchild, Charles S.,	10 West 8th Street, " " "
Faure, John P.,	346 Broadway, " " "
Fay, Charles J.,	49 Wall Street, " " "
Field, Hamilton E.,	106 Columbia Heights, Brooklyn
Finch, Edward R.,	53 Washington Square, New York City

Fisher, George H., . . E. 28th Street and Emmons Avenue, Brooklyn
Folks, Homer, ... 105 E. 22nd Street, New York City
Ford, Worthington C., . Care Library of Congress, Washington, D. C.
Forrest, C. R., ... Asylum Avenue, Hartford, Conn.
Fox, Alan, ... 52 William Street, New York City
Fox, Austen G., (Life), . . . 45 W. 33d Street, " " "
Frankenheimer, John, ... 25 Broad Street, " " "
Frankfurter, Felix, . U. S. District Attorney's Office, " " "
Frissell, H. B. . . . . Hampton, Va.
Frothingham, Howard P., . . . 2 Wall Street, New York City
Fuller, Frank, ... , . 61 Fifth Avenue, " " "
Fuller, Paul, ... 71 Broadway. " " "
Fullerton, Alexander, (Life), . . 7 W. 8th Street, " " "
Funk, I. K., ... 195 Washington Park, Brooklyn

Gaillard, William D., ... 141 Broadway, New York City
Garver, John A., ... 44 Wall Street, " " "
Gasser, Roy C., ... 35 Wall Street, " " "
Germond, H. S., ... 44 Broad Street, " " "
Getzelsohn, J. A., ... 810 E. 134th Street, " " "
Gibbons, George W , ... 198 Broadway, " " "
Gibson, William J., ... 26 Liberty Street, " " "
Gitterman, John M., . . . 1317 F Street, N. W., Washington, D C.
Goadby, Clarence, . . . 21 W. 35th Street, New York City
Goddard, George A., ... 10 Tremont Street, Boston, Mass.
Godkin, Laurence, ... 30 Pine Street, New York City
Goldman, Julius, ... 31 Nassau Street, " " "
Goldmark, James, . . . 67 Cortlandt Street, " " "
Goodale, John McGregor, . . . 42 Broadway, " " "
Goodnow, Frank J., . . . 49 Riverside Drive, " " "
Goodwin, Elliot H., ... 79 Wall Street, " " "
Gottheil, Paul, ... Produce Exchange, " " "
Gottsberger, Francis, ... 156 Broadway, " " "
Gould, Elgin R. L., ... 281 Fourth Avenue, " " "
Grant, De Forest, ... 22 E. 49th Street, " " "
Grant, Percy S., ... 7 W. 10th Street, " " "
Gray, Henry G., ... 161 Madison Avenue, " " "
Green, Noah, ... 478 Central Park, West, " " "
Greenbaum, Samuel, County Court House, B'way & Chambers St., " "
Greene, Francis V., ... 816 Fidelity Building, Buffalo, N. Y.
Greenough, John, ... 38 E. 63rd Street, New York City
Greer, David H., ... 7 Gramercy Park, " " "
Gulliver, W. C., ... 120 Broadway, " " "
Guthrie, William D., . . . 52 William Street, " " "
Gwynne, Arthur C., ... Rye, N. Y.

Hagemeyer, F. E., . . . F 15, Produce Exchange, New York City
Hague, James D., ... 18 Wall Street, " " "

Haines, C. G.,	Ursinus College, Collegeville, Pa.
Haines, Henry F.,	2 Wall Street, New York City
Hall, Valentine G.,	Tivoli, Duchess Co., N. Y.
Halsey, Robert H.,	118 W. 58th Street, New York City
Halsted, John F.,	93 Remsen Street, Brooklyn, N. Y.
Hamlin, Frank H.,	Canandaigua, N. Y.
Hand, Learned,	2 Wall Street, New York City
Harbeck, Charles T.,	32 Broadway, " " "
Harding, Edward,	43 Exchange Place, " " "
Hardon, Henry Winthrop,	60 Wall Street, " " "
Harrison, Robert L.,	59 Wall Street, " " "
Hart, John Wilson,	District Attorney's Office, " " "
Haskin, William H.,	42 East 41st Street, " " "
Hasslacher, Jacob,	100 William Street, " " "
Hastings, Thomas S.,	27 W. 46th Street, " " "
Hayes, J. Noble,	68 William, " " "
Heath, Frank E.,	95 Liberty Street, " " "
Healy, A. Augustus,	198 Columbia Heights, Brooklyn
Heinze, Arthur P.,	31 Nassau Street, New York City
Henderson, Harold G.,	80 Irving Place,, " " "
Hendrick, Ellwood,	139 E. 40th Street, " " "
Hentz, Leonard S.,	769 St. Mark's Avenue, Brooklyn
Herbert, William,	11 Pine Street, New York City
Hess, Henry E.,	32 Nassau Street, " " "
Higginson, James J.,	16 E. 41st Street, " " "
Hill, William B.,	68 William Street, " " "
Hinkley, Samuel Neilson,	166 E. 61st Street, " " "
Hinrichs, Frederick W.,	76 William Street, " " "
Hitchcock, Welcome G., (Life)	453 Broome Street, " " "
Hobart, Henry L.,	120 Front Street, " " "
Hodges, Harrison B.,	16 Gramercy Park, " " "
Hoe, Richard M.,	Room 102, Produce Exchange, " " "
Hoffman, Frank S.,	Schenectady, N. Y.
Hoe, Robert,	504 Grand Street, New York City
Holt, Henry,	29 W. 23d Street, " " "
Holt, Roland,	29 W. 23d Street, " " "
Hopkins, J. A. H.,	51 West 11th Street, " " "
Hoppin, Frederick S., Jr.,	131 E. 19th Street, " " "
Hoppin, William W.,	54 William Street, " " "
Hornblower, William B.,	24 Broad Street, " " "
Howe, Daniel R.,	Asylum Avenue, Hartford, Conn.
Howe, Horace J.,	25 Gold Street, Yonkers, N. Y.
Howe, Walter B.,	Criminal Court Building, New York City
Howe, Wirt,	135 Broadway, " " "
Howland, Charles P.,	35 Wall Street, " " "
Hoyt, Francis D.,	69 Wall Street, " " "
Hoyt, Gerald L.,	28 E. 36th Street, " " "

Hubbard, Thomas H.,	16 W. 58th Street, New York City
Hughes, Charles E.,	96 Broadway, " " "
Hull, Charles A.,	95 William Street, " " "
Huntington, Francis C.,	54 William Street, " " "
Huntington, Samuel,	146 Broadway, " " "
Huntington, William R.,	804 Broadway, " " "
Huyler, John S.,	64 Irving Place, " " "
Ide, Robert L.,	7 Nassau Street, New York City
Ireland, F. G.,	299 Broadway, " " "
Ireland, John B,	15 E. 47th Street, " " "
Iselin, John H.,	27 William Street, " " "
Isham, Samuel.	6th Avenue and 40th Street, " " "
Jackson, Frederick W.,	Westchester, N. Y.
Jackson, John G.,	35 Wall Street, New York City
Jacob, Lawrence,	52 Broadway, " " "
James, D. Willis,	99 John Street, " " "
Jameson. E. C.,	76 William Street, " " "
Jaretzki, Alfred.	49 Wall Street, " " "
Jay, Pierre,	Hyde Park, Mass.
Jay, William,	48 Wall Street, New York City
Jellenix, Felix,	17 William Street, " " "
Jennings, Frederick B.,	15 Broad Street, " " "
Jesup, Morris K.,	195 Madison Avenue, " " "
Johnson, Willis Fletcher,	154 Nassau Street, " " "
Joline, Adrian, H.,	54 Wall Street, " " "
Jones. Oliver Livingston, Jr.,	116 W. 72d Street, " " "
Josephthal, Sidney L.,	43 Cedar Street, " " "
Kahn, Otto H., (Life),	54 William Street, New York City
Kellogg, Francis B.,	Temple Auditorium, Los Angeles, Cal.
Kelsey, Clarence H.,	146 Broadway, New York City
Kennaday, Paul,	88 Grove Street, " " "
Kennedy, Edward G.,	220 Fifth Avenue, " " "
Kennedy, Elijah R.,	29 & 31 Liberty Street, " " "
Kenneson, Thaddeus D.,	13 William Street, " " "
Kenyon, Alan D.,	49 Wall Street, " " "
Kenyon, William Houston.	49 Wall Street, " " "
Keogh, Alexander,	Criminal Court Building, " " "
Keppler, Rudolph,	25 Broad Street, " " "
Kernan, John D.,	37 Liberty Street, " " "
Kerr, Albert B.,	49 Wall Street, " " "
Kidder, Camillus G.,	27 William Street, " " "
Kidder, Edward H.,	170 Broadway. " " "
Kilmer, Alfred G.,	80 Broadway, " " "
Kimball, A. R.,	Orange, N. J.
Kimball, Daniel T..	198 Broadway, New York City

King, Delcevare, ... 126 Summer Street, Boston, Mass.
King, William F., ... 410 Broadway, New York City
Kinnicutt, Francis H:. . . . . 2 Rector Street, " " "
Kinnicutt, Francis P., ... 42 W. 37th Street, " " "
Kinnicutt, G Herman, . . . 39 E. 35th Street, " " "
Kirchhoff, Charles, ... 14 & 16 Park Place, " " "
Kissell, Gustav E., (Life), . . . 1 Nassau Street, " " "
Klein, Isaac H., ... 45 Cedar Street, " " "
Klupfel, Charles, Care North German Lloyd, 5 Broadway, " " "
Knapp, Shepherd, ... 266 Lexington Avenue, " " "
Knauth, Antonio, ... 233 West 70th Street, " " "
Knauth, Theodor W., . . . Wadsworth House, Cambridge, Mass.
Knox, Herbert H., ... 30 Broad Street, New York City
Koehler, Jerome H., . . , . . 47 Cedar Street, " " "
Kohler, Max J., ... 42 Broadway, " " "
Kuehnle, Frederick C., . . . 629 W. 51st Street, " " "
Kuhne, Percival, ... 13 William Street, " " "
Kunhardt, William B., ... 100 Broadway, " " "
Kunstlich, Samuel H., ... 302 Broadway, " " "

Laimbeer, Francis E., ... 99 Nassau Street, New York City
Lambert, William B., ... Highland Street, Cambridge Mass.
Langdon, William Chauncy, . District Attorney's Office, New York City
Lansing, J. Townsend, ... 82 State Street, Albany, N. Y.
Large, Walter, . , . . 15 William Street, New York City
Larocque, Joseph, ... 40 Wall Street, " " "
Larremore, Wilbur, ... 32 Nassau Street, " " "
Lawrence, Walter B., . . . 35 Wall Street, " " "
Lawshe, Jay E., ... 60 Wall Street, " " "
Lea, Henry Charles, . . . 2000 Walnut Street, Philadelphia, Pa.
Leavitt, John Brooks, . . . 115 Broadway, New York City
Leaycraft, J. Edgar, . . - . . 19 W. 42nd Street, " " "
Lederle, Ernest J., ... 471 W. 143d Street, " " "
Ledoux, Albert R., ... 9 Cliff Street, " " "
Lee, W. H. L., , ... 25 Pine Street, " " "
Lefferts, Marsnall C., . . . 30 Washington Place, " " "
Leffingwell, R. C , ... 52 William Street, " " "
Le Gendre, William, . . . 59 Wall Street, " " "
Lehmaier, Louis A., ... 78 Beekman Street, " " "
Lethbridge, R. P., ... 49 Wall Street, " " "
Levi, Albert A., ... 108 Exchange Court, " " "
Lewis, Richard V., . . - . . 130 W. 42d Street, " " "
Lindenthal, Gustav, ... 45 Cedar Street, " " "
Lindsay, Alexander M., . . . 373 East Avenue, Rochester, N. Y.
Littauer, Lucius N., ... Gloversville, N. Y.
Livingston, Goodhue, . . . 38 E. 65th Street, New York City
Livingston, Julius I., ... 52 Broadway, " " "
Lockwood, Benoni. . . . . 56 Irving Place, " " "

Loines, Russell H.,	27 W. 11th Street, New York City
Lomb, Adolph,	48 Cumberland Street, Rochester, N. Y.
Lomb, Henry,	48 Cumberland Street, " "
Lomb, Henry C.,	48 Cumberland Street, " "
Lord, Franklin B., Jr..	49 Wall Street, New York City
Lounsbery, Richard P.,	15 Broad Street, " " "
Lovell, Joseph J.,	Avondale Place, Woodhaven, N. Y.
Low, C. Adolph,	41 Liberty Street, New York City
Lowe, William E.,	49 Wall Street, " " "
Lowndes, James,	1515 Massachusetts Avenue, Washington, D. C.
Ludlow, James B.,	45 Cedar Street, New York City
Luther, George Martin,	25 Broad Street, " " "
Lyall, Arthur V.,	25 Pine Street, " " "
Lyman, Frank,	34 Remsen Street, Brooklyn
Lyman, George T.,	Bellport, N. Y.
Lyman, Theodore,	Woodland Street, Hartford, Conn.
Lynch, J. De P.,	Utica, N. Y.
Lynde, Rollin H.,	82 Beaver Street, New York City
Macdonough, A. R.,	105 E. 15th Street, New York City
Macfarlane, Wallace,	32 Liberty Street, " " "
MacMullen, C. W.,	20 Broad Street, " " "
MacVeagh, Charles,	15 Broad Street, " " "
Mallet-Prevost, Severo,	30 Broad Street, " " "
Mallinckrodt, Edward,	Mallinckrodt Chemical Works, St. Louis, Mo.
Mansfield, Howard,	49 Wall Street, New York City
Mapes, Charles V.,	143 Liberty Street, " " "
Markoe, Francis H.,	15 E. 49th Street, " " "
Marling, Alfred E.,	21 Liberty Street, " " "
Marshall, Charles H.,	45 William Street, " " "
Marshall, Fielding L.,	35 Nassau Street, " " "
Marshall, Harford,	District Attorney's Office, " " "
Marshall, Louis,	30 Broad Street, " " "
Marsters, A., A.,	125 Milk Street, Boston, Mass.
Martin, John,	Grymes Hill, Staten Island, N. Y.
Martin, Newell,	25 Broad Street, New York City
Martin, T. Comerford,	114 Liberty Street, " " "
Mason, Alexander T.,	13 William Street, " " "
Mason, Alfred Bishop.	Apartado 130, City of Mexico
Masten, Arthur H.,	49 Wall Street, New York City
Mathews, Robert,	135 Spring Street, Rochester, N. Y.
Mathews W. K.,	36 Wall Street, New York City
Matthews, Brander,	681 West End Avenue, " " "
Matthewson, Arthur,	South Woodstock, Conn.
Maxwell, William H.,	500 Park Avenue, New York City
Meacham, Alfred B,	59 Wall Street, " " "
Meehan, Thomas J.,	38 Park Row " " "
Mellen, Chase,	52 William Street, " " "

Merck, George, ... 15 University Place, New York City
Merrill, Charles E., ... 44 E. 23d Street, " " "
Merrill, Payson, ... 31 Nassau Street, " " "
Millbank, Albert G., , , . . 49 Wall Street, " " "
Milburn, John G., ... 54 Wall Street, " " "
Miller, Clifford L., ... 62 West 89th Street, " " "
Miller, George Douglas, . . . 125 State Street, Albany, N. Y.
Miller, Hoffman, ... 80 Broadway, New York City
Mills, L. H., ... 473 Broome Street, " " "
Mitchell, Edward, ... 44 Wall Street, " " "
Moffat, George B., ... 1 Nassau Street, " " "
Moffat, R. Burnham, ... 63 Wall Street, " " "
Montgomery, Robert H., . . , 43 Exchange Place, " " "
Montgomery, R. M., ... 27 Pine Street, " " "
Moore, W. H. H., ... Box 402, " " "
Morris, Ray, ... 81 Fulton Street, " " "
Morrow, Dwight, , ... Englewood, N. J.
Morse, Horace J., ... 820 St. Mark's Avenue, Brooklyn
Morse, Richard C., ... 35 Sidney Place, "
Mortimer, Richard, ... 11 Wall Street, New York City
Mosenthal, P. J., ... 93 William Street, " " "
Mosle, A. Henry, ... 30 Broad Street, " " "
Mott, William F., ... Toms River, N. J.
Munro, J. G., ... 61 Erie County Bank Building, Buffalo, N. Y.
Munro, John R., ... 132 Remsen Street, Brooklyn, N. Y.
Munro, Willis, ... 1088 Trinity Building, New York City
Munroe, Vernon, ... 45 William Street, " " "
Murphy, Daniel F., . . . Criminal Court Building, " " "
Murray, James B., . . . 23 Belmont Terrace, Yonkers, "
Murray, Joseph K., ... 90 Wall Street, New York City
McAlpin, George L., ... 9 E. 90th Street, " " "
McCagg, Louis Butler, . . . 18 E. 84th Street, " " "
McCandless, Charles W., . . . 60 Wall Street, " " "
McCook, Philip J., ... 15 William Street, " " "
McDowell, H. G., ... 50 Broadway, " " "
McGinness, Remsen, . . . 42 East 41st Street, " " "
McKeen, James, ... 58 Clark Street, Brooklyn
McKeever, J. Lawrence, . . . 164 Lexington Avenue, New York City
McMahon, Fulton, ... 54 William Street, " " "

Nadal, Charles C., ... 142 E. 35th Street, New York City
Nash, Francis Philip, ... Geneva, N. Y.
Naumberg, Elkan, ... 48 W. 58th Street, New York City
Naumberg, George W., . . . 33 Wall Street, " " "
Naumberg, Walter W., . . . 33 Wall Street, " " "
Nelson, Henry Loomis, . . Williams College, Williamstown, Mass.
Nelson, H. W., Jr., ... Marshfield Hills, "
Nevin, A. Parker, ... 149 Broadway, New York City

Newton Albro J., ... 528 Union Street, Brooklyn, N. Y.
Newton, R. Heber, ... East Hampton, N. Y.
Nichols, George M., ... 277 Adelphi Street, Brooklyn, N. Y.
Nichols, W. N., ... 25 Broad Street, New York City
Nicoll, James C., ... 51 W. 10th Street, " " "
Nordlinger, Abraham E., . . . 143 West Broadway, " " "
North, Thomas M., ... 160 Central Park South, " " "
Notman, George, ... 99 John Street, " " "
Nourse, Charles J., Jr., ... 82 Beaver Street, " " "

Oakes, Charles, ... 9 Pine Street, New York City
O'Connor, John A., ... 12 E. 44th Street. " " "
Ogden, Rollo, ... 206 Broadway, " " "
Olin, Stephen H., ... 32 Nassau Street, " " "
Olney, Peter B., Jr., ... 68 William Street, " " "
Oltman, H. H., ... 20 Broad Street, " " "
Olyphant, Robert, ... 17 Battery Place, " " "
Opdyke, William S., ... 20 Nassau Street, " " "
Oppenheim, Edward L., . . . 80 Broad Street, " " "
Oppenheimer, Henry S., . . . 741 Madison Avenue. " " "
Orcutt C. Blake, ... Hudson River Day Line, " " "
Ordway, Edward W., ... 1098 Dean Street, Brooklyn
Orr, Alexander E., ... 102 Remsen Street, "
Osborn, Perry, ... 52 Brattle Street, Cambridge, Mass.
Osborne, Thomas M., ... Auburn, N. Y.

Packard, Edwin, ... 241 Henry Street, Brooklyn
Page, Walter H., ... 34 Union Square, New York City
Parker, Frederick S., ... 32 Garden Place, Brooklyn
Parks, J. Waring, ... 49 Wall Street, New York City
Parsons, Herbert, ... 52 William Street, " " "
Parsons, John E., ... 52 William Street, " " "
Paulding, James Kirk, ... 130 E. 24th Street, " " "
Pauli, H. G., ... 15 S. William Street, " " "
Peabody, George Foster, . . . 2 Rector Street. " " "
Peck, George G., ... 18 East 65th Street, " " "
Pedersen, James, ... 20 E. 46th Street, " " "
Pell, Frederick A., ... Lakewood, N. J.
Pendleton, Francis K., . . . 25 Broad Street, New York City
Perrine, William A., . . . 2440 N. Marshall Street, Philadelphia, Pa.
Phillips, Lee, ... 438 W. 116th Street, New York City
Phoenix, Phillips, ... 68 Broad Street, " " "
Pierce, Franklin, ... 27 Pine Street, " " "
Pierce, Henry H., ... 120 Broadway, " " "
Pierrepont, Henry E., . . . 216 Columbia Heights, Brooklyn
Pierrepont, John J., . . . 66 & 68 Broad Street, New York City
Pierrepont, Robert Low, ... Box 449, Bay Shore, N. Y.

Pinchot, Amos R. E.,	Criminal Court Building, New York City
Pinchot, Gifford,	1615 Rhode Island Avenue, Washington, D. C.
Pollak, Francis D.,	49 Wall Street, New York City
Pope, A. A.,	Box 11, Jerusalem Road, Cohasset, Mass.
Pope, George A.,	926 St. Paul Street, Baltimore, Md.
Potter, Frederick,	71 Broadway, New York City
Potter, Henry C.,	113 W. 40th Street, " " "
Potts, William,	7 W. 43rd Street, " " "
Powell, Wilson M., Jr.,	29 Wall Street. " " "
Pratt, Frederic B.,	Pratt Institute, Brooklyn, N. Y.
Prentice, William P.,	52 Broadway, New York City
Prentiss, George H.,	108 Pierrepont Street, Brooklyn, N Y.
Price, Joseph M.,	158 West Broadway, New York City
Pryer, Charles,	New Rochelle, N. Y.
Pryor, James W.,	99 Nassau Street, New York City
Putnam, George Haven,	27 W. 23d Street, " " "
Putnam, George P.,	160 Fifth Avenue, " " "
Putnam, Harrington,	404 Washington Avenue, Brooklyn
Putnam, Irving,	27 W. 23rd Street, New York City
Pyne, Moses Taylor,	263 Madison Avenue, " " "
Rainsford, W. S.,	209 E. 16th Street, New York City
Rand, George C.,	107 Wall Street, " " "
Rand, William H., Jr.	63 Wall Street, " " "
Raven, A. A.,	51 Wall Street, " " "
Raymond, Charles H.,	26 Liberty Street, " " "
Raymond, Rossiter W.	123 Henry Street, Brooklyn
Reichhelm, Edward P.,	90 West 34th Street, Bayonne, N. J.
Reynolds, James B.,	55 W. 44th Street, New York City
Rice, Edwin T., Jr.,	59 Wall Street, " " "
Richards, C. A. L.,	169 Power Street, Providence, R. I.
Rives, George L.,	14 W. 38th Street. New York City
Robb, J. Hampden,	23 Park Avenue, " " "
Robinson, Beverly R.,	42 W. 37th Street, " " "
Robinson, Moncure,	7 E. 42d Street. " " "
Romaine, Louis Tyson,	84 Beaver Street, " " "
Roome, W. Harris,	287 Fourth Avenue, " " "
Roosevelt, Franklin D,	125 E. 36th Street, " " "
Roosevelt, Theodore,	Oyster Bay, N. Y.
Root, Elihu,	State Department, Washington, D. C.
Rose, Arthur P.,	Geneva, N. Y.
Rosenbaum, S. D.,	201 Wooster Street, New York City
Rosendale, Simon W.,	57 State Street, Albany, N. Y.
Rosenfeld, George,	27 Pine Street, New York City
Rounds, Arthur C.,	96 Broadway, " " "
Rowe, William V.,	51 Wall Street, " " "
Rublee, George,	15 Broad Street, " " "
Russell, J. Townsend,	170 Remsen Street, Brooklyn, N. Y.

Sackett, Henry W., ... 154 Nassau Street, New York City
Sage, Dean, ... 49 Wall Street, " " "
Saint Gaudens, Augustus, ... Windsor, Vt.
Salomon, William, ... 25 Broad Street, New York City
Sand, Henry A. L., ... , 43 Cedar Street, " " "
Sanger, William Cary, ... Sangerfield, N. Y.
Savage, Minot J., . . 34th Street and Park Avenue, New York City
Sayer, W. Murray, Jr., ... 398 Washington Avenue, Brooklyn
Schafer, Samuel M., ... 35 Wall Street, New York City
Scharmann, Hermann B., . . . 170 W. 59th Street, " " "
Schieren, Charles A. . . . . . 405 Clinton Avenue, Brooklyn
Schnakenberg, D., ... 6 Hanover Street, New York City
Schrader, George H. F., ... 32 Rose Street, " "
Schurman, George W., . . . 15 W. 57th Street, " " "
Schurz, Carl Lincoln, ... 19 William Street, " " "
Scott, J. F., . . . , . . 349 W. 121st Street, " " "
Scott, William, ... 25 Duane Street, " " "
Scribner, Arthur H., ... 153 Fifth Avenue, " " "
Scribner, Charles, ... 153 Fifth Avenue, " " "
Seaman, Louis L., ... 247 Fifth Avenue, " " "
Searle, Arthur, ... 41 Concord Avenue, Cambridge, Mass.
Seaver, Benjamin F., ... 111 Pierrepont Street, Brooklyn
Sedgwick, Arthur G., . . . 52 William Street, New York City
Sedgwick, Ellery, ... 143 Fifth Avenue, " " "
Sedgwick, Henry D., ... 120 E. 22d Street, " " "
Seligman, E. R. A., ... 324 W. 86th Street, " " "
Seligman, Jefferson, ... 15 Broad Street, " " "
Serven, A. Ralph, ... 1419 "F" Street, N. W., Washington, D. C.
Seward, George F., ... 97 Cedar Street, New York City
Sexton, Lawrence E., ... 34 Pine Street, " " "
Seymour, Origen S., . . . 54 William Street, " " "
Shainwald, Ralph L., . . . 100 William Street, " " "
Shaw, Albert, ... 13 Astor Place, " " "
Sheldon, Edward W., ... 45 Wall Street, " " "
Sheppard, John S., Jr., ... 26 Liberty Street, " " "
Sherman, Arnold W, ... 265 Henry Street, Brooklyn
Shillaber, William Jr., ... 1 Broadway, New York City
Shortt, W. A., ... 32 Broadway, " " "
Siedenberg, Reinhard, ... Cotton Exchange, " " "
Simes, William, ... Box 3084, Boston, Mass.
Sinclair, John, ... 16 E. 66th Street, New York City
Skillin, Augustus H., ... 34 Pine Street, " " "
Slade, Francis Louis, ... 49 Cedar Street, " " "
Sleicher, John A., . . . 225 Fourth Avenue, " " "
Slicer, Thomas R., ... 156 E. 38th Street, " " "
Smillie, James D., ... 440 West End Avenue, " " "
Smith, Adelbert J., ... 15 William Street, " " "
Smith, Bryan H., ... Brooklyn Savings Bank, Brooklyn, N. Y.

Smith, Charles Robinson,	25 Broad Street, New York City
Smith, Charles Stewart,	25 W. 47th Street, " " "
Smith, Clarence B.,	71 E. 87th Street, " " "
Smith, F. Hopkinson,	150 E. 34th Street, " " "
Smith, Frederick J.,	278 Mulberry Street, " " "
Smith, Howard M.,	Brevoort Savings Bank. Brooklyn, N. Y.
Smith, James E.,	38 Park Row, New York City
Smith, William Alexander,	412 Madison Avenue, " " "
Smyth, Nathan A.,	Criminal Court Building, " " "
Snow, Henry Sanger,	81 Willoughby Street, Brooklyn
Southard, George H., Jr.,	164 Montague Street, Brooklyn, N. Y.
Spaulding, Henry K.,	501 W. 120th Street, New York City
St. John, William M.,	Union League Club, " " "
Stanton, George, A.,	45 Cedar Street, " " "
Stapler, H. B. B.,	32 Liberty Street, " " "
Stark, Joshua,	176 Martin Street, Milwaukee, Wis.
Stedman, Edmund C.,	2643 Broadway, New York City
Steers, James R.,	31 Nassau Street, " " "
Steinway, Frederick T.,	53rd Street and Park Avenue, " " "
Stern, Benjamin,	32 W. 23rd Street, " " "
Stewart, William R.,	31 Nassau Street, " " "
Stimson, Daniel M.,	28 W. 37th Street, " " "
Stokes, Anson Phelps, Jr., (Life),	Yale University, New Haven, Conn.
Stokes, Harold M. Phelps, (Life),	229 Madison Avenue, New York City
Stokes, I. N. Phelps, (Life),	229 Madison Avenue, " " "
Stokes, James,	49 Cedar Street, " " "
Stokes, J. G. Phelps, (Life),	229 Madison Avenue, " " "
Strauss, Albert,	15 Broad Street, " " "
Strauss, Frederick,	15 Broad Street, " " "
Strong, George A.,	50 Wall Street, " " "
Strong, Theron G.,	49 Wall Street, " " "
Sturges, S. Perry,	305 Washington Avenue, Brooklyn
Sturgis, F. K.,	36 Broad Street, New York City
Sturgis, Russell,	307 E. 17th Street, " " "
Stuyvesant, Rutherford,	16 Exchange Place, " " "
Sulzberger, Cyrus L.,	516 West End Avenue, " " "
Sulzberger, Ferdinand,	45th Street and First Avenue, " " "
Symonds, Joseph H. A.,	Criminal Court Building, " " "
Taft, Henry W.,	40 Wall Street, New York City
Taggart, Rush,	195 Broadway, " " "
Tatham, Charles,	465 W. 23rd Street, " " "
Tatham, Edwin,	82 Beekman Street, " " "
Taussig, Walter M.,	9-15 Murray Street, " " "
Taylor, E. P., Jr.,	25 Pine Street, " " "
Taylor, Stevenson,	123 W. 85th Street, " " "
Taylor, Thomas Fenton,	552 Center Street, Orange. N. J.
Taylor, Walter F.,	54 Wall Street, New York City

Taylor, William C.,	25 So. Portland Avenue, Brooklyn
Terry, Roderick,	169 Madison Avenue, New York City
Terry, Seth Sprague,	126 E. 34th Street, " " "
Thacher, George O.,	2 E. 86th Street, " " "
Thacher, Thomas,	62 Cedar Street, " " "
Thacher, Thomas, Jr.,	U. S District Attorney's Office, " " "
Thorne, Robert,	30 Broad Street, " " "
Thorne, Samuel, Jr.,	54 Wall Street, " " "
Thornton, William,	117 Prince Street, " " "
Thurber, Francis B.,	90 West Broadway, " " "
Tiebout, Charles H.,	31 Grand Street, Brooklyn
Tinker, Edward L.,	Criminal Court Building, New York City
Tinkham, Julian R.,	42 Broadway, " " "
Tison, Alexander,	11 William Street, " " "
Tod, J. Kennedy,	45 Wall Street, " " "
Todd, Henry A.,	824 West End Avenue, " " "
Tomkins, Calvin,	17 Battery Place, " " "
Tompkins, Hamilton B.,	229 Broadway, " " "
Train, Arthur C.,	Criminal Court Building, " " "
Trotter, William,	124 E. 30th Street, " " "
Trowbridge, Mason,	Criminal Court Building, " " "
Tuckerman, Alfred,	1123 Broadway, " " "
Tuckerman, Eliot,	44 Pine Street, " " "
Turnbull, George R.,	33 Mercer Street, " " "
Unckles, D. S.,	957 St. Mark's Avenue, Brooklyn
Vail, Charles D.,	Geneva, N. Y.
Valentine, Charles A.,	1 E. 27th Street, New York City
Valentine, Henry C., (Life),	257 Broadway, " " "
Valentine, Robert G.	Office of Indian Affairs, Washington, D. C.
Vallandingham, Edward N.,	Reform Club, New York City
Vandiver, Almuth C.,	District Attorney's Office, New York City
Van Dusen, Samuel C.,	27 Cliff Street, " " "
Van Ingen, Edward H.,	9 E. 71st Street, " " "
Van Nest, George W.,	20 Broad Street, " " "
Villard, Harold G.	43 Cedar Street, " " "
Villard, Oswald Garrison, (Life),	206 Broadway, " " "
Wadsworth, James W.,	Geneseo, N. Y.
Wagener, August P.,	51 Chambers Street, New York City
Walcott, Philip K.,	111 Broadway, " " "
Walker, John,	1231 Western Avenue, Alleghany City, Pa.
Walker, Samuel C.,	Harbison & Walker, Pittsburg, "
Walker, William,	" " " " "
Wallace, Jackson,	26 Liberty Street, New York City

Wallace, William H.,	66 Broadway, New York City
Wallace, W. J.,	203 W. 80th Street, " " "
Walling, William English,	8 Fifth Avenue, " " "
Warburg, F. M., (Life),	52 William Street, " " "
Ward, Henry Galbreath,	79 Wall Street, " " "
Ward, J. H.,	34 Kenyon Bldg., Louisville, Ky.
Ward, J. Q. A.,	119 W. 52nd Street, New York City
Warren, George A.,	1118 20th Street, N. W., Washington, D. C.
Warren, H. Langford,	120 Boylston Street, Boston, Mass.
Wasson, James B.,	154 Nassau Street, New York City
Watson, Charles W.,	500 Madison Avenue, " " "
Webb, Willoughby L.,	63 Wall Street, " " "
Weed, John W.,	62 William Street, " " "
Weeks, E. R.,	3408 Harrison Street, Kansas City, Mo.
Weeks, Rufus W.,	P. O. Box 1663, New York City
Welch, Archibald A.,	Woodland Street, Hartford, Conn.
Weld, Francis M.,	5 Nassau Street, New York City
Welling, R. W. G.,	2 Wall Street, " " "
Werthein, H. P.,	27 William Street, " " "
Wetmore, Edmund,	34 Pine Street, " " "
Wheeler, Everett P.,	21 State Street, " " "
Wheeler, James R.,	Columbia College, " " "
White, Alexander M.,	52 Remsen Street, Brooklyn
White, Andrew D., (Life),	Ithaca, N. Y.
White, George C.,	Glen Ridge, N. J.
Whiteside, George W.,	District Attorney's Office, New York City
Whitney, Edward B.,	26 Liberty Street, " " "
Whitridge, Frederick W.,	59 Wall Street, " " "
Wickersham, C. W.,	Hastings Hall, Cambridge, Mass.
Wickersham, George W.,	40 Wall Street. New York City
Wilcox, Ansley,	295 Main Street, Buffalo, N. Y.
Wilder, William R.,	45 Cedar Street, New York City
Wilds, Howard Payson,	University Club, " " "
Williams, L. L.,	Care E. C. Williams, 135 Broadway, " " "
Williams, Norman A.,	42 E. 41st Street, " " "
Williams, Perry P.,	Produce Exchange, " " "
Williams, Richard H.,	1 Broadway, " " "
Williams, Stephen G.,	953 Madison Avenue, " " "
Williams, William,	35 Wall Street, " " "
Willis, Albert L.,	124 W. 183rd Street, " " "
Wilson, George Augustus,	37 Liberty Street, " " "
Wilson, Richard T.,	511 Fifth Avenue, " " "
Wilson, Theodore,	Orange, N. J.
Winthrop, Bronson,	32 Liberty Street, New York City
Wise, B. E.,	21 Broad Street, " " "
Wisner, Charles,	Cotton Exchange, " ". "
Wisner, H. G.,	18 W. 12th Street, " " "
Witherbee, F. S,	71 Broadway, " " "

Wolff, Lewis S., ... 12 E. 70th Street, New York City
Woodbridge, Charles E., ... 8 Bridge Street, " " "
Worcester, Edwin D., Jr., ... 35 Nassau Street, " " "
Wright, Jonathan, ... 44 W. 49th Street, " " "

Yates, Arthur G., . . . 130 So. Fitzhugh Street, Rochester, N.Y.
Yonge, Henry, ... Hotel Margaret, Brooklyn

Zabriskie, George, ... 49 Wall Street, New York City
Zerega, Richard A., ... 101 Classon Avenue, Brooklyn

ARTICLES OF INCORPORATION

OF

THE NEW YORK CIVIL SERVICE REFORM ASSOCIATION

[Filed May 11, 1900.]

KNOW ALL MEN BY THESE PRESENTS: That we, the undersigned, being persons of full age and all citizens of the United States, a majority of whom are also citizens of the State of New York, and being now Directors of an unincorporated association known as the New York Civil Service Reform Association, and organized for the purposes hereinafter mentioned; being desirous of incorporation for the same purposes under the Membership Corporations Law of the State of New York, do hereby, pursuant to unanimous vote of all the members of the said Association, present and voting at a regularly called meeting thereof, and pursuant to authority given by the said unanimous vote at the said meeting, of which meeting notice of the intention so to incorporate was given personally or by mail to each member of such Association whose residence or Post Office address was known, at least thirty days before said meeting, and at which meeting the corporate name stated in paragraph First was by unanimous vote adopted, do hereby certify as follows

FIRST.—The name or title by which the Association in which we desire to form ourselves as aforesaid shall be known in law, shall be the Civil Service Reform Association.

SECOND.—The territory in which its operations are to be principally conducted shall be the City of New York.

THIRD.—The city in which its principal office is to be located is the City of New York.

FOURTH.—The objects of the Association shall be to further the establishment of a system of appointment, promotion and removal in the civil service, founded upon the principle that public office is a public trust, admission to and retention in which should depend upon proven fitness; and to take such action as may tend to secure the honest and efficient execution of laws and rules relating to the civil service, and to the proper administration thereof.

FIFTH.—The number of its directors shall be twenty-eight.

SIXTH.—The names of the persons to be its directors until its first annual meeting are as follows:

Samuel P. Avery, Truman J. Backus, Henry De Forest Baldwin, Edward Cary, Charles Collins, W. Bayard Cutting, Horace E. Deming, A. S. Frissell, Richard Watson Gilder, Edwin L. Godkin, J. Warren Greene, George McAneny, James McKeen, Jacob F. Miller, Samuel H. Ordway, William A. Perrine, George Foster Peabody, William J. Schieffelin, Carl Schurz, Charles A. Schieren, Thomas R. Slicer, Henry Sanger Snow, Anson Phelps Stokes, S. Perry Sturges, Henry W. Taft, William H. Thomson, Charles W. Watson and Everett P. Wheeler.

In WITNESS WHEREOF we have made, signed, acknowledged and filed this certificate in duplicate.

Dated this Eighth day of May, 1900.

C. SCHURZ,	WILLIAM H. THOMSON,
JACOB F. MILLER,	A. S. FRISSELL,
ANSON PHELPS STOKES,	GEORGE MCANENY,
EVERETT P. WHEELER,	CHARLES A. SCHIEREN,
CHARLES COLLINS,	SAMUEL P. AVERY,
SAMUEL H. ORDWAY,	GEORGE FOSTER PEABODY.
J. WARREN GREENE,	

STATE OF NEW YORK, } ss.
COUNTY OF NEW YORK,

On this eighth day of May, one thousand and nine hundred, before me personally came Carl Schurz, Jacob F. Miller, Anson Phelps Stokes, Everett P. Wheeler, Charles Collins, J. Warren Greene, William H. Thomson, Samuel H. Ordway, A. S. Frissell, George McAneny, Charles A. Schieren, Samuel P. Avery and George Foster Peabody, to me personally known to be the persons described in and who made and signed the foregoing certificate, and severally duly acknowledged to me that they had made, signed and executed the same for the uses and purposes therein set forth.

F. W. HOERSCHGEN,
Notary Public, Kings County. (149)
(Certificate filed in New York County.)

Approved, May 9, 1900.

DAVID LEVINTRITT,
Justice of the Supreme Court of the State of New York.

REPORT

OF THE

Executive Committee

OF THE

New York Civil Service Reform Association

Read at the Annual Meeting, May 13, 1908.

LIST OF MEMBERS, ETC.

NEW YORK
PUBLISHED FOR THE
CIVIL SERVICE REFORM ASSOCIATION
79 Wall Street
1908

CONTENTS

Annual Report of the Executive Committee - 5
Annual Report of the Treasurer - - - 19
Constitution and By Laws - - - . 21
Roll of Officers and Members - - - - 29
Articles of Incorporation - - - - - 51

ANNUAL REPORT

OF THE

Executive Committee of the Civil Service Reform Association.

Twenty-five years ago, on January 16th, 1883, the first real civil service law in this country was passed. It was drafted by the Committee on Legislation of this Association, of which the late Dorman B. Eaton was the Chairman, and was introduced by Senator Pendleton of Ohio, by whose name the law has ever since been known. That it was drawn with rare judgment and with careful regard to future development is demonstrated by the fact that although the number of government employees subject to its jurisdiction has grown from 13,000 in 1883 to approximately 200,000 in 1908, it has never been amended and is considered to-day by many as the best civil service law of any now in force. In the same year, on May 4, the New York Civil Service Law was approved by Governor Cleveland. The Association which had so much to do with their creation and subsequent adoption may well take pride in its achievement.

Though the extension of the classified service under the jurisdiction of the civil service law has progressed rapidly, the growth of public opinion in support of the merit system has more than kept pace with it. The success of the Pendleton Act in promoting economy and efficiency in the public service, compared with the extravagance and waste resulting from fifty years of the spoils system, has provided an unanswerable argument 1st those who for personal or political reasons wished the progress of the merit system by proclaiming it ideal and impractical, and unfitted to American political conditions. Had the law added not a whit to the efficiency of the public service, it would, nevertheless, have justified itself many times over by what it has done to purify those political conditions.

The experience with the merit system in the Federal Service has been, in lesser degree, the experience in states and cities in which it has been introduced. Once introduced, it has, with rare exceptions, steadily grown in popular favor and justified its existence. No one to-day would seriously consider the possibility of the repeal of the Federal Law—even those who harangue the loudest against it in legislative halls, do so with a sure conviction that they may safely so indulge themselves without running any chance of having the burden of distributing the spoils thrust back upon them.

The Federal Law was followed in 1883 and 1884 by the New York and Massachusetts Laws, which extend to the cities as well as to the state service. The merit system is now in force in six states, and in over a score of cities in addition to those in New York and Massachusetts. Extension has been particularly rapid in the last five years, and each year sees new jurisdictions added to the list. This year, the State of New Jersey has fallen into line with a law that is mandatory for the state service, and optional for cities and other civil divisions.

The adoption of civil service laws is, however, but the first step. Honest, sane and energetic enforcement is essential in order that they may accomplish results. To secure this, the Civil Service Reform Association has maintained its organization and its activity. It is to-day the main reliance of those in this State who are seeking to administer the law in accordance with its spirit in spite of pressure to let down the bars, and the frank critic of those who yield to such pressure, or who, through fear of bringing down upon themselves political disfavor, seek means of avoiding a full and proper enforcement of the law.

Your Committee reports with deep regret the death, during the past year, of one of the Vice-Presidents of the Association, D. Willis James, who throughout his connection with the Association, which began in 1882, was one of its most faithful and generous supporters.

THE FEDERAL SERVICE.

In the absence of any recent additions by the President to the classified service, interest has chiefly centred in action by Congress on the various measures pending before it affecting the administration of the civil service law. That body has refused to consider favorably the reasonable request that the salaries of the Civil Service Commissioners should be increased to $5,000, merely making provision for a $500 increase in the salary of the President of the Commission. It has granted, with manifest reluctance, the salaries of thirteen additional clerks, much needed in order that the Commission may keep pace with the demands made upon it.

A strong effort has been made by the civil service reformers throughout the country to defeat the provisions in the bill for the taking of the decennial census, that the additional clerical force, numbering about 4,000, should be recruited outside the civil service law through noncompetitive examinations. In a special message to Congress the President characterized these non-competitive examinations as merely "a cloak to hide the nakedness of the spoils system," and called attention to the extravagance and delay which had resulted from their use in previous censuses. The National Civil Service Reform League appealed to the members of all its constituent associations to write to their Senators and Representatives, and brought the matter forcibly to the attention of commercial organizations and the press. Although the bill was reported with this vicious clause included, its promoters have not dared to bring it to a vote, fearing the effect upon public opinion that its passage might have in a campaign year. It is not expected to come up again during the present session, but, in all probability, the fight against this clause will have to be renewed with the opening of the short session.

In his annual message to Congress, the President recommended legislation providing for the classification of fourth-class postmasters, who number nearly 60,000. The recommendation has, however, been wholly ignored, and it is hoped that this fact may lead the President to use his own power to classify under existing law. The President has also transmitted to Congress a report by the Keep Committee on Department Methods, recommending the passage of a bill providing for the retirement of government employees upon annuities, a certain proportion to be withheld from the salary of every classified employee each month. The bill has been the subject of hearings, and has been amended, but not, as yet, reported.

The National Assembly of Civil Service Commissions held its second biennial meeting in Chicago on May 7th and 8th. These meetings of representatives of commissions throughout the country are extremely valuable in that they provide an opportunity for the discussion of the practical problems of administration and lead to the adoption of new and improved methods of examination.

THE STATE SERVICE.
ATTITUDE OF GOVERNOR HUGHES.

The enforcement of the civil service law in the State Service reflects the favorable attitude of Governor Hughes toward the merit system, which he so forcibly expressed in his address before the National Civil Service Reform League in Buffalo last November. Such unqualified endorsement of the system as a pre-requisite of efficient public service, coming from the chief executive of a state in which it has been in force for years, has given added impetus to the movement for its extension. A concrete example of the Governor's stand in favor of thorough enforcement was his refusal to re-appoint Harry H. Bender as Fiscal Supervisor of State Charities, whom Governor Higgins had merely reprimanded for his notorious activity as a collector of campaign assessments from state employees.

THE STATE CIVIL SERVICE COMMISSION.

Governor Hughes has made no change in the composition of the State Civil Service Commission. The continuous growth of the service, and the increase in the work of the Commission emphasizes the desirability of the adoption of the suggestion made in our last report in favor of more frequent meetings of the board and of a president resident in Albany to supervise and direct the executive work. The present custom of the Commissioners of holding meetings in Albany only once a month leads, we are compelled to feel, to hasty and not well-considered action in some important cases; and to an undue delay in others which may prove extremely embarrassing to an appointing officer, who is entitled to a prompt decision of the question at issue. Observations of the enforcement of civil service laws elsewhere have led us to the opinion that the best results are obtained where the Commission, or its President, is in direct and constant executive control of the administration. That administration is likely to work much more smoothly and successfully if heads of departments, when questions involving action by the Civil Service Commission arise, can confer with some one possessing authority to act rather than with subordinate officers who must refer every important matter to their superiors for decision.

INVESTIGATIONS.

The investigations carried on by the State Commission have been of the highest importance in securing enforcement of the law. During the past year, the Commission has inquired into the employment of persons as unskilled laborers, who in the State and County services are not required to submit to examination or registration, and their subsequent assignment to positions which the law provides shall be filled through competitive examinations.

This abuse had grown to large proportions; in the State Engineer's department alone over four hundred of these so-called laborers were found to be thus illegally employed, and similar conditions were found to exist, in lesser degree, in other departments, particularly in the Kings County offices. The Commission with, in most cases, the cooperation of the heads of departments involved, took action to end this abuse, with the result that, by the end of the year, two hundred names had been stricken from the roster of laborers and their places filled from eligible lists.

The investigations of municipal commissions by the State Commissioners or by their able Secretary and Chief Examiner have been continued. These have proved of great value in correcting abuses, and in establishing a correct system of administration and uniform standards of examination throughout the State.

EXEMPTIONS FROM COMPETITIVE EXAMINATION.

The law, as interpreted by the courts in their later decisions, now gives very great discretion to the Commission in deciding the question of the practicability of competitive examinations for a given position. Unless it flagrantly departs from what experience has proved to be right, or from the clear intent of the law, its decision is not subject to review.

The responsibility thus placed upon the state Commissioners is great. It makes them the final judge, in practically every case, of the classification, not only of the state and county services, but of all municipal services as well. The Commission promises, in its latest report, "a thorough and systematic reclassification of the whole service to the end that such classification may be made uniform as affecting different departments and institutions and that the proportion of exemptions be minimized."

This is official recognition of the justice of the claim, so frequently advanced by the Association, that the exempt class, through the discretionary action of the Commission, has increased beyond its due proportion. Improved methods of examination now practised by the State and other Commissions have done away with the reason for many exemptions which existed at the time they were granted, and we are strongly of the conviction that a thorough reclassification along modern lines is an urgent need.

A popular error exists to the effect that examinations must of necessity consist of academic written tests and that they are, therefore, practically applicable only to subordinate positions, in which executive ability, trust and confidence, or proof of character and integrity, are not required. As a matter of fact, the Commission may apply precisely similar tests for the selection of candidates for positions of this character that a private employer would make use of, and in so doing has a much wider scope of selection. As this is the main function for which the Commission exists, it can, in most cases, examine much more thoroughly into the requisite qualifications than any private employer or appointing officer, with his other executive duties, could afford to, or in actual practice would, do. That this erroneous point of view in regard to the scope of competition should be held by new and inexperienced commissioners might perhaps be expected, but that it is not shared in by the present State Commission is made clear in the following emphatic statement in its last report:

"The Commission is insisting more and more that the rule of competition which the State constitution declares shall prevail in making appointments and promotions in the civil service is practicable for the filling of all public positions outside those which the legislature in its wisdom has directly or by plain inference declared to be exempt. It insists that competition shall be the rule, exemption the exception, as was clearly the intent of the framers of the constitution and of the law."

But it is difficult to reconcile this positive declaration

of its policy with the favorable action by the State Commission upon requests for exemptions during the past year, and particularly with the granting at a recent meeting, from which Commissioner Brown was unavoidably absent, of requests for thirty exempt positions, in addition to those which the legislature has declared to be exempt, in the municipal courts of New York City, and for ten additional auditors, who handle no money, but simply pass on claims, in the Finance Department, New York City. The State Commission has certainly laid itself open to very serious criticism in thus falling so far below the proper standard it had officially raised for itself.

APPROPRIATIONS FOR THE STATE COMMISSION.

The State Commission justly complains of the small allowance made by the Legislature for the carrying on of its examining work. In securing the needed increase, the Association will cooperate to the extent of its power. The Legislature should be made to realize that to hamper the Civil Service Commission by denying it the necessary funds is false economy, which results in hampering and delaying the work of all departments of the State government.

MEASURES IN THE STATE LEGISLATURE.
SPANISH WAR VETERAN PREFERENCE.

In the session of the Legislature which closed on April 23rd, a measure was introduced, and came very near passing, which, if enacted into law, would go far toward setting aside the merit system and substituting in its stead a system of appointment to office based on military service. This was the concurrent resolution, introduced in the Senate by Mr. Cobb of Watertown, and in the Assembly by Mr. Fowler of Ulster County, to amend the civil service section of the Constitution by granting to veterans of the Spanish War, the Philippine insurrection and the Boxer Uprising a preference in appointment by adding ten per cent to their average ratings in civil service examinations. There are approximately 30,000 of these veterans in this State, and, under such a handicap, it would be practically useless for a civilian to attempt to compete for public office.

The influence behind the bill was that of the Spanish War Veterans' organization, which, before the session opened, had secured pledges from a number of the members of the legislature. These members failed to realize the results which would follow such legislation, and were drawn to its support by the plausible argument that this would be doing for the veterans of later wars only what had years ago been done in recognition of the services of veterans of the Civil War. They did not take account of the fact that the Civil War preference was wholly wrong in principle, and injurious to the service, but that that injury is reduced to a minimum as, owing to advanced age, few of them can undertake to compete for public office. This disability would not, of course, apply to veterans of the Spanish War.

The Association was represented at the hearings on this bill, and in addition conducted an extensive campaign of education through the press. It had the cordial co-operation of the Buffalo Association, the State Civil Service Commission, which, in its last report, condemned the plan from the point of view of its effect upon the administration of the merit system; the New York City Commission, the City Club and the Citizens' Union. The attention of civil employees was called to the injustice which would result from the enactment of this measure to all those now in office by placing them under a serious disadvantage in competitive examinations for promotion. After being reported, it was recommitted in the Assembly for a further hearing at which, in addition to the organizations named above, associations of patrolmen and firemen were represented in opposition.

Toward the close of the session the resolution passed the Senate, Senators Agnew, Armstrong, Davis, Dunn, Fancher, Fuller, Hinman and White being the only ones recorded in the negative. It was reported by the Committee on Rules to the Assembly on the closing day, and was there defeated by the adoption of an amendment, at too late an hour to permit of its reprinting and repassage. For this defeat, Assemblymen John Lord O'Brian of Erie, Republican, and William Allaire Shortt of Richmond, Alfred E. Smith of New York, and David C. Robinson of Chemung, Democrats, are entitled to great credit. It is safe to assume, however, that the measure will again be introduced at future sessions of the legislature.

OTHER BILLS AFFECTING THE CIVIL SERVICE.

Every bill introduced was subjected to scrutiny, and measures of any importance affecting the merit system were either advocated or opposed, on the advice of the Law Committee. The number of these bills was much less than in former sessions. Of the measures advocated by the Association, one only secured passage,—a bill to prevent any but bona-fide exempt volunteer firemen from securing any advantage under Section 21 of the Civil Service Law. If this bill is signed by the Governor, it will end an abuse of the law under which civil employees in large numbers have joined volunteer fire companies immediately prior to their disbandment, and by this means have sought to gain an unmerited and improper security against removal.

It is too early as yet to report the fate of all the bills opposed by the Law Committee of the Association, as the thirty days allowed to the Governor for action have not yet expired. Many failed of passage, and briefs have been filed with the Governor in opposition to those awaiting his action.

NEW YORK CITY.

THE MUNICIPAL CIVIL SERVICE COMMISSION.

On July 8, the Mayor suddenly called for the resignation of Commissioner Alfred J. Talley, who was originally appointed October 5th, 1904, on the recommendation of former Corporation Counsel Delany, alleging neglect of duty. In his place he appointed Frank L. Polk, a young lawyer of standing, a graduate of Yale and the Columbia Law School. On January 9, Hon. William F. Baker, President of the Commission, resigned to become First Deputy Police Commissioner of Brooklyn and Queens, succeeding Hon. Arthur J. O'Keefe, who was in turn appointed Civil Service Commissioner. We cannot pass over the resignation of Commissioner Baker without a word of recognition of the faithfulness, impartiality and efficiency with which he administered his office during his three years of service as President of the Commission. Commissioner Polk has succeeded him as President.

Since these changes in the composition of two-thirds of the Commission have taken place, too little time has elapsed to attempt to pass judgment upon its administration of the law. Generally speaking, the policy of former President Baker has been adhered to, but in the matter of the granting of exemptions of positions from competitive examination there has been a decided lowering of the standard. The Commission reports the number of employees in the exempt class at the close of 1907 as 727. Since that time, the Commission has granted over sixty additional exemptions, and now has under consideration the exemption of all court interpreters subject to their jurisdiction, in number about forty-three. What has been said above in regard to exemptions by the State Commission, and the urgent need for reduction, applies with equal force to the New York City Commission.

THE FINANCE DEPARTMENT.

During the year new positions have been added to the exempt list in the Finance Department, making a total of 152, and the Comptroller has asked for twelve more, which the Municipal Commission has already granted. The State Commission has taken the stand that the number now existing, nearly one in four, (152 to 679), is out of all due proportion and, before granting the additions requested, has asked the Comptroller to consider a proper re-classification, in accordance with the plans formulated by the Comptroller, with the aid of the Bureau of Municipal Research, for a thorough reorganization of the department. The matter has been the subject of conference between the Comptroller and the State Commission, but the result has not yet been announced.

Under Comptroller Grout's administration, the Association brought forward and published facts pointing to the use of these exempt positions in the interest of the Democratic organization of Kings County, presided over by Hon. Patrick H. McCarren. The same charge has been frequently heard against Comptroller Metz. On the day on which the Spring primaries were held, he removed from office William E. Melody, Deputy Collector of Assessments and Arrears, and one of the leaders of the revolt against McCarren, for "disloyalty."

The most flagrant disregard for the civil service law was, however, shown in the employment of so-called "temporary expert clerks" to make up new records of assessments and arrears in the Finance Department, for which a special appropriation of $48,000 had been secured. The new Chief of the Bureau originally requested that these positions should be exempt, but after a conference, in which President Baker of the Municipal Commission, Commissioner Brown of the State Commission, and the Secretary of the Association took part, he agreed to appoint as many as he could secure from the existing eligible list for Searcher. He stated that he would wish to employ about forty at an average salary of $1,200, and, in view of his assertions in regard to the need for employing experts, and that much of the work would have to be done at night, it was agreed that he should be allowed to appoint the balance under Clause 6 of Rule 12, permitting the Commission to except from competition "any person engaged in private business who shall render any professional, scientific, technical or expert service of an occasional and exceptional character, to any city officer and the amount of whose compensation in any one year shall not exceed $750."

For this service, twelve men were secured from the searchers' list. The work began in March, 1907, and in four months the force was increased to over one hundred. Subsequent appropriations have been secured, and the work is not yet finished. A preliminary investigation shows that night work was kept up for a short time only; that the duties performed by most of these men have been of the simplest clerical nature, and that this so-called "expert" force was made up in part of saloon keepers, mechanics, barbers, laborers, milk men, ice men, deputy sheriffs, etc. Of 144 men so employed, 78 were appointed from Brooklyn. The City Record enrollment transcripts show that 107 enrolled as Democrats, 6 as Republicans, 1 as an Independent, and that 30 did not enroll. After the matter had been called to its attention by President Coler of the Borough of Brooklyn, the Commission ordered the payrolls of these employees held up on the first of April, and called upon the Comptroller to furnish proof of their capacity as experts; but that it should have accepted appointments in such number, and of such character, is almost inconceivable. The investigation by the Association will be continued.

INVESTIGATIONS.

In July last, the Association presented charges to the Mayor against Joseph I. Berry, Commissioner of Parks for the Borough of the Bronx, for violation of the civil service law in the appointment of laborers. At the same time, it sent to the Civil Service Commission, for investigation, a list of irregularities and fraudulent representations in applications for laboring positions discovered in the course of the investigation. The charges were referred by the Mayor to the Commissioners of Accounts, who, after a long series of hearings, made a report upon which the charges were dismissed by the Mayor. The Civil Service Commission has not as yet seen fit to take any positive action looking to the annulment of the employment of those who received and still retain their positions through fraud and false representations.

Last summer, at the request of the Commissioner of Health, the Secretary of the Association made an investigation of the employment of persons through noncompetitive examination in the contagious disease hospitals. A number of irregularities and violations of law were discovered, and reported to the Commissioner who replied stating that he had ordered all the charges made which the report recommended.

The Executive Committee expresses its thanks to the Women's Auxiliary for the assistance and support it has so generously given to the Association in its work. It reports that the membership of the Association numbers 869. Of these, 15 are life members, 77 sustaining members, and 777 regular members.

Respectfully submitted.:

SAMUEL H. ORDWAY,
Chairman.

ELLIOT H. GOODWIN,
Secretary.

ANNUAL REPORT
OF THE
CIVIL SERVICE REFORM ASSOCIATION.

MAY 1, 1908.

Balance on hand May 1, 1907			$ 249.42
RECEIPTS:			
From Annual Dues		$3,505.00	
" Sustaining Membership Dues		1,770.00	
" Subscriptions		923.84	
" Women's Auxiliary		300.00	
" A. S. Frissell, Treasurer, a/c Interest on Elial F. Hall Bequest		655.48	7,154.32
			$7,403.74
DISBURSEMENTS:			
Salary of Secretary		$1,650.00	
" " Assistant Secretary		962.50	
" " Second Assistant Secretary		159.62	
" " Charles W. McCandless "of Counsel"		100.00	
" " Clerks		1,113.50	
Rent of Office		550.00	
Expenses of Litigation		58.93	
Expenses of Annual Dinner		132.62	
Subscription to GOOD GOVERNMENT		561.46	
Legislation Information		270.55	
Stationery		169.88	
Printing		318.54	
Postage and Stamped Envelopes		285.25	
Telephone Service		167.99	
Traveling Expenses		134.77	
Office Expenses		200.48	
Tax on Elial F. Hall Bequest		528.00	7,364.09
Balance on hand			$ 39.65

E. & O. E.

A. S. FRISSELL, *Treasurer.*

ELIAL F. HALL FUND.

Held as a special deposit at the Fifth Avenue Bank, certificate No. 5844 for sixteen shares Title Guarantee & Trust Company stock.

The above stock pays dividends of 16% per annum, namely, $256.

A. S. FRISSELL, *Treasurer.*

The above account examined and found correct, May 11, 1908.

GEORGE R. BISHOP,
ELLWOOD HENDRICK, } *Auditing Committee.*

ORGANIZATION
OF
THE NEW YORK CIVIL SERVICE REFORM ASSOCIATION

CONSTITUTION.

ARTICLE I.

The name of this organization shall be The Civil Service Reform Association.

ARTICLE II.

The object of the Association shall be to establish a system of appointment, promotion, and removal in the civil service, founded upon the principle that public office is a public trust, admission to which should depend upon proven fitness. To this end the Association will demand that appointments to subordinate executive offices, with such exceptions as may be expedient, not inconsistent with the principle already mentioned, shall be made from persons whose fitness has been ascertained by competitive examinations open to all applicants properly qualified, and that removals shall be made for legitimate cause only, such as dishonesty, negligence, or inefficiency, but not for political opinion or refusal to render party service; and the Association will advocate all other appropriate measures for securing integrity, intelligence, efficiency, good order, and due discipline in the civil service.

ARTICLE III.

The Association will hold meetings, raise funds, publish and circulate appropriate information, correspond and cooperate with associations organized elsewhere for the objects set forth in this Constitution, and support all executive and legislative action which promote its purposes.

Article IV.

The conditions of membership shall be wholly independent of party preference. Questions shall not be discussed in the debate or in the publications of the Association upon party grounds. Neither the name nor influence of the Association shall be used on behalf of any party, or for procuring office or promotion for any person. But nothing in this article shall be construed to prevent the Association from opposing any candidate when in its opinion, or in that of three-fourths of the members of the Executive Committee, such course is demanded by the objects of the Association.

Article V.

There shall be a President, to be elected by the Association at the annual meeting, who shall perform the usual and prescribed duties of that office. He shall be, ex-officio, a member of all committees, with a casting vote only, and he may call special meetings of the Executive Committee whenever he thinks it necessary, and, with the assent of two members of the Executive Committee, special meetings of the Association.

There shall be ten Vice-Presidents, to be annually elected by the Association.

There shall be a Treasurer and Secretary and such other officers as the Executive Committee may from time to time designate, who shall perform the usual and prescribed duties of such officers. They shall be respectively appointed by the Executive Committee, and may be removed by them. The Treasurer shall be, ex-officio, a member of the Finance Committee of the Association.

There shall be an Executive Committee of twenty-five members, to be elected annually by the Association. Subject to these articles, the Executive Committee shall manage the affairs of the Association, direct and dispose of its funds, and from time to time make and modify by-laws for the Association and for its own action. The Executive Committee shall keep a record of its proceedings, and shall make a report to the Association at the annual meeting. No appropriation of

money by the Executive Committee beyond the amount in the hands of the Treasurer at the time shall bind any member of the Association, excepting those members of the Executive Committee who shall vote for it. Vacancies in the Executive Committee may be filled by the President for the remainder of the term. Other vacancies may be filled by the Executive Committee.

All the officers of the Association and members of the several Standing Committees shall be, ex-officio, members of the Executive Committee.

Article VI.

Each officer of the Association shall continue to hold office until his successor has been selected and is ready to enter upon the duties of the office.

Article VII.

There shall be an annual meeting of the Association on the second Wednesday of May, at which officers shall be elected for the ensuing year, and other appropriate business may be transacted; except in the year 1898, when the annual meeting shall be held on the second Wednesday of January.

Article VIII.

Any person may be proposed in writing for membership by any member of the Association, and shall be admitted upon approval of the Executive Committee. Members failing to pay their dues may be dropped from the roll by the Executive Committee.

Article IX.

The annual dues of each member shall be $5, payable on the 1st of May, and each member shall receive the annual report and all other publications of the Association. Sustaining members, on payment of twenty-five dollars annually, and Life members, exempt from annual dues on payment of one hundred dollars, may be elected by the Executive Committee at any regular meeting thereof.

Article X.

All provisions of this Constitution, except those relating to the rights of members, and the term of officers, may be suspended or amended by a vote of two-thirds of the Executive Committee, subject to the approval of the Association by a two-thirds vote of the members present either at the annual meeting or at a special meeting duly called. Due notice shall be given before any such annual or special meeting that the approval of the Association will, thereat, be asked for such action of the Executive Committee, and the notice shall clearly state the effect of such suspension or amendment in the text of the Constitution. Any member of the Association may propose amendments to the Constitution, which may be approved under the same conditions.

BY-LAWS.

FOR THE GOVERNMENT OF THE ASSOCIATION AND ITS COMMITTEES.

§ 1. The Annual meeting of the Association shall be held at such hour and place as the Executive Committee shall designate. The election of officers shall be by ballot, but any member not present may declare his vote by letter to the Secretary and it shall be counted.

§ 2. The meetings of each committee, unless otherwise especially provided for, shall be at half-past eight P. M., at which time the chairman shall direct the call of the names of its members and the Secretary shall record the names of those present and others as they appear.

§ 3. The order of business, before each committee shall be:
    1. The reading and correction of the records of the last meeting.

And, thereafter, unless otherwise ordered, as follows:
    2. Any statement due from the Treasurer.
    3. Unfinished business from the last meeting.
    4. Report from the Secretary's office.
    5. Reports of standing committees.
    6. Reports of special committees.
    7. Proposals of new members and their election.
    8. Miscellaneous business.

§ 4. Regular meetings of the Executive Committee shall be held on the second Wednesday of every month except July and August, but if that day be a holiday, then on the third Wednesday. Ten members of the Executive Committee shall constitute a quorum.

§ 5. Neither in the meetings of the Association nor of any committee shall any member speak more than once on any motion nor more than ten minutes at one time, without unanimous consent, nor shall any person, or his actions, be characterized on party grounds.

§ 6. Special meetings of any committee may be called by its chairman or by any three members, and due notice thereof shall be given by the Secretary.

§ 7. All notices to a member shall be sent to his address filed with the Secretary.

§ 8. On the demand of one-fifth of the members present, at any meeting of the Association or of a committee, the ayes and nays shall be called and recorded on any motion.

§ 9. All committees shall be appointed by the chair unless their selection shall be otherwise provided for.

§ 10. At each regular meeting of the Executive Committee, it shall be the duty of the Treasurer to make a statement of the amount of money in the treasury and of the place of its deposit, and, at the annual meeting, he shall state the source of all moneys received and the use made of the same during the past year.

§ 11. The Secretary shall keep a record of the proceedings of the Association and of the Executive Committee, and perform the other duties assigned him.

§ 12. Without the consent of three-fourths of the members present, no vote which will declare or fill a vacancy or elect a member of the Association shall be deemed carried, at the same meeting in which it was first moved.

§ 13. It shall require a vote of two-thirds of the members of the Executive Committee present to pass any vote under which more than $100 will be appropriated or the Association be pledged for more than that amount, and the Executive Committee alone shall have authority to create any charge upon the funds of the Association. But neither said committee nor any officer or officers of the Association shall be authorized to create a personal liability against any members but themselves.

§ 14. There shall be the following Standing Committees, of seven members each, which shall be selected annually by the Executive Committee:

(1) A Finance Committee, whose duty it shall be to devise and carry into effect, subject to the direction of the Executive Committee, suitable measures for raising funds, and to supervise and report upon the income and expenditures of the Association. The Chairman of the Executive Committee shall, in advance of each annual meeting of the Association, appoint an Auditing Committee from among the members of the Association, whose duty it shall be to examine all vouchers and audit the accounts of the Treasurer, and to report thereon at the annual meeting.

(2) A Publication Committee, whose duty it shall be to prepare and recommend matters suitable for publication by the Association, and to take charge of the printing and distribution of whatever may be ordered printed.

(3) A Committee on Correspondence, whose duty it shall be to promote the objects of the Association through correspondence and co-operation with other organizations.

(4) A Committee on Administration, whose duty it shall be to investigate and report upon the administration of the civil service law and rules and to consider and recommend suitable methods of examination for admission to and promotion in the public service, and suitable procedure tending to make the system more efficient.

There shall also be a Standing Committee on Law of nine members, which shall be selected annually by the Executive Committee. Its duty shall be to consider all legislation affecting the civil service, to promote such as may be approved, and to oppose such as may be disapproved by the Executive Committee, and to prepare and recommend such amendments to the law as in their opinion will advance the purposes of the Association. The Law Committee shall have power to represent the Association in any legal proceedings which may be necessary in order to maintain or enforce the laws affecting the State or Municipal civil service.

There shall also be a Standing Committee on Membership

of fifteen members, which shall be selected annually by the Executive Committee. Its duties shall be to devise and carry into effect measures for increasing the membership of the Association.

Each Standing Committee shall be competent to fix the number of its own quorum; but such quorum shall in no case be less than three.

§ 15. These By-Laws may be amended, or new By-Laws added, by a four-fifths vote at any meeting of the Executive Committee; or by a two-thirds vote, provided a statement of the proposed change had been entered on the minutes at the last meeting.

§ 16. Amendments proposed under the last clause of the tenth section of the constitution shall be first submitted to the Executive Committee.

OFFICERS—1908-1909.

PRESIDENT:

SILAS W. BURT

VICE-PRESIDENTS:

DAVID H. GREER
WILLIAM G. LOW
LEVI P. MORTON
THEODORE ROOSEVELT
ELIHU ROOT

EDWARD M. SHEPARD
ANSON PHELPS STOKES
OSCAR S. STRAUS
EVERETT P. WHEELER
HORACE WHITE

SECRETARY:

ELLIOT H. GOODWIN

ASSISTANT SECRETARY:

ALBERT DE ROODE

TREASURER:

A. S. FRISSELL

2ND ASSISTANT SECRETARY:

CHARLES B. MARBLE

EXECUTIVE COMMITTEE:

SAMUEL H. ORDWAY, *Chairman.*
HENRY De FOREST BALDWIN
THEODORE M. BANTA
GEORGE R. BISHOP
CHARLES C. BURLINGHAM
EDWARD CARY
LEANDER T. CHAMBERLAIN
CHARLES COLLINS
JOSEPH P. COTTON, Jr.
HORACE E. DEMING
SAMUEL B. DONNELLY
HOMER FOLKS

J. WARREN GREENE
GEORGE J. GREENFIELD
HENRY W. HARDON
ABRAHAM JACOBI
JACOB W. MACK
GEORGE McANENY
JOHN G. MILBURN
GEORGE FOSTER PEABODY
WILLIAM JAY SCHIEFFELIN
NELSON S. SPENCER
WILLIAM H. THOMSON
CHARLES W. WATSON

STANDING COMMITTEES.

FINANCE:

L. T. CHAMBERLAIN, Chairman.
JOHN G. AGAR
A. S. FRISSELL, ex-officio
ISAAC N. SELIGMAN
JACOB W. MACK
HORACE WHITE

PUBLICATION:

EDWARD CARY, Chairman.
GROSVENOR H. BACKUS
GEORGE R. BISHOP
ROB'T UNDERWOOD JOHNSON
WILSON M. POWELL, JR.
CARL L. SCHURZ
JOHN A. SLEICHER

CORRESPONDENCE:

EVERETT V. ABBOT, Chairman.
ALBERT S. BARD
LEARNED HAND
NATHAN A. SMYTH
CORNELIUS B. SMITH
WALTER F. TAYLOR

ADMINISTRATION:

SILAS W. BURT, Chairman.
CHARLES COLLINS
FRANCIS H. KINNICUTT
GEORGE McANENY
PHILIP J. McCOOK
CLARENCE BISHOP SMITH
NELSON S. SPENCER

LAW:

SAMUEL H. ORDWAY, Chairman.
HENRY De FOREST BALDWIN
CHARLES C. BURLINGHAM
JOSEPH P. COTTON, JR.
WINFRED T. DENISON
A. LEO EVERETT
J. WARREN GREENE
HENRY W. HARDON
CHARLES P. HOWLAND

MEMBERSHIP:

RUSSELL H. LOINES, Chairman,
FRANCIS W. BIRD
CHARLES WHITNEY DALL
CHARLES J. FAY
ROY C. GASSER
GEORGE J. GREENFIELD
ELLWOOD HENDRICK
SAMUEL N. HINCKLEY
JOHN G. JACKSON
PERCY H. JENNINGS
JAY E. LAWSHE
JOSIAH O. LOW
CHARLES W. McCANDLESS
ALFRED B. MEACHAM
ROGER H. WILLIAMS

MEMBERSHIP ROLL.

SUSTAINING MEMBERS.

AMEND, BERNARD G., ... 205 Third Avenue, New York City
APPLETON, R. ROSS, . . 146 Joralemon Street, Brooklyn, N. Y.

BEHR, HERMAN, . , . . 75 Beekman Street, New York City
BURLINGHAM, CHARLES C., . . 27 William Street, " " "

CARY, EDWARD, ... The "Times," New York City
CHAPLIN, DUNCAN D., ... 64 Worth Street, " " "
CLYDE, WILLIAM P., . . . 19 State Street,. " " "
COCHRAN, ALEX. SMITH. . . . . . . Yonkers, N. Y.
COLLARD, GEORGE W., . . . 884 Fifth Avenue, New York City
COLLINS, CHARLES, . . . 33 E. 17th Street, " " "
CONNOR, W. E., . . . 31 Nassau Street, " " "
CRANE, RICHARD T., . . 2541 Michigan Avenue, Chicago, Ill.
CURTIS, W. J., ... 49 Wall Street, New York City
CUTTING, R. FULTON, ... 32 Nassau Street. " " "

DAY, WILLIAM S., . . . 220 Hobart Avenue, Summit, N. J.
DE COPPET, E. J., ... 42 Broadway, New York City
DEERING, JAMES, . Fullerton and Clybourne Avenues, Chicago, Ill.
DELANO, WARREN Jr., . . . 1 Broadway, New York City
DEMUTH, WILLIAM, ... 524 Fifth Avenue, " " "
DENISON, WINFRED T., . Room 50, Post Office Building, " " "
DIMOCK, HENRY F., ... 60 Wall Street, " " "

FINCH, EDWARD R., . . 53 Washington Square, New York City
FRISSELL, A. S., ... 530 Fifth Avenue, New York City

GILDER, RICHARD WATSON, . . 33 E. 17th Street, New York City
GOODMAN, A. L, . . . 263 W. 113th Street' " " "
GOODWIN, J. J., ... 11 W. 54th Street, " " "
GREENE, J. WARREN, . . . 3 Broad Street, " " "
GREENFIELD, GEORGE J., . . 32 Broadway, " " "

HARRIOT, S. CARMAN, . . . 57 W. 39th Street, New York City
HEMENWAY, AUGUSTUS, . . . 10 Tremont Street, Boston, Mass.
HENTZ, HENRY, ... 769 St. Mark's Avenue, Brooklyn
HOPKINS, GEORGE B., ... 52 Broadway, New York City
HUBER, JACQUES, ... 472 Broome Street, " " "

JACOBI, A., ... 19 E. 47th Street, New York City
JAMES, DARWIN R., . . . 226 Gates Avenue. Brooklyn, N. Y.

KENNEDY, JOHN S.,	31 Nassau Street. New York City
LOEB, JAMES,	52 William Street, New York City
LOEB, MORRIS,	278 Madison Avenue, " " "
LOINES, STEPHEN,	152 Columbia Heights, Brooklyn
LOW, SETH,	30 E. 64th Street, New York City
LOW, WILLIAM G.,	58 Remsen Street, Brooklyn
MACK, JACOB W.,	92 Liberty Street, New York City
MACY, V. EVERIT,	68 Broad Street, " " "
MINTURN, ROBERT SHAW,	116 E. 22d Street, " " "
MORTON, LEVI P.,	35 Nassau Street, " " "
MOSLE, GEORGE R.,	16-18 Exchange Place, " " "
McANENY, GEORGE,	19 E. 47th Street, New York City
McKIM, JOHN A.,	6 E. 74th Street, " " "
ORDWAY, SAMUEL H.,	27 William Street, New York City
OSBORN, WILLIAM CHURCH,	71 Broadway, " " "
PAGE, EDWARD D.,	60 Worth Street, New York City
PAGE, WILLIAM H., Jr.,	32 Liberty Street, " " "
PAGENSTECHER, A.,	P. O. Box 683, " " "
PHIPP, HENRY,	6 E. 87th Street, " " "
RANDOLPH, STUART F.,	31 Nassau Street, New York City
RUSSELL, CHARLES H.,	15 Broad Street, " " "
SANDS, B. AYMAR,	31 Nassau Street, New York City
SCHEFER, CARL,	476 Broome Street, " " "
SCHIEFFELIN, WILLIAM JAY,	5 E. 66th Street, " " "
SCHIFF, JACOB H.,	P. O. Box 1198, " " "
SCHWAB, GUSTAV H.,	5 Broadway, " " "
SELIGMAN, ISAAC N.,	1 William Street, " " "
SHEPARD, EDWARD M.,	128 Broadway, " " "
SMITH, CORNELIUS B.,	101 E. 69th Street, " " "
SPENCER, NELSON S.,	27 William Street, " " "
SPEYER, JAMES,	257 Madison Avenue, " " "
STETSON, FRANCIS LYNDE,	15 Broad Street, " " "
STOKES, ANSON PHELPS,	100 William Street, " " "
STRAUS, OSCAR S.,	Dep't of Commerce and Labor, Washington, D. C.
STURHAHN, C. F.,	84 William Street, New York City
THOMSON, WILLIAM H.,	23 E. 47th Street. New York City
TRASK, SPENCER,	54 William Street, " " "
VOSS, F. G.,	40 Wall Street, New York City
WARE, WILLIAM R.,	Milton, Mass.
WHITE, ALFRED T.,	5 Nassau Street, New York City
WHITE, HORACE,	18 W. 69th Street, " " "
WUNDERLICH, F. W.,	165 Remsen Street, Brooklyn.

Abbot, Everett V., ... 45 Cedar Street, New York City
Abbott, Lawrence F., ... "The Outlook," " " "
Abbott, Lyman, ... 287 Fourth Avenue, " " "
Achelis, John, ... 68 Leonard Street, " " "
Adams, Edward D., ... 71 Broadway, " " "
Adams, Elbridge L., ... 299 Broadway, " " "
Adams, Joseph, ... Union Stock Yards, Chicago, Ill.
Adams, Thatcher M., ... 36 Wall Street, New York City
Adler, Felix, ... 152 W. 77th Street, " " "
Affeld, Francis O., ... 873 President Street, Brooklyn
Agar, John G., ... 31 Nassau Street, New York City
Agnew, Andrew Gifford, . . . 22 William Street, " " "
Aitken, John W., ... 873 Broadway, " " "
Allen, Calvin H., ... 1 W. 72nd Street, " " "
Allen, Elmer A., ... 42 Broadway, " " "
Allen, Franklin, ... 371 Fulton Street, Brooklyn
Alling, Joseph T., ... 400 Oxford Street, Rochester, N. Y.
Allison, Charles R., ... 60 Wall Street, New York City
Alsop, Reese F., ... 96 Remsen Street, Brooklyn
Amundson, John A., ... 146 Broadway, New York City
Anderson, Frank E., ... 486 Broadway, " " "
Andrews, J. Sherlock, . . . 111 St. Paul Street, Rochester, N. Y.
Arend, F. J., ... 165 Broadway, New York City
Armstrong, James, ... 71 Nassau Street, " " "
Armstrong, S. T., ... 144 E. 37th Street, " " "
Atterbury, Grosvenor, ... 20 W. 43rd Street, " " "
Auchincloss, John, ... 27 Pine Street, " " "
Avery, Samuel P., ... 4 E. 38th Street, " " "

Babbott, Frank L., ... 346 Broadway, New York City
Backus, Grosvenor H, ... 32 Liberty Street, " " "
Bacon, Gorham, ... 47 W. 54th Street, " " "
Bagley, Valentine N., . . . 641 Washington Street, " " "
Baker, William F., ... 450 Greene Avenue, Brooklyn, N. Y.
Baldwin, Elbert F., ... "The Outlook," New York City
Baldwin, Henry de Forest, . . 49 Wall Street, " " "
Bangs, L. Bolton, ... 39 E. 72nd Street, " " "
Bannard, Otto T., ... 24 Broad Street, " " "
Banta, Theodore M., ... 348 Broadway, " " "
Bard, Albert Sprague, ... 25 Broad Street, " " "
Barnes, Henry B., Jr., . . . 48 Wall Street, " " "
Barney, A. H., (Life) . . . 101 E. 38th Street, " " "
Barrett, Frank R., ... Box 105, Portland, Me.
Barrett, John D. . . . . . 49 Wall Street, New York City
Bartlett, P. G., ... 62 Cedar Street, " " "
Baruch, Bernard M., ... 111 Broadway, " " "
Batterman, Henry, ... 21 Clinton Street, Brooklyn
Bausch, Edward, ... Rochester, N. Y.

Bausch, Henry,	746 St. Paul Street, Rochester, N. Y.
Bausch, J. J.,	13 Hyde Park, " "
Bausch, William,	745 St. Paul Street, " "
Baylies, Edmund L.,	54 Wall Street, New York City
Bayne, Hugh,	40 Wall Street, " " "
Beekman, Gerard,	7 E. 42d Street, " " "
Beer, George Lewis,	329 W. 71st Street, " " "
Beers, E. Le Grand,	131 Remsen Street, Brooklyn
Beers, Lucius H.,	49 Wall Street, New York City
Bell, Gordon Knox,	22 William Street, " " "
Bellamy, Frederick P.,	204 Montague Street, Brooklyn
Bennecke, Henry,	219 Congress Street, "
Benedict, Elliot S.,	60 Wall Street, New York City
Bernard, William,	206 Broadway, " " "
Bijur, Nathan,	34 Nassau Street, " " "
Bird, Francis W.,	40 W. 59th Street, " " "
Bisbee, Ralph,	63 Wall Street, " " "
Bishop, George R.,	142 E. 18th Street, " " "
Bispham, William,	66 Broadway, " " "
Blagden, Arthur C.,	Dunster Hall, Cambridge, Mass.
Boas, Franz,	123 W. 82d Street, New York City
Bode, Frederick H.,	129 Michigan Avenue, Chicago, Ill.
Bogert, Eugene T.,	66 Broadway, New York City
Bogert, Theodore L.,	194 Broadway, " " "
Borden, M. C. D.,	Box 1794, " " "
Bottome, Harry H.,	49 Exchange Place, " " "
Bowen, C. Winthrop,	5 E. 63rd Street, " " "
Bowker, R. R.,	298 Broadway, " " "
Brachhausen, G. A.,	Rahway, N. J.
Brackett, George C.,	50 Remsen Street, Brooklyn
Bradt, Herbert S.,	120 Broadway, New York City
Brady, William H.,	17 Battery Place, " " "
Briesen, Arthur von, (Life)	49 Wall Street, " " "
Briscoe, S. William,	20 Sanford Avenue, Flushing, N. Y.
Brookfield, Frank,	2 Rector Street, New York City
Brown, Addison,	45 W. 89th Street, " " "
Brown, Augustus H.,	262 W. 136th Street, " " "
Brown, Edwin H.,	141 Broadway, " " "
Brown, Everit,	27 William Street, " " "
Brown, Roscoe C. E.,	"Tribune" Office, " " "
Brown, Thatcher M.,	36 E. 37th Street, " " "
Brownell, William C.,	153 Fifth Avenue, " " "
Brush, W. Franklin,	16 E. 37th Street, " " "
Buckingham, C. L.,	38 Park Row, " " "
Bulkley, Edwin M.,	54 William Street, " " "
Burke, J. A.,	149 W. 48th Street, " " "
Burr, Winthrop,	7 Wall Street, " " "
Burt, Silas W.,	30 Broad Street, " " "

Butler, Howard R., ... 131 E. 66th Street, New York City
Buttfield. William J., . . . 96 Wall Street, " " "
Byram, L. Winters, ... Manaca;Temple, Waverly, N. Y.
Byrne, James, ... 26 Broad Street, New York City

Cadwalader, John L., . . . 40 Wall Street, New York City
Cahen, I. J., ... 1 Madison Avenue, " " "
Canfield, George F., . . . 49 Wall Street, " " "
Carr, William, ... 35 W. 46th Street, " " "
Carnegie, Andrew, (Life) . . 2 E. 91st Street, " " "
Cary, Clarence, . . . 59 Wall Street, " " "
Cassatt, George M., . . . 327 Broadway, " " "
Cauldwell, S. Millbank, ... Pelham Manor, N. Y
Chadbourne, William M , . . . 49 Wall Street. New York City
Chaffee, J. Irwin, . Sedgwick Avenue, Fordham Heights, " " "
Chamberlain, L. T., . . . 222 W. 23 Street, " " "
Chapman, Henry G., . . . care Baring Bros & Co., London, Eng.
Chapman, J. W., ... 35 Nassau Street, " " "
Chase, George, ... 35 Nassau Street, " " "
Chauncey, Daniel, ... 129 Joralemon Street, Brooklyn
Chauncey, Elihu, ... 11 W. 38th Street, New York City
Cheney, F. W., ... South Manchester, Conn.
Childs, Edwards H., . . . 59 Wall Street, New York City
Choate, Joseph H., ... 60 Wall Street, " " "
Choate, Joseph H. Jr., . . . 60 Wall Street, " " "
Choate, William G., . . . 40 Wall Street, " " "
Cillis, Hubert, ... 20 Nassau Street, " " "
Claflin, John, ... 224 Church Street, " " "
Clark, George H.. . . . . 154 Nassau Street, " " "
Clark, Grenville, . . . 21 W. 47th Street, " " "
Clarke, Samuel B., ... 32 Nassau Street, " " "
Clay, George E., . . . 9 Jackson Avenue, Long Island City
Cleveland, Treadwell, . . . 27 William Street, New York City
Coleman, Edwin S., ... 17 Battery Place, " " "
Codington, Perley M., . . . 1487 Broadway, " " "
Coffin, I. Sherwood, . . . 30 Cliff Street, " " "
Cohen, William N., ... 22 William Street, " " "
Collins, Atwood, ... Asylum Avenue, Hartford, Conn.
Collins, Minturn Past, . . . 1 W. 34th Street, New York City
Collins, Stephen W., . . . 69 Wall Street, " " "
Collyer, Robert, . . . 201 W. 55th Street, " " "
Conant, Charles A., . . . 38 Nassau Street, " " "
Conger, Clarence R., . . . 37 Liberty Street, " " "
Conger, Henry Rutgers, . . . 40 Wall Street, " " "
Cook, Walter, ... 3 W. 29th Street, " " "
Cooley, Alford Warriner, . D epartment of Justice, Washington, D C.
Cope, Francis R., . . 508 West End Trust Building, Philadelphia, Pa.
Corbett, George J., ... 54 Wall Street, New York City

Corrigan, Joseph E.,	District Attorney's Office, New York City
Corwine, William R.,	11 Broadway, " " "
Cotton, Joseph P., Jr.,	52 William Street, " " "
Coudert, Frederick R., Jr.,	71 Broadway, " " "
Coverley, William,	19 Broadway, " " "
Cowdin, Wintrop, The Algonquin Company,	Passaic, N. J.
Cowperthwait, J. Howard,	195 Park Row, New York City
Coxe, Macgrane,	50 Church Street, " " "
Coykendall, S. D.,	Rondout, N. Y.
Crandall, Floyd M.,	113 W. 95th Street, New York City
Crane, Frederick,	Bloomfield, N. J.
Crane, Leroy B.,	277 Broadway, New York City
Cranford, Walter V.,	215 Montague Street, Brooklyn
Cravath, Paul D.,	52 William Street, New York City
Crawford, Gilbert H.,	32 Liberty Street, " " "
Croly, Herbert D.,	19 E. 24th Street, " " "
Cromwell, Frederic,	32 Nassau Street, " " "
Cromwell, Lincoln,	1 Greene Street, " " "
Croswell, J. G.,	17 W. 44th Street, " " "
Currie, J. W.,	144 Remsen Street, Brooklyn, N. Y.
Curtis, William E.,	30 Broad Street, " " "
Cushing, H. A,	43 Cedar Street, " " "
Cushing, William E.,	Society for Savings Bldg., Cleveland, O.
Cutting, R. Bayard,	32 Nassau Street, " " "
Cutting, W. Bayard,	24 E. 72nd Street, " " "
Cuyler, C. C.,	44 Pine Street, " " "
Daboll, Henry E.,	Plainfield, N. J.
Dall, C. Whitney,	44 Leonard Street, New York City
Dana, Charles A.,	District Attorney's office, " " "
Dana, Charles L.,	53 W. 53rd Street, " " "
Davidge, William H.,	49 Wall Street, " " "
Davies, Julien T.,	32 Nassau Street, " " "
Davies, William Gilbert,	32 Nassau Street, " " "
Davis, G. Pierrepont,	Woodland Street, Hartford, Conn.
Davis, Horace A.,	185 Broadway, New York City
Davis John, H.,	10 Wall Street, " " "
Davison, Charles Stewart,	60 Wall Street, " " "
Day, Clarence S.,	45 Wall Street, " " "
DeForest, R. W.,	30 Broad Street, " " "
Deming, Horace E.,	13 William Street, " " "
Demorest, William C.,	60 Liberty Street, " " "
de Roode, Albert,	79 Wall Street, " " "
Despard, W. D.,	6 Hanover Street, " " "
Devine, Thomas J.,	19 Portsmouth Terrace, Rochester, N. Y.
DeWitt, Theodore,	88 Nassau Street, New York City
Dickinson, A. Lowes,	54 William Street, " " "
Dickinson, Robert L.,	168 Clinton Street, **Brooklyn**

Dickson, James B., ... 49 Wall Street, New York City
Dittenhoefer, A. J., ... 96 Broadway, " " "
Dix, John A., ... Care L. Thomson & Co., Albany, N. Y.
Dodge, Cleveland H., ... 99 John Street, New York City
Dominick, H. B., . . . , . . 3 W. 29th Street, " " "
Dommerich, L. F., ... 57 Greene Street, " " "
Donnelly, Samuel B., . -. . . 571 Putnam Avenue, Brooklyn
Dougherty, J. Hampden, . . . 27 William Street, New York City
Dows, Tracy, ... Room 102, Produce Exchange, " " "
Dreier, H. E., ... 129 West 20th Street, " " "
Drescher, William, ... 715 St. Paul Street, Rochester, N. Y.
Driggs, Laurence, ... 43 Cedar Street, New York City
Dunham, Edward K., ... 338 E. 26th Street, " " "
Dunning, S. Wright, ... 80 Madison Avenue, " " "
Dutton, George D., , . . . 40 W. 59th Street, " " "

Eastman, George, . . . 400 East Avenue, Rochester, N. Y.
Eaton, Henry W., ... 45 William Street, New York City
Ecaubert, F., ... 18 Rose Street, " " "
Elderkin, John, . . . Lotos Club, 558 Fifth Avenue, " " "
Eliot, Charles W., ... Cambridge, Mass.
Elkins, Stephen B., ... 1626 K Street, Washington, D. C.
Ely, Arthur H., ... 56 Wall Street, New York City
Ely, Moses, ... 2 Rector Street, " " "
Ely, Robert E., ... 23 West 44th Street, " " "
Emmons, Arthur B., ... 60 Park Avenue, " " "
Emmons, Samuel F., . . U. S. Geological Survey, Washington, D. C.
Erbe, Gustav, ... 344 St. Paul Street, Rochester, N. Y.
Erbslöh, R., ... 364 Broadway, New York City
Everest, Charles M., . . . 506 West Avenue, Rochester, N. Y.
Everett, A. Leo, ... 49 Wall Street, New York City
Ewart, Richard H., ... 115 Franklin Street, " " "
Ewing, Thomas, Jr., ... 67 Wall Street, " " "

Fabbri, Alessandro, ... 11 E. 62d Street, New York City
Fabbri, Ernesto G., ... 11 E. 62d Street, " " "
Fahnestock, Gates D., . . . 214 Hicks Street, Brooklyn, N. Y.
Fahnestock, H. C., ... 2 Wall Street, New York City
Fairchild, Benjamin T., ... P. O. Box 1120, " " "
Fairchild, Charles S., . . . 10 West 8th Street, " " "
Faure, John P., ... 346 Broadway, " " "
Fay, Charles J., ... 31 Nassau Street, " " "
Field, Hamilton E., ... 106 Columbia Heights, Brooklyn
Fisher, George H., . E. 28th Street and Emmons Avenue, Brooklyn
Folks, Homer, ... 105 E. 22nd Street, New York City
Ford, Worthington C., . Care Library of Congress, Washington, D. C.
Forrest, C. R., ... Asylum Avenue, Hartford, Conn.
Fox, Alan, ... 52 William Street, New York City

Fox, Austen G., (Life), ... 45 W. 33d Street, New York City
Frankenheimer, John, ... 25 Broad Street, " " "
Frankfurter, Felix, . U. S. District Attorney's Office, " " "
Frissell, H. B., ... Hampton, Va.
Frothingham, John W., ... 68 Broad Street, New York City
Fuller, Frank, ... , . 61 Fifth Avenue, " " "
Fuller, Paul, ... 71 Broadway. " " "
Fullerton, Alexander, (Life), . . 7 W. 8th Street, " " "
Funk, I. K., ... 195 Washington Park, Brooklyn

Gaillard, William D., ... 141 Broadway, New York City
Garver, John A., ... 44 Wall Street, " " "
Gasser, Roy C., ... 35 Wall Street, " " "
Germond, H. S., ... 44 Broad Street, " " "
Gerrish, Frank Scott, ... 17 E. 76th Street, " " "
Getzelsohn, J. A., ... 810 E. 134th Street, " " "
Gibbons, George W , ... 198 Broadway, " " "
Gibson, William J., ... 26 Liberty Street, " " "
Gitterman, John M., . . . 1317 F Street, N. W., Washington, D C.
Goadby, Clarence, ... 21 W. 35th Street, New York City
Goddard, George A., ... 10 Tremont Street, Boston, Mass.
Godkin, Laurence, ... 30 Pine Street, New York City
Goetze, Otto, ... 142 Amity Street, Brooklyn, N. Y.
Goldman, Julius, ... 31 Nassau Street, New York City
Goldmark, James, ... 83 Warren Street, " " "
Goodale, John McGregor, ... 42 Broadway, " " "
Goodnow, Frank J., ... 49 Riverside Drive, " " "
Goodwin, Elliot H., ... 79 Wall Street, " " "
Gottheil, Paul, ... Produce Exchange, " " "
Gottsberger, Francis, ... 156 Broadway, " " "
Gould, Elgin R. L., ... 281 Fourth Avenue, " " "
Grant, De Forest, ... 22 E. 49th Street, " " "
Grant Percy S., ... 7 W. 10th Street, " " "
Gray, Henry G., ... 161 Madison Avenue, " " "
Green, Noah, ... 478 Central Park, West, " " "
Greenbaum, Samuel, County Court House, B'way & Chambers St., " "
Greene, Francis V., ... 816 Fidelity Building, Buffalo, N. Y.
Greenough, John, ... 38 E. 63rd Street, New York City
Greer, David H., ... 7 Gramercy Park, " " "
Gulliver, W. C., ... 120 Broadway, " " "
Guthrie, William D., ... 45 Pine Street, " " "
Gwynne, Arthur C., ... Rye, N. Y.

Hague, James D., . . . 18 Wall Street, " " "
Haines, Henry F., ... 2 Wall Street, New York City
Hall, Valentine G., ... Tivoli, Duchess Co., N. Y.
Halsey, Robert H., . . . 118 W. 58th Street, New York City
Halsted, John F., ... 93 Remsen Street, Brooklyn, N. Y.

Hamlin, Frank H.,	Canandaigua, N. Y.
Hand, Learned,	2 Wall Street, New York City
Hand, Richard L.,	Elizabethtown, N. Y.
Harbeck, Charles T.,	306 Lexington Avenue, New York City
Harding, Edward,	43 Exchange Place, " " "
Hardon, Henry Winthrop,	60 Wall Street, " " "
Harrison, Robert L.,	59 Wall Street, " " "
Hart, John Wilson,	District Attorney's Office, " " "
Hart, W. O.,	134 Carondelet Street, New Orleans La.
Hartwell, John A.,	50 E. 53d Street, New York City
Hasslacher, Jacob,	100 William Street, " " "
Hastings, Thomas S.,	27 W. 46th Street, " " "
Haupt, Louis,	1232 E. 19th Street, " " "
Hayes, J. Noble,	68 William, " " "
Heath, Frank E.,	95 Liberty Street, " " "
Healy, A. Augustus,	198 Columbia Heights, Brooklyn
Heinze, Arthur P.,	31 Nassau Street, New York City
Henderson, Harold G.,	80 Irving Place,, " " "
Hendrick, Ellwood,	139 E. 40th Street, " " "
Hentz, Leonard S.,	769 St. Mark's Avenue, Brooklyn
Herbert, William,	11 Pine Street, New York City
Higginson, James J.,	16 E. 41st Street, " " "
Hinkley, Samuel Neilson,	166 E. 61st Street, " " "
Hinrichs, Frederick W.,	76 William Street, " " "
Hitchcock, Welcome G., (Life)	453 Broome Street, " " "
Hobart, Henry L.,	120 Front Street, " " "
Hodges, Harrison B.,	16 Gramercy Park, " " "
Hoe, Richard M.,	Room 102, Produce Exchange, " " "
Hoffman, Frank S.,	Schenectady, N. Y.
Hollister, H. H.,	17 Broad Street, New York City
Holt, Henry,	29 W. 23d Street, " " "
Holt, Roland,	29 W. 23d Street, " " "
Hopkins, J. A. H,	51 West 11th Street, " " "
Hoppin, Frederick S., Jr.,	131 E. 19th Street, " " "
Hoppin, William W.,	54 William Street, " " "
Hornblower, William B.,	24 Broad Street, " " "
Howe, Daniel R.,	Asylum Avenue, Hartford, Conn.
Howe, Horace J.,	25 Gold Street, Yonkers, N. Y.
Howe, Walter B.,	Criminal Court Building, New York City
Howe, Wirt,	135 Broadway, " " "
Howland, Charles P.,	35 Wall Street, " " "
Hoyt, Francis D.,	69 Wall Street, " " "
Hoyt, Gerald L.,	28 E. 36th Street, " " "
Hubbard, Thomas H.,	16 W. 58th Street, " " "
Hughes, Charles E.,	96 Broadway, " " "
Hull, Charles A.,	95 William Street, " " "
Hunt, Leavitt J.,	111 Broadway, " " "
Huntington, Francis C.,	54 William Street, " " "

Huntington, Samuel,	176 Broadway, New York City
Huntington, William R.,	804 Broadway, " " "
Huyler, John S.,	64 Irving Place, " " "
Ide, Robert L.,	7 Nassau Street, New York City
Ireland, F. G.,	299 Broadway, " " "
Ireland, John B.,	15 E. 47th Street, " " "
Iselin, John H.,	27 William Street, " " "
Isham, Samuel.	6th Avenue and 40th Street, " " "
Jackson, John G.,	35 Wall Street, New York City
Jacob, Lawrence.	52 Broadway, " " "
Jacobson, Samuel A.,	132 Nassau Street, " " "
Jameson, E. C.,	76 William Street, " " "
Jaretzki, Alfred,	49 Wall Street, " " "
Jay, William,	48 Wall Street, " " "
Jellenix, Felix,	17 William Street, " " "
Jennings, Frederick B.,	15 Broad Street, " " "
Jennings, Percy H.,	25 Broad Street, " " "
Johnson, Burgess.	225 5th Avenue, " " "
Johnson, Robert Underwood,	33 E. 17th Street, " " "
Johnson, Willis Fletcher,	154 Nassau Street, " " "
Joline, Adrian, H,	54 Wall Street, " " "
Jones, Oliver Livingston, Jr.,	116 W. 72d Street, " " "
Josephthal, Sidney L.,	43 Cedar Street, " . " "
Kahn, Otto H., (Life),	54 William Street, New York City
Kellogg, Francis B.,	Temple Auditorium, Los Angeles, Cal.
Kelsey, Clarence H.,	146 Broadway, New York City
Kennedy, Edward G.,	220 Fifth Avenue, " " "
Kennedy, Elijah R.,	29 & 31 Liberty Street, " " "
Kenneson, Thaddeus D.,	13 William Street, " " "
Kenyon, Alan D.,	49 Wall Street, " " "
Kenyon, William Houston.	49 Wall Street, " " "
Keogh, Alexander,	Criminal Court Building, " " "
Keppler, Rudolph,	25 Broad Street, " " "
Kernan, John D,	37 Liberty Street, " " "
Kerr, Albert B.	49 Wall Street, " " "
Kidder, Camillus G,	27 William Street, " " "
Kidder, Edward H.,	170 Broadway. " " "
Kilmer, Alfred G.,	80 Broadway, " " "
Kimball, A. R.,	Orange, N. J.
Kimball, Daniel T,	198 Broadway, New York City
King, Le Roy,	20 E. 84th Street, " " "
King, William F.,	410 Broadway, " " "
Kinnicutt, Francis H.,	2 Rector Street, " " "
Kinnicutt, Francis P.,	42 W. 37th Street, " " "
Kinnicutt, G Herman,	39 E. 35th Street, " " "

Kirchhoff, Charles, ... 14 & 16 Park Place, " " "
Kissell, Gustav E., (Life), ... 1 Nassau Street, " " "
Klein, Isaac H., ... 8 Broad Street, " " "
Klupfel, Charles, Care North German Lloyd, 5 Broadway, " " "
Knapp, Shepherd, ... 266 Lexington Avenue, " " "
Knauth, Antonio, ... 233 West 70th Street, " " "
Knauth, Theodor W., . . . Wadsworth House, Cambridge, Mass.
Knox, Herbert H., ... 30 Broad Street, New York City
Koehler, Jerome H., . . , . . 47 Cedar Street, " " "
Kohler, Max J., ... 42 Broadway, " " "
Kuehnle, Frederick C., . . . 629 W. 51st Street. " " "
Kuhne, Percival, ... 13 William Street, " " "
Kunhardt, William B., ... 100 Broadway, " " "
Kunstlich, Samuel H., . . . 302 Broadway, " " "

La Fetra, Linnaeus E., ... 58 W. 58th Street. New York City
Laimbeer, Francis E., ... 290 Broadway, " " "
Lambert, William B., ... Highland Street, Cambridge Mass.
Landsman, S. M., ... 220 E. 19th Street, New York City
Langdon, William Chauncy, . District Attorney's Office, " " "
Langmann, G., ... 121 W. 57th Street, " " "
Lansing, J. Townsend, ... 82 State Street, Albany, N. Y.
Large, Walter, . , . . 15 William Street, New York City
Larremore, Wilbur, ... 82 Nassau Street. " " "
Law, James, ... 15 E. 127th Street, " " "
Lawrence, Walter B., ... 35 Wall Street, " " "
Lawshe, Jay E., ... 60 Wall Street, " " "
Lea, Henry Charles, . . . 2000 Walnut Street, Philadelphia, Pa.
Leavitt, John Brooks, ... 115 Broadway, New York City
Leaycraft, J. Edgar, ... 19 W. 42nd Street, " " "
Lederle, Ernest J., ... 471 W. 143d Street, " " "
Ledoux, Albert R., ... 9 Cliff Street, " " "
Lee, W. H. L., ... 25 Pine Street, " " "
Leffingwell, R. C , ... 52 William Street, " " "
Le Gendre, William, ... 59 Wall Street, " " "
Lehmaier, Louis A., ... 78 Beekman Street, " " "
Lethbridge, R. P., ... 49 Wall Street, " " "
Levi, Albert A., ... 52 Broadway, " " "
Lewis, Richard V., ... 130 W. 42d Street, " " "
Lindenthal, Gustav, ... 45 Cedar Street. " " "
Lindsay, Alexander M., . . . 373 East Avenue, Rochester, N. Y.
Littauer, Lucius N., ... Gloversville, N. Y.
Livingston, Goodhue, . . . 38 E. 65th Street, New York City
Livingston, Julius I., ... 33 Bethune Street, " " "
Lockwood, Benoni, ... 56 Irving Place, " " "
Loines, Russell H., ... 131 E. 66th Street, New York City
Lomb, Adolph, ... 48 Cumberland Street, Rochester, N. Y.
Lomb Henry, ... 48 Cumberland Street, " "

Lomb, Henry C., . . . 48 Cumberland Street, Rochester, N. Y.
Lord, Franklin B., Jr.. . . . 49 Wall Street, New York City
Lounsbery, Richard P., . . . 15 Broad Street, " " "
Lovell, Joseph J., ... Avondale Place, Woodhaven, N. Y.
Low, Josiah O., ... 56 William Street, New York City
Lowe, William E., ... 49 Wall Street, " " "
Lowndes, James, . . 1515 Massachusetts Avenue, Washington, D. C.
Ludlow, James B., ... 45 Cedar Street, New York City
Luther, George Martin, . . . 25 Broad Street, " " "
Lyall, Arthur V., ... 25 Pine Street, " " "
Lyman, Frank, ... 34 Remsen Street, Brooklyn
Lyman, George T., ... Bellport, N. Y.
Lyman, Theodore, ... Woodland Street, Hartford, Conn.
Lynch, J. De P., . . . , . , . . . Utica, N. Y.

Macfarlane, Wallace, ... 32 Liberty Street, New York City
MacVeagh, Charles, ... 15 Broad Street, " " "
Mallet-Prevost, Severo, ... 30 Broad Street, " " "
Mallinckrodt, Edward, . Mallinckrodt Chemical Works, St. Louis, Mo.
Mansfield, Howard, ... 49 Wall Street, New York City
Mapes, Charles V., . . . 143 Liberty Street, " " "
Markoe, Francis H., . . . 15 E. 49th Street, " " "
Marling, Alfred E., . . . 21 Liberty Street, " " "
Marshall, Charles H., ... 45 William Street, " " "
Marshall, Fielding L., ... 35 Nassau Street, " " "
Marshall, Harford, . . District Attorney's Office, " " "
Marshall, Louis, ... 30 Broad Street, " " "
Marsters, A., A., ... 125 Milk Street, Boston, Mass.
Martin, John, ... Grymes Hill, Staten Island, N. Y.
Martin, Newell, ... 25 Broad Street, New York City
Martin, T. Comerford, . . . 114 Liberty Street, " " "
Mason, Alexander T., ... 13 William Street, " " "
Mason, Alfred Bishop, ... Apartado 130, City of Mexico
Masten, Arthur H., ... 49 Wall Street, New York City
Matthew, William B., . . . 319 W. 112th Street, " " "
Mathews, Robert, ... 135 Spring Street, Rochester, N. Y.
Mathews W. K., ... 36 Wall Street, New York City
Matthews, Brander, . . . 681 West End Avenue, " " "
Matthewson, Arthur, ... South Woodstock, Conn.
Maxwell, William H., ... 500 Park Avenue, New York City
Meacham, Alfred B , ... 59 Wall Street, " " "
Medina, J. L., ... 2 Stone Street, " " "
Mechan, Thomas J., ... 38 Park Row " " "
Mellen, Chase, ... 52 William Street, " " "
Merck, George, ... 15 University Place, New York City
Merrill, Charles E., ... 44 E. 23d Street, " " "
Merrill, Payson, ... 31 Nassau Street, " " "
Meyer, Adolph, ... 35 Mount Morris Park, " " "

Meyer, Alfred, ... 785 Madison Avenue, New York City
Milbank, Albert G., , , . . . 49 Wall Street. " " "
Milburn, John G., ... 54 Wall Street, " " "
Miller, Clifford L., ... 62 West 89th Street, " " "
Miller, George Douglas, . . . 125 State Street, Albany, N. Y.
Miller, Hoffman, ... 80 Broadway, New York City
Mills, L. H., ... 473 Broome Street, . " " "
Mitchell, Edward, ... 44 Wall Street, " " "
Moffat, George B., ... 1 Nassau Street, " " "
Moffat, R. Burnham, ... 63 Wall Street, " " "
Montgomery, Robert H., . . , . 165 Broadway, " " "
Montgomery, R. M., ... 51 Wall Street, " " "
Moore, W. H. H., ... Box 402, " " "
Morris, Ray, ... 81 Fulton Street, " " "
Morrow, Dwight, , ... Englewood, N. J.
Morse, Horace J., ... 820 St. Mark's Avenue, Brooklyn
Morse, Richard C., ... 35 Sidney Place, "
Mortimer, Richard, ... 11 Wall Street, New York City
Mosenthal, P. J., ... 95 William Street, " " "
Mosle, A. Henry, ... 30 Broad Street, " " "
Mott, William F., ... Toms River, N. J
Munro, J. G., . . . 61 Erie County Bank Building, Buffalo. N. Y.
Munro, John R., ... 132 Remsen Street. Brooklyn. N. Y.
Munroe, Vernon, ... 45 William Street, New York City
Murphy, Daniel F., . . . Criminal Court Building, " " "
Murray, James B., ... 23 Belmont Terrace, Yonkers, "
Murray, Joseph K., . . ., . 90 Wall Street, New York City
McAlpin, George L., ... 55 W. 33d Street, " " "
McCagg, Louis Butler, . . . 18 E. 84th Street, " " "
McCandless, Charles W., . . . 60 Wall Street, " " "
McCook, Philip J., ... 15 William Street, " " "
McDowell, H. G., ... 87 Nassau Street, " " "
McGinness. Remsen, ... 42 East 41st Street, " " "
McKeen, James, ... 58 Clark Street, Brooklyn
McKeever, J. Lawrence, . . . 164 Lexington Avenue, New York City
McMahon, Fulton. . . . . 54 William Street. " " "

Nadal, Charles C , ... 142 E. 35th Street, New York City
Nash, Francis Philip, ... Geneva, N. Y.
Naumberg, Elkan, ... 48 W. 58th Street, New York City
Naumberg, George W., . . . 33 Wall Street, " " '
Nelson, H. W., Jr., ... Marshfield Hills, Mass.
Nevin, A. Parker, ... 149 Broadway, New York City
Newton Albro J., ... 528 Union Street, Brooklyn, N. Y.
Newton, R. Heber, ... East Hampton, N. Y.
Nichols, George M., . . . 277 Adelphi Street, Brooklyn, N. Y.
Nichols, W. N., ... 25 Broad Street, New York City
Nicoll, James C., ... 51 W. 10th Street, " " "

Nordlinger, Abraham E., . . . 143 West Broadway, New York City
North, Thomas M., . . . 160 Central Park South, " " "
Notman, George, ... 99 John Street, " " "

Oakes, Charles, ... 49 Wall Street, New York City
O'Connor, John A., ... Box H, Tarrytown, N. Y.
Ogden, Rollo, ... 206 Broadway, New York City
Olin, Stephen H., ... 32 Nassau Street, " " "
Olney, Peter B., Jr., ... 68 William Street, " " "
Oltman, H. H., ... 20 Broad Street, " " "
Olyphant, Robert, ... 17 Battery Place, " " "
Opdyke, William S., ... 20 Nassau Street, " " "
Oppenheim, Edward L., . . . 30 Broad Street, " " "
Oppenheimer, Henry S., . . . 741 Madison Avenue, " " "
Orcutt C. Blake, . . . Hudson River Day Line, " " "
Ordway, Edward W., ... 1093 Dean Street, Brooklyn
Orr, Alexander E., ... 102 Remsen Street, "
Osborn, Perry, ... 52 Brattle Street, Cambridge, Mass.
Osborne, Thomas M., ... Auburn, N. Y.

Paffard, Frederic C., ... 238 Clinton Street, Brooklyn, N. Y.
Page, Walter H., ... 34 Union Square, New York City
Parker, Frederick S., ... 32 Garden Place, Brooklyn
Parks, J. Waring, . . . 56 Pine Street, New York City
Parsons, Herbert, . . . 52 William Street, " " "
Parsons, John E., . . . 52 William Street, " " "
Parsons, Ralph S., ... Ossining, N. Y.
Paulding, James Kirk, . . . 130 E. 24th Street, New York City
Pauli, H. G., ... 15 S. William Street, " " "
Peabody, George Foster, . . . 2 Rector Street, " " "
Peck, George G., ... 117 Chambers Street, " " "
Pedesen, James, . . . 20 E. 46th Street, " " "
Pederson, Victor C., . . . 45 W. 9th Street, " " "
Pell, Frederick A., ... Lakewood, N. J.
Pendleton, Francis K., . . . 25 Broad Street, New York City
Perrine, William A., . . . 2440 N. Marshall Street, Philadelphia, Pa.
Phillips, Lee, . . . 438 W. 116th Street, New York City
Phoenix, Phillips, ... 68 Broad Street, " " "
Pierce, Franklin, ... 27 Pine Street, " " "
Pierce, Henry H., . . . 49 Wall Street, " " "
Pierrepont, Henry E., . . . 216 Columbia Heights, Brooklyn
Pierrepont, John J., . . . 66 & 68 Broad Street, New York City
Pierrepont, Robert Low, ... Box 449, Bay Shore, N. Y.
Pinchot, Amos R. E., . . . Criminal Court Building, New York City
Pinchot, Gifford, . . . 1615 Rhode Island Avenue, Washington, D. C.
Plaut, Albert, . . . 120 William Street, New York City
Pollak, Francis D., . . . 49 Wall Street, " " "
Pope, A. A., . . . Box 11, Jerusalem Road, Cohasset, Mass

Pope, George A., ... 926 St. Paul Street, Baltimore, Md.
Potter, Frederick, ... 71 Broadway, New York City
Potter, Henry C., ... 113 W. 40th Street, " " "
Potts, William, ... 7 W. 43rd Street, " " "
Powell, Wilson M., Jr., . . . 29 Wall Street. " " "
Pratt, Frederic B., ... Pratt Institute, Brooklyn, N. Y.
Prentice, William P., ... 52 Broadway, New York City
Prentiss, George H., . . . 108 Pierrepont Street, Brooklyn, N Y.
Price, Joseph M., ... 158 West Broadway, New York City
Proskauer, Joseph M , ... 170 Broadway, " " "
Pryer, Charles, ... New Rochelle, N. Y.
Pryor, James W., ... 99 Nassau Street, New York City
Putnam, George Haven, . . . 27 W. 23d Street, " " "
Putnam, George P., ... 160 Fifth Avenue, " " "
Putnam, Harrington, ... 404 Washington Avenue, Brooklyn
Putnam, Irving, ... 27 W. 23rd Street, New York City
Pyne, Moses Taylor, ... 30 Pine Street, " " "

Rand, William H., Jr. . . . . 63 Wall Street, New York City
Raven, A. A., ... 51 Wall Street, " " "
Raymond, Charles H., ... 11 Pine Street, " " "
Raymond, Rossiter W. . . . . 123 Henry Street, Brooklyn, N. Y.
Read, J. Sturdivant, ... 228 Clinton Street. " "
Reichhelm, Edward P., . . . 90 West 34th Street, Bayonne, N. J.
Reid, Wallace, ... 56 Maiden Lane, New York City
Reynolds, James B., ... 55 W. 44th Street, " " "
Rice, Edwin T., Jr., ... 59 Wall Street, " " "
Richards, C. A. L., . . 169 Power Street, Providence, R. I.
Richards, William R., . . . 14 E. 37th Street, New York City
Rives, George L., ... 14 W. 38th Street. " " "
Robb, J. Hampden, ... 23 Park Avenue, " " "
Robinson, Beverly R., . . . 42 W. 37th Street, " " "
Robinson, Moncure, ... 7 E. 42d Street. " " "
Roome, W. Harris, ... 287 Fourth Avenue, " " "
Roosevelt, Franklin D., . . . 125 E 36th Street, " " "
Roosevelt, Theodore, ... Oyster Bay, N. Y.
Root, Elihu, ... State Department, Washington, D. C.
Rose, Arthur P., ... Geneva, N. Y.
Rosendale, Simon W., ... 57 State Street, Albany, N. Y.
Rosenfeld, George, ... 58 New Street, New York City
Rounds, Arthur C., ... 96 Broadway, " " "
Rowe, William V., ... 51 Wall Street, " " "
Rublee, George, ... 15 Broad Street, " " "
Russell, J. Townsend, . . . 170 Remsen Street, Brooklyn, N. Y.

Sachs, Walter E., ... 43 Exchange Place, New York City
Sackett, Henry W., ... 154 Nassau Street, " " "
Sage, Dean, ... 49 Wall Street, " " "

Salomon, William, ... 25 Broad Street, New York City
Sand, Henry A. L., ... 120 Broadway, " " "
Sanger, William Cary, ... Sangerfield, N. Y.
Sayer, W. Murray, Jr., . . . 398 Washington Avenue, Brooklyn
Schafer, Samuel M., ... 35 Wall Street, New York City
Scharmann, Hermann B., . . 170 W. 59th Street, " " "
Schieren, Charles A. . . . . . 405 Clinton Avenue, Brooklyn
Schnakenberg, D., ... 6 Hanover Street, New York City
Schneidenbach, Arthur Jaques, . . 75 E. 82d Street, " " "
Schrader, George H. F., ... 32 Rose Street, " "
Schurman, George W., . . . 15 W. 57th Street, " " "
Schurz, Carl Lincoln, ... 49 Wall Street, " " "
Scott, J. F., ... 40 Greenridge Avenue, White Plains, N. Y.
Scott, William, ... 25 Duane Street, New York City
Scribner, Arthur H., ... 153 Fifth Avenue, " " "
Scribner, Charles, ... 153 Fifth Avenue, " " "
Seaman, Louis L., ... 247 Fifth Avenue, " " "
Searle, Arthur, ... 41 Concord Avenue, Cambridge, Mass.
Seaver, Benjamin F., ... 111 Pierrepont Street, Brooklyn
Seaver, Oscar S., ... 35 E. 31st Street, New York City
Sedgwick, Arthur G., ... 52 William Street, " " "
Sedgwick, Ellery, ... 1020 Park Avenue, " " "
Sedgwick, Henry D., ... 120 E. 22d Street, " " "
Seligman, E. R. A., ... 324 W. 86th Street, " " "
Seligman, Jefferson, ... 15 Broad Street, " " "
Serven, A. Ralph, . . . 1419 "F" Street, N. W., Washington, D. C.
Seward George F., ... 97 Cedar Street, New York City
Sexton, Lawrence E., ... 34 Pine Street, " " "
Seymour, Origen S., ... 54 William Street, " " "
Shainwald, Ralph L., ... 100 William Street, " " "
Shaw, Albert, ... 13 Astor Place, " " "
Sheldon, Edward W., ... 45 Wall Street, " " "
Sheppard, John S., Jr., ... 26 Liberty Street, " " "
Shillaber, William Jr., ... 1 Broadway, " " "
Shortt, W. A., ... 32 Broadway, " " "
Siedenberg, Reinhard, ... Cotton Exchange, " " "
Silverman, M. J., ... 218 Alexander Avenue, " " "
Simes, William, ... Box 3084, Boston, Mass.
Sinclair, John, ... 16 E. 66th Street, New York City
Skillin, Augustus H., ... 34 Pine Street, " " "
Skuse, Thomas J, . . Naval Office, Customs House, " " "
Slade Francis Louis, ... 49 Cedar Street, " " "
Sleicher, John A., ... 225 Fifth Avenue, " " "
Slicer, Thomas R., ... 156 E. 38th Street, " " "
Smillie, James D., ... 440 West End Avenue, " " "
Smith, Adelbert J., ... 15 William Street, " " "
Smith, Bryan H., . . . Brooklyn Savings Bank, Brookly
Smith, Charles Robinson, . . . 25 Broad Street, New

Smith, Charles Stewart,   25 W. 47th Street, New York City
Smith, Clarence B.,   71 E. 87th Street,   "   "   "
Smith, F. Hopkinson,   150 E. 34th Street, "   "   "
Smith, Frederick J.,   278 Mulberry Street, "   "   "
Smith, Howard M,   Brevoort Savings Bank. Brooklyn, N. Y.
Smith, James E.,   38 Park Row, New York City
Smith, William Alexander,   412 Madison Avenue, "   "   "
Smyth, Nathan A.,   Criminal Court Building, "   "   "
Southard, George H., Jr.,   164 Montague Street, Brooklyn, N. Y.
Spiegelberg, Frederick,   36 W. 76th Street, New York City
Stedman, Edmund C.,   2643 Broadway,   "   "   "
Steers, James R.,   31 Nassau Street,   "   "   "
Steinway, Frederick T.,   53rd Street and Park Avenue, " " "
Stern, Benjamin,   32 W. 23rd Street,   "   "   "
Stern, Henry Root,   40 Wall Street.   "   "   "
Stewart, William R.,   31 Nassau Street,   "   "   "
Stimson, Daniel M.,   28 W. 37th Street,   "   "   "
Stokes, Anson Phelps, Jr., (Life),   Yale University, New Haven, Conn.
Stokes, Harold M. Phelps, (Life),   229 Madison Avenue, New York City
Stokes, I. N. Phelps, (Life),   229 Madison Avenue, "   "   "
Stokes. James,   49 Cedar Street,   "   "   "
Stokes. J. G. Phelps, (Life),   229 Madison Avenue, "   "   "
Strasbourger, Samuel,   74 Broadway,   "   "   "
Strauss, Albert,   15 Broad Street,   "   "   "
Strauss. Frederick,   15 Broad Street,   "   "   "
Strong, George A.,   50 Wall Street,   "   "   "
Strong, Theron G.,   49 Wall Street,   "   "   "
Sturges, S. Perry,   305 Washington Avenue, Brooklyn
Sturgis, F. K.,   36 Broad Street, New York City
Sturgis, Russell,   307 E. 17th Street, "   "   "
Stuyvesant, Rutherford,   32 Liberty Street,   "   "   "
Sulzberger, Cyrus L.,   516 West End Avenue, "   "   "
Sulzberger, Ferdinand,   802 First Avenue,   "   "   "
Symonds, Joseph H. A,   Criminal Court Building, " " "

Taft, Henry W.,   40 Wall Street, New York City
Taggart, Rush,   195 Broadway,   "   "   "
Tappan, J. B. Coles,   49 Wall Street,   "   "   "
Tatham, Charles,   465 W. 23rd Street, "   "   "
Tatham, Edwin,   82 Beekman Street,   "   "   "
Taussig, Walter M.,   9-15 Murray Street, "   "   "
Taylor, E. P., Jr.,   25 Pine Street,   "   "   "
Taylor, Thomas Fenton,   130 E. 67th Street, "   "   "
Taylor, Walter F.,   54 Wall Street,   "   "   "
Taylor, William C.,   25 So. Portland Avenue, Brooklyn
Terry, Roderick,   169 Madison Avenue, New York City
Terry, Seth Sprague,   126 E. 34th Street, "   "   "
       go O.,   2 E. 86th Street,   "   "   "

Thacher, Thomas,	62 Cedar Street, New York City
Thacher, Thomas, Jr.,	U. S District Attorney's Office, " " "
Thatcher, John S ,	839 Madison Avenue. " " "
Thomson, George G ,	412 Bergen Street, Brooklyn, N. Y.
Thorne, Robert,	30 Broad Street, New York City
Thomas, John H.,	9 Broadway. " " "
Thorne, Samuel, Jr.,	43 Cedar Street, " " "
Thornton, William,	117 Prince Street, " " "
Thurber, Francis B.,	90 West Broadway, " " "
Tiebout, Charles H.,	31 Grand Street. Brooklyn
Tinker, Edward L.,	Criminal Court Building, New York City
Tinkham, Julian R.,	42 Broadway, " " "
Tison, Alexander.	11 William Street, " " "
Tod, J. Kennedy,	5 Nassau Street, " " "
Todd, Henry A.,	824 West End Avenue, " " "
Tomkins, Calvin,	17 Battery Place, " " "
Tompkins, Hamilton B.,	229 Broadway, " " "
Train, Arthur C.,	Criminal Court Building, " " "
Trotter, William,	124 E. 30th Street, " " "
Trowbridge, Mason.	Criminal Court Building. " " "
Tuckerman, Alfred,	1123 Broadway, " " "
Tuckerman, Eliot,	44 Pine Street, " " "
Turnbull, George R..	33 Mercer Street, " " "
Unckles, D. S.,	957 St. Mark's Avenue, Brooklyn
Vail, Charles D.,	Geneva, N. Y.
Valentine, Charles A.,	1 E. 27th Street. New York City
Valentine, Henry C., (Life),	257 Broadway, " " "
Valentine, Robert G.	Office of Indian Affairs, Washington, D. C.
Van Dusen, Samuel C.,	27 Cliff Street, " " "
Van Ingen, Edward H.,	9 E. 71st Street, " " "
Van Nest, George W.,	20 Broad Street, " " "
Van Santvoord, R.,	10 W. 122nd Street, " " "
Vidal, J. E ,	68 Beach Street, Stapleton, S. I.
Villard, Harold G.	43 Cedar Street, New York City
Villard, Oswald Garrison, (Life),	206 Broadway, " " "
Wadsworth, James W.,	Geneseo, N. Y.
Wagener, August P.,	51 Chambers Street, New York City
Walker, John,	1231 Western Avenue, Alleghany City, Pa.
Walker, William,	Harbison & Walker, Pittsburg, Pa.
Wallace, William H.,	66 Broadway, New York City
Wallace, W. J.,	209 W. 81st Street, " " "
Walling, William English,	8 Fifth Avenue, " " "
Warburg, F. M., (Life),	52 William Street, " " "
Ward, Henry Galbreath,	79 Wall Street, " " "

Ward, J. Q. A.,	119 W. 52nd Street, New York City
Warren, George A.,	1118 20th Street, N. W., Washington, D. C.
Warren, H. Langford,	120 Boylston Street, Boston, Mass.
Watson, Charles W.,	500 Madison Avenue, " " "
Webb, Willoughby L.,	63 Wall Street, " " "
Weed, John W.,	62 William Street, " " "
Weeks, E R.,	3408 Harrison Street, Kansas City, Mo
Weeks, John E.,	46 E. 57th Street, New York City
Welch, Archibald A.,	Woodland Street, Hartford, Conn
Weld, Francis M.,	5 Nassau Street, New York City
Welling, R. W. G.,	2 Wall Street, " " "
Werthein, H. P.,	27 William Street, " " "
Wetmore, Edmund,	34 Pine Street, " " "
Wheeler, Everett P.,	21 State Street, " " "
Wheeler, James R.,	Columbia College, " " "
White, Alexander M.,	52 Remsen Street, Brooklyn
White, Andrew D., (Life).	Ithaca, N Y.
Whiteside, George W.,	District Attorney's Office, New York City
Whiton, John M,	73 Williams Street, " " "
Whitney, Edward B.,	26 Liberty Street, " " "
Whitridge, Frederick W.,	59 Wall Street, " " "
Wickersham, C. W.,	Hastings Hall, Cambridge, Mass
Wickersham, George W.,	40 Wall Street. New York City
Wilcox, Ansley,	295 Main Street, Buffalo, N. Y.
Wilder, William R.,	45 Cedar Street, New York City
Wilds, Howard Payson,	University Club, " " "
Williams, L. L.,	Care E C Williams, 135 Broadway, " " "
Williams, Norman A.,	42 E. 41st Street, " " "
Williams, Perry P.,	Produce Exchange, " " "
Williams, Richard H.,	1 Broadway. " " "
Williams, Roger H.,	31 W. 12th Street, " " "
Williams, Stephen G.,	953 Madison Avenue, " " "
Williams, William,	35 Wall Street. " " "
Willis, Albert L.,	124 W. 183rd Street, " " "
Wilson, George Augustus,	37 Liberty Street, " " "
Wilson, Richard T.,	511 Fifth Avenue, " " "
Winston, G. Owen,	936 Broadway, " " "
Winters, Joseph E.,	25 W. 37th Street, " " "
Winters, Byram M.,	Manoca Temple, Waverly, N Y.
Winthrop, Bronson,	32 Liberty Street, New York City
Wise, B. E.,	21 Broad Street, " " "
Wisner, Charles,	Cotton Exchange, " " "
Wisner, H. G,	18 W. 12th Street, " " "
Witherbee F. S.,	71 Broadway, " " "
Wolff. Lewis S.,	12 E. 70th Street, " " "
Woodbridge, Charles E.,	8 Bridge Street, " " "
Worcester, Edwin D., Jr.,	35 Nassau Street, " " "
Wright, Jonathan,	44 W. 49th Street, " " "

Yates, Arthur G., . . . 130 So. Fitzhugh Street, Rochester, N.Y.
Yongo, Henry, ... 169 Columbia Heights, Brooklyn

Zabriskie, George, ... 49 Wall Street, New York City
Zerega, Richard A., ... 101 Classon Avenue, Brooklyn
Ziegel, H. Fred Lange, . . . 218 W. 14th Street, New York City

ARTICLES OF INCORPORATION

OF

THE NEW YORK CIVIL SERVICE REFORM ASSOCIATION

[Filed May 11, 1900.]

KNOW ALL MEN BY THESE PRESENTS: That we, the undersigned, being persons of full age and all citizens of the United States, a majority of whom are also citizens of the State of New York, and being now Directors of an unincorporated association known as the New York Civil Service Reform Association, and organized for the purposes hereinafter mentioned; being desirous of incorporation for the same purposes under the Membership Corporations Law of the State of New York, do hereby, pursuant to unanimous vote of all the members of the said Association, present and voting at a regularly called meeting thereof, and pursuant to authority given by the said unanimous vote at the said meeting, of which meeting notice of the intention so to incorporate was given personally or by mail to each member of such Association whose residence or Post Office address was known, at least thirty days before said meeting, and at which meeting the corporate name stated in paragraph First was by unanimous vote adopted, do hereby certify as follows

FIRST.—The name or title by which the Association in which we desire to form ourselves as aforesaid shall be known in law, shall be the Civil Service Reform Association.

SECOND.—The territory in which its operations are to be principally conducted shall be the City of New York.

THIRD.—The city in which its principal office is to be located is the City of New York.

FOURTH.—The objects of the Association shall be to further the establishment of a system of appointment, promotion and removal in the civil service, founded upon the principle that public office is a public trust, admission to and retention in which should depend upon proven fitness; and to take such action as may tend to secure the honest and efficient execution of laws and rules relating to the civil service, and to the proper administration thereof.

FIFTH.—The number of its directors shall be twenty-eight.

SIXTH.—The names of the persons to be its directors until its first annual meeting are as follows :

Samuel P. Avery, Truman J. Backus, Henry De Forest Baldwin, Edward Cary, Charles Collins, W. Bayard Cutting, Horace E. Deming, A. S. Frissell, Richard Watson Gilder, Edwin L. Godkin, J. Warren Greene, George McAneny, James McKeen, Jacob F. Miller, Samuel H. Ordway, William A. Perrine, George Foster Peabody, William J. Schieffelin, Carl Schurz, Charles A. Schieren, Thomas R. Slicer, Henry Sanger Snow, Anson Phelps Stokes, S. Perry Sturges, Henry W. Taft, William H. Thomson, Charles W. Watson and Everett P. Wheeler.

In WITNESS WHEREOF we have made, signed, acknowledged and filed this certificate in duplicate.

Dated this Eighth day of May, 1900.

<blockquote>
C. SCHURZ,
JACOB F. MILLER,
ANSON PHELPS STOKES,
EVERETT P. WHEELER,
CHARLES COLLINS,
SAMUEL H. ORDWAY,
J. WARREN GREENE,

WILLIAM H. THOMSON,
A. S. FRISSELL,
GEORGE MCANENY,
CHARLES A. SCHIEREN,
SAMUEL P. AVERY,
GEORGE FOSTER PEABODY.
</blockquote>

STATE OF NEW YORK, } ss.
COUNTY OF NEW YORK, }

On this eighth day of May, one thousand and nine hundred, before me personally came Carl Schurz, Jacob F. Miller, Anson Phelps Stokes, Everett P. Wheeler, Charles Collins, J. Warren Greene, William H. Thomson, Samuel H. Ordway, A. S. Frissell, George McAneny, Charles A. Schieren, Samuel P. Avery and George Foster Peabody, to me personally known to be the persons described in and who made and signed the foregoing certificate, and severally duly acknowledged to me that they had made, signed and executed the same for the uses and purposes therein set forth.

<blockquote>
F. W. HOERSCHGEN,
Notary Public, Kings County. (149)
(Certificate filed in New York County.)
</blockquote>

Approved, May 9, 1900.

<blockquote>
DAVID LEVINTRITT,
Justice of the Supreme Court of the State of New York.
</blockquote>

REPORT

OF THE

Executive Committee

OF THE

New York

Civil Service Reform Association

READ AT THE ANNUAL MEETING, MAY 12, 1909.

LIST OF MEMBERS, ETC.

NEW YORK
PUBLISHED FOR THE
CIVIL SERVICE REFORM ASSOCIATION
79 WALL STREET
1909

CONTENTS

Annual Report of the Executive Committee - 5
Annual Report of the Treasurer - - - 23
Constitution and By Laws - - - . 25
Roll of Officers and Members - - - - 33
Articles of Incorporation - - - - - 55

ANNUAL REPORT

OF THE

Executive Committee of the Civil Service Reform Association.

The election of President Taft and the re-election of Governor Hughes, pronounced advocates, both in and out of office, of the merit system, insured continued progress for civil service reform in nation and state. In the past twelve months covered by this report there have been important extensions in both jurisdictions and, as a result of the attitude of the national and state administrations, the civil service laws have been better enforced and the merit principle has received wider acceptance.

Before proceeding to review the work of the Association during the year, we desire to record our deep regret at the loss of such staunch supporters of the merit system and former members of the Association as Grover Cleveland, Bishop Henry C. Potter and William Potts.

THE FEDERAL SERVICE

A complete review of the progress of civil service reform under President Roosevelt was presented in President Choate's address before the National Civil Service Reform League at its annual meeting in Pittsburgh last December. Since the classification of the fourth-class postmasters in all states north of the Ohio and east of the Mississippi on December 1, 1908, and the adoption of regulations to govern the appointments on January 20, 1909, no important changes in the federal service have taken place.

THE UNITED STATES COMMISSION

The change in the national administration has brought about one change in the personnel of the United States Civil Service Commission. The resignation of Commissioner Henry F. Greene took effect on May 1, and he has been succeeded by James T. Williams of South Carolina. During his six years of service on the Commission, Mr. Greene had shown himself at all times in thorough accord with the principles upon which the law is based, and had been a constant advocate of enforcement and extension. Mr. Williams is a young newspaper man who served for a time as Secretary to the Chairman of the Republican National Committee and later accompanied President Taft on his campaign tour. He is without previous experience in civil service reform work, but the appointment is understood to be a personal selection by President Taft and we are assured that the new commissioner will be found to be in entire sympathy with the reform.

THE CENSUS BILL

Last year every member of the Association was asked to write his senators and representative in Congress to vote against the clause in the bill for the taking of the census of 1910 providing for the appointment of the additional clerical force, on the recommendation of senators and representatives, after non-competitive examination. The failure of the bill to pass in 1908; its subsequent passage in the early part of 1909 and the veto of President Roosevelt on February 5, are past history; but the subsequent course of census legislation is not so well known. At the opening of the special session called for the purpose of revising the tariff, a new census bill providing for appointment of the additional force after *competitive* examination was introduced and immediately passed the House. The Senate amended the bill further to safeguard competition and to regulate the apportionment of appointments under the civil service law. The conference committee, at the request of the House conferees, struck out the amendment in regard to the apportionment, on the ground that it was an attempt to amend the general law through a special act, and, because of this action, the report of the conference committee was rejected in the Senate and sent back. As the House is not disposed to consent to this amendment, the bill will in all probability remain in committee until the tariff legislation is disposed of.

THE STATE SERVICE

THE CAMPAIGN

In the state campaign which resulted in the election of Governor Hughes, civil service reform was not an issue. The Republican platform was silent on the subject; the Democratic platform demanded the enforcement of the law. Both candidates for Governor thoroughly endorsed the merit system. • The Association addressed letters to candidates of both parties for Senate and Assembly asking them to state their attitude upon the proposed constitutional amendment granting to Spanish War veterans a ten per cent preference in rating in civil service examinations. The Association also called the attention of heads of departments to the provision of the civil service law prohibiting political assessments and sent notices to be posted in the offices. Governor Hughes issued a warning against violations of this provision, and the State Commission sent out a circular requesting information as to violations. A few cases were brought to light, in one of which the evidence was sufficient to warrant the presentation of the matter to the District Attorney of Monroe County for prosecution.

THE STATE CIVIL SERVICE COMMISSION

The personnel of the State Civil Service Commission remains the same as for several years past. The President is Hon. Charles F. Milliken of Canandaigua, the other Republican member is Hon. Roscoe C. E. Brown of

New York and the minority member is Hon. John E. Kraft of Kingston. All three are newspaper editors. Through this composition the Commission loses the decided advantage of having a lawyer as a member of the board to aid in the solution of the many legal problems which must inevitably arise in the construction and enforcement of the civil service law and rules. As none of the commissioners is resident in Albany and all are actively engaged in private business in places at a considerable distance from the Capital, the executive direction of the office work has been confided to the secretary and chief examiner.

REORGANIZATION OF POSITIONS IN THE OFFICE

In March Mr. Charles S. Fowler, who had been the Chief Examiner of the State Commission since 1896, resigned to become a Deputy Superintendent of the Insurance Department. Mr. Fowler was originally selected through competitive examination. In addition to being a graduate of Cornell, Mr. Fowler had received a legal training and in the discharge of his duties during his thirteen years of service showed great ability in conducting the work of this most important division of the Commission's duties.

In anticipation of a new appointment, the Commission secured the introduction of a bill amending the civil service law so as to make the secretary the chief executive officer under the Commission. In so doing they struck out the clause providing for a chief examiner at a fixed salary of $3,600. The object was to avoid the possibility of future conflict of authority between the chief examiner and the secretary. To correspond with this bill the appropriation bill carried an increase in the salary of the secretary to $4,000, and reduced the salary of the chief examiner to $3,000.

To your Committee this seemed a serious error in judgment. The chief examiner is the key to the success of the Commission's work. His position and salary should not be subject to the annual whims of an appropriation committee. The position requires the services of an expert and a man of high educational attainments. To subordinate the position to that of the secretary, who need not and, in the long run, will not possess these qualifications is to degrade the chief examinership and make it less attractive to the right kind of candidates.

These arguments were presented to the Commission. It was pointed out that by regulation, and without amendment to the law, the Commission could fix authority as they saw fit, and that in other commissions the possibility of conflict was met by the commission itself, or its president, taking executive control of the office. This plan would require more frequent meetings or the residence of the President in Albany, but the Association has been urging these changes for some years past. As the Commission was unwilling to withdraw its bill, a memorandum in opposition to it has been filed by the Association with the Governor who has not acted upon it as yet. If the bill is signed we fear difficulty in securing a properly qualified person to fill the chief examinership.

CONFERENCE OF CIVIL SERVICE COMMISSIONERS

At the invitation of the State Commission, the second conference of representatives of civil service commissions throughout the State was held in Albany, October 1 and 2. Practical questions of administration were discussed and, before adjourning, the conference adopted a resolution in favor of fixed terms of office for civil service commissioners, so arranged that the terms should overlap, in order that the commission should be a continuous body. These conferences are of great value in standardizing the examinations and bringing about uniformity in the enforcement of the law.

RECLASSIFICATION

The State Commission took action in December, 1907, looking to a reclassification and a reduction in the number of positions in the exempt class. Its work was finished last August and received the approval of the Governor, with but slight changes, on December 28th. A number of positions paid wholly by fees were dropped from the classification altogether. Thirty-nine positions in the state service and 131 in the county services were transferred from the exempt to the competitive class. Commissioner Kraft opposed 24 out of the 39 transfers in the state service, and 106 out of the 131 in the county services. One hundred and forty-six positions were transferred from the non-competitive to the competitive class.

Full credit should be given to the Commission,—or, in this case, to Commissioners Milliken and Brown,—for this progressive action. The result is to leave 650 positions in the state service exempt and, approximately, 4,000 competitive. In the state and county services combined there remain 1,182 exempt positions.

With the approval of the Governor the State Commission has extended the competitive classification to the position of county superintendent of highways in all counties of the state, thus establishing a new precedent for extension to particular positions instead of by civil divisions. It has, in addition, decided, subject to the approval of the Governor, to extend the classification to the counties of Niagara, Oneida, Orange, Oswego and Ulster.

INVESTIGATIONS

The Commission during the past twelve months has, through its own members and its secretary and chief examiner, inspected the methods of administration of the municipal commissions in twenty-one cities. The need for such investigations is strikingly shown by the case of Plattsburg, where the representatives of the State Commission found that the municipal commission had held no meetings and conducted no examinations in the course of a year. The failure to secure results in small cities is more often due to ignorance of methods of administration than to bad intentions. There are 48 cities in the state all subject to the civil service law and possessing local commissions. This Association would be glad to see the State Commission in a position to make inspections of the work in all cities at least once a year.

ADMINISTRATIVE METHODS OF STATE COMMISSION

Since the passage of the White Law in 1899, the duties and responsibilities of the State Commission have largely increased. The efficiency and success of the work of municipal commissions is dependent to a large extent upon the State Commission, for no change, however slight, in rules or classification can be made without the consent of the State Commission, and the municipal commission in all it does is subject to the supervision and investigation of the State Commission. This plan leads to uniformity and stability and prevents the upsetting of the local service with a change of administration.

We submit, however, that in order to avoid hampering the work of local commissions, and in order to meet its increased responsibilities, the State Commission should hold more frequent meetings, and we renew our previous recommendation that there should be a President residing in Albany to take executive control of the work. The Commission is by law required to meet at least once a month in Albany, except in August. In 1905 it held 16 meetings, in 1906 13 meetings, in 1907 16 meetings. During the past twelve months it has held 19 meetings.

The Commission has no fixed dates for its Albany meetings, but meetings are held to suit the convenience of the commissioners. No notice of matters to come before the meeting is published, and frequently local commissions have only a few days' notice before a meeting is held. The time is often inadequate to get important matters approved by the mayor and arrange for the appearance of the officials interested. Moreover, the State Commission seldom acts on an important matter at the same meeting at which it is presented, but it is laid over for further consideration at the next meeting. This almost invariably means a delay of from two weeks to a month. In this connection some comparisons with the practice of other commissions is valuable.

The New York City Commission holds stated meetings on Wednesday morning of each week. All matters involving change of rules or classification are set down for public hearing and are advertised in advance in the *City Record*. It holds such additional meetings as it finds necessary and publishes its minutes. Its president is in executive control of the office work and visits the office daily. In the last twelve months 54 meetings have been held.

The New Jersey State Commission meets once a week.

The Massachusetts Commission holds stated meetings on Tuesday and Friday afternoons of each week, and on Monday, Wednesday and Thursday one of the commissioners visits the office. In 1908 there were 99 regular meetings and at least one commissioner was in attendance at the office on 86 other days.

The Chicago Commission holds regular meetings every Monday, Wednesday and Friday, and special meetings are frequently held on Tuesday and Thursday. The president devotes all of his time to the work of the Commission. During 1908, 194 meetings were held.

The delay in the determination of executive matters which may result from the custom of the State Commission of holding meetings only at long intervals and laying things over from meeting to meeting is strikingly exemplified in the case of the investigation of the Finance Department in New York City:

The Association's letter specifying the abuses and requesting a general investigation was sent under date of July 1. The first meeting held thereafter was on July 31, when a reply by the Deputy Comptroller was presented by counsel. Action was postponed to August 13.

On August 13, the Commission met

City. The Comptroller was present and argued for dismissal. Action was postponed in order to permit the Comptroller to file a further answer.

The Commission met again on September 17. The Comptroller's answer was presented. Action was postponed until the next meeting.

On October 7 the Commission voted to conduct an investigation.

On November 13 Secretary Birdseye came to New York City to investigate records and witnesses.

On December 3 the Commission began taking testimony, continued the hearing on the next day and completed the taking of testimony on December 9.

The report was published on January 11, six months after the presentation of the complaint.

INVESTIGATION OF THE FINANCE DEPARTMENT.

The request of the New York Association that the State Commission should investigate the administration of the civil service law and rules in the Department of Finance, New York City, was based on specifications showing:

(1) That of 63 appointments by the Comptroller to exempt positions, 54 of the appointees were enrolled as Democrats, of whom 42 resided in Brooklyn, and 5 were district leaders. Appointment for political considerations is a violation of section 24 of the civil service law.
(2) That 144 persons had been appointed as "expert searchers" without examination under pretense that the work was temporary, expert in character, and had to be carried on at night. Political appointments had been made to these positions. The work required of these men was, in fact, of a simple, clerical character, little night work had been demanded, the employment had continued over a year, and the work was not completed.
(3) That 11 cashiers had been illegally transferred from the exempt class to competitive positions, and the vacancies thus created had been filled by political appointees without examination.
(4) That certain removals had been made for political reasons.

ation of witnesses, Mr. Joseph P. Cotton, Jr., of the Law Committee, acted as counsel for the Association, and every opportunity was given to him, as well as to counsel for the Comptroller, to cross-examine. The Comptroller himself was frank in admitting appointments on party recommendations. The testimony fully bore out the allegations of the Association in regard to the appointments of "expert searchers" and cashiers, and indicated that political considerations had weight in the matter of the removals. The report of the Commission, however, was a compromise.

Commissioners Milliken and Brown signed the report. Commissioner Kraft, the minority member, made a dissenting report exonerating the Comptroller altogether. The majority report was interpreted by the newspapers at will for one side or the other on every question considered. In the face of the records and testimony as to political appointments to exempt places, the report excused the Comptroller on the ground that many other heads of departments, both in the state and city service, were doing the same thing. For the appointments without examination of expert searchers and cashiers no one was to be dismissed or reprimanded, but the Commission proposed, as a panacea, a thorough investigation and reclassification of positions in the Comptroller's office by the Municipal Commission. This, while of undoubted advantage for the future, and therefore having the support of the Association, will result at present in "covering in" to the competitive class without examination many whose title to office was seriously questioned in this investigation.

MEASURES IN THE STATE LEGISLATURE

The Association secured the introduction of a number of bills this year designed to strengthen and perfect the civil service law. All the Association's bills, with the exception of one, the purpose of which was to limit the political activity of employees in the classified service, received the endorsement of the State Commission in its last annual report. Only one bill was reported from committee; a bill to grant all municipal commissions the same powers of investigation that are now possessed by the State Commission and by the New York City Commission under the Charter. This passed the Assembly and was favorably reported by the Senate Judiciary Committee, but was defeated on third reading in the Senate, receiving only ten votes in its favor. The Legislature this year did not prove favorably disposed toward bills intended only to improve the public service and limit the scope of patronage.

The Association has pursued its usual course in carefully scrutinizing all bills introduced in the Legislature and filing memoranda with the appropriate committees in the case of all bills affecting the civil service law or its administration. It is too early yet to speak of results as a number of these bills are still awaiting action by the Mayor or Governor. Notable among them is a bill providing for a crude system of retirement on pension of employees of the City of Buffalo which has received the approval of the mayor of that city. Its enactment into law would serve as an unfortunate precedent.

The Constitutional amendment providing for a ten per cent. preference in rating in all civil service examinations for veterans of the Spanish War, the Philippine Insurrection and the Boxer Uprising, which came so close to passage last year, was not reported from committee in either house during the last session. Hearings were held before both committees at which, in addition to the President of the Buffalo Association and the Secretary of the New York Association, representatives of the State and New York City Commissions and of the civil employees in New York and Buffalo appeared in opposition.

PROPOSED NEW CHARTER FOR NEW YORK CITY

At the request of Commissioner McAneny, of the New York Charter Commission, the Association, through its Law Committee, prepared and submitted a number of amendments to the charter, almost all of which were accepted by the Commission. The Law Committee was then requested by the Chairman of the Charter Commission to draft a civil service chapter for the new charter, including therein all the scattered civil service provisions of the present charter which it considered desirable to retain. This was also done; but the Legislature failed to act on the charter after it was introduced.

NEW YORK CITY

THE MUNICIPAL CIVIL SERVICE COMMISSION

No change has been made in the Municipal Commission. The results of more than a year's work under the presidency of Hon. Frank L. Polk, who succeeded President Baker as executive head of the Commission in January, 1908, show steadily increased efficiency and an ability to cope with new problems. The fullest publicity is given to all that the Commission does or proposes to do.

NEW PROMOTION BUREAU

There is no more difficult problem in the administration of the civil service system than the question how to regulate promotions so as to exclude politics and at the same time get the best results. Some of those who heartily subscribe to the principle of competition for original appointment believe that this principle cannot be practically applied in selecting candidates for promotion, because so much depends on the spirit and manner in which the candidate performs his work. Nevertheless, the New York Constitution provides for competitive promotions and the civil service law requires that the examination shall take into account the record of performance of duty and seniority of service as well as the rating on written papers.

The Commission has done what it proper grading of salaries as a neces lated promotions. In view of the difficulty encountered in securing proper records of efficiency and conduct from the departments, the Commission established a promotion bureau and placed in charge one of its ablest examiners, Mr. Thomas C. Murray. Mr. Murray revised the rules governing the keeping of efficiency records, called together all the department officers engaged in marking efficiency and thoroughly explained the system to them, established standards for marking and provided for boards of promotion in each department in order to secure uniformity in the marking of different bureaus. The Association aided in this work. It is not too much to say that the New York City Commission has done more than any other in the country toward solving the problem of promotion through competition.

FOREMAN AND ASSISTANT FOREMAN MADE COMPETITIVE.

The Commission took another important step to place the service on a higher plane when it adopted the plan, which the Association has been advocating for years past, of transferring the positions of foreman and assistant foreman from the labor to the competitive class. Hitherto assignments to these positions had been matters of favor or political influence. In order to provide against being swamped by the number of candidates in open competitive examination for these positions, the Commission has arranged for the filling of these positions by promotion from laborer, under proper safeguards. In certain other cases the Commission, in its discretion, allows promotion from the labor class to the lowest grade of the competitive class after three years of service upon competitive examination and, although this plan has been severely criticised and is open to some theoretical objections, it has worked well in practice.

CLASSIFICATION OF FERRY SERVICE

A further improvement was made by transferring pilots from the non-competitive to the competitive class.

The new municipal ferry service has been graded to provide for promotions, and the Commission now proposes to classify as competitive the positions of superintendent and assistant superintendent of ferries. With this change the entire ferry service, from superintendent to deckhand and stoker, will be removed from political influence; a matter of immense importance to the thousands of citizens who are daily dependent upon the municipal ferry for transportation.

RECLASSIFICATION OF EXEMPT POSITIONS

The State Commission, in its report upon the investigation of the Finance Department, recommended to the Municipal Commission a reclassification of the exempt positions in the department. The Municipal Commission decided to take this up on a broader basis and, so far as possible, to eliminate from the exempt class in all departments the positions which can practically be filled through competition. It is unfortunate that this could not have been done before so as to avoid the inevitable charge that these changes in the last year of an administration were for the purpose of "covering in" political favorites, but the proposed transfers are justified on their merits, and the Commission is prepared to consider them with sole regard to the duties performed and the practicability of competition, entirely aside from the wishes of present incumbents. The first hearing on changes in eleven departments and offices involving the transfer of 57 positions from the exempt to the competitive class was held May 5; the second, affecting an equal number of positions in 12 other departments and offices was held May 10. The Finance Department will probably be considered separately next week. The full plan involves the transfer of over 140 positions from the exempt to the competitive class.

NEW FORM OF PAYROLLS

The segregated budget and the new forms of payrolls—both results of the far-reaching work of the Bureau of Municipal Research—have brought to light many violations of the civil service law of long standing. Month after month for years past, appointing officers have been certifying—contrary to the facts in many cases —that employees were performing the duties of the positions legally held by them, when in fact many of them have been illegally assigned to perform entirely different duties. The best that can be said in their excuse is that they were ignorant of what was going on in their own departments and, before attaching their signatures, did not take the pains to inquire as to the facts to which they made certification. As soon as these cases were brought to light an outcry was raised against the new payrolls as impracticable. They have been continued, however, and even strengthened, at the suggestion of the Association, by including in all forms of payrolls instead of only in that form used for the labor service, a column in which the appointing officer should be required to state the precise duties performed by each person on the payroll during the time for which he seeks pay. The Commission has required the dismissal or reassignment of many employees improperly employed and is engaged in making the necessary readjustments in classification. At the hearings and in the inspections of departments the Association has taken part. The results have shown a necessity for a bureau of inspection in the Civil Service Commission.

REAPPOINTMENT OF BRIDGE EMPLOYEES

The action of the Municipal Commission in permitting the reappointment of twenty-two former employees of the New York and Brooklyn Bridge who had been out of the city service for eleven years is open to severe criticism. The Association has brought the matter to the attention of the State Commission, with a request that they should rescind their approval of the resolution of the Municipal Commission allowing reappointment. The State Commission has questioned the legality of the adoption of this resolution. The men are now at work and no definite action has been taken.

CRITICISMS OF CIVIL SERVICE LAW

In speeches at the Budget Exhibit held at 135 Broadway last Fall, certain department heads,—notably the Comptroller,—showed a disposition to attribute dereliction of duty and failure to get results to the operation of the civil service law. It was stated that civil service employees could not be kept at work after four; that they could not be removed for inefficiency except after a trial, and removal generally resulted in reinstatement through the courts; that it was impossible to lay off civil service men in case of lack of work or lack of appropriation.

An opportunity to reply to these charges at a later meeting was given to the advocates of the law, and the representatives of the Commission and the Association showed them to be wholly baseless. The civil service law does not fix the hours of labor, which are subject to ordinance and the will of the head of department; it places no restriction on removal of city employees and provides for no appeal to the courts except in the case of veterans and veteran volunteer firemen, and it permits the utmost freedom in laying off men for lack of work or lack of appropriation. The New York City Charter contains special provisions regulating the removal of policemen and firemen and certain other employees, but in the case of ordinary civil service employees places the power of removal in the head of department, and requires him only to present and record his reasons for removal and allow the employee a reasonable opportunity to reply in writing. This procedure complied with, the head of department is free to act as he sees fit and, unless the reasons were mere generalizations or utterly frivolous on their face the employee has no room for hope of reinstatement through the courts. The right of appointing officers to make removals, as above described, has been placed beyond all question by frequent decisions of the courts.

LITIGATION

Only one important case has engaged the attention of the Law Committee this year, and in its presentation the Association had no part. In Flaherty *vs.* Milliken the Court of Appeals reversed the decision of the Appellate Division and held that the employees of the Sheriff, who were in any way connected with the civil side of the Sheriff's duties, were his personal appointees, responsible solely to him, and, therefore, not subject to the civil service law. The effect will be to withdraw from the classification a large majority of the positions under the Sheriff's in every county.

The Executive Committee expresses its appreciation of the work for civil service reform performed by the Women's Auxiliary, and thanks the members of the standing committees of the Association for the attention they have given to the details of the Association's work. The membership of the Association numbers 894, against 869 at the end of the previous year. There are 16 life members, 77 sustaining members and 801 regular members.

Respectfully submitted,

SAMUEL H. ORDWAY,
Chairman.

ELLIOT H. GOODWIN,
Secretary.

ANNUAL REPORT OF THE TREASURER.

MAY 1, 1909.

Balance on hand May 1, 1908		$ 39.65
RECEIPTS:		
From Annual Dues	$3,530.00	
" Sustaining Membership Dues	1,890.00	
" Subscriptions	747.50	
" Title Guarantee & Trust Company, Interest on Elial F. Hall Bequest	272.00	
" Women's Auxiliary	100.00	6,539.50
		$6,579.15
DISBURSEMENTS:		
Salary of Secretary	$1,474.49	
" " Assistant Secretary	962.50	
" " Second Assistant Secretary	550.00	
" " Clerks	1,080.00	
Expenses of Litigation	41.74	
Expenses of Annual Dinner	76.40	
Subscription to GOOD GOVERNMENT	507.04	
Legislative Information	150.00	
Stationery	95.33	
Printing	378.55	
Postage and Stamped Envelopes	344.36	
Telephone Service	97.60	
Office Rent	550.00	
Travelling Expenses	69.52	
Office Expenses	174.42	6,551.95
Balance on hand		$ 27.20

E. & O. E.   A. S. FRISSELL, *Treasurer.*

ELIAL F. HALL FUND.

Held as a special deposit at the Fifth Avenue Bank, certificate No. 5844 for sixteen shares Title Guarantee & Trust Company stock.

The above stock paid 5% on the last quarterly dividend or at the rate of 20% per annum, namely, $320.

A. S. FRISSELL, *Treasurer.*

The above account examined and found correct, May 11, 1909.

ELLWOOD HENDRICK,
PHILIP J. MCCOOK, } *Auditing Committee.*

ORGANIZATION

OF

THE NEW YORK CIVIL SERVICE REFORM ASSOCIATION

CONSTITUTION.

ARTICLE I.

The name of this organization shall be The Civil Service Reform Association.

ARTICLE II.

The object of the Association shall be to establish a system of appointment, promotion, and removal in the civil service, founded upon the principle that public office is a public trust, admission to which should depend upon proven fitness. To this end the Association will demand that appointments to subordinate executive offices, with such exceptions as may be expedient, not inconsistent with the principle already mentioned, shall be made from persons whose fitness has been ascertained by competitive examinations open to all applicants properly qualified, and that removals shall be made for legitimate cause only, such as dishonesty, negligence, or inefficiency, but not for political opinion or refusal to render party service; and the Association will advocate all other appropriate measures for securing integrity, intelligence, efficiency, good order, and due discipline in the civil service.

ARTICLE III.

The Association will hold meetings, raise funds, publish and circulate appropriate information, correspond and co-operate with associations organized elsewhere for the objects set forth in this Constitution, and support all executive and legislative action which promote its purposes.

Article IV.

The conditions of membership shall be wholly independent of party preference. Questions shall not be discussed in the debate or in the publications of the Association upon party grounds. Neither the name nor influence of the Association shall be used on behalf of any party, or for procuring office or promotion for any person. But nothing in this article shall be construed to prevent the Association from opposing any candidate when in its opinion, or in that of three-fourths of the members of the Executive Committee, such course is demanded by the objects of the Association.

Article V.

There shall be a President, to be elected by the Association at the annual meeting, who shall perform the usual and prescribed duties of that office. He shall be, ex-officio, a member of all committees, with a casting vote only, and he may call special meetings of the Executive Committee whenever he thinks it necessary, and, with the assent of two members of the Executive Committee, special meetings of the Association.

There shall be ten Vice-Presidents, to be annually elected by the Association.

There shall be a Treasurer and Secretary and such other officers as the Executive Committee may from time to time designate, who shall perform the usual and prescribed duties of such officers. They shall be respectively appointed by the Executive Committee, and may be removed by them. The Treasurer shall be, ex-officio, a member of the Finance Committee of the Association.

There shall be an Executive Committee of twenty five members, to be elected annually by the Association. Subject to these articles, the Executive Committee shall manage the affairs of the Association, direct and dispose of its funds, and from time to time make and modify by-laws for the Association and for its own action. The Executive Committee shall keep a record of its proceedings, and shall make a report to the Association at the annual meeting. No appropriation of

money by the Executive Committee beyond the amount in the hands of the Treasurer at the time shall bind any member of the Association, excepting those members of the Executive Committee who shall vote for it. Vacancies in the Executive Committee may be filled by the President for the remainder of the term. Other vacancies may be filled by the Executive Committee.

All the officers of the Association and members of the several Standing Committees shall be, ex-officio, members of the Executive Committee.

Article VI.

Each officer of the Association shall continue to hold office until his successor has been selected and is ready to enter upon the duties of the office.

Article VII.

There shall be an annual meeting of the Association on the second Wednesday of May, at which officers shall be elected for the ensuing year, and other appropriate business may be transacted; except in the year 1898, when the annual meeting shall be held on the second Wednesday of January.

Article VIII.

Any person may be proposed in writing for membership by any member of the Association, and shall be admitted upon approval of the Executive Committee. Members failing to pay their dues may be dropped from the roll by the Executive Committee.

Article IX.

The annual dues of each member shall be $5, payable on the 1st of May, and each member shall receive the annual report and all other publications of the Association. Sustaining members, on payment of twenty-five dollars annually, and Life members, exempt from annual dues on payment of one hundred dollars, may be elected by the Executive Committee at any regular meeting thereof.

Article X.

All provisions of this Constitution, except those relating to the rights of members, and the term of officers, may be suspended or amended by a vote of two-thirds of the Executive Committee, subject to the approval of the Association by a two-thirds vote of the members present either at the annual meeting or at a special meeting duly called. Due notice shall be given before any such annual or special meeting that the approval of the Association will, thereat, be asked for such action of the Executive Committee, and the notice shall clearly state the effect of such suspension or amendment in the text of the Constitution. Any member of the Association may propose amendments to the Constitution, which may be approved under the same conditions.

BY-LAWS.

FOR THE GOVERNMENT OF THE ASSOCIATION AND ITS COMMITTEES.

§ 1. The Annual meeting of the Association shall be held at such hour and place as the Executive Committee shall designate. The election of officers shall be by ballot, but any member not present may declare his vote by letter to the Secretary and it shall be counted.

§ 2. The meetings of each committee, unless otherwise especially provided for, shall be at half-past eight P. M., at which time the chairman shall direct the call of the names of its members and the Secretary shall record the names of those present and others as they appear.

§ 3. The order of business, before each committee shall be :
1. The reading and correction of the records of the last meeting.

And, thereafter, unless otherwise ordered, as follows:
2. Any statement due from the Treasurer.
3. Unfinished business from the last meeting.
4. Report from the Secretary's office.
5. Reports of standing committees.
6. Reports of special committees.
7. Proposals of new members and their election.
8. Miscellaneous business.

§ 4. Regular meetings of the Executive Committee shall be held on the second Wednesday of every month except July and August, but if that day be a holiday, then on the third Wednesday. Ten members of the Executive Committee shall constitute a quorum.

§ 5. Neither in the meetings of the Association nor of any committee shall any member speak more than once on any motion nor more than ten minutes at one time, without unanimous consent, nor shall any person, or his actions, be characterized on party grounds.

§ 6. Special meetings of any committee may be called by its chairman or by any three members, and due notice thereof shall be given by the Secretary.

§ 7. All notices to a member shall be sent to his address filed with the Secretary.

§ 8. On the demand of one-fifth of the members present, at any meeting of the Association or of a committee, the ayes and nays shall be called and recorded on any motion.

§ 9. All committees shall be appointed by the chair unless their selection shall be otherwise provided for.

§ 10. At each regular meeting of the Executive Committee, it shall be the duty of the Treasurer to make a statement of the amount of money in the treasury and of the place of its deposit, and, at the annual meeting, he shall state the source of all moneys received and the use made of the same during the past year.

§ 11. The Secretary shall keep a record of the proceedings of the Association and of the Executive Committee, and perform the other duties assigned him.

§ 12. Without the consent of three-fourths of the members present, no vote which will declare or fill a vacancy or elect a member of the Association shall be deemed carried, at the same meeting in which it was first moved.

§ 13. It shall require a vote of two-thirds of the members of the Executive Committee present to pass any vote under which more than $100 will be appropriated or the Association be pledged for more than that amount, and the Executive Committee alone shall have authority to create any charge upon the funds of the Association. But neither said committee nor any officer or officers of the Association shall be authorized to create a personal liability against any members but themselves.

§ 14. There shall be the following Standing Committees, of seven members each, which shall be selected annually by the Executive Committee:

(1) A Finance Committee, whose duty it shall be to devise and carry into effect, subject to the direction of the Executive Committee, suitable measures for raising funds, and to supervise and report upon the income and expenditures of the Association. The Chairman of the Executive Committee shall, in advance of each annual meeting of the Association, appoint an Auditing Committee from among the members of the Association, whose duty it shall be to examine all vouchers and audit the accounts of the Treasurer, and to report thereon at the annual meeting.

(2) A Publication Committee, whose duty it shall be to prepare and recommend matters suitable for publication by the Association, and to take charge of the printing and distribution of whatever may be ordered printed.

(3) A Committee on Correspondence, whose duty it shall be to promote the objects of the Association through correspondence and co-operation with other organizations.

(4) A Committee on Administration, whose duty it shall be to investigate and report upon the administration of the civil service law and rules and to consider and recommend suitable methods of examination for admission to and promotion in the public service, and suitable procedure tending to make the system more efficient.

There shall also be a Standing Committee on Law of nine members, which shall be selected annually by the Executive Committee. Its duty shall be to consider all legislation affecting the civil service, to promote such as may be approved, and to oppose such as may be disapproved by the Executive Committee, and to prepare and recommend such amendments to the law as in their opinion will advance the purposes of the Association. The Law Committee shall have power to represent the Association in any legal proceedings which may be necessary in order to maintain or enforce the laws affecting the State or Municipal civil service.

There shall also be a Standing Committee on Membership

ORGANIZATION

OF

THE NEW YORK CIVIL SERVICE REFORM ASSOCIATION

CONSTITUTION.

Article I.

The name of this organization shall be The Civil Service Reform Association.

Article II.

The object of the Association shall be to establish a system of appointment, promotion, and removal in the civil service, founded upon the principle that public office is a public trust, admission to which should depend upon proven fitness. To this end the Association will demand that appointments to subordinate executive offices, with such exceptions as may be expedient, not inconsistent with the principle already mentioned, shall be made from persons whose fitness has been ascertained by competitive examinations open to all applicants properly qualified, and that removals shall be made for legitimate cause only, such as dishonesty, negligence, or inefficiency, but not for political opinion or refusal to render party service; and the Association will advocate all other appropriate measures for securing integrity, intelligence, efficiency, good order, and due discipline in the civil service.

Article III.

The Association will hold meetings, raise funds, publish and circulate appropriate information, correspond and co-operate with associations organized elsewhere for the objects set forth in this Constitution, and support all executive and legislative action which promote its purposes.

Article IV.

The conditions of membership shall be wholly independent of party preference. Questions shall not be discussed in the debate or in the publications of the Association upon party grounds. Neither the name nor influence of the Association shall be used on behalf of any party, or for procuring office or promotion for any person. But nothing in this article shall be construed to prevent the Association from opposing any candidate when in its opinion, or in that of three-fourths of the members of the Executive Committee, such course is demanded by the objects of the Association.

Article V.

There shall be a President, to be elected by the Association at the annual meeting, who shall perform the usual and prescribed duties of that office. He shall be, ex-officio, a member of all committees, with a casting vote only, and he may call special meetings of the Executive Committee whenever he thinks it necessary, and, with the assent of two members of the Executive Committee, special meetings of the Association.

There shall be ten Vice-Presidents, to be annually elected by the Association.

There shall be a Treasurer and Secretary and such other officers as the Executive Committee may from time to time designate, who shall perform the usual and prescribed duties of such officers. They shall be respectively appointed by the Executive Committee, and may be removed by them. The Treasurer shall be, ex-officio, a member of the Finance Committee of the Association.

There shall be an Executive Committee of twenty five members, to be elected annually by the Association. Subject to these articles, the Executive Committee shall manage the affairs of the Association, direct and dispose of its funds, and from time to time make and modify by-laws for the Association and for its own action. The Executive Committee shall keep a record of its proceedings, and shall make a report to the Association at the annual meeting. No appropriation of

money by the Executive Committee beyond the amount in the hands of the Treasurer at the time shall bind any member of the Association, excepting those members of the Executive Committee who shall vote for it. Vacancies in the Executive Committee may be filled by the President for the remainder of the term. Other vacancies may be filled by the Executive Committee.

All the officers of the Association and members of the several Standing Committees shall be, ex-officio, members of the Executive Committee.

Article VI.

Each officer of the Association shall continue to hold office until his successor has been selected and is ready to enter upon the duties of the office.

Article VII.

There shall be an annual meeting of the Association on the second Wednesday of May, at which officers shall be elected for the ensuing year, and other appropriate business may be transacted; except in the year 1898, when the annual meeting shall be held on the second Wednesday of January.

Article VIII.

Any person may be proposed in writing for membership by any member of the Association, and shall be admitted upon approval of the Executive Committee. Members failing to pay their dues may be dropped from the roll by the Executive Committee.

Article IX.

The annual dues of each member shall be $5, payable on the 1st of May, and each member shall receive the annual report and all other publications of the Association. Sustaining members, on payment of twenty-five dollars annually, and Life members, exempt from annual dues on payment of one hundred dollars, may be elected by the Executive Committee at any regular meeting thereof.

Article X.

All provisions of this Constitution, except those relating to the rights of members, and the term of officers, may be suspended or amended by a vote of two-thirds of the Executive Committee, subject to the approval of the Association by a two-thirds vote of the members present either at the annual meeting or at a special meeting duly called. Due notice shall be given before any such annual or special meeting that the approval of the Association will, thereat, be asked for such action of the Executive Committee, and the notice shall clearly state the effect of such suspension or amendment in the text of the Constitution. Any member of the Association may propose amendments to the Constitution, which may be approved under the same conditions.

BY-LAWS.

FOR THE GOVERNMENT OF THE ASSOCIATION AND ITS COMMITTEES.

§ 1. The Annual meeting of the Association shall be held at such hour and place as the Executive Committee shall designate. The election of officers shall be by ballot, but any member not present may declare his vote by letter to the Secretary and it shall be counted.

§ 2. The meetings of each committee, unless otherwise especially provided for, shall be at half-past eight P. M., at which time the chairman shall direct the call of the names of its members and the Secretary shall record the names of those present and others as they appear.

§ 3. The order of business, before each committee shall be:
    1. The reading and correction of the records of the last meeting.

And, thereafter, unless otherwise ordered, as follows:
    2. Any statement due from the Treasurer.
    3. Unfinished business from the last meeting.
    4. Report from the Secretary's office.
    5. Reports of standing committees.
    6. Reports of special committees.
    7. Proposals of new members and their election.
    8. Miscellaneous business.

§ 4. Regular meetings of the Executive Committee shall be held on the second Wednesday of every month except but if that day be a holiday, then on the mbers of the Executive Commit-

§ 5. Neither in the meetings of the Association nor of any committee shall any member speak more than once on any motion nor more than ten minutes at one time, without unanimous consent, nor shall any person, or his actions, be characterized on party grounds.

§ 6. Special meetings of any committee may be called by its chairman or by any three members, and due notice thereof shall be given by the Secretary.

§ 7. All notices to a member shall be sent to his address filed with the Secretary.

§ 8. On the demand of one-fifth of the members present, at any meeting of the Association or of a committee, the ayes and nays shall be called and recorded on any motion.

§ 9. All committees shall be appointed by the chair unless their selection shall be otherwise provided for.

§ 10. At each regular meeting of the Executive Committee, it shall be the duty of the Treasurer to make a statement of the amount of money in the treasury and of the place of its deposit, and, at the annual meeting, he shall state the source of all moneys received and the use made of the same during the past year.

§ 11. The Secretary shall keep a record of the proceedings of the Association and of the Executive Committee, and perform the other duties assigned him.

§ 12. Without the consent of three-fourths of the members present, no vote which will declare or fill a vacancy or elect a member of the Association shall be deemed carried, at the same meeting in which it was first moved.

§ 13. It shall require a vote of two-thirds of the members of the Executive Committee present to pass any vote under which more than $100 will be appropriated or the Association be pledged for more than that amount, and the Executive Committee alone shall have authority to create any charge upon the funds of the Association. But neither said committee nor any officer or officers of the Association shall be authorized to create a personal liability against any members but themselves.

§ 14. There shall be the following Standing Committees, of seven members each, which shall be selected annually by the Executive Committee:

(1) A Finance Committee, whose duty it shall be to devise and carry into effect, subject to the direction of the Executive Committee, suitable measures for raising funds, and to supervise and report upon the income and expenditures of the Association. The Chairman of the Executive Committee shall, in advance of each annual meeting of the Association, appoint an Auditing Committee from among the members of the Association, whose duty it shall be to examine all vouchers and audit the accounts of the Treasurer, and to report thereon at the annual meeting.

(2) A Publication Committee, whose duty it shall be to prepare and recommend matters suitable for publication by the Association, and to take charge of the printing and distribution of whatever may be ordered printed.

(3) A Committee on Correspondence, whose duty it shall be to promote the objects of the Association through correspondence and co-operation with other organizations.

(4) A Committee on Administration, whose duty it shall be to investigate and report upon the administration of the civil service law and rules and to consider and recommend suitable methods of examination for admission to and promotion in the public service, and suitable procedure tending to make the system more efficient.

There shall also be a Standing Committee on Law of nine members, which shall be selected annually by the Executive Committee. Its duty shall be to consider all legislation affecting the civil service, to promote such as may be approved, and to oppose such as may be disapproved by the Executive Committee, and to prepare and recommend such amendments to the law as in their opinion will advance the purposes of the Association. The Law Committee shall have power to represent the Association in any legal proceedings which may be necessary in order to maintain or enforce the laws affecting the State or Municipal civil service.

There shall also be a Standing Committee on Membership

of fifteen members, which shall be selected annually by the Executive Committee. Its duties shall be to devise and carry into effect measures for increasing the membership of the Association.

Each Standing Committee shall be competent to fix the number of its own quorum; but such quorum shall in no case be less than three.

§ 15. These By-Laws may be amended, or new By-Laws added, by a four-fifths vote at any meeting of the Executive Committee; or by a two-thirds vote, provided a statement of the proposed change had been entered on the minutes at the last meeting.

§ 16. Amendments proposed under the last clause of the tenth section of the constitution shall be first submitted to the Executive Committee.

OFFICERS—1909-1910.

PRESIDENT:
SILAS W. BURT

VICE-PRESIDENTS:

DAVID H. GREER
WILLIAM G. LOW
LEVI P. MORTON
ELIHU ROOT
EDWARD M. SHEPARD

ANSON PHELPS STOKES
OSCAR S. STRAUS
EVERETT P. WHEELER
HORACE WHITE
GEORGE W. WICKERSHAM

EXECUTIVE COMMITTEE:

SAMUEL H. ORDWAY, *Chairman.*
HENRY De FOREST BALDWIN
GEORGE R. BISHOP
CHARLES C. BURLINGHAM
EDWARD CARY
LEANDER T. CHAMBERLAIN
CHARLES COLLINS
JOSEPH P. COTTON, Jr.
HORACE E. DEMING
HOMER FOLKS
J. WARREN GREENE
GEORGE J. GREENFIELD

LEARNED HAND
HENRY W. HARDON
ABRAHAM JACOBI
RUSSELL H. LOINES
JACOB W. MACK
GEORGE McANENY
JOHN G. MILBURN
LUDWIG NISSEN
GEORGE FOSTER PEABODY
CARL L. SCHURZ
NELSON S. SPENCER
WILLIAM H. THOMSON

CHARLES W. WATSON

SECRETARY:
ELLIOT H. GOODWIN

TREASURER:
A. S. FRISSELL

ASSISTANT SECRETARIES:
ALBERT DE ROODE
CHARLES B. MARBLE

STANDING COMMITTEES.

FINANCE:

L. T. CHAMBERLAIN, *Chairman.*
JOHN G. AGAR
CHARLES A. CONANT
A. S. FRISSELL, *ex-officio*
ISAAC N. SELIGMAN
JACOB W. MACK
HORACE WHITE

PUBLICATION:

EDWARD CARY, *Chairman.*
GROSVENOR H. BACKUS
GEORGE R. BISHOP
CHARLES J. FAY
ROB'T UNDERWOOD JOHNSON
WILSON M. POWELL, JR.
JOHN A. SLEICHER

CORRESPONDENCE:

EVERETT V. ABBOT, *Chairman.*
ELBRIDGE L. ADAMS
ALBERT S. BARD
WILLIAM M. CHADBOURNE
NATHAN A. SMYTH
CORNELIUS B. SMITH
WALTER F. TAYLOR

ADMINISTRATION:

SILAS W. BURT, *Chairman.*
CHARLES COLLINS
FRANCIS H. KINNICUTT
PHILIP J. McCOOK
CLARENCE BISHOP SMITH
NELSON S. SPENCER

LAW:

SAMUEL H. ORDWAY, *Chairman.*
HENRY De FOREST BALDWIN
CHARLES C. BURLINGHAM
JOSEPH P. COTTON, JR.
WINFRED T. DENISON
A. LEO EVERETT
J. WARREN GREENE
HENRY W. HARDON
CHARLES P. HOWLAND

MEMBERSHIP:

RUSSELL H. LOINES, *Chairman,*
FRANCIS W. BIRD
CHARLES WHITNEY DALL
FELIX FRANKFURTER
ROY C. GASSER
GEORGE J. GREENFIELD
ELLWOOD HENDRICK
SAMUEL N. HINCKLEY
JOHN G. JACKSON
PERCY H. JENNINGS
CHARLES W. McCANDLESS
ALFRED B. MEACHAM
THOMAS D. THACHER
ROGER H. WILLIAMS

MEMBERSHIP ROLL.

SUSTAINING MEMBERS.

AMEND, BERNARD G., ... 205 Third Avenue, New York City
APPLETON, R. ROSS, . . 146 Joralemon Street, Brooklyn, N. Y.
BEHR, HERMAN, . , . . 75 Beekman Street, New York City
BURLINGHAM, CHARLES C., . . 27 William Street, " " "
CARY, EDWARD, ... The "Times," New York City
CHAPLIN, DUNCAN D., ... 64 Worth Street, " " "
CHUBB, PERCY, ... Glen Cove, L. I.
CLYDE, WILLIAM P., ... 24 State Street, New York City
COCHRAN, ALEX. SMITH. . . . . . . Yonkers, N. Y.
COLLARD, GEORGE W., . . . 884 Fifth Avenue, New York City
COLLINS, CHARLES, . . . 33 E. 17th Street, " " "
CONNOR, W. E., . . . 31 Nassau Street, " " "
CRANE, RICHARD T., . . . 2541 Michigan Avenue, Chicago, Ill.
CURTIS, W. J., ... 49 Wall Street, New York City
CUTTING, R. FULTON, ... 82 Nassau Street. " " "
DAY, WILLIAM S., ... 220 Hobart Avenue, Summit, N. J.
DE COPPET, E. J., ... 42 Broadway, New York City
DEERING, JAMES, . Fullerton and Clybourne Avenues, Chicago, Ill.
DE LAMAR, J. R., ... 43 Exchange Place, New York City
DELANO, WARREN Jr., ... 1 Broadway, " " "
DEMUTH, WILLIAM, ... 524 Fifth Avenue, " " "
DENISON, WINFRED T., . . . 82 Beaver Street, " " "
DIMOCK, HENRY F., ... 60 Wall Street, " " "
FINCH, EDWARD R., ... , 82 Nassau Street, New York City
FRISSELL, A. S., ... 530 Fifth Avenue, " " "
GILDER, RICHARD WATSON, . . 33 E. 17th Street, New York City
GOODMAN, A. L., ... 263 W. 113th Street' " " "
GOODWIN, J. J., ... 11 W. 54th Street, " " "
GREENE, J. WARREN, . . . 111 Broadway, " " "
GREENFIELD, GEORGE J., . . 82 Broadway, " " "
HARRIOT, S. CARMAN, . . . 57 W. 39th Street, New York City
HEMENWAY, AUGUSTUS, . . . 10 Tremont Street, Boston, Mass.
HENTZ, HENRY, ... 769 St. Mark's Avenue, Brooklyn
HOPKINS, GEORGE B., ... 52 Broadway, New York City
HUBER, JACQUES, ... 472 Broome Street, " " "
JACOBI, A., ... 19 E. 47th Street, New York City
KENNEDY, JOHN S., ... 31 Nassau Street. New York City

LOEB, JAMES,	52 William Street, New York City
LOEB, MORRIS,	273 Madison Avenue, " " "
LOINES, STEPHEN,	152 Columbia Heights, Brooklyn
LOW, SETH,	30 E. 64th Street, New York City
LOW, WILLIAM G.,	58 Remsen Street, Brooklyn
MACK, JACOB W.,	92 Liberty Street, New York City
MACY, V. EVERIT,	68 Broad Street, " " "
MARTIN, BRADLEY, Jr.,	6 E. 87th Street, " " "
MINTURN, ROBERT SHAW,	116 E. 22d Street, " " "
MORTON, LEVI P.,	38 Nassau Street, " " "
MOSLE, GEORGE R.,	16-18 Exchange Place, " " "
McANENY, GEORGE,	19 E. 47th Street, New York City
McKIM, JOHN A.,	6 E. 74th Street, " " "
ORDWAY, SAMUEL H.,	27 William Street, New York City
OSBORN, WILLIAM CHURCH,	71 Broadway, " " "
PAGE, EDWARD D.,	60 Worth Street, New York City
PAGE, WILLIAM H., Jr.,	32 Liberty Street, " " "
PAGENSTECHER, A.,	P. O. Box 683, " " "
PHIPPS, HENRY,	6 E. 87th Street, " " "
RANDOLPH, STUART F.,	31 Nassau Street, New York City
READ, WILLIAM A.,	25 Nassau Street, " " "
ROBINSON, NELSON,	23 E. 55th Street, " " "
ROSSBACH, LEOPOLD,	42 E. 75th Street, " " "
RUSSELL, CHARLES H.,	15 Broad Street, " " "
SCHEFER, CARL,	476 Broome Street, New York City
SCHIEFFELIN, WILLIAM JAY,	5 E. 66th Street, " " "
SCHIFF, JACOB H.,	P. O. Box 1198, " " "
SCHWAB, GUSTAV H.,	5 Broadway, " " "
SELIGMAN, ISAAC N.,	1 William Street, " " "
SHEPARD, EDWARD M.,	128 Broadway, " " "
SMITH, CORNELIUS B.,	101 E. 69th Street, " " "
SMITH, J. HOPKINS,	17 E. 47th Street, " " "
SPENCER, NELSON S.,	27 William Street, " " "
SPEYER, JAMES,	257 Madison Avenue, " " "
STETSON, FRANCIS LYNDE,	15 Broad Street, " " "
STOKES, ANSON PHELPS,	100 William Street, " " "
STRAUS, OSCAR S.,	Dep't of Commerce and Labor, Washington, D. C.
STURHAHN, C. F.,	84 William Street, New York City
THOMSON, WILLIAM H.,	23 E. 47th Street, New York City
TRASK, SPENCER,	54 William Street, " " "
VOSS, F. G.,	128 Pall Mall, London, S. W., England
WHITE, ALFRED T.,	5 Nassau Street, New York
WHITE, HORACE,	18 W. 69th Street
WUNDERLICH, F. W.,	165 Remsen

Abbot, Everett V.,	45 Cedar Street, New York City
Abbott, Lawrence F.,	"The Outlook," " " "
Abbott, Lyman,	287 Fourth Avenue, " " "
Achelis, John,	68 Leonard Street. " " "
Adams, Edward D.,	71 Broadway, " " "
Adams, Elbridge L.,	299 Broadway, " " "
Adams, Joseph,	Union Stock Yards, Chicago, Ill.
Adams, Thatcher M.,	36 Wall Street, New York City
Adler, Felix,	152 W. 77th Street. " " "
Affeld, Francis O.,	873 President Street, Brooklyn
Agar, John G.,	31 Nassau Street. New York City
Agnew, Andrew Gifford,	22 William Street, " " "
Aitken, John W.	873 Broadway, " " "
Albers, Julius,	64 Wall Street, " " "
Allen, Calvin H.,	1 W. 72nd Street, " " "
Allen, Elmer A.,	42 Broadway, " " "
Allen, Franklin,	371 Fulton Street, Brooklyn
Alling, Joseph T.,	400 Oxford Street, Rochester, N. Y.
Allison, Charles R.,	60 Wall Street, New York City
Alsop, Reese F.,	96 Remsen Street, Brooklyn
Ambrose, John F.,	10 E. 130th Street, New York City
Amundson, John A.,	146 Broadway, " " "
Anderson, Frank E.,	486 Broadway, " " "
Andrews, J. Sherlock,	111 St. Paul Street, Rochester, N. Y.
Arend F. J.,	165 Broadway, New York City
Armstrong, James,	71 Nassau Street, " " "
Atterbury, Grosvenor,	20 W. 43rd Street. " " "
Auchincloss, John,	27 Pine Street, " " "
Avery, Samuel P.,	61 Woodland Street, Hartford, Conn.
Babbott, Frank L.	346 Broadway, New York City
Backus, Grosvenor H,	32 Liberty Street, " " "
Bacon, Gorham,	47 W. 54th Street, " " "
Bagley, Valentine N.,	641 Washington Street, " " "
Baker, William F.,	379 Washington Avenue, Brooklyn, N. Y.
Baldwin, Elbert F.,	"The Outlook," New York City
Baldwin, Henry de Forest,	49 Wall Street, " " "
Bangs, L. Bolton,	32 E. 51st Street, " " "
Bannard, Otto T.,	24 Broad Street, " " "
Banta, Theodore M.,	348 Broadway, " " "
Bard, Albert Sprague,	25 Broad Street, " " "
Barnes, Henry B., Jr.,	48 Wall Street, " " "
Barney, A. H., (Life)	101 E. 38th Street, " " "
Barrett, Frank R.,	Box 105, Portland, Me.
Barrett, John D.	49 Wall Street, New York City
Bartlett, P. G.,	62 Cedar Street, " " "
Baruch, Bernard M.,	111 Broadway, " " "
Batterman, Henry,	21 Clinton Street, Brooklyn

Bausch, Edward,		Rochester, N. Y.
Bausch, Henry,	746 St. Paul Street,	" "
Bausch, J. J.,	13 Hyde Park,	" "
Bausch, William,	745 St. Paul Street,	" "
Baylies, Edmund L.,	54 Wall Street,	New York City
Bayne, Hugh,	40 Wall Street,	" " "
Beekman, Gerard,	7 E. 42d Street,	" " "
Beer, George Lewis,	329 W. 71st Street,	" " "
Beers, E. Le Grand,	131 Remsen Street, Brooklyn
Beers, Lucius H.,	49 Wall Street, New York City
Bell, Gordon Knox,	22 William Street,	" " "
Bellamy, Frederick P.,	204 Montague Street, Brooklyn
Bennecke, Henry,	219 Congress Street,	"
Benedict, Elliot S.,	60 Wall Street, New York City
Bernard, William.	206 Broadway,	" " "
Bijur, Nathan,	34 Nassau Street,	" " "
Binkerd, R. S.,	care Citizens Union,	" " "
Bird, Francis W.,	101 E. 62nd Street,	" " "
Bisbee, Ralph,	63 Wall Street,	" " "
Bishop, George R.,	142 E. 18th Street,	" " "
Bispham, William,	66 Broadway,	" " "
Blagden, Arthur C.,	Hyde Park, Mass.
Boas, Franz,	123 W. 82d Street, New York City
Bode, Frederick H.,	129 Michigan Avenue, Chicago, Ill.
Bogert, Eugene T.,	66 Broadway, New York City
Bogert, Theodore L.,	194 Broadway,	" " "
Borden, M. C. D.,	Box 1794,	" " "
Borkel, John,	42 E. Houston Street,	" " "
Bottome, Harry H.,	49 Exchange Place,	" " "
Bowen, C. Winthrop,	5 E. 63rd Street,	" " "
Bowker, R. R.,	298 Broadway,	" " "
Brachhausen, G. A.,	Rahway, N. J.
Brackett, George C.,	50 Remsen Street, Brooklyn
Bradt, Herbert S.,	120 Broadway, New York City
Bradley, S. R.,	Nyack, N. Y.
Brady, William H.,	17 Battery Place New York City
Briesen, Arthur von, (Life)	49 Wall Street,	" " "
Briscoe, S. William,	Room 1606, 299 Broadway,	" " "
Brookfield, Frank,	2 Rector Street,	" " "
Brown, Addison,	45 W. 89th Street,	" " "
Brown, Augustus H.,	262 W. 136th Street,	" " "
Brown, Edwin H.,	141 Broadway.	" " "
Brown, Everit,	12 Broadway,	" " "
Brown, Roscoe C. E.,	"Tribune" Office,	" " "
Brown, Thatcher M.,	36 E. 37th Street,	" " "
Brownell, William C.,	153 Fifth Avenue,	" " "
Brush, W. Franklin,	16 E. 37th Street,	" " "
Buckingham, C. L.,	38 Park Row,	" " "

Bulkley, Edwin M., ... 54 William Street, New York City
Burke, J. A., ... 149 W 48th Street, " " "
Burr, Winthrop, ... 7 Wall Street, " " "
Burt, Silas W., ... 30 Broad Street, " " "
Butler, Howard R., ... 131 E. 66th Street, " " "
Buttfield, William J., . . . 96 Wall Street, " " "
Byrne, James, ... 26 Broad Street, " " "

Cadwalader, John L., ... 40 Wall Street, New York City
Cahen, I. J., ... 1 Madison Avenue, " " "
Campbell, John A., ... New Cumberland, West Va.
Canfield, George F., ... 49 Wall Street, New York City
Carnegie, Andrew, (Life) . . . 2 E. 91st Street, " " "
Carr, William, ... 35 W. 46th Street, " " "
Cary, Clarence, ... 59 Wall Street, " " "
Cassatt, George M., ... 327 Broadway, " " "
Cauldwell, S. Millbank, ... Pelham Manor, N. Y.
Chadbourne, William M., . . . 49 Wall Street, New York City
Chaffee, J. Irwin, . Sedgwick Avenue, Fordham Heights, " " "
Chamberlain, L. T., ... 222 W. 23 Street, " " "
Chapman, Henry G., . . . 135 Madison Avenue, " " "
Chapman, J. W., ... 35 Nassau Street, " " "
Chase, George, ... 174 Fulton Street, " " "
Chauncey, Daniel, ... 129 Joralemon Street, Brooklyn
Chauncey, Elihu, ... 11 W. 38th Street, New York City
Cheney, F. W., ... South Manchester, Conn.
Childs, Edwards H., ... 59 Wall Street, New York City
Choate, Joseph H., ... 60 Wall Street, " " "
Choate, Joseph H. Jr., ... 60 Wall Street, " " "
Choate, William G., ... 40 Wall Street, " " "
Cillis, Hubert, ... 20 Nassau Street, " " "
Claflin, John, ... 224 Church Street, " " "
Clark, George H., ... 154 Nassau Street, " " "
Clark, Grenville, ... 21 W. 47th Street, " " "
Clarke, Samuel B., ... 32 Nassau Street, " " "
Clay, George E., ... 9 Jackson Avenue, Long Island City
Cleveland, Treadwell, . . . 27 William Street, New York City
Codington, Perley M., . . . 1487 Broadway, " " "
Coffin, I. Sherwood, ... 30 Cliff Street, " " "
Cohen, William N., ... 22 William Street, " " "
Coleman, Edwin S., ... 17 Battery Place, " " "
Collins, Atwood, ... Asylum Avenue, Hartford, Conn.
Collins, Minturn Post, . . . 1 W. 34th Street, New York City
Collins, Stephen W., ... 69 Wall Street, " " "
Conant, Charles A., ... 38 Nassau Street, " " "
Conger, Clarence R., ... 37 Liberty Street, " " "
Cook, Walter, ... 3 W. 29th Street, " " "
Cooley, Alford Warriner, . Department of Justice, Washington, D C.

Cope, Francis R.,	503 West End Trust Building, Philadelphia, Pa.
Copeland, Henry C.,	242 W. 101st Street, New York City
Corbett, George J.,	54 Wall Street, " " "
Corrigan, Joseph E.,	District Attorney's Office, " " "
Corwine, William R.,	11 Broadway, " " "
Cotton, Joseph P., Jr.,	165 Broadway, " " "
Coudert, Frederick R., Jr.,	2 Rector Street, " " "
Coverley, William,	19 Broadway, " " "
Cowdin, Wintrop, The Algonquin Company,	Passaic, N. J.
Cowperthwait, J. Howard,	195 Park Row, New York City
Coxe, Macgrane,	50 Church Street, " " "
Coykendall, S. D.,	Rondout, N. Y.
Crandall, Floyd M.,	113 W. 95th Street, New York City
Crane, Frederick,	"The Schuyler," 46th Street. " " "
Crane, Leroy B.,	277 Broadway, " " "
Cranford, Walter V.,	215 Montague Street, Brooklyn
Cravath, Paul D.,	52 William Street, New York City
Crawford, Gilbert H.,	32 Liberty Street, " " "
Croly, Herbert D.,	11 E. 24th Street, " " "
Cromwell, Frederic,	32 Nassau Street, " " "
Cromwell, Lincoln,	1 Greene Street, " " "
Crosby, John Schuyler,	206 W. 50th Street, " " "
Croswell, J. G.,	17 W. 44th Street, " " "
Currie, J. W.,	144 Remsen Street, Brooklyn, N. Y.
Curtis, Warren, Sr.,	30 Broad Street, New York City
Curtis, William E.,	30 Broad Street, " " "
Cushing, H. A.,	43 Cedar Street, " " "
Cushing, William E.,	Society for Savings Bldg., Cleveland, O.
Cutting, R. Bayard,	32 Nassau Street, New York City
Cutting, W. Bayard,	24 E. 72nd Street, " " ".
Cuyler, C. C.,	44 Pine Street, " " "
Daboll, Henry E.,	New London, Conn.
Dall, C Whitney,	44 Leonard Street, New York City
Dana, Charles A.,	District Attorney's Office, " " "
Dana, Charles L.,	53 W. 53rd Street, " " "
Davidge, William H.,	49 Wall Street, " " "
Davies, J. Clarence,	149th Street and 3rd Avenue, " " "
Davies, Julien T.,	32 Nassau Street, " " "
Davies, William Gilbert,	32 Nassau Street, " " "
Davis, G. Pierrepont,	Woodland Street, Hartford, Conn.
Davis, Horace A.,	135 Broadway, New York City
Davis John, H.,	10 Wall Street, " " "
Davison, Charles Stewart,	60 Wall Street, " " "
Day, Clarence S.,	45 Wall Street, " " "
de Copper, H,	754 Park Avenue, " " "
DeForest, R. W.,	30 Broad Street, " " "
de Milhau, Louis J.,	119 E. 19th Street, " " "

Deming, Horace E., ... 13 William Street, New York City
Demorest, William C., ... 60 Liberty Street, " " "
de Roode, Albert, ... 79 Wall Street, " " "
Despard, W. D., ... 6 Hanover Street, " " "
Devine. Thomas J., . . . 19 Portsmouth Terrace, Rochester, N. Y.
DeWitt, Theodore, ... 88 Nassau Street, New York City
Dickinson, A. Lowes, ... 54 William Street, " " "
Dickinson, Robert L., ... 168 Clinton Street, Brooklyn
Dickons, James B., ... 49 Wall Street, New York City
Dittenhoefer, A. J., ... 96 Broadway, " " "
Dix, John A., ... Care L. Thomson & Co., Albany, N. Y.
Dodd, Leo W., . . , . 257 W. 86th Street, New York City
Dodge, Cleveland H., ... 99 John Street, " " "
Dommerich, L. F., ... 57 Greene Street, " " "
Donnelly, Samuel B., ... Public Printer, Washington, D. C.
Dougherty, J. Hampden, . . . 27 William Street, New York City
Dows, Tracy, . . . Room 102, Produce Exchange, " " "
Dreier, H. E., ... 129 West 20th Street, " " "
Drescher, William A. E., . . 715 St. Paul Street, Rochester, N. Y.
Driggs, Laurence, ... 43 Cedar Street, New York City
Dunham, Edward K., ... 338 E. 26th Street, " " "
Dunning, S. Wright, ... 80 Madison Avenue, " " "
Dutton, George D., , . . . 101 E. 62nd Street, " " "

Eastman, George, ... 400 East Avenue, Rochester, N. Y.
Eaton, Henry W., ... 45 William Street, New York City
Ecaubert, F., ... 18 Rose Street, " " "
Ehrich, Louis R., ... 463 Fifth Avenue, " " "
Elderkin, John, . . . Lotos Club, 558 Fifth Avenue, " " "
Eliot, Charles W., ... Cambridge, Mass.
Elkins, Stephen B., ... 1626 K Street, Washington, D. C.
Ely, Arthur H., ... 56 Wall Street, New York City
Ely, Robert E., ... 23 West 44th Street, " " "
Emmons, Arthur B., . . . 3 Westmoreland Pl., Pasadena, Cal.
Emmons, Samuel F., . . U. S. Geological Survey, Washington, D. C.
Erbe, Gustav, ... 344 St. Paul Street, Rochester, N. Y.
Erbslöh, R., ... Box 16, Station A, New York City
Evans, George, ... 55 West 39th Street, " " "
Everest, Charles M., . . . 506 West Avenue, Rochester, N. Y.
Everott, A. Leo, ... 49 Wall Street, New York City
Ewart, Richard H., . . . 115 Franklin Street, " " "
Ewing, Thomas, Jr., . . . 67 Wall Street, " " "

Fabbri, Alessandro, ... 11 E. 62d Street, New York City
Fabbri, Ernesto G., ... 11 E. 62d Street, " " "
Fahnestock, Gates D., ... 214 Hicks Street, Brooklyn, N. Y.
Fairchild, Benjamin T., . . . P. O. Box 1120, New York City
Fairchild, Charles S., . . . 10 West 8th Street, " " "

Faure, John P., ... 346 Broadway, New York City
Fay, Charles J., ... 31 Nassau Street, " " "
Field, Hamilton E., ... 106 Columbia Heights, Brooklyn
Fisher, George H., . . E. 28th Street and Emmons Avenue, "
Folks, Homer, ... 105 E. 22nd Street, New York City
Ford, Worthington C., . Care Library of Congress, Washington, D. C.
Forrest. C. R., ... Asylum Avenue, Hartford. Conn.
Foster, Macom G., ... P. O. Box 1120, New York City
Fox, Alan, ... 52 William Street, " " "
Fox, Austen G., (Life), . . . 37 E. 39th Street, " " "
Frankenheimer, John, ... 25 Broad Street, " " "
Frankfort, M., ... C 22 Produce Exchange, " " "
Frankfurter, Felix, . U. S. District Attorney's Office, " " "
Frissell. H. B... . . . . Hampton, Va.
Frothingham, John W., ... 68 Broad Street, New York City
Fuller, Frank, ... 61 Fifth Avenue, " " "
Fuller, Paul, ... 71 Broadway. " " "
Fullerton. Alexander, (Life), . . 5 W. 8th Street, " " "
Funk, I. K., ... 22 Upper Mountain Ave., Montclair, N. J.

Gaillard, William D., ... 141 Broadway, New York City
Gallagher, Patrick, ... 1181 Broadway, " " "
Garver, John A., ... 44 Wall Street, " " "
Gasser, Roy C., ... 35 Wall Street, " " "
Germond, H. S., ... 44 Broad Street, " " "
Gerrish, Frank Scott, ... 17 E. 76th Street, " " "
Getzelsohn, J. A., ... 1065 Prospect Avenue, " " "
Gibbons. George W , ... 198 Broadway, " " "
Gibson, William J., ... 26 Liberty Street, " " "
Glenn, John M., ... 152 E. 35th Street, " " "
Goadby, Clarence, ... 21 W. 35th Street, " " "
Goddard, George A., ... 10 Tremont Street, Boston, Mass.
Godkin, Laurence, ... 30 Pine Street, New York City
Goetze, Otto, ... 142 Amity Street, Brooklyn, N. Y.
Goldman, Julius, ... 31 Nassau Street, New York City
Goldmark, James, ... 83 Warren Street, " " "
Goodale, John McGregor, . . . 42 Broadway, " " "
Goodnow, Frank J., ... 49 Riverside Drive, " " "
Goodwin, Elliot H., ... 79 Wall Street, " " "
Goodwin, H. L.. . . . . . 170 Broadway, " " "
Gottheil, Paul, ... Produce Exchange, " " "
Gottsberger, Francis, ... 156 Broadway, " " "
Gould, Elgin R. L., ... 281 Fourth Avenue, " " "
Grant, De Forest, ... 22 E. 46th Street, " " "
Grant. Percy S., ... 7 W. 10th Street, " " "
Gray, Henry G., ... 161 Madison Avenue, " " "
Green, Noah, ... 478 Central Park, West, " " "
Greenbaum, Samuel. County Court House, B'way & Chambers St., ' "

Greene, Francis V., ... 816 Fidelity Building, Buffalo, N. Y.
Greenough, John, ... 38 E. 63rd Street, New York City
Greer, David H., ... 7 Gramercy Park, " " "
Gregory, E. C., ... 54 W. 47th Street, " " "
Gulliver, W. C., ... 120 Broadway, " " "
Gunther, J. J., ... 4 E. 81st Street, " " "
Guthrie, William D., ... 28 Park Place, " " "
Gwynne, Arthur C., ... Rye, N. Y.

Haan, R. M., ... Hotel St. Regis New York City
Haines, Henry F., ... 660 W. Princess Street, York, Penn.
Hall, Frank L., ... 30 Broad Street, New York City
Hall, Valentine G., ... Tivoli, Duchess Co., N Y.
Halsey, Robert H., . . . 118 W. 58th Street, New York City
Halsted, John F., ... 93 Remsen Street, Brooklyn, N. Y.
Hamlin, Frank H., ... Canandaigua, N. Y.
Hand, Learned, ... 2 Wall Street, New York City
Hand, O K., ... 68 Columbia Heights, Brooklyn
Hand, Richard L , ... Elizabethtown, N. Y.
Harbeck, Charles T., . . . 306 Lexington Avenue, New York City
Harding, Edward, ... 43 Exchange Place, " " "
Hardon, Henry Winthrop, . . 60 Wall Street, " " "
Harlan, Richard D., George Washington University, Washington, D. C.
Harrison, Robert L., ... 59 Wall Street, New York City
Hart, John Wilson, . . . District Attorney's Office, " " "
Hart, W. O., ... 134 Carondelet Street, New Orleans La.
Hartwell, John A., ... 50 E. 53d Street, New York City
Hasslacher, Jacob, ... 100 William Street, " " "
Hastings, Thomas S., ... 27 W. 46th Street, " " "
Haupt, Louis, ... 232 E. 19th Street, " " "
Hayes, J. Noble, ... 68 William, " " "
Heath, Frank E., ... 95 Liberty Street, " " "
Healy, A. Augustus, ... 198 Columbia Heights, Brooklyn
Heinze, Arthur P., ... 31 Nassau Street, New York City
Henderson, Harold G.. . . . . 80 Irving Place,, " " "
Hendrick, Ellwood, ... 139 E. 40th Street, " " "
Hentz, Leonard S., ... 769 St. Mark's Avenue, Brooklyn
Herbert, William, ... 11 Pine Street, New York City
Hewlett, Mortimer C., . . . 900 Broadway, " " "
Hey, George, ... 3630 Park Avenue, " " "
Higginson, James J., ... 16 E. 41st Street, " " "
Hinkley, Samuel Neilson, ... Lawrence, L. I.
Hinrichs, Frederick W., : . . 76 William Street, New York City
Hitchcock, Welcome G., (Life) . . 69 E. 11th Street, " " "
Hobart, Henry L., ... 120 Front Street, " " "
Hodges, Harrison B., ... 16 Gramercy Park, " " "
Hoe, Richard M., . . . Room 102, Produce Exchange, " " "
Hollister, H. H., ... 17 Broad Street, " " "

Holt, Henry,	34 W. 33rd Street, New York City
Holt, Roland,	34 W. 33rd Street, " " "
Hooper, Parker Morse,	169 Grammercy Park, " " "
Hopkins, J. A. H.,	51 West 11th Street, " " "
Hoppin, Frederick S., Jr.,	131 E. 19th Street, " " "
Hoppin, William W.,	54 William Street, " " "
Hornblower, William B.,	24 Broad Street, " " "
Howe, Daniel R.,	Asylum Avenue. Hartford, Conn.
Howe, Horace J.,	25 Gold Street, Yonkers, N. Y.
Howe, Walter B.,	Criminal Court Building, New York City
Howe, Wirt,	135 Broadway, " " "
Howland, Charles P.,	35 Wall Street, " " "
Hoyt, Francis D.,	69 Wall Street, " " "
Hubbard, Thomas H.,	16 W. 58th Street, " " "
Hughes, Charles E.,	96 Broadway, " " "
Hull, Charles A.,	95 William Street, " " "
Hunt. Leavitt J.,	165 Broadway, " " "
Huntington, Francis C.,	54 William Street, " " "
Huntington, Samuel,	176 Broadway, " " "
Huntington, William R.,	804 Broadway, " " "
Huyler, John S.,	64 Irving Place, " " "
Ide, Robert L.,	7 Nassau Street, New York City
Ijams, J. Horton,	56 William Street, " " "
Ingraham, Edward,	69 Worth Street, " " "
Ireland, F. G.,	299 Broadway, " " "
Ireland. John B.,	15 E. 47th Street, " " "
Iselin, John H.,	27 William Street, " " "
Isham, Samuel.	6th Avenue and 40th Street, " " "
Jackson, John G.,	35 Wall Street, New York City
Jacob, Lawrence.	52 Broadway, " " "
Jacobson, Samuel A.,	132 Nassau Street, " " "
Jameson. E. C.,	76 William Street, " " "
Jaretzki, Alfred,	49 Wall Street, " " "
Jay, William,	48 Wall Street, " " "
Jellenix, Felix,	17 William Street, " " "
Jennings, Frederick B.,	15 Broad Street, " " "
Jennings, Percy H.,	25 Broad Street, " " "
Johnson, Burgess,	225 5th Avenue, " " "
Johnson, Robert Underwood,	33 E. 17th Street, " " "
Johnson, Willis Fletcher,	154 Nassau Street, " " "
Joline, Adrian, H.,	54 Wall Street, " " "
Jones. Oliver Livingston, Jr.,	116 W. 72d Street, " " "
Josephthal, Sidney L.,	43 Cedar Street, " " "
Kahn, Otto H.. (Life),	54 William Street, New York City
Kellogg, Francis B.,	Temple Auditorium, Los Angeles, Cal.
Kelsey, Clarence H.,	146 Broadway, New York City

Kemp, Edward, ... 135 Water Street, New York City
Kennedy, Edward G., ... 220 Fifth Avenue, " " "
Kennedy, Elijah R., ... 29 & 31 Liberty Street, " " "
Kenneson, Thaddeus D., ... 13 William Street, " " "
Kenyon, Alan D., ... 49 Wall Street, " " "
Kenyon, William Houston. . . . . 49 Wall Street, " " "
Keogh, Alexander, . . . Criminal Court Building, " " "
Keppler, Rudolph, ... , . . 25 Broad Street, " " "
Kernan, John D. . . . . . 37 Liberty Street, " " "
Kernochan, J Frederic, . . . 44 Pine Street, " " "
Kerr, Albert B., ... 49 Wall Street, " " "
Keyes, E. L., ... Tuxedo Park N. Y.
Kidder Camillus G., ... 27 William Street, New York City
Kiernan, Patrick, ... 14 E. 83rd Street, " " "
Kilmer, Alfred G., ... 12 William Street, " " "
Kimball, A. R., ... Orange, N. J.
Kimball, Daniel T., ... 198 Broadway, New York City
King, Le Roy, ... 20 E. 84th Street, " " "
King, William F., ... 410 Broadway, " " "
Kinnicutt, Francis H.. . . . 165 Broadway, " " "
Kinnicutt, Francis P., ... 42 W 37th Street, " " "
Kinnicutt, G Herman, ... 39 E. 35th Street, " " "
Kirchhoff, Charles, ... 14 & 16 Park Place, " " "
Kissell, Gustav E., (Life), ... 1 Nassau Street, " " "
Klein, Isaac H., ... 30 Broad Street, " " "
Klupfel, Charles, Care North German Lloyd, 5 Broadway, " " "
Knapp, Horace Greeley, ... 5 E. 42nd Street, " " "
Knapp, Shepherd, ... 8 Institute Road, Worcester, Mass.
Knauth, Antonio, ... 233 West 70th Street, New York City
Knauth, Oswald W., ... 302 W. 76th Street, " " "
Knauth, Theodor W., ... 15 William Street, " " "
Koehler, Jerome H , . . . , . . 47 Cedar Street, " " "
Kohler, Max J., ... 42 Broadway, " " "
Kuehnle, Frederick C., ... 629 W. 51st Street, " " "
Kuhne, Percival, ... 13 William Street, " " "
Kunhardt, William B., ... 100 Broadway, " " "
Kunstlich, Samuel H., ... 256 Broadway, " " "

La Fetra, Linnaeus E , . . . 110 E. 62nd Street, New York City
Laimbeer, Francis E., ... 290 Broadway, " " "
Lambert, William B., ... Highland Street, Cambridge Mass.
Landsman, S. M., ... 220 E. 19th Street, New York City
Langmann, G., ... 121 W. 57th Street, " " "
Lansing, J. Townsend. . . . . . 82 State Street, Albany, N. Y.
Large, Walter, , . . . 15 William Street, New York City
Larremore, Wilbur . . . . . 32 Nassau Street, " " "
Law, James, ... 15 E. 127th Street, " " "
Lawrence, John Burling, ... 136 E. 30th Street, " " "

Lawrence, Walter B.,	85 Wall Street, New York City
Lea, Henry Charles,	2000 Walnut Street, Philadelphia, Pa.
Leavitt, John Brooks,	115 Broadway, New York City
Leaycraft, J. Edgar,	19 W. 42nd Street, " " "
Lederle, Ernest J.,	471 W. 143d Street, " " "
Ledoux, Albert R.,	9 Cliff Street, " " "
Lee, W. H. L.,	25 Pine Street, " " "
Leech, John E,	94 Remsen Street, Brooklyn, N. Y.
Leffingwell, R. C,	52 William Street, New York City
Le Gendre, William,	59 Wall Street, " " "
Lehmaier, Louis A.,	78 Beekman Street, " " "
Levi, Albert A.,	52 Broadway, " " "
Lewis, Richard V.,	130 W. 42d Street, " " "
Lindenthal, Gustav,	45 Cedar Street, " " "
Lindsay, Alexander M.,	378 East Avenue, Rochester, N. Y.
Littauer, Lucius N.,	Gloversville, N. Y.
Livingston, Goodhue,	38 E. 65th Street, New York City
Livingston, Julius I.,	110 Liberty Street, " " "
Lobenstein, William C.,	245 Central Park West, " " "
Loines, Russell H.,	131 E. 66th Street, " " "
Lomb, Adolph,	48 Cumberland Street, Rochester, N. Y.
Lomb, Henry C.,	48 Cumberland Street, " "
Lord, Franklin B., Jr.,	49 Wall Street, New York City
Lord, Frederic W.,	126 E. 65th Street, " " "
Lounsbery, Richard P.,	15 Broad Street, " " "
Lovell, Joseph J.,	Avondale Place, Woodhaven, N. Y.
Low, Josiah O.,	56 William Street, New York City
Lowndes, James,	1515 Massachusetts Avenue, Washington, D. C.
Ludlow, James B.,	45 Cedar Street, New York City
Luther, George Martin,	25 Broad Street, " " "
Lyall, Arthur V.,	7 Pine Street, " " "
Lyman, Frank,	88 Wall Street, " " "
Lyman, Theodore,	Woodland Street, Hartford, Conn.
Lynch, J. De P.,	Utica, N. Y.
Macfarlane, Wallace,	32 Liberty Street, New York City
MacVeagh, Charles,	15 Broad Street, " " "
Mallet-Prevost, Severo,	30 Broad Street, " " "
Mallinckrodt, Edward,	Mallinckrodt Chemical Works, St. Louis, Mo.
Mansfield, Howard,	49 Wall Street, New York City
Marble, Charles B.,	79 Wall Street, " " "
Markoe, Francis H.,	15 E. 49th Street, " " "
Marling, Alfred E.,	21 Liberty Street, " " "
Marshall, Charles H.,	45 William Street, " " "
Marshall, Fielding L.,	1440 Sheridan Road, Chicago, Ills.
Marshall, Harford,	District Attorney's Office, New York City
Marshall, Louis,	37 Wall Street, " " "
Marsters, A., A.,	125 Milk Street, Boston, Mass.

Martin, Alfred W., 995 Madison Avenue, New York City
Martin, John, Grymes Hill, Staten Island, N. Y.
Martin, Newell, 1 Nassau Street, New York City
Martin, T. Comerford, 114 Liberty Street, " " "
Mason, Alexander T., 13 William Street, " " "
Mason, Alfred Bishop, Apartado 130, City of Mexico
Mathews, Robert, 135 Spring Street, Rochester, N. Y.
Mathews W. K., 36 Wall Street, New York City
Matthew, William B., 319 W. 112th Street, " " "
Matthews, Brander, 681 West End Avenue, " " "
Matthewson, Arthur, South Woodstock, Conn.
Maxwell, William H., 500 Park Avenue, New York City
Meacham, Alfred B, 59 Wall Street, " " "
Meehan, Thomas J., 2 Rector Street, " " "
Mellen, Chase, 32 Nassau Street, " " "
Merck, George, Llewelyn Park, West Orange, N. J.
Merrill, Charles E., 44 E. 23d Street, New York City
Merrill, Payson, 31 Nassau Street, " " "
Meyer, Adolph, 35 Mount Morris Park, " " "
Meyer, Alfred, 785 Madison Avenue, " " "
Milbank, Albert G., 49 Wall Street, " " "
Milburn, John G., 54 Wall Street, " " "
Miller, Clifford L., 62 West 89th Street, " " "
Miller, Daniel S., 150 Central Park S., " " "
Miller, George Douglas, 125 State Street, Albany, N. Y.
Milliken, Hugh K., 51 Leonard Street, New York City
Mills, L H., 473 Broome Street, " " "
Moffat, George B., 1 Nassau Street, " " "
Moffat, R. Burnham, 63 Wall Street, " " "
Montgomery, Robert H, 165 Broadway, " " "
Montgomery, R. M., 27 Pine Street, " " "
Moore, W. H. H., 51 Wall Street, " " "
Morris, Ray, 81 Fulton Street, " " "
Morrow, Dwight, Englewood, N. J.
Morse, Horace J., 820 St. Mark's Avenue, Brooklyn
Morse, Richard C., 35 Sidney Place, "
Mortimer, Richard, 11 Wall Street, New York City
Mosenthal, P. J., 95 William Street, " " "
Mosle, A. Henry, 30 Broad Street, " " "
Mott, William F., Toms River, N. J.
Munro, J. G., 61 Erie County Bank Building, Buffalo, N. Y.
Munro, John R., 132 Remsen Street, Brooklyn, N. Y.
Munroe, Vernon, 45 William Street, New York City
Murphy, Daniel F., Criminal Court Building, " " "
Murray, James B., 23 Belmont Terrace, Yonkers, N. Y.
Murray, Joseph K., 90 Wall Street, New York City
McAlpin, George L., 55 W. 33d Street, " " "
McCagg, Louis Butler, 18 E. 84th Street, " " "

Lawrence, Walter B.,	35 Wall Street, New York City
Lea, Henry Charles,	2000 Walnut Street, Philadelphia, Pa.
Leavitt, John Brooks,	115 Broadway, New York City
Leaycraft, J. Edgar,	19 W. 42nd Street, " " "
Lederle, Ernest J.,	471 W. 143d Street, " " . "
Ledoux, Albert R.,	9 Cliff Street, " " "
Lee, W. H. L.,	25 Pine Street, " " "
Leech, John E.,	94 Remsen Street, Brooklyn, N. Y.
Leffingwell, R. C,	52 William Street, New York City
Le Gendre, William,	59 Wall Street, " " "
Lehmaier, Louis A.,	78 Beekman Street, " " "
Levi, Albert A.,	52 Broadway, " " "
Lewis, Richard V.,	130 W. 42d Street, " " "
Lindenthal, Gustav,	45 Cedar Street, " " "
Lindsay, Alexander M.,	373 East Avenue, Rochester, N. Y.
Littauer, Lucius N.,	Gloversville, N. Y.
Livingston, Goodhue,	38 E. 65th Street, New York City
Livingston, Julius I.,	110 Liberty Street, " " "
Lobenstein, William C.,	245 Central Park West, " " "
Loines, Russell H.,	131 E. 66th Street, " " "
Lomb, Adolph,	48 Cumberland Street, Rochester, N. Y.
Lomb, Henry C.,	48 Cumberland Street, " "
Lord, Franklin B., Jr.,	49 Wall Street, New York City
Lord, Frederic W.,	126 E. 65th Street, " " "
Lounsbery, Richard P.,	15 Broad Street, " " "
Lovell, Joseph J.,	Avondale Place, Woodhaven, N. Y.
Low, Josiah O.,	56 William Street, New York City
Lowndes, James,	1515 Massachusetts Avenue, Washington, D. C.
Ludlow, James B.,	45 Cedar Street, New York City
Luther, George Martin,	25 Broad Street, " " "
Lyall, Arthur V.,	7 Pine Street, " " "
Lyman, Frank,	88 Wall Street, " " "
Lyman, Theodore,	Woodland Street, Hartford, Conn.
Lynch, J. De P.,	Utica, N. Y.
Macfarlane, Wallace,	82 Liberty Street, New York City
MacVeagh, Charles,	15 Broad Street, " " "
Mallet-Prevost, Severo,	30 Broad Street, " " "
Mallinckrodt, Edward,	Mallinckrodt Chemical Works, St. Louis, Mo.
Mansfield, Howard,	49 Wall Street, New York City
Marble, Charles B.,	79 Wall Street, " " "
Markoe, Francis H.,	15 E. 49th Street, " " "
Marling, Alfred E.,	21 Liberty Street, " " "
Marshall, Charles H.,	45 William Street, " " "
Marshall, Fielding L.,	1440 Sheridan Road, Chicago, Ills.
Marshall, Harford,	District Attorney's Office, New York City
Marshall, Louis,	37 Wall Street, " " "
Marsters, A., A.,	125 Milk Street, Boston, Mass.

Martin, Alfred W., ... 995 Madison Avenue, New York City
Martin, John, ... Grymes Hill, Staten Island, N. Y.
Martin, Newell, ... 1 Nassau Street, New York City
Martin, T. Comerford, ... 114 Liberty Street, " " "
Mason, Alexander T., ... 13 William Street, " " "
Mason, Alfred Bishop. . . . . . Apartado 130, City of Mexico
Mathews, Robert, ... 135 Spring Street, Rochester, N. Y.
Mathews W. K., ... 36 Wall Street, New York City
Matthew, William B., ... 319 W. 112th Street, " " "
Matthews, Brander, . . . 681 West End Avenue, " " "
Matthewson, Arthur, ... South Woodstock, Conn.
Maxwell, William H., ... 500 Park Avenue, New York City
Meacham, Alfred B, ... 59 Wall Street, " " "
Meehan, Thomas J., ... 2 Rector Street. " " "
Mellen, Chase, ... 32 Nassau Street. " " "
Merck, George, ... Llewelyn Park, West Orange, N. J.
Merrill, Charles E., ... 44 E. 23d Street, New York City
Merrill, Payson, ... 31 Nassau Street, " " "
Meyer, Adolph, ... 35 Mount Morris Park, " " "
Meyer, Alfred, ... 785 Madison Avenue, " " "
Milbank, Albert G., , , . . . 49 Wall Street, " " "
Milburn, John G., ... 54 Wall Street, " " "
Miller, Clifford L., ... 62 West 89th Street, " " "
Miller, Daniel S., ... 150 Central Park S., " " "
Miller, George Douglas, ... 125 State Street, Albany, N. Y.
Milliken, Hugh K., ... 51 Leonard Street, New York City
Mills, L H., ... 473 Broome Street, " " "
Moffat, George B., ... 1 Nassau Street, " " "
Moffat, R. Burnham, ... 63 Wall Street, " " "
Montgomery, Robert H , . . , . . 165 Broadway, " " "
Montgomery, R. M., ... 27 Pine Street, " " "
Moore, W. H. H., ... 51 Wall Street, " " "
Morris, Ray, ... 81 Fulton Street, " " "
Morrow, Dwight, , ... Englewood, N. J.
Morse, Horace J., ... 820 St. Mark's Avenue, Brooklyn
Morse, Richard C., ... 35 Sidney Place, "
Mortimer, Richard, ... 11 Wall Street, New York City
Mosenthal, P. J., ... 95 William Street, " " "
Mosle, A. Henry, ... 30 Broad Street, " " "
Mott, William F., ... Toms River, N. J.
Munro, J. G., ... 61 Erie County Bank Building, Buffalo, N. Y.
Munro, John R., ... 132 Remsen Street, Brooklyn, N. Y.
Munroe, Vernon, ... 45 William Street, New York City
Murphy, Daniel F., . . . Criminal Court Building, " " "
Murray, James B., ... 23 Belmont Terrace, Yonkers, N. Y.
Murray, Joseph K., ... 90 Wall Street, New York City
McAlpin, George L., ... 55 W. 33d Street, " " "
McCagg, Louis Butler, ... 18 E. 84th Street, " " "

McCandless, Charles W., . . . 15 William Street, New York City
McCook, Philip J., ... 15 William Street, " " "
McDowell, H. G., ... 87 Nassau Street, " " "
McGinness, Remsen, . . . 42 East 41st Street, " " "
McKeen, James, ... 58 Clark Street, Brooklyn
McKeever, J. Lawrence, . . 164 Lexington Avenue, New York City
McMahon, Fulton, ... 54 William Street. " " "

Nadal, Charles C., . . . 142 E. 35th Street, New York City
Nash, Francis Philip, ... Geneva, N. Y.
Naumberg, Elkan, . . . 48 W. 58th Street, New York City
Naumberg, George W., . . 33 Wall Street, " " "
Nelson, H. W., Jr., ... Marshfield Hills, Mass.
Nevin, A. Parker, ... 149 Broadway, New York City
Newton Albro J., ... 528 Union Street, Brooklyn, N. Y.
Newton, R. Heber, ... East Hampton, N. Y.
Nichols, George M., . . . 277 Adelphi Street, Brooklyn, N. Y.
Nichols, W. N., ... 25 Broad Street, New York City
Nicoll, James C., ... 51 W. 10th Street, " " "
Nissen, Ludwig, ... 182 Broadway, " " "
Nordlinger, Abraham E., . . 143 West Broadway, " " "
Notman, George, ... 99 John Street, " " "

Oakes, Charles, ... 49 Wall Street, New York City
O'Connor, John A., ... Box H, Tarrytown, N. Y.
Ogden, Charles W., . . . 14 E. 79th Street, New York City
Ogden, Rollo, ... 206 Broadway, " " "
Olin, Stephen H., ... 32 Nassau Street, " " "
Olney, Peter B., Jr., . . . 68 William Street, " " "
Oltman, H. H., ... 42 Broadway, " " "
Olyphant, Robert, ... 17 Battery Place, " " "
Opdyke, William S., . . . 20 Nassau Street, " " "
Oppenheim, Edward L., . . 30 Broad Street, " " "
Oppenheimer, Henry S., . . 741 Madison Avenue. " " "
Orcutt C. Blake, . . . Hudson River Day Line, " " "
Ordway, Edward W., . . . 1093 Dean Street, Brooklyn
Orr, Alexander E., ... 102 Remsen Street, "
Osborn, Perry, ... 52 Brattle Street, Cambridge, Mass.
Osborne, Thomas M., ... Auburn, N. Y.

Paffard, Frederic C., . . . 238 Clinton Street, Brooklyn, N. Y.
Page, Walter H., ... 34 Union Square, New York City
Parker, Frederick S., . . . 32 Garden Place, Brooklyn
Parks, J. Waring, ... 56 Pine Street, New York City
Parsons, Herbert, ... 52 William Street, " " "
Parsons, John E., ... 52 William Street, " " "
Paulding, James Kirk, . . 130 E. 24th Street, " " "
Pauli, H. G., ... 116 Broad Street, " " "

Peabody, George Foster,	2 Rector Street. New York City
Peck, George G.,	117 Chambers Street, " " "
Pedersen, James,	20 E. 46th Street, " " "
Pederson, Victor C.,	45 W. 9th Street, " " "
Pell, Frederick A.,	Lakewood, N. J.
Pendleton, Francis K.,	25 Broad Street, New York City
Perrine, William A.,	2440 N. Marshall Street, Philadelphia, Pa.
Phoenix, Phillips,	68 Broad Street, New York City
Pierce, Franklin,	27 Pine Street, " " "
Pierce, Henry H.,	49 Wall Street, " " "
Pierrepont, Henry E.,	216 Columbia Heights, Brooklyn
Pierrepont, Robert Low,	Box 449, Bay Shore, N. Y.
Pinchot, Amos R. E.,	Criminal Court Building, New York City
Pinchot, Gifford,	1615 Rhode Island Avenue, Washington, D. C.
Planten, John R.,	44 Eighth Avenue. Brooklyn, N. Y.
Planten, W. R. J.,	44 Eighth Avenue, " "
Plaut, Albert,	120 William Street, New York City
Poillon, Cornelius,	125 E. 70th Street, " " "
Pollak, Francis D.,	49 Wall Street, " " "
Pope, A. A.,	Box 11, Jerusalem Road, Cohasset, Mass.
Pope, George A.,	926 St. Paul Street, Baltimore, Md.
Potter, Frederick,	71 Broadway, New York City
Powell, Wilson M., Jr.,	29 Wall Street. " " "
Pratt, Frederic B.,	215 Ryerson Street, Brooklyn, N. Y.
Prentice, William P.,	52 Broadway, New York City
Prentiss, George H.,	108 Pierrepont Street, Brooklyn, N Y.
Price, Joseph M.,	158 West Broadway, New York City
Proskauer, Joseph M.,	170 Broadway, " " "
Pruden, W. Edgar,	162 W. 120th Street, " " "
Pryer, Charles,	New Rochelle, N. Y.
Pryor, James W.,	99 Nassau Street, New York City
Putnam, George Haven,	27 W. 23d Street, " " "
Putnam, George P.,	160 Fifth Avenue, " " "
Putnam, Harrington,	404 Washington Avenue, Brooklyn
Putnam, Irving,	27 W. 23rd Street, New York City
Pyne, Moses Taylor,	30 Pine Street, " " "
Rand, William H., Jr.	63 Wall Street, New York City
Raven, A. A.,	51 Wall Street, " " "
Raymond, Charles H.,	11 Pine Street, " " "
Raymond, Rossiter W.	123 Henry Street, Brooklyn, N. Y.
Read, J. Sturdivant,	228 Clinton Street. " "
Reed, Lansing P.,	15 Broad Street, New York City
Rees, Norman L.,	39 Frankford Street, " " "
Reichhelm, Edward P.,	90 West 34th Street, Bayonne, N. J.
	56 Maiden Lane, New York City
	500 Fifth Avenue, " " "
	59 Wall Street, " " "

Richards, C. A. L., ... 169 Power Street, Providence, R. I.
Richards, William R., . . . 14 E. 37th Street, New York City
Rives, George L., ... 14 W. 38th Street. " " "
Robb, J. Hampden, ... 23 Park Avenue, " " "
Robinson, Beverly R., ... 42 W. 37th Street, " " "
Robinson, Moncure, ... 7 E. 42d Street. " " "
Rogers, Robert, , ... 48 E. 61st Street, " " "
Roome, W. Harris, . . . 287 Fourth Avenue, " " "
Roosevelt, Franklin D., . . . 125 E 36th Street, " " "
Roosevelt, Theodore, ... Oyster Bay, N. Y.
Root, Elihu. . . . . Washington, D. C.
Root, Elihu, Jr., ... 31 Nassau Street, New York City
Rose, Arthur P , ... Geneva, N. Y.
Rosendale, Simon W., ... 57 State Street, Albany, N Y
Rosenfeld, George, ... 58 New Street, New York City
Rounds, Arthur C., ... 96 Broadway, " " "
Rowe, Basil W.. . . . . . . 71 Broadway, " " "
Rowe, William V., ... 51 Wall Street, " " "
Rublee, George, ... 30 Pine Street, " " "
Runyon, Carman R , . . . 87 Locust Hill Avenue, Yonkers. N. Y.
Russell, J. Townsend, . . . 170 Remsen Street, Brooklyn, N. Y.

Sachs, Walter E , ... 43 Exchange Place, New York City
Sackett, Henry W. . . . . 154 Nassau Street, " " "
Sage, Dean. . . . . . 49 Wall Street, " " "
Salomon, William, ... 25 Broad Street, " " "
Sand, Henry A. L., ... 120 Broadway, " " "
Sands, B. Aymar, ... 31 Nassau Street. " " "
Sanger, William Cary, ... Sangerfield. N. Y
Sayer, W. Murray, Jr., . . . 398 Washington Avenue, Brooklyn
Schafer, Samuel M., . . . 5 Wall Street. New York City
Scharmann, Hermann B., . . 170 W. 59th Street, " " "
Schieren, Charles A. . . . . 405 Clinton Avenue, Brooklyn
Schnakenberg, D., ... 6 Hanover Street, New York City
Schneidenbach, Arthur Jaques, . . 75 E. 82d Street, " " "
Schrader, George H. F., ... 32 Rose Street, " "
Schurman, George W., . . . 15 W. 57th Street, " " "
Schurz, Carl Lincoln, ... 49 Wall Street, " " "
Scott, J. F., ... 40 Greenridge Avenue, White Plains, N, Y.
Scott, William, ... 25 Duane Street, New York City
Scribner, Arthur H., ... 153 Fifth Avenue, " " "
Scribner. Charles, ... 153 Fifth Avenue, " " "
Seaman, Louis L., ... 247 Fifth Avenue. " " "
Searle. Arthur, ... 41 Concord Avenue, Cambridge, Mass,
Seaver, Benjamin F., ... 111 Pierrepont Street, Brooklyn
Seaver, Oscar S., ... 263 Fifth Avenue, New York City
Sedgwick, Arthur G , . . . 52 William Street, " " "
Sedgwick, Ellery, ... 1020 Park Avenue, " " "

Sedgwick, Henry D.,	120 E. 22d Street, New York City
Seligman, E. R. A.,	324 W. 86th Street, " " "
Seligman, George W,	3 S. William Street, " " "
Seligman, Jefferson,	15 Broad Street, " " "
Serveu, A. Ralph,	1419 "F" Street, N. W., Washington, D. C.
Seward George F.,	97 Cedar Street, New York City
Sexton, Lawrence E.,	34 Pine Street, " " "
Seymour, Origen S.,	54 William Street, " " "
Shainwald, Ralph L.,	100 William Street, " " "
Shaw, Albert,	13 Astor Place, " " "
Sheldon, Edward W.,	45 Wall Street, " " "
Sheppard, John S., Jr.,	26 Liberty Street, " " "
Shillaber, William Jr.,	1 Broadway, " " "
Shortt, W. A.,	32 Broadway, " " "
Siedenberg, Reinhard,	Cotton Exchange, " " "
Silverman, M. J.,	213 Alexander Avenue, " " "
Simes, William,	Box 3084, Boston, Mass.
Skidmore, William L.,	39 W. 52nd Street, New York City
Skuse, Thomas J,	Naval Office, Customs House, " " "
Slade, Francis Louis,	49 Cedar Street, " " "
Sleicher, John A.,	225 Fifth Avenue, " " "
Slicer, Thomas R.,	156 E. 38th Street, " " "
Smillie, James D.,	440 West End Avenue, " " "
Smith, Adelbert J.,	15 William Street, " " "
Smith, Bryan H.,	Brooklyn Savings Bank, Brooklyn, N. Y.
Smith, Charles Robinson,	25 Broad Street, New York City
Smith, Charles Stewart,	25 W. 47th Street, " " "
Smith, Clarence B.,	21 State Street, " " "
Smith, Edgar L.,	31 W. 45th Street, " " "
Smith, F. Hopkinson,	150 E. 34th Street, " " "
Smith, Frederick J.,	278 Mulberry Street, " " "
Smith, Howard M.,	Brevoort Savings Bank, Brooklyn, N. Y.
Smith, James E.,	38 Park Row, New York City
Smith, William Alexander,	412 Madison Avenue, " " "
Smyth, Nathan A.,	Criminal Court Building, " " "
Southard, George H., Jr.,	164 Montague Street, Brooklyn, N. Y.
Spector, Joseph,	241 E. 68th Street, New York City
Spiegelberg, Frederick,	36 W. 76th Street, " " "
Spingarn, J. E.,	9 W. 73rd Street, " " "
Stebbins, H. C.,	718 Fifth Avenue, " " "
Steers, James R.,	101 Park Avenue, " " "
Steinway, Frederick T.,	53rd Street and Park Avenue, " " "
Stern, Benjamin,	32 W. 23rd Street, " " "
Stern, Henry Root,	40 Wall Street, " " "
Stevens, Gorham P.,	107 E. 16th Street, " " "
Stewart, William R.,	31 Nassau Street, " " "
Stimson, Daniel M.,	28 W. 37th Street, " " "
Stokes, Anson Phelps, Jr., (Life),	Yale University, New Haven, Conn.

Stokes, Harold M. Phelps, (Life),	229 Madison Avenue,	New York City
Stokes, I. N. Phelps, (Life),	229 Madison Avenue,	" " "
Stokes, James,	49 Cedar Street,	" " "
Stokes, J. G. Phelps, (Life),	229 Madison Avenue,	" " "
Straus, Isador,	Broadway and 34th Street,	" " "
Strasbourger, Samuel,	74 Broadway,	" " "
Strauss, Albert,	15 Broad Street,	" " "
Strauss, Frederick,	15 Broad Street,	" " "
Strobel, Emil L.,	307 W. 103rd Street,	" " "
Strong, George A.,	50 Wall Street,	" " "
Strong, Theron G.,	49 Wall Street,	" " "
Sturges, S. Perry,	305 Washington Avenue,	Brooklyn
Sturgis, F. K.,	36 Broad Street,	New York City
Sturgis, Russell,	307 E. 17th Street,	" " "
Stuyvesant, Rutherford,	32 Liberty Street,	" " "
Sulzberger, Cyrus L.,	516 West End Avenue,	" " "
Sulzberger, Ferdinand,	802 First Avenue,	" " "
Symonds, Joseph H. A.,	Criminal Court Building,	" " "
Taft, Henry W.,	40 Wall Street,	New York City
Taggart, Rush,	195 Broadway,	" " "
Tappan, J. B. Coles,	49 Wall Street,	" " "
Tatham, Charles,	82 Beekman Street,	" " "
Tatham, Edwin,	82 Beekman Street,	" " "
Taussig, Walter M.,	9-15 Murray Street,	" " "
Taylor, E. P., Jr.,	7 Pine Street,	" " "
Taylor, Thomas Fenton,	130 E 67th Street,	" " "
Taylor, Walter F.,	54 Wall Street,	" " "
Terry, Roderick,		Newport, R. I.
Terry, Seth Sprague,	126 E. 34th Street,	New York City
Thacher, George O.,	157 Chambers Street,	" " "
Thacher, Thomas,	62 Cedar Street,	" " "
Thacher, Thomas, D.,	U. S. District Attorney's Office,	" " "
Thatcher, John S.,	839 Madison Avenue.	" " "
Thomas, John H.,	9 Broadway,	" " "
Thomson, George G.,	412 Bergen Street,	Brooklyn, N. Y.
Thorne, Robert,	30 Broad Street,	New York City
Thorne, Samuel, Jr.,	43 Cedar Street,	" " "
Thornton, William,	117 Prince Street,	" " "
Tiebout, Charles H.,	31 Grand Street,	Brooklyn
Tinker, Edward L.,	70 West 55th Street.	New York City
Tinkham, Julian R.,	42 Broadway,	" " "
Tison, Alexander,	11 William Street,	" " "
Tod, J. Kennedy,	5 Nassau Street,	" " "
Todd, Henry A.,	824 West End Avenue,	" " "
Tomkins, Calvin,	17 Battery Place,	" " "
Tompkins, Hamilton B.,	229 Broadway,	" " "
Tower, George H.,	35 Wall Street,	" " "

Train, Arthur C., . . . Criminal Court Building, New York City
Trowbridge, Alexander B., . . . 114 E. 28th Street, " " "
Trowbridge, Mason, . . . Criminal Court Building. " " "
Tuckerman, Alfred, . . . 1737 H Street, N. W., Washington, D. C.
Tuckerman, Eliot, ... 44 Pine Street, New York City
Turnbull, George R.. . . . . 33 Mercer Street, " " "
Tweedy, J. F., ... 11 Pine Street, " " "

Unckles, D. S., ... 957 St. Mark's Avenue, Brooklyn

Vail, Charles D., ... Geneva, N. Y.
Valentine, Charles A., ... 1 E. 27th Street, New York City
Valentine, Henry C., (Life), ... 257 Broadway, " " "
Valentine, Robert G. . . . Office of Indian Affairs, Washington, D. C.
Van Dusen, Samuel C., ... 27 Cliff Street, New York City
Van Ingen, Edward H., ... 9 E. 71st Street, " " "
Van Nest, George W., ... 20 Broad Street, " " "
Van Santvoord, R., ... 10 W. 122nd Street, " " "
Vidal, J. E , ... 68 Beach Street, Stapleton, S. I.
Villard, Harold G. . . . . . 43 Cedar Street, New York City
Villard, Oswald Garrison, (Life), . . . 206 Broadway, " " "

Wadsworth, James W., ... Geneseo, N. Y.
Wagener, August P., . . . 51 Chambers Street, New York City
Walker, John, . . . 1231 Western Avenue, Allegheny City, Pa.
Walker, William, ... Harbison & Walker, Pittsburg, Pa.
Wallace, William H., ... 66 Broadway. New York City
Wallace, W. J., ... 209 W. 81st Street, " " "
Walling, William English, . . . 3 Fifth Avenue, " " "
Warburg, F. M., (Life), . . . 52 William Street, " " "
Warburg, Paul M., ... 52 William Street, " " "
Ward, Henry Galbreath, . . . 79 Wall Street, " " "
Ward, J. Q. A., ... 618 W. 147th Street, " " "
Warren, George A., . . . 1301 K Street, N. W., Washington, D. C.
Warren, H. Langford, ... 120 Boylston Street, Boston, Mass.
Watson, Charles W., ... 500 Madison Avenue, New York City
Webb, Willoughby L., ... 63 Wall Street, " " "
Weed, John W., ... 62 William Street, " " "
Weeks, John E., ... 46 E. 57th Street, " " "
Welch, Archibald A., . . . Woodland Street, Hartford, Conn.
Weld, Francis M., ... 5 Nassau Street, New York City
Welling, R. W. G., ... 2 Wall Street, " " "
Werthein, H. P., ... 27 William Street, " " "
Wetmore, Edmund, ... 34 Pine Street, " " "
Wheeler, Everett P., ... 21 State Street, " " "
Wheeler, James R., ... Columbia College, " " "
White, Alexander M., ... 52 Remsen Street, Brooklyn
White, Andrew D., (Life). . . . . . . Ithaca, N. Y.

White, Harold T.,	5 Nassau Street, New York City
Whiteside, George W.,	District Attorney's Office, " " "
Whiton, John M.,	73 William Street, " " "
Whitridge, Frederick W.,	59 Wall Street, " " "
Wickersham, C W.,	Hastings Hall, Cambridge, Mass.
Wickersham, George W.,	40 Wall Street. New York City
Wilcox, Ansley,	295 Main Street, Buffalo, N. Y.
Wilder, William R.,	45 Cedar Street, New York City
Wilds, Howard Payson,	University Club, " " "
Williams, Benjamin A.,	22 E. 82nd Street, " " "
Williams, L. L.,	Care E C Williams, 135 Broadway, " " "
Williams, Norman A.,	42 E. 41st Street, " " "
Williams, Perry P.,	Produce Exchange, " " "
Williams, Richard H.,	1 Broadway. " " "
Williams, Roger H.,	31 W. 12th Street, " " "
Williams, Stephen G.,	953 Madison Avenue, " " "
Williams, William,	35 Wall Street, " " "
Willis, Albert L.,	124 W. 183rd Street, " " "
Wilson, George Augustus,	37 Liberty Street, " " "
Wilson, Richard T.,	511 Fifth Avenue, " " "
Winston, G. Owen,	936 Broadway, " " "
Winters, Joseph E.,	25 W. 37th Street, " " "
Winters, Byram L.,	Manoca Temple, Waverly, N. Y.
Winthrop, Bronson,	32 Liberty Street, New York City
Wise, E. E.,	19 William Street, " " "
Wisner, Charles,	Cotton Exchange, " " "
Wisner, H. G.,	18 W. 12th Street, " " "
Witherbee F. S.,	71 Broadway, " " "
Wolff, Lewis S.,	12 E. 70th Street, " " "
Wood, L. Hollingsworth,	2 Wall Street, " " "
Woodbridge, Charles E.,	17 Battery Place, " " "
Worcester, Edwin D., Jr.,	35 Nassau Street, " " "
Wright, Jonathan,	44 W. 49th Street, " " "
Yonge, Henry,	169 Columbia Heights, Brooklyn
Zabriskie, George,	49 Wall Street, New York City
Zerega, Richard A.,	35 Caryl Street, Yonkers, N. Y.
Ziegel, H. Fred Lange,	8 W. 86th Street, New York City

ARTICLES OF INCORPORATION

OF

THE NEW YORK CIVIL SERVICE REFORM ASSOCIATION

[Filed May 11, 1900.]

KNOW ALL MEN BY THESE PRESENTS: That we, the undersigned, being persons of full age and all citizens of the United States, a majority of whom are also citizens of the State of New York, and being now Directors of an unincorporated association known as the New York Civil Service Reform Association, and organized for the purposes hereinafter mentioned; being desirous of incorporation for the same purposes under the Membership Corporations Law of the State of New York, do hereby, pursuant to unanimous vote of all the members of the said Association, present and voting at a regularly called meeting thereof, and pursuant to authority given by the said unanimous vote at the said meeting, of which meeting notice of the intention so to incorporate was given personally or by mail to each member of such Association whose residence or Post Office address was known, at least thirty days before said meeting, and at which meeting the corporate name stated in paragraph First was by unanimous vote adopted, do hereby certify as follows:

FIRST.—The name or title by which the Association in which we desire to form ourselves as aforesaid shall be known in law, shall be the Civil Service Reform Association.

SECOND.—The territory in which its operations are to be principally conducted shall be the City of New York.

THIRD.—The city in which its principal office is to be located is the City of New York.

FOURTH.—The objects of the Association shall be to further the establishment of a system of appointment, promotion and removal in the civil service, founded upon the principle that public office is a public trust, admission to and retention in which should depend upon proven fitness; and to take such action as may tend to secure the honest and efficient execution of laws and rules relating to the civil service, and to the proper administration thereof.

FIFTH.—The number of its directors shall be twenty-eight.

REPORT

OF THE

Executive Committee

OF THE

New York Civil Service Reform Association

READ AT THE ANNUAL MEETING, MAY 11, 1910.

LIST OF MEMBERS, ETC.

NEW YORK
PUBLISHED FOR THE
CIVIL SERVICE REFORM ASSOCIATION
79 WALL STREET
1910

REPORT

OF THE

Executive Committee

OF THE

New York

Civil Service Reform Association

READ AT THE ANNUAL MEETING, MAY 11, 1910.

LIST OF MEMBERS, ETC.

NEW YORK
PUBLISHED FOR THE
CIVIL SERVICE REFORM ASSOCIATION
79 WALL STREET
1910

CONTENTS

Annual Report of the Executive Committee -
Annual Report of the Treasurer - - -
Constitution and By-Laws - - - .
Roll of Officers and Members - - - -
Articles of Incorporation - - - - -

ANNUAL REPORT

OF THE

Executive Committee of the Civil Service Reform Association.

Before reviewing the work of the year, the Committee records its sense of deep loss in the death of Richard Watson Gilder, long a member of the Association and for eight years a member of this Committee.

As evidence of popular support, the Committee has pleasure in reporting an increase in the Association's membership, which numbers 948 against 894 at the end of the previous year. There are 84 sustaining members, 16 life members and 848 regular members.

In December the Association had the pleasure of entertaining the National Civil Service Reform League on the occasion of its annual meeting. The meeting was a memorable one and the public banquet to the delegates was one of the most successful in the history of the League.

THE FEDERAL SERVICE

The Association takes cognizance of the progress of the reform in the federal service only in so far as it relates to the federal offices within the state. To review the progress made throughout the federal service is the province of the National Civil Service Reform League.

FOURTH CLASS POSTMASTERS

The success of the movement inaugurated by President Roosevelt's order of December, 1908, which placed under competition the fourth class postmasters in states north of the Ohio and east of the Mississippi, while of general interest, has a special interest for this Association, for the most marked success has been in this state. In New York, Illinois, Massachusetts and Ohio all positions paying less than $500 a year are filled after examination by postoffice inspectors, while those fourth class offices paying over $500 are filled subject to competitive examinations conducted by the civil service commission. In the first year under the operation of the new order, 27 competitive examinations were held in New York State, through which all vacancies have been filled. There were 119 applicants in these examinations, of whom 91 passed and of whom 28 have been appointed. There has been an average of over four applicants for each position, thus insuring real competition. In only five cases has there been but one applicant, and in no case was it necessary to hold more than one examination to secure a qualified postmaster. The people of New York have become accustomed to the merit system as a means of entering public service. Although the statistics for the other states under the new order are not so favorable to competition as in New York, nevertheless they show that the system has worked successfully and has not placed too great a burden upon the civil service commission.

CUSTOM HOUSE FRAUDS

Although a number of competitive employees were involved in the recent weighing frauds in the customs service at New York City, in justice to the merit system it should be kept in mind that the executive officers in charge of the customs service were the products of the spoils system. And that this was largely responsible for the frauds has apparently been recognized by the surveyor of the port, General J. S. Clarkson, who, as first assistant postmaster-general under President Harrison, gained an unenviable reputation as a spoilsman, for in a manifesto issued at the expiration of his term of office, he stated:

The customs service will never attain its rightful and possible efficiency until it is completely separated from political influence and entirely removed from partisan politics, and personal ambition.

James F. Vail, the deputy surveyor in charge of the weighing division, was promoted to that position by Surveyor Clarkson without examination, by special dispensation of President Roosevelt. Mr. Vail was dismissed for negligence and incompetency because, while there were no proofs of any actual corruption on his part, "he was in charge of the weighing division during the time that the extensive underweighing frauds were perpetrated." John M. Bishop, the deputy surveyor in charge of the inspection division, was also promoted by Surveyor Clarkson through a special waiver of the rules. Collector Loeb insisted that he be transferred, which led to his resignation. Within a few weeks, serious frauds dating back to his administration had been discovered. In the Appraiser's Department, likewise concerned in the frauds, the chief officials are political henchmen and leaders. Where the spoils system in the selection of executive officers thus dominates the service, the failure of subordinates to remain honest and efficient cannot fairly be charged to the merit system.

FEDERAL APPOINTMENTS

Certain appointments by President Taft to federal offices have come as a distinct surprise to the Committee. In Brooklyn, Edmund W. Voorhies, a minor Republican district leader, was appointed postmaster to succeed George H. Roberts, whose second term of office had expired. Mr. Voorhies at the time of his appointment was serving as private secretary to Naval Officer Frederick J. H. Kracke, a more powerful Republican district leader in Kings County. In Yonkers, Dr. Nathan A. Warren, practicing physician, active politician and defeated Republican candidate for mayor, was appointed postmaster to succeed John N. Parsons. William J. Maxwell was appointed collector of internal revenue to succeed Edward

V. Jordan of Brooklyn. All the displaced officials had made conspicuously creditable records. It is reported that Mr. Maxwell's appointment was made at the suggestion of Congressman Calder, who wished by such appointment to remove a dangerous candidate for his own position. Recently, Naval Officer Kracke was reappointed, for obvious political reasons.

Another outright political appointment is that of J. B. H. Mongin, the Republican boss of Seneca County, who was removed from the position of court and trust fund examiner by State Comptroller Williams. Immediately upon his removal a federal position was found for him as postmaster of Seneca Falls.

THE STATE SERVICE

EXTENSION OF THE SYSTEM

A notable extension of the competitive system has been made during the past year. On March 23d, under power given by the civil service law, the state commission by resolution, subsequently approved by Governor Hughes, extended the civil service rules to the seven villages of Batavia, Canandaigua, Ossining, Peekskill, Portchester, Saratoga Springs and White Plains. This is the first attempt made to apply the comprehensive principle of the state constitution to civil divisions of the state other than cities and counties and is comparable to the action taken by the commission under Governor Roosevelt, which first extended the civil service rules to counties.

There are 47 cities in the state, each with a local civil service commission. In only 19 of these cities is the competitive service larger than in the largest of the villages. Opportunity will therefore be afforded for comparing the administration of the civil service law in villages by the state commission, with the administration of the same law in cities by local commissons.

SUCCESSFUL COMPETITIVE EXAMINATIONS

The past year has seen in the state service the successful application of competitive examinations to the filling of responsible and important positions. The commission in its reports has constantly testified to the fallacy of excluding from the realm of competition positions of a so-called "confidential" nature. As a matter of fact, while in every request for exemption the confidential nature of the position is urged as a reason for exemption, there are extremely few requiring such confidence as to preclude competition. By its conduct of high class and advanced examinations for positions involving more than the ordinary amount of ability and discretion, the commission has removed any real basis of opposition to competition for the great majority of positions now exempt or filled through special exception. Illustrative of positions of responsibility filled through competition are, among others, those of transfer tax appraiser, deputy attorney-general and superintendent of the new state institution for the epileptic and feeble-minded.

That employees obtained through competitive examination are efficient and trustworthy has been amply proved in the state service. Perhaps the most notable instance was in connection with the administration of the insolvent Binghamton Trust Company. Upon the failure of this company, the state banking department undertook the administration of the bank's assets. Over $1,500,000 was collected in five months as a cost of two-thirds of one per cent of the amount collected. Contrasted with the cost of other methods of winding up insolvent banks the result is striking. Official figures show that during a period of ten years preceding 1902 the cost of liquidating insolvent banks, other than national banks, had ranged from 20 to 90 per cent of the receipts and that in the case of national banks the ratio was 8.7 per cent. Yet the administration of the affairs of the Binghamton company was entirely in charge of an examiner selected through competitive examination.

Unexpected approval of the competitive system came from the chairman of the state highways commission, Hon. S. Percy Hooker, a former state senator. Mr. Hooker at first had objected to the competitive classification of the county superintendents of highways, but was so pleased with the results of the examination that he wrote to the state civil service commission:

I had at first some hesitation about endorsing the view taken by your commission that this position was properly a civil service position. * * * After meeting these gentlemen [the superintendents selected from the eligible lists] * * * I feel that I must cordially endorse your position in regard to the examination. * * * The examination in its result has done much to remove from my mind the fear of competitive examination.

ADMINISTRATIVE METHODS OF THE COMMISSION

In its last report the Executive Committee urged the necessity for more frequent and regular meetings of the state commission. We are glad to note that since the first of the year the commission has decided to meet regularly twice a month. The more expeditious transaction of business resulting from this arrangement justifies the position taken by the Committee. The commission's work has grown to such proportions that the original plan of administration is inadequate. The commission not only has immediate jurisdiction over the state service but also the services of seventeen counties and seven villages, with prospects of further extensions. Under a recent opinion of the attorney-general it has also immediate jurisdiction over the classified service of the board of education of the city of New York. It has supervisory jurisdiction over the municipal commissions in 47 cities and this requires extensive investigation. Believing that there should be a president residing in Albany to take executive charge of the work, this Committee caused to be introduced at the present session of the Legislature a bill amending the civil service law by increasing the salary of the president from $3,000 to $5,000 and specifically providing that he should take executive charge. The Association's bill also provided for overlapping terms of six years for each of the commissioners and for their removal only after stated reasons and an opportunity to reply. These amendments would secure a continuity in administrative policy and prevent an entire change, for political reasons, in the commission upon a change of state administration. This bill was reported from the Ways and Means Committee of the Assembly but was subsequently recommitted.

The Committee urges upon the Legislature that it make increased and adequate appropriation for the state commission, which is now hampered in its administration by lack of funds.

INVESTIGATIONS INTO ADMINISTRATION OF THE LAW.

The Committee has had occasion in previous reports to refer to the partisan attitude of commissioners in investigations into the administration of the civil service law. This attitude was again shown by Commissioner Kraft in connection with the investigation of the Utica municipal civil service commission, which was ordered to appear before the state commission to show cause why it should not be removed for failure to observe the provisions of the civil service law. The new Utica administration was Democratic, and was found by the majority of the state commission to have violated the civil service law persistently since January 1st, and the evidence seems amply to warrant this finding. As it requires the unanimous vote of the state commission to remove a municipal commission, Commissioner Kraft by his vote prevented the removal of the Utica commission.

During the year covered by this report the state commission investigated the charge made by one Earl H. Gallup that he had been removed by State Comptroller Gaus for political reasons. Comptroller Gaus was a Republican and Commissioner Kraft experienced no difficulty in joining in a majority report which found that Mr. Gallup had been removed for political reasons, a fact which was subsequently substantiated by the finding of a jury in the courts. In spite of the clear evidence Commissioner Milliken, the Republican president, found in a minority report that Mr. Gallup had not been removed for political reasons and announced the doctrine that since Mr. Gallup had been originally appointed for political reasons "he should be precluded from invoking for his own protection the law's prohibition against removal on account of political opinions or affiliations."

LEGISLATION

In addition to the bill reorganizing the state commission, the Committee secured the introduction of a number of bills to strengthen and perfect the civil service law. One of these, giving powers of investigation to municipal commissions, has passed the Assembly and is now before the Senate. The other bills have not been reported from committee. The Association's bill extending to competitive employees throughout the state, the method of removal now obtaining in the services of New York City and the counties comprised therein, was defeated through the selfish opposition of the organized employees of New York City. This organization attempted to force an amendment which would give to competitive employees who had served five years the right to a formal trial before removal. As a provision for a formal trial before removal has been found in practice to make it impossible to maintain discipline the Association could not accept the proposed amendment.

Except for this opposition, there was no open objection made to the legislation proposed by the Association, other than by the various members of legislative committees. The refusal to pass our proposed legislation may be ascribed to a general disinclination to strengthen the civil service law.

An ill-considered pension plan for civil employees of New York City was introduced by Assemblyman Conklin on behalf of the organization of New York City employees. The bill was crudely drawn and its defects were obvious. It proposed a retirement fund made up by contributions from the employees themselves, without any contribution from the city. Advocates of the bill contended that this fund would be self-supporting, but a report of an actuary obtained by the Association showed that the fund would be hopelessly bankrupt from the outset, as in order to be self-supporting, it would be necessary for 870 employees out of every 1,000 contributing to forfeit their contributions either by death or other separation from the service. This bill was defeated by the opposition of the Association.

The movement to pension employees is rapidly growing in favor. In the judgment of the Committee the main reason for a retirement system for civil employees is the resulting improvement of the public service. This will be accomplished if a retirement plan attracts a higher class of applicants and through its operation provides for retiring superannuated employees and thus facilitates earlier promotion. We believe, however, that it is of high importance to oppose retirement systems which instead of accomplishing these results tend to the contrary.

The Association has been able to do important constructive work in connection with the proposed revision of the New York City charter. Recommendations for improvements were submitted to the committee in charge of drafting the charter and we found them anxious to accept the suggestions and meet our views. The charter as presented to the legislature represents a decided improvement in civil service details over the present one and in many cases signal advances.

THE CITY SERVICE

THE NEW ADMINISTRATION

The attitude of the new administration appears to be highly favorable toward the merit system. In response to letters sent by the Association, Comptroller Prendergast, President of the Board of Aldermen Mitchel and

Borough Presidents McAneny, Miller, Steers and Cromwell expressed their approval and support of the merit system.

With the change of administration came a change in the personnel of the civil service commission. Hon. John C. McGuire was appointed president and Messrs. R. W. G. Welling and Alexander Keogh the other commissioners. Mr. Welling has long been a member of this Association and an active advocate of the merit system during its earlier years. The new commission has received the representatives of the Association with marked cordiality and is, we believe, in thorough sympathy with the principles for which we stand.

MAYOR GAYNOR'S ATTITUDE.

In his appointment of heads of departments Mayor Gaynor has, to a remarkable degree, disregarded partisan affiliations, more so, perhaps than any other mayor in recent years. From the outset, he has shown a determination to abolish political influence in appointments to the civil service. In a letter to his commissioner of parks for the Borough of The Bronx, the Mayor ordered that the prior practice in that department of coercing employees to join political clubs be stopped. The Association had called this practice to the attention of Mayor McClellan without effect. In his letter, Mayor Gaynor stated:

No political interference or influence whatever shall hereafter be suffered in any department of the government of the city of New York.

The mayor also ordered the fire commissioner to prevent political influence in the filling of positions in that department and recommended the appointment of eligibles in the order of their rating. Your Committee adopted a resolution commending this attitude and in acknowledging its receipt the mayor declared that this was the policy of his administration in all departments.

THE PRIOR ADMINISTRATION

Under the prior administration during the period covered by this report two important advances were made. The Association has long advocated a considerable reduction of the exempt class and the commission, after careful investigation, during the early summer transferred over 80 positions to the competitive class. Among the positions thus transferred were many of a highly responsible character. A careful regrading of the various positions of the city service was also made, which placed in the graded service subject to competitive examinations for promotion over 100 positions previously in the ungraded service. Besides this, a comprehensive classification of grades for the purposes of promotion was adopted. This classification established primary grades based upon the relative duties of the positions and secondary grades based upon salaries. The number of additional employees who have thus been brought under an orderly classification of grades is estimated at over 10,000. This action of the Commission makes for good administration and, if carried into effect, will simplify the difficult problem of promotions.

This regrading has been attacked in a suit brought in the interest of certain city employees who find their chances for increases of salary through favoritism curtailed. The case is being vigorously defended by the corporation counsel's office which has cordially received the suggestions of your Committee.

THE SKELLY INCIDENT

Too much importance should not be attached to the letters to a political boss written by the assistant secretary of the municipal commission, which were published in the New York American. While these letters reflected seriously upon the integrity of the commission, investigations by both the municipal and state commissions showed that there had been nothing improper actually done except by the assistant secretary, who explained that the letters were written in a humorous vein. The publication of the letters, however, created public distrust in the work of the commission and as successful administration of the merit system depends largely upon popular confidence in its integrity, it is to be regretted that only a suspension of a few days without pay was imposed upon Mr. Skelly.

THE EXEMPT CLASS

The great number of positions in the exempt class is a serious obstacle to separating purely administrative functions of the city government from political influence. It is a matter of common notoriety that these positions are used in the majority of cases as political spoil in spite of the prohibition of the civil service law. Figures compiled by the Association show that the salaries of these positions amount to about $2,500,000 a year, at least, and constitute a patronage fund of cogent incentive in a municipal election. More far-reaching even than the cash value of these positions is the control and sinister influence exerted through them over the entire civil service. An important function of the Committee is to oppose unwarranted requests for further exemptions and in this opposition the Committee has made no distinction between good and bad officials, believing that the character of men appointing or appointed under an exemption is not the proper criterion. It is difficult, however, to convince an official, who sincerely wishes for the public good to make an appointment exempt from examination, that in opposing the exemption the Association is not trying to hamper the efficient administration of his department.

POLITICAL ACTIVITY

During the recent campaign the activity of officeholders was notorious. The most conspicuous examples were in the finance department among the holders of positions exempted from competition because of their confidential and responsible duties. From the deputy comptroller down, the campaign witnessed the activity of officeholders in all departments, from running as candidates for elective offices to acting as election district captains and street spellbinders. That officeholders paid by the entire body of taxpayers should engage in working to defeat the wishes of at least a very large minority of these taxpayers, justifies the Association in its efforts to prohibit by law such activity.

The growing demand of the average citizen to be represented in party management is a hopeful augury for the full development of democratic government. But the average citizen in trying to engage in party activity is met by the fact that the party machinery is run almost entirely by officeholders, who can devote all their time outside of office hours, and even a considerable portion of their office hours, to partisan work. No movement to give to the average citizen a fuller participation in party management can be successful until public officeholders, who have more or less selfish interest in party success, are forbidden to engage in partisan activity.

CORPORATION INSPECTORS

An unalloyed form of political patronage is the anomalous position of "corporation inspector." Corporation inspectors are designated by a borough president to inspect the restoration of streets and pavements removed by various public service corporations, but are paid by the corporations whose work they are supposed to inspect. The commissioners of accounts in the last administration characterized this system as "licensed blackmail." For many years the Association has urged the passage of legislation to remedy this situation, and again this year such legislation was introduced. Letters were sent to the various borough presidents, asking their views as to selecting these inspectors under civil service rules. Favorable replies were received from Borough Presidents Cromwell of Richmond and McAneny of Manhattan. President

Miller, of The Bronx, disapproved of the plan, alleging that these inspectors were confidential agents. The proposed legislation has not been enacted.

In its successful work along educational lines and in stimulating public interest, the Women's Auxiliary has contributed in no small measure to the progress of the reform and the Executive Committee thanks the Auxiliary heartily for its work in this direction, as well as for generous financial support.

The Committee records its appreciation of the public spirit shown by Senators Newcomb and Wainwright and Assemblymen Bates and Bennet in introducing in the Legislature the various bills of the Association.

The Executive Committee reports with regret the resignation of Mr. Charles B. Marble, who has been second assistant secretary for over two years. Mr. Marble has served the Association faithfully and intelligently and bears with him the best wishes of this Committee.

Respectfully submitted,

SAMUEL H. ORDWAY,
Chairman.

ELLIOT H. GOODWIN,
Secretary.

ALBERT DE ROODE,
Assistant Secretary.

ANNUAL REPORT OF THE TREASURER.

MAY 1, 1910.

Balance on hand May 1, 1909		$ 27.20
RECEIPTS:		
From Annual Dues	$3,655.00	
" Sustaining Membership Dues	2,175.00	
" Subscriptions	795.00	
" Title Guarantee & Trust Company, Interest on Elial F. Hall Bequest	320.00	
" Women's Auxiliary	200.00	7,145.00
		$7,172.20
DISBURSEMENTS:		
Salary of Secretary	$1,108.30	
" " Assistant Secretary	1,320.82	
" " Second Assistant Secretary	787.50	
" " Clerks	1,138.91	
Expenses of Litigation	23.68	
Subscription to GOOD GOVERNMENT	521.06	
Legislative Information	150.00	
Stationery	130.22	
Printing	351.18	
Postage and Stamped Envelopes	433.05	
Telephone Service	180.00	
Office Rent	550.00	
Travelling Expenses	104.30	
Office Expenses	316.62	7,115.64
Balance on hand		$ 56.56

E. & O. E.   A. S. FRISSELL, *Treasurer.*

ELIAL F. HALL FUND.

Held as a special deposit at the Fifth Avenue Bank, certificate No. 5844 for sixteen shares Title Guarantee & Trust Company stock. The above stock pays dividends of 20% per annum, namely $320.

A. S. FRISSELL, *Treasurer.*

The above account examined and found correct.

New York, May 6, 1910.

GEO. R. BISHOP,
THOMAS D. THACHER, } *Auditing Committee.*

ORGANIZATION

OF

THE NEW YORK CIVIL SERVICE REFORM ASSOCIATION

CONSTITUTION.

ARTICLE I.

The name of this organization shall be The Civil Service Reform Association.

ARTICLE II.

The object of the Association shall be to establish a system of appointment, promotion, and removal in the civil service, founded upon the principle that public office is a public trust, admission to which should depend upon proven fitness. To this end the Association will demand that appointments to subordinate executive offices, with such exceptions as may be expedient, not inconsistent with the principle already mentioned, shall be made from persons whose fitness has been ascertained by competitive examinations open to all applicants properly qualified, and that removals shall be made for legitimate cause only, such as dishonesty, negligence, or inefficiency, but not for political opinion or refusal to render party service; and the Association will advocate all other appropriate measures for securing integrity, intelligence, efficiency, good order, and due discipline in the civil service.

ARTICLE III.

The Association will hold meetings, raise funds, publish and circulate appropriate information, correspond and co-operate with associations organized elsewhere for the objects set forth in this Constitution, and support all executive and ~hich promote its purposes.

Article IV.

The conditions of membership shall be wholly independent of party preference. Questions shall not be discussed in the debate or in the publications of the Association upon party grounds. Neither the name nor influence of the Association shall be used on behalf of any party, or for procuring office or promotion for any person. But nothing in this article shall be construed to prevent the Association from opposing any candidate when in its opinion, or in that of three-fourths of the members of the Executive Committee, such course is demanded by the objects of the Association.

Article V.

There shall be a President, to be elected by the Association at the annual meeting, who shall perform the usual and prescribed duties of that office. He shall be, ex-officio, a member of all committees, with a casting vote only, and he may call special meetings of the Executive Committee whenever he thinks it necessary, and, with the assent of two members of the Executive Committee, special meetings of the Association.

There shall be ten Vice-Presidents, to be annually elected by the Association.

There shall be a Treasurer and Secretary and such other officers as the Executive Committee may from time to time designate, who shall perform the usual and prescribed duties of such officers. They shall be respectively appointed by the Executive Committee, and may be removed by them. The Treasurer shall be, ex-officio, a member of the Finance Committee of the Association.

There shall be an Executive Committee of twenty-five members, to be elected annually by the Association. Subject to these articles, the Executive Committee shall manage the affairs of the Association, direct and dispose of its funds, and from time to time make and modify by-laws for the Association and for its own action. The Executive Committee shall keep a record of its proceedings, and shall make a report to the Association at the annual meeting. No appropriation of

money by the Executive Committee beyond the amount in the hands of the Treasurer at the time shall bind any member of the Association, excepting those members of the Executive Committee who shall vote for it. Vacancies in the Executive Committee may be filled by the President for the remainder of the term. Other vacancies may be filled by the Executive Committee.

All the officers of the Association and members of the several Standing Committees shall be, ex-officio, members of the Executive Committee.

Article VI.

Each officer of the Association shall continue to hold office until his successor has been selected and is ready to enter upon the duties of the office.

Article VII.

There shall be an annual meeting of the Association on the second Wednesday of May, at which officers shall be elected for the ensuing year, and other appropriate business may be transacted; except in the year 1898, when the annual meeting shall be held on the second Wednesday of January.

Article VIII.

Any person may be proposed in writing for membership by any member of the Association, and shall be admitted upon approval of the Executive Committee. Members failing to pay their dues may be dropped from the roll by the Executive Committee.

Article IX.

The annual dues of each member shall be $5, payable on the 1st of May, and each member shall receive the annual report and all other publications of the Association. Sustaining members, on payment of twenty-five dollars annually, and Life members, exempt from annual dues on payment of one hundred dollars, may be elected by the Executive Committee at any regular meeting thereof.

Article X.

All provisions of this Constitution, except those relating to the rights of members, and the term of officers, may be suspended or amended by a vote of two-thirds of the Executive Committee, subject to the approval of the Association by a two-thirds vote of the members present either at the annual meeting or at a special meeting duly called. Due notice shall be given before any such annual or special meeting that the approval of the Association will, thereat, be asked for such action of the Executive Committee, and the notice shall clearly state the effect of such suspension or amendment in the text of the Constitution. Any member of the Association may propose amendments to the Constitution, which may be approved under the same conditions.

BY-LAWS.

FOR THE GOVERNMENT OF THE ASSOCIATION AND ITS COMMITTEES.

§ 1. The Annual meeting of the Association shall be held at such hour and place as the Executive Committee shall designate. The election of officers shall be by ballot, but any member not present may declare his vote by letter to the Secretary and it shall be counted.

§ 2. The meetings of each committee, unless otherwise especially provided for, shall be at half-past eight P. M., at which time the chairman shall direct the call of the names of its members and the Secretary shall record the names of those present and others as they appear.

§ 3. The order of business, before each committee shall be :
1. The reading and correction of the records of the last meeting.

And, thereafter, unless otherwise ordered, as follows:
2. Any statement due from the Treasurer.
3. Unfinished business from the last meeting.
4. Report from the Secretary's office.
5. Reports of standing committees.
6. Reports of special committees.
7. Proposals of new members and their election.
8. Miscellaneous business.

§ 4. Regular meetings of the Executive Committee shall be held on the second Wednesday of every month except July and August, but if that day be a holiday, then on the third Wednesday. Ten members of the Executive Committee shall constitute a quorum.

§ 5. Neither in the meetings of the Association nor of any committee shall any member speak more than once on any motion nor more than ten minutes at one time, without unanimous consent, nor shall any person, or his actions, be characterized on party grounds.

§ 6. Special meetings of any committee may be called by its chairman or by any three members, and due notice thereof shall be given by the Secretary.

§ 7. All notices to a member shall be sent to his address filed with the Secretary.

§ 8. On the demand of one-fifth of the members present, at any meeting of the Association or of a committee, the ayes and nays shall be called and recorded on any motion.

§ 9. All committees shall be appointed by the chair unless their selection shall be otherwise provided for.

§ 10. At each regular meeting of the Executive Committee, it shall be the duty of the Treasurer to make a statement of the amount of money in the treasury and of the place of its deposit, and, at the annual meeting, he shall state the source of all moneys received and the use made of the same during the past year.

§ 11. The Secretary shall keep a record of the proceedings of the Association and of the Executive Committee, and perform the other duties assigned him.

§ 12. Without the consent of three-fourths of the members present, no vote which will declare or fill a vacancy or elect a member of the Association shall be deemed carried, at the same meeting in which it was first moved.

§ 13. It shall require a vote of two-thirds of the members of the Executive Committee present to pass any vote under which more than $100 will be appropriated or the Association be pledged for more than that amount, and the Executive Committee alone shall have authority to create any charge upon the funds of the Association. But neither said committee nor any officer or officers of the Association shall be authorized to create a personal liability against any members but themselves.

§ 14. There shall be the following Standing Committees, of seven members each, which shall be selected annually by the Executive Committee:

(1) A Finance Committee, whose duty it shall be to devise and carry into effect, subject to the direction of the Executive Committee, suitable measures for raising funds, and to supervise and report upon the income and expenditures of the Association. The Chairman of the Executive Committee shall, in advance of each annual meeting of the Association, appoint an Auditing Committee from among the members of the Association, whose duty it shall be to examine all vouchers and audit the accounts of the Treasurer, and to report thereon at the annual meeting.

(2) A Publication Committee, whose duty it shall be to prepare and recommend matters suitable for publication by the Association, and to take charge of the printing and distribution of whatever may be ordered printed.

(3) A Committee on Correspondence, whose duty it shall be to promote the objects of the Association through correspondence and co-operation with other organizations.

(4) A Committee on Administration, whose duty it shall be to investigate and report upon the administration of the civil service law and rules and to consider and recommend suitable methods of examination for admission to and promotion in the public service, and suitable procedure tending to make the system more efficient.

There shall also be a Standing Committee on Law of nine members, which shall be selected annually by the Executive Committee. Its duty shall be to consider all legislation affecting the civil service, to promote such as may be approved, and to oppose such as may be disapproved by the Executive Committee, and to prepare and recommend such amendments to the law as in their opinion will advance the purposes of the Association. The Law Committee shall have power to represent the Association in any legal proceedings which may be necessary in order to maintain or enforce the laws affecting the State or Municipal civil service.

There shall also be a Standing Committee on Membership

of fifteen members, which shall be selected annually by the Executive Committee. Its duties shall be to devise and carry into effect measures for increasing the membership of the Association.

Each Standing Committee shall be competent to fix the number of its own quorum; but such quorum shall in no case be less than three.

§ 15. These By-Laws may be amended, or new By-Laws added, by a four-fifths vote at any meeting of the Executive Committee; or by a two-thirds vote, provided a statement of the proposed change had been entered on the minutes at the last meeting.

§ 16. Amendments proposed under the last clause of the tenth section of the constitution shall be first submitted to the Executive Committee.

OFFICERS—1910-1911.

PRESIDENT:
SILAS W. BURT

VICE-PRESIDENTS:

DAVID H. GREER
WILLIAM G. LOW
LEVI P. MORTON
ELIHU ROOT

EDWARD M. SHEPARD
ANSON PHELPS STOKES
OSCAR S. STRAUS
EVERETT P. WHEELER

HORACE WHITE

EXECUTIVE COMMITTEE:

SAMUEL H. ORDWAY, *Chairman.*
HENRY De FOREST BALDWIN
GEORGE R. BISHOP
CHARLES C. BURLINGHAM
EDWARD CARY
LEANDER T. CHAMBERLAIN
CHARLES COLLINS
JOSEPH P. COTTON, Jr.
HORACE E. DEMING
HOMER FOLKS
A. S. FRISSELL
J. WARREN GREENE

GEORGE J. GREENFIELD
LEARNED HAND
HENRY W. HARDON
ABRAHAM JACOBI
RUSSELL H. LOINES
JACOB W. MACK
JOHN G. MILBURN
LUDWIG NISSEN
CARL L. SCHURZ
ISAAC N. SELIGMAN
NELSON S. SPENCER
WILLIAM H. THOMSON

CHARLES W. WATSON

SECRETARY:
ELLIOT H. GOODWIN

TREASURER:
A. S. FRISSELL

ASSISTANT SECRETARIES:
ALBERT DE ROODE
ROBT. W. BELCHER

STANDING COMMITTEES.

FINANCE:

CHARLES A. CONANT, *Chairman.*
R. ROSS APPLETON
L. T. CHAMBERLAIN
A. S. FRISSELL, *ex-officio*
ISAAC N. SELIGMAN
JACOB W. MACK
HORACE WHITE

PUBLICATION:

EDWARD CARY, *Chairman.*
GROSVENOR H. BACKUS
GEORGE R. BISHOP
CHARLES J. FAY
LAURENCE GODKIN
WILSON M. POWELL, JR.
JOHN A. SLEICHER

CORRESPONDENCE:

EVERETT V. ABBOT, *Chairman.*
ELBRIDGE L. ADAMS
ALBERT S. BARD
WILLIAM M. CHADBOURNE
NATHAN A. SMYTH
CORNELIUS B. SMITH
WALTER F. TAYLOR

ADMINISTRATION:

NELSON S. SPENCER, *Chairman.*
FELIX FRANKFURTER
ELLWOOD HENDRICK
FRANCIS H. KINNICUTT
RUSSELL H. LOINES
PHILIP J. McCOOK
CLARENCE BISHOP SMITH

LAW:

SAMUEL H. ORDWAY, *Chairman.*
HENRY DE FOREST BALDWIN
CHARLES C. BURLINGHAM
JOSEPH P. COTTON, JR.
A. LEO EVERETT
J. WARREN GREENE
HENRY W. HARDON
CHARLES P. HOWLAND

MEMBERSHIP:

FRANCIS W. BIRD, *Chairman,*
CHARLES BURLINGHAM
CHARLES WHITNEY DALL
ALAN FOX
ROY C. GASSER
SAMUEL N. HINCKLEY
JOHN G. JACKSON
PERCY H. JENNINGS
NICHOLAS KELLEY
LEONARD G. McANENY
CHARLES W. McCANDLESS
CHARLES B. MARBLE
ALFRED B. MEACHAM
THOMAS D. THACHER
ROGER H. WILLIAMS

MEMBERSHIP ROLL.

SUSTAINING MEMBERS.

AMEND, BERNARD G.,	205 Third Avenue, New York City
APPLETON, R. ROSS,	146 Joralemon Street, Brooklyn, N. Y.
BEHR, HERMAN,	75 Beekman Street, New York City
BURLINGHAM, CHARLES C.,	27 William Street, " " "
CARY, EDWARD,	The "Times," New York City
CHAPLIN, DUNCAN D.,	817 Broadway, " " "
CHUBB, PERCY,	Glen Cove, L. I.
CLYDE, WILLIAM P.,	24 State Street, New York City
COCHRAN, ALEX. SMITH.	Yonkers, N. Y.
COLLARD, GEORGE W.,	884 Fifth Avenue, New York City
COLLINS, CHARLES,	33 E. 17th Street, " " "
CONNOR, W. E.,	31 Nassau Street, " " "
CRANE, RICHARD T.,	2541 Michigan Avenue, Chicago, Ill.
CURTIS, W. J.,	49 Wall Street, New York City
CUTTING, R. FULTON,	32 Nassau Street. " " "
DAY, WILLIAM S.,	220 Hobart Avenue, Summit, N. J.
DE COPPET, E. J.,	42 Broadway, New York City
DEERING, JAMES,	Fullerton and Clybourne Avenues, Chicago, Ill.
DE LAMAR, J. R.,	43 Exchange Place, New York City
DELANO, WARREN Jr.,	1 Broadway, " " "
DEMUTH, WILLIAM,	524 Fifth Avenue, " " "
DENISON, WINFRED T.,	32 Liberty Street, " " "
DIMOCK, HENRY F.,	44 Pine Street, " " "
FINCH, EDWARD R.,	32 Nassau Street, New York City
FORD, JAMES B.	4 E. 43rd Street, " " "
FRISSELL, A. S.,	530 Fifth Avenue, " " "
FROTHINGHAM, JOHN W,	5 Nassau Street, " " "
GOODMAN, A. L,	263 W. 113th Street' " " "
GOODWIN, J. J.,	11 W. 54th Street, " " "
GREENE, J. WARREN,	111 Broadway, " " "
GREENFIELD, GEORGE J.,	32 Broadway, " " "
HARRIOT, S. CARMAN,	57 W. 39th Street, New York City
HEMENWAY, AUGUSTUS,	10 Tremont Street, Boston, Mass.
HENTZ, HENRY,	760 St. Mark's Avenue, Brooklyn
HOPKINS, GEORGE B.,	52 Broadway, New York City
ISELIN, ADRIAN, Jr.,	711 Fifth Avenue, New York City
JACOBI, A.,	19 E. 47th Street, New York City
LOEB, JAMES,	52 William Street, New York City
LOEB, MORRIS,	273 Madison Avenue, " " "
LOINES, STEPHEN,	152 Columbia Heights, Brooklyn

LOW, SETH,	30 E. 64th Street, New York City
LOW, WILLIAM G.,	58 Remsen Street, Brooklyn
MACK, JACOB W.,	85 Liberty Street, New York City
MACY, V. EVERIT,	68 Broad Street, " " "
MARTIN, BRADLEY, Jr.,	6 E. 87th Street, " " "
MINTURN, ROBERT SHAW,	116 E. 22d Street, " " "
MORTON, LEVI P.,	38 Nassau Street, " " "
MOSLE, GEORGE R.,	16-18 Exchange Place, " " "
MUSCHENHEIM, WILLIAM C.,	Hotel Astor, " " "
McANENY, GEORGE,	19 E. 47th Street, New York City
McKIM, JOHN A.,	6 E. 74th Street, " " "
ORDWAY, SAMUEL H.,	27 William Street, New York City
OSBORN, WILLIAM CHURCH,	71 Broadway, " " "
PAGE, EDWARD D.,	Oakland, New Jersey
PAGE, WILLIAM H., Jr.,	32 Liberty Street, New York City
PAGENSTECHER, A.,	P. O. Box 683, " " "
PAYNE, GEORGE E.,	251 Nott Avenue, Long Island City
PHIPPS, HENRY,	6 E. 87th Street, New York City
PIERCE, H. CLAY,	25 Broad Street, " " "
RANDOLPH, STUART F.,	31 Nassau Street, New York City
READ, WILLIAM A.,	25 Nassau Street, " " "
ROBINSON, NELSON,	23 E. 55th Street, " " "
ROSSBACH, LEOPOLD,	42 E. 75th Street, " " "
RUSSELL, CHARLES H.,	15 Broad Street, " " "
SCHEFER, CARL,	476 Broome Street, New York City
SCHIEFFELIN, WILLIAM JAY,	5 E. 66th Street, " " "
SCHIFF, JACOB H.,	P. O. Box 1193, " " "
SCHWAB, GUSTAV H.,	5 Broadway, " " "
SELIGMAN, ISAAC N.,	1 William Street, " " "
SHEPARD, EDWARD M.,	128 Broadway, " " "
SMITH, CORNELIUS B.,	101 E. 69th Street, " " "
SMITH, J. HOPKINS,	17 E. 47th Street, " " "
SPENCER, NELSON S.,	27 William Street, " " "
SPEYER, JAMES,	257 Madison Avenue, " " "
STETSON, FRANCIS LYNDE,	15 Broad Street, " " "
STEVENS, BYAM R,	11 E. 78th Street, " " "
STOKES, ANSON PHELPS,	100 William Street, " " "
STRAUS, OSCAR S.,	42 Warren Street, " " "
STURHAHN, C. F.,	84 William Street, " " "
THOMSON, WILLIAM H.,	70 E. 54th Street, New York City
von POST, H. C.,	32 W. 57th Street, New York City
VOSS, F. G.,	123 Pall Mall, London, S. W., England
WHITE, ALFRED T.,	5 Nassau Street, New York City
WHITE, HORACE,	18 W. 69th Street, " " "
WUNDERLICH, F. W,	165 Remsen Street, Brooklyn

Abbot, Everett V.,	45 Cedar Street, New York City
Abbott, Lawrence F.,	"The Outlook," " " "
Abbott, Lyman,	287 Fourth Avenue, " " "
Achelis, John,	68 Leonard Street, " " "
Adams, Edward D.,	71 Broadway, " " "
Adams, Elbridge L.,	299 Broadway, " " "
Adams, Joseph,	Union Stock Yards, Chicago, Ill.
Adams, Thatcher M.,	36 Wall Street, New York City
Adler, Felix,	152 W. 77th Street, " " "
Affeld, Francis O.,	873 President Street, Brooklyn
Agar, John G.,	31 Nassau Street, New York City
Agnew, Andrew Gifford,	22 William Street, " " "
Albers, Julius,	64 Wall Street, " " "
Allen, Calvin H.,	1 W. 72nd Street, " " "
Allen, Elmer A.,	42 Broadway, " " "
Allen, Franklin,	371 Fulton Street, Brooklyn
Alling, Joseph T.,	400 Oxford Street, Rochester, N. Y.
Allison, Charles R.,	60 Wall Street, New York City
Alsop, Reese F.,	96 Remsen Street, Brooklyn
Ambrose, John F.,	10 E. 130th Street, New York City
Ames, John McE.,	165 Broadway, " " "
Anderson, Frank E.,	486 Broadway, " " "
Andrews, J. Sherlock,	111 St. Paul Street, Rochester, N. Y.
Arend, F. J.,	165 Broadway, New York City
Armstrong, James,	71 Nassau Street, " " "
Armstrong, S. T.,	1744 Broadway, " " "
Atterbury, Grosvenor,	20 W. 43rd Street, " " "
Auchincloss, John,	27 Pine Street, " " "
Avery, Samuel P.,	61 Woodland Street, Hartford, Conn.
Babbott, Frank L.,	346 Broadway, New York City
Backus, Grosvenor H.,	154 Nassau Street, " " "
Bacon, Gorham,	47 W. 54th Street, " " "
Bagley, Valentine N.,	641 Washington Street, " " "
Baker, William F.,	379 Washington Avenue, Brooklyn, N. Y.
Baldwin, Elbert F.,	"The Outlook," New York City
Baldwin, Henry de Forest,	49 Wall Street, " " "
Baldwin, William D.,	175 W. 58th Street, " " "
Bangs, L. Bolton,	32 E. 51st Street, " " "
Bannard, Otto T.,	24 Broad Street, " " "
Banta, Theodore M.,	348 Broadway, " " "
Bard, Albert Sprague,	25 Broad Street, " " "
Barkley, C. B.,	14 E. 60th Street, " " "
Barnes, Henry B., Jr.,	48 Wall Street, " " "
Barney, A. H., (Life)	101 E. 38th Street, " " "
Barrett, Frank R.,	Box 105, Portland, Me.
Barrett, John D.	49 Wall Street, New York City
Bartlett, P. G.,	62 Cedar Street, " " "

Baruch, Bernard M.,	111 Broadway, New York City
Batterman, Henry,	Hotel Bossert, Brooklyn
Bausch, J. J.,	13 Hyde Park, Rochester, N.Y.
Bausch, William,	745 St. Paul Street, " "
Baylies, Edmund L.,	54 Wall Street, New York City
Beekman, Gerard,	7 E. 42d Street, " " "
Beer, George Lewis,	329 W. 71st Street, " " "
Beers, E. Le Grand,	131 Remsen Street, Brooklyn
Beers, Lucius H.,	49 Wall Street, New York City
Bell, Gordon Knox,	22 William Street, " " "
Bellamy, Frederick P.,	204 Montague Street, Brooklyn
Bennecke, Henry,	219 Congress Street, "
Benedict, Elliot S.,	60 Wall Street, New York City
Bernard. William.	206 Broadway, " " "
Betts, Samuel R.,	52 William Street, " " "
Bijur, Nathan,	34 Nassau Street, " " "
Binkerd, R. S.,	City Club, " " "
Bird, Francis W.,	101 E. 62nd Street, " " "
Bisbee, Ralph,	63 Wall Street, " " "
Bishop, George R.,	142 E. 18th Street, " " "
Blagden. Arthur C.,	Hyde Park, Mass.
Boas, Franz,	Columbia University, New York City
Bode, Frederick H.,	129 Michigan Avenue, Chicago, Ill.
Bogert, Eugene T.,	66 Broadway, New York City
Borden, M. C. D.,	Box 1794, " " "
Borkel, John,	42 E. Houston Street, " " "
Bowen, C. Winthrop,	5 E. 63rd Street, " " "
Bowker, R. R.,	298 Broadway, " " "
Bowler, R. P.,	2 Rector Street, " " "
Brachhausen, G. A.,	Rahway, N. J.
Brackett, George C.,	50 Remsen Street, Brooklyn
Bradley, S. R.,	Nyack, N. Y.
Bradt, Herbert S.,	120 Broadway, New York City
Brady, William H.,	17 Battery Place, " " "
Briesen, Arthur von, (Life)	49 Wall Street, " " "
Briscoe, S. William,	Room 1606, 299 Broadway, " " "
Brookfield, Frank,	2 Rector Street, " " "
Brown, Addison,	45 W. 89th Street, " " "
Brown, Edwin H.,	141 Broadway. " " "
Brown, Everit,	12 Broadway, " " "
Brown, Franklin Q.,	33 Pine Street, " " "
Brown. F. Tilden,	14 E. 58th Street, " " "
Brown, Roscoe C. E.,	" Tribune " Office, " " "
Brown, Thatcher M.,	1024 Park Avenue, Plainfield, N. J.
Brownell, William C.,	153 Fifth Avenue, New York City
Brush, W. Franklin,	16 E. 37th Street, " " "
Bulkley, Edwin M.,	54 William Street, " " "
Bulkley, Johathan,	75 Duane Street, " " "

Burlingham, Charles,	52 William Street, New York City
Burr, Winthrop,	7 Wall Street, " " "
Burt, Silas W.,	Hotel Hargrave, " " "
Butler, Howard R.,	131 E. 66th Street, " " "
Buttfield. William J.,	96 Wall Street, " " "
Byrne, James,	26 Broad Street, " " "
Cadwalader, John L.,	40 Wall Street, New York City
Cahen, I. J.,	1 Madison Avenue, " " "
Campbell, Frederick B.,	54 Wall Street, " " "
Campbell, John A.,	New Cumberland, West Va.
Canfield, George F.,	49 Wall Street, New York City
Carey, Samuel.	170 Broadway, " " "
Carnegie, Andrew, (Life)	2 E. 91st Street, " " "
Carr, William,	35 W. 46th Street. " " "
Cary, Clarence,	59 Wall Street, " " "
Cassatt, George M.,	327 Broadway, " " "
Cauldwell, S. Millbank,	Pelham Manor, N. Y.
Cerf, L. A.,	135 Broadway, New York City
Chadbourne, William M.,	49 Wall Street. " " "
Chaffee, J. Irwin,	Sedgwick Avenue, Fordham Heights, " " "
Chamberlain, L. T.,	222 W. 23 Street, " " "
Chapman, John Jay,	35 Wall Street, " " "
Chapman, Henry G.,	135 Madison Avenue. " " "
Chase, George,	174 Fulton Street, " " "
Chauncey, Daniel,	129 Joralemon Street, Brooklyn
Chauncey, Elihu,	208 Madison Avenue. New York City
Childs, Edwards H.,	59 Wall Street, " " "
Childs, Richard S.,	353 Fourth Avenue, " " "
Choate, Joseph H.,	60 Wall Street, " " "
Choate, Joseph H. Jr.,	60 Wall Street, " " "
Choate, William G.,	40 Wall Street, " " "
Cilis, Hubert,	20 Nassau Street, " " "
Claflin, John,	224 Church Street, " " "
Clark, Grenville,	21 W. 47th Street, " " "
Clarke, Samuel B.,	32 Nassau Street, " " "
Clarkson, Banyer,	26 W. 50th Street, " " "
Clay, George E.,	9 Jackson Avenue, Long Island City
Cleveland, Treadwell,	27 William Street, New York City
Codington, Perley M.,	1437 Broadway, " " "
Coffin, C A.,	30 Church Street, " " "
Coffin, I. Sherwood,	30 Cliff Street, " " "
Cohen, William N.,	22 William Street, " " "
Coleman, Edwin S.,	17 Battery Place, " " "
Collins, Atwood,	Asylum Avenue, Hartford, Conn.
Collins, Minturn Post,	1 W. 34th Street, New York City
Collins, Stephen W.,	63 Wall Street, " " "
Comstock, C. B.,	124 E. 27th Street, " " "

Conant, Charles A.,	38 Nassau Street, New York City
Conger, Clarence R.,	37 Liberty Street, " " "
Conner, Lewis A.,	53 E. 49th Street, " " "
Cook, Walter,	3 W. 29th Street, " " "
Cooley, Alford Warriner,	Department of Justice, Washington, D C.
Copeland, Henry C.,	242 W. 101st Street, New York City
Corbett, George J.,	54 Wall Street, " " "
Corning, C. R.,	36 Wall Street, " " "
Corrigan, Joseph E.,	39 E. 10th Street, " " "
Corwine, William R.,	11 Broadway, " " "
Cotton, Joseph P., Jr.,	165 Broadway, " " "
Coudert, Frederick R., Jr.,	2 Rector Street, " " "
Coverley, William,	19 Broadway, " " "
Cowdin, Wintrop, The Algonquin Company,	Passaic, N. J.
Cowperthwait, J. Howard,	195 Park Row, New York City
Coxe, Macgrane,	50 Church Street,
Coykendall, S. D.,	Rondout, N. Y.
Crandall, Floyd M.,	113 W. 95th Street, New York City
Crane, Frederick,	"The Schuyler,' 46th Street. " " "
Crane, Leroy B.,	277 Broadway, " " "
Cranford, Walter V.,	215 Montague Street, Brooklyn
Cravath, Paul D.,	52 William Street, New York City
Crawford, Gilbert H.,	32 Liberty Street, " " "
Croly, Herbert D.,	11 E. 24th Street, " " "
Cromwell, Frederic,	32 Nassau Street, " " "
Cromwell, Lincoln,	1 Greene Street, " " "
Crosby, John Schuyler,	206 W. 50th Street. " " "
Croswell, J. G.,	17 W. 44th Street, " " "
Curtis, F. Kingsbury,	30 Broad Street, " " "
Curtis, Warren, Sr.,	30 Broad Street, " " "
Curtis, William E.,	30 Broad Street, " " "
Cushing, H. A,	43 Cedar Street, " " "
Cushing, William E.,	Society for Savings Bldg, Cleveland, O.
Cutting, R. Bayard,	32 Nassau Street. New York City
Cutting, W. Bayard,	24 E. 72nd Street, " " "
Cuyler, C. C.,	55 Cedar Street, " " "
Dall, C. Whitney,	44 Leonard Street, New York City
Dana, Charles A.,	55 West 51st Street, " " "
Dana, Charles L.,	53 W. 53rd Street, " " "
Dana, Richard H., Jr.,	103 Park Avenue, " " "
Davidge, William H.,	49 Wall Street, " " "
Davies, J. Clarence,	149th Street and 3rd Avenue, " " "
Davies, Julien T.,	32 Nassau Street, " " "
Davies, William Gilbert,	32 Nassau Street. " " "
Davis, G. Pierrepont,	Woodland Street, Hartford, Conn.
Davis, Horace A.,	135 Broadway, New York City
Davis John, H.,	10 Wall Street, " " "

Davison, Charles Stewart,	60 Wall Street, New York City
Day, Clarence S.,	45 Wall Street, " " "
de Coppet, H.,	754 Park Avenue, " " "
DeForest, R. W.,	30 Broad Street, " " "
de Milhau, Louis J.,	119 E 19th Street, " " "
Deming, Horace E.,	13 William Street, " " "
Demorest, William C.,	60 Liberty Street, " " "
de Roode, Albert,	79 Wall Street, " " "
Despard, W. D.,	6 Hanover Street, " " "
Devine, Thomas J.,	19 Portsmouth Terrace, Rochester, N. Y.
DeWitt, Theodore,	88 Nassau Street, New York City
Dickinson, A. Lowes,	54 William Street, " " "
Dickinson, Robert L.,	168 Clinton Street, Brooklyn
Dickson, James B.,	49 Wall Street, New York City
Dittenhoefer, A. J.,	96 Broadway, " " "
Dix, John A.,	Care L. Thomson & Co., Albany, N. Y.
Dodd, Lee W.,	257 W. 86th Street, New York City
Dodge, Cleveland H.,	99 John Street, " " "
Dommerich, L. F.,	57 Greene Street, " " "
Donnelly, Samuel B.,	Public Printer, Washington, D. C.
Dormitzer, Henry,	27 E. 74th Street, New York City
Dougherty, J. Hampden,	27 William Street, " " "
Dows, Tracy,	Room 102, Produce Exchange, " " "
Dreier, H. E.,	129 West 20th Street, " " "
Drescher, William, A. E.,	715 St. Paul Street, Rochester, N. Y.
Drew, John,	Racquet and Tennis Club, New York City
Driggs, Laurence,	43 Cedar Street, " " "
Drucklieb, Charles G.,	178 Washington Street, " " "
Dunham, Edward K.,	338 E. 26th Street, " " "
Dunning, S. Wright,	80 Madison Avenue, " " "
Dutton, George D.,	101 E. 62nd Street, " " "
Eastman, George,	400 East Avenue, Rochester, N. Y.
Eaton, Henry W.,	45 William Street, New York City
Ehrich, Louis R,	463 Fifth Avenue, " " "
Elderkin, John,	Lotos Club, 558 Fifth Avenue, " " "
Eliot, Charles W.,	Cambridge, Mass.
Elkins, Stephen B.,	1626 K Street, Washington, D. C.
Elliot, Daniel G,	77th Street and 8th Avenue, New York City
Ely, Arthur H.,	56 Wall Street, " " "
Ely, Robert E.,	23 West 44th Street, " " "
Emmons, Arthur B.,	3 Westmoreland Pl, Pasadena, Cal.
Emmons, Samuel F.,	U. S. Geological Survey, Washington, D. C.
Erbe, Gustav,	344 St. Paul Street, Rochester, N. Y.
Erbslöh, R.,	Box 16, Station A, New York City
Estes, Webster C.,	74 Warren Street, " " "
Evans, George,	55 West 39th Street, " " "
Evans, Selah O.,	118 W. Houston Street, " " "

Everest, Charles M., ... 506 West Avenue, Rochester, N. Y.
Everett, A. Leo, ... 49 Wall Street, New York City
Ewart, Richard H., ... 115 Franklin Street, " " "
Ewing, Thomas, Jr., ... 67 Wall Street, " " "

Fabhri, Alessandro, ... 11 E. 62d Street, New York City
Fabbri, Ernesto G., ... 11 E. 62d Street, " " "
Fahnestock, Gates D., ... 214 Hicks Street, Brooklyn, N. Y.
Fairchild, Benjamin T.. . . . P. O. Box 1120, New York City
Fairchild, Charles S., ... 10 West 8th Street, " " "
Fay, Charles J., ... 31 Nassau Street. " " "
Ferguson, William C., ... Garden City, New York
Field, Hamilton E., ... 106 Columbia Heights, Brooklyn
Fisher, George H., ... 84 Broadway, New York City
Folks, Homer, ... 105 E. 22nd Street, " " "
Ford, Worthington C., . Care Library of Congress, Washington, D. C.
Forrest, C. R., ... Asylum Avenue, Hartford, Conn.
Foster, Macom G., ... P. O. Box 1120, New York City
Fox, Alan, ... 50 Pine Street, " " "
Fox, Austen G., (Life), . . . 37 E. 39th Street, " " "
Frankenheimer, John, ... 25 Broad Street, " " "
Frankfort, M., ... C 22 Produce Exchange, " " "
Frankfurter, Felix, . . . 82 Liberty Street, " " "
French, Daniel E., ... 125 W. 11th Street, " " "
Frissell, H. B... . . . . . Hampton, Va.
Fuld, Leonard Felix, . . . 130 E. 110th Street, New York City
Fuller, Frank, ... , . 61 Fifth Avenue, " " "
Fuller, Paul, ... 71 Broadway. " " "
Fullerton, Alexander, (Life), . . . 5 W. 8th Street, " " "
Funk, I. K., ... 22 Upper Mountain Ave., Montclair, N. J.

Gaillard, William D., ... 141 Broadway, New York City
Gallagher, Patrick, ... 1181 Broadway, " " "
Garver, John A., ... 44 Wall Street, " " "
Gasser, Roy C., ... 35 Wall Street, " " "
Germond, H. S., ... 44 Broad Street, " " "
Gerrish, Frank Scott, ... 17 E. 76th Street, " " "
Getzelsohn, J. A., ... 1065 Prospect Avenue, " " "
Gibbons, George W., ... 198 Broadway, " " "
Gibson, William J., ... 26 Liberty Street, " " "
Gilbert, Cass, ... 11 E. 24th Street, " " "
Gilliss, Walter, ... 150 Fifth Avenue, " " "
Glenn, John M., ... 152 E. 35th Street, " " "
Goadby, Clarence, ... 21 W. 35th Street, " " "
Goddard, George A., ... 10 Tremont Street, Boston, Mass.
Godkin, Laurence, ... 36 W. 10th Street, New York City
Goetze, Otto, ... 60 Remsen Street, Brooklyn, N. Y.
Goldman, Julius, ... 31 Nassau Street, New York City

Goldmark, James, ... 88 Warren Street, New York City
Goodale, John McGregor, ... 43 Broadway, " " "
Goodnow, Frank J., ... 49 Riverside Drive, " " "
Goodrich, David M., ... 2 Rector Street, " " "
Goodwin, Elliot H., ... 79 Wall Street, " " "
Goodwin, H. L., ... 170 Broadway, " " "
Gotthell, Paul, ... Produce Exchange, " " "
Gottsberger, Francis, ... 156 Broadway, " " "
Gould, Elgin R. L., ... 281 Fourth Avenue, " " "
Grant, De Forest, ... 2½ E. 45th Street, " " "
Grant, Percy S., ... 7 W. 10th Street, " " "
Gray, Henry G., ... 161 Madison Avenue, " " "
Green, Noah, ... 478 Central Park, West, " " "
Greenbaum, Samuel, County Court House, B'way & Chambers St., " "
Greene, Francis V., ... 816 Fidelity Building, Buffalo, N. Y.
Greenough, John, ... 38 E. 63rd Street, New York City
Greer, David H., ... 7 Gramercy Park, " " "
Gregory, E. C., ... 54 W. 47th Street, " " "
Gunther, J. J., ... 45 E. 81st Street, " " "
Guthrie, William D., ... 28 Park Place, " " "
Gwynne, Arthur C., ... Rye, N. Y.

Haan, R. M., ... Hotel St. Regis New York City
Hall, Frank L., ... 30 Broad Street, " " "
Hall, Thomas C., ... 700 Park Avenue, " " "
Halsey, Robert H., ... 118 W. 58th Street, " " "
Halsted, John F., ... 93 Remsen Street, Brooklyn, N. Y.
Hamlin, Frank H., ... Canandaigus, N. Y.
Hammond, John Henry, ... 40 Wall Street, New York City
Hand, Learned, ... 2 Wall Street, " " "
Hand, O K., ... 68 Columbia Heights, Brooklyn
Hand, Richard L., ... Elizabethtown, N. Y.
Hansmann, Carl A., ... 96 Broadway, New York City
Harbeck, Charles T., . . . 306 Lexington Avenue, " " "
Harding, Edward, ... 43 Exchange Place, " " "
Hardon, Henry Winthrop, . . . 60 Wall Street, " " "
Harlan, Richard D., George Washington University, Washington, D. C.
Harrison, Robert L., ... 59 Wall Street, New York City
Hart, John Wilson, . . District Attorney's Office, " " "
Hart, W. O., ... 134 Carondelet Street, New Orleans La.
Hartwell, John A., ... 50 E. 53d Street, New York City
Hasslacher, Jacob, ... 100 William Street, " " "
Haupt, Louis, ... 232 E. 19th Street, " " "
Hayes, J. Noble, ... 68 William, " " "
Healy, A. Augustus, ... 198 Columbia Heights, Brooklyn
Heath, Frank E., ... 95 Liberty Street, New York City
Heckscher, A., ... 576 Fifth Avenue, " " "
Heimann, Julius, ... 315 W. 105th Street, " " "

Heinze, Arthur P.,	31 Nassau Street,	New York City
Henderson, Harold G.,	80 Irving Place,,	" " "
Hendrick, Ellwood,	139 E. 40th Street,	" " "
Hentz, Leonard S.,	769 St. Mark's Avenue,	Brooklyn
Herbert, William,	11 Pine Street,	New York City
Hess, Selmar,	151 W. 25th Street,	" " "
Hewlett, Mortimer C.,	900 Broadway,	" " "
Hey, George,	3630 Park Avenue,	" " "
Higginson, James J.,	16 E. 41st Street,	" " "
Hildreth, P. S,	135 Broadway,	" " "
Hinkley, Samuel Neilson,		Lawrence, L. I.
Hinrichs, Frederick W.,	76 William Street,	New York City
Hitchcock, Welcome G., (Life)	69 E. 11th Street,	" " "
Hobart, Henry L.,	120 Front Street,	" " "
Hodges, Harrison B.,	16 Gramercy Park,	" " "
Hoe, Richard M.,	Room 102, Produce Exchange,	" " "
Holt, Henry,	34 W. 33rd Street,	" " "
Holt, Roland,	34 W. 33rd Street,	" " "
Holter, Edwin O,	40 Wall Street,	" " "
Hooper, Parker Morse,	169 Grammercy Park,	" " "
Hoppin, Frederick S., Jr.,	131 E. 19th Street,	" " "
Hoppin, William W.,	54 William Street,	" " "
Hornblower, William B.,	24 Broad Street,	" " "
Howe, Daniel R.,	Asylum Avenue,	Hartford, Conn.
Howe, Horace J.,	25 Gold Street,	Yonkers, N. Y.
Howe, J. Morgan,	12 W. 46th Street,	New York City
Howe, Walter B.,	Criminal Court Building,	" " "
Howe, Wirt,	135 Broadway,	" " "
Howell, Wilson S.,	80th Street, East End Avenue,	" " "
Howland, Charles P.,	35 Wall Street,	" " "
Hoyt, Allen G.,	49 Wall Street,	" " "
Hoyt, Francis D.,	69 Wall Street,	" " "
Hubbard, Thomas H.,	16 W. 58th Street,	" " "
Hughes, Charles E.,		Albany, N.Y.
Hull, Charles A.,	95 William Street,	New York City
Hunt, Leavitt J.,	165 Broadway,	" " "
Huntington, Francis C.,	54 William Street,	" " "
Huntington, Samuel,	176 Broadway,	" " "
Huyler, John S.,	64 Irving Place,	" " "
Hyde, A. F.,	90 West Street,	" " "
Ide, Robert L.,	7 Nassau Street,	New York City
Ijams, J. Horton,	56 William Street,	" " "
Ingraham, Edward,	69 Worth Street,	" " "
Insley, Robert B.,		Westfield, N. J.
Ireland, F. G.,	299 Broadway,	New York City
Ireland, John B.,	15 E. 47th Street,	" " "
Iselin, C. Oliver,	36 Wall Street,	" " "

Iselin, John H., 27 William Street, New York City
Isham, Samuel. 471 Park Avenue, " " "

Jackson, John G., 71 Broadway, New York City
Jacob, Lawrence. 68 Broad Street, " " "
Jacobson, Samuel A., 132 Nassau Street, " " "
James, Walter B., 17 W. 54th Street, " " "
Jameson, E. C., 76 William Street, " " "
Jaretzki, Alfred, 49 Wall Street, " " "
Jay, William, 48 Wall Street, " " "
Jellenix, Felix, 17 William Street, " " "
Jennings, Frederick B., 15 Broad Street, " " "
Jennings, Percy H., 25 Broad Street, " " "
Johnson, Burgess. 3 E. 14th Street, " " "
Johnson, Robert Underwood, 33 E. 17th Street, " " "
Johnson, Willis Fletcher, 154 Nassau Street, " " "
Joline, Adrian, H., 54 Wall Street, " " "
Jones, Oliver Livingston, Jr., 116 W. 72d Street, " " "
Josephthal, Sidney L., 43 Cedar Street, " " "

Kahn, Otto H., (Life), 54 William Street, New York City
Kelley, Nicholas, 52 William Street, " " "
Kellogg, Francis B., Temple Auditorium, Los Angeles, Cal.
Kelsey, Clarence H., 146 Broadway, New York City
Kemp, Edward, 135 Water Street, " " "
Kennedy, Elijah R., 29 & 31 Liberty Street, " " "
Kenneson, Thaddeus D., 13 William Street, " " "
Kenyon, Alan D., 49 Wall Street, " " "
Kenyon, William Houston, 49 Wall Street, " " "
Keppler, Rudolph, 25 Broad Street, " " "
Kernan, John D., Utica, N.Y.
Kernochan, J. Frederic, 44 Pine Street, New York City
Keyes, E L., Tuxedo Park, N. Y.
Kidder, Camillus G., 27 William Street, New York City
Kiernan, Patrick, 14 E. 83rd Street, " " "
Kilbreth, James T., 45 Broadway, " " "
Kilmer, Alfred G, 15 William Street, " " "
Kimball, A. R., Orange, N. J.
Kimball, Daniel T., 198 Broadway, New York City
King, Le Roy, 20 E. 84th Street, " " "
Kinnicutt, Francis H., 165 Broadway, " " "
Kinnicutt, Francis P., 39 E. 35th Street, " " "
Kinnicutt, G. Herman, 39 E. 35th Street, " " "
Kirchhoff, Charles, 14 & 16 Park Place, " " "
Kissell, Gustav E., (Life), 37 Wall Street, " " "
Klein, Isaac H., 30 Broad Street, " " "
Knapp, Horace Greeley, 5 E. 42nd Street, " " "
Knapp, James R., 60 Wall Street, " " "

Knapp, Shepherd,	8 Institute Road, Worcester, Mass.
Knauth, Antonio,	39 West 76th Street, New York City
Knauth, Theodor W.,	15 William Street, " " "
Koehler, Jerome H,	47 Cedar Street, " " "
Kohler, Max J.,	42 Broadway, " " "
Kuehnle, Frederick C.,	629 W. 51st Street, " " "
Kuhne, Percival,	13 William Street, " " "
Kunhardt, William B.,	100 Broadway, " " "
Kunstlich, Samuel H.,	256 Broadway, " " "
La Fetra, Linnaeus E.,	110 E. 62nd Street, New York City
Laimbeer, Francis E.,	299 Broadway, " " "
Lambert, William B.,	Highland Street, Cambridge Mass.
Landes, Leonard,	140 E. 22nd Street, New York City
Landsman, S. M.,	220 E. 19th Street, " " "
Langmann, G.,	121 W. 57th Street, " " "
Lansing, J. Townsend,	82 State Street, Albany, N. Y.
Large, Walter,	15 William Street, New York City
Larremore, Wilbur,	32 Nassau Street. " " "
Law, James,	15 E. 127th Street, " " "
Lawrence, John Burling,	136 E. 30th Street, " " "
Lawrence, Walter B.,	35 Wall Street, " " "
Leavitt, John Brooks,	115 Broadway, " " "
Leaycraft, J. Edgar,	19 W. 42nd Street, " " "
Lederle, Ernest J.,	471 W. 143d Street, " " "
Ledoux, Albert R.,	9 Cliff Street, " " "
Lee, Frederick S.,	125 E. 65th Street, " " "
Lee, Henry T.,	54 E. 52nd Street, " " "
Lee, W. H. L.,	45 Pine Street, " " "
Leech, John E,	94 Remsen Street, Brooklyn, N. Y.
Leffingwell, R. C,	52 William Street, New York City
Le Gendre, William,	59 Wall Street, " " "
Lehmaier, James M..	215 E. 22nd Street, " " "
Lehmaier, Louis A.,	78 Beekman Street, " " "
Levi, Albert A.,	52 Broadway, " " "
Lewis, Richard V.,	130 W. 42d Street, " " "
Lichtenstein, Paul,	304 W. 78th Street, " " "
Lindenthal, Gustav,	45 Cedar Street, " " "
Lindsay, Alexander M.,	373 East Avenue, Rochester, N. Y.
Littauer, Lucius N.,	Gloversville, N. Y.
Livingston, Goodhue,	38 E. 65th Street, New York City
Lobenstein, William C.,	245 Central Park West, " " "
Loines, Russell H.,	131 E. 66th Street, " " "
Lomb, Adolph,	48 Cumberland Street, Rochester, N. Y.
Lomb, Henry C.,	281 Barrington Street, " "
Lord, Franklin B.,	49 Wall Street, New York City
Lord, Frederic W..	126 E. 65th Street, "
Lounsbery, Richard P.,	15 Broad Street

Low, Josiah O., ... 56 William Street, New York City
Lowndes, James, . . . 1515 Massachusetts Avenue, Washington, D. C.
Ludington, A. C.. . . . . 56 W. 10th Street, New York City
Ludlow, James B., ... 45 Cedar Street, " " "
Luther, George Martin, ... 25 Broad Street, " " "
Lyall, Arthur V., ... 7 Pine Street, " " "
Lyman, Frank, ... 88 Wall Street, " " "
Lyman, Theodore, . . . Woodland Street, Hartford, Conn.
Lynch, J. De P., ... Utica, N. Y.

Macfarlane, Wallace, ... 82 Liberty Street, New York City
MacVeagh, Charles, ... 15 Broad Street, " " "
MacKenzie, James C., ... Dobbs Ferry, N. Y.
Mallet-Prevost, Severo, . . . 30 Broad Street, New York City
Mallinckrodt, Edward, . Mallinckrodt Chemical Works, St. Louis, Mo.
Mansfield, Howard, ... 49 Wall Street, New York City
Marble, Charles B., . . . 58 Morningside Avenue, " " "
Marling, Alfred E., ... 21 Liberty Street, " " "
Marshall, Charles H., ... 45 William Street, " " "
Marshall, Fielding L., . . . 1440 Sheridan Road, Chicago, Ill.
Marshall, Louis, ... 37 Wall Street, New York City
Marsters, A., A., ... 15 Dey Street, " " "
Martin, Alfred W., ... 995 Madison Avenue, " " "
Martin, John, ... Grymes Hill, Staten Island, N. Y.
Martin, Newell, ... 20 Exchange Place, New York City
Martin, T. Comerford, ... 114 Liberty Street, " " "
Mason, Alexander T., ... 13 William Street, " " "
Mason, Alfred Bishop. . . . . . . Tuxedo, New York
Mathews, Robert, . . . 135 Spring Street, Rochester, N. Y.
Mathews W. K., ... 36 Wall Street, New York City
Matthew, William B., ... 319 W. 112th Street, " " "
Matthews, Brander, . . . 681 West End Avenue, " " "
Matthewson, Arthur, ... South Woodstock, Conn.
Maxwell, William H., ... 500 Park Avenue, New York City
Maynard, Walter E., . . . Fifth Avenue Building, " " "
Meacham, Alfred B., ... 59 Wall Street, " " "
Meehan, Thomas J., ... 2 Rector Street, " " "
Mellen, Chase, ... 32 Nassau Street, " " "
Merck, George, ... Llewelyn Park, West Orange, N. J.
Merrill, Charles E., ... 44 E. 23d Street, New York City
Merrill, Payson, ... 31 Nassau Street, " " "
Metcalfe, Henry, ... 147 Fourth Avenue, " " "
Meyer, Alfred, ... 785 Madison Avenue, " " "
Milbank, Albert G., , , . . . 49 Wall Street, " " "
Milburn, John G., ... 54 Wall Street, " " "
Miller, Clifford L., ... 62 West 89th Street, " " "
Miller, Daniel S., ... 150 Central Park S., " " "
Miller, George Douglas, ... 125 State Street, Albany, N. Y.

Milliken, Hugh K.,	51 Leonard Street, New York City
Mills, L. H.,	478 Broome Street, " " "
Moffat, George B.,	5 Nassau Street, " " "
Moffat, R. Burnham,	63 Wall Street, " " "
Montgomery, R. M.,	27 Pine Street, " "
Morgan, W. Fellows,	Arch 5, Brooklyn Bridge, " " "
Morgan, W. Forbes, Jr.,	49 Broadway, " " "
Morris, Ray,	81 Fulton Street, " " "
Morrow, Dwight,	Englewood, N. J.
Morse, Horace J.,	820 St. Mark's Avenue, Brooklyn
Morse, Richard C.,	85 Sidney Place, "
Mortimer, Richard,	11 Wall Street, New York City
Mosenthal, P. J.,	9½ William Street, " " "
Mosle, A. Henry,	30 Broad Street, " " "
Mott, William F.,	Toms River, N. J.
Munro, J. G.,	61 Erie County Bank Building, Buffalo, N. Y.
Munro, John R.,	132 Remsen Street, Brooklyn, N. Y.
Munroe, Vernon,	45 William Street, New York City
Murphy, Daniel F.,	165 Broadway, " " "
Murray, Joseph K.,	Broadway, opposite 16th Street, Flushing, N. Y.
McAlpin, George L.,	55 W. 33d Street, New York City
McAneny, Leonard G.,	2 Rector Street, " " "
McCagg, Louis Butler,	18 E. 84th Street, " " "
McCandless, Charles W.,	15 William Street, " " "
McCarroll, William,	Tribune Building, " " "
McCobb, James S.,	44 W. 44th Street, " " "
McCook, Philip J.,	15 William Street, " " "
McDowell, H. G.,	87 Nassau Street, " " "
McGinness, Remsen,	42 East 41st Street, " " "
McKeen, James,	58 Clark Street, Brooklyn
McKeever, J. Lawrence,	164 Lexington Avenue, New York City
McMahon, Fulton,	54 William Street, " " "
Nadal, Charles C.,	142 E. 35th Street, New York City
Nash, Francis Philip,	Geneva, N. Y.
Naumberg, Elkan,	48 W. 58th Street, New York City
Nelson, H. W., Jr.,	Marshfield Hills, Mass.
Nevin, A. Parker,	149 Broadway, New York City
Newton Albro J.,	528 Union Street, Brooklyn, N. Y.
Newton, R. Heber,	East Hampton, N. Y.
Nichols, George M.,	277 Adelphi Street, Brooklyn, N. Y.
Nichols, W. N.,	25 Broad Street, New York City
Nicoll, James C.,	51 W. 10th Street, " " "
Nissen, Ludwig,	182 Broadway, " " "
Nordlinger, Abraham E.,	143 West Broadway, " " "
Norris, Henry S.,	10 W. 49th Street, " " "
Notman, George,	99 John Street, " " "
Oakes, Charles,	49 Wall Street. " " "

O'Connor, John A., ... , Box H. Tarrytown, N. Y.
Ogden, Charles W., ... 14 E. 79th Street, New York City
Ogden, Rollo, ... 20 Vesey Street, " " "
Olin, Stephen H., ... 82 Nassau Street, " " "
Olney, Peter B., Jr., ... 68 William Street, " " "
Oltman, H. H., ... 42 Broadway, " " "
Olyphant, Robert, ... 17 Battery Place, " " "
Opdyke, William S., ... 20 Nassau Street, " " "
Oppenheim, Edward L., ... 30 Broad Street, " " "
Oppenheimer, Henry S., ... 5 E. 43rd Street, " " "
Orcutt C. Blake, ... Hudson River Day Line, ". " "
Ordway, Edward W., ... 1093 Dean Street, Brooklyn
Orr, Alexander E., ... 102 Remsen Street, "
Osborn, Perry, ... 52 Brattle Street, Cambridge, Mass.
Osborne, Thomas M., ... Auburn, N. Y.

Paffard, Frederic C., ... 238 Clinton Street, Brooklyn, N. Y.
Page, Walter H., ... 34 Union Square, New York City
Parker, Frederick S., ... 32 Garden Place, Brooklyn
Parks, J. Waring, ... 56 Pine Street, New York City
Parsons, Herbert, ... 52 William Street, " " "
Parsons, John E., ... 52 William Street, " " "
Partridge, John N., ... Hamilton Club, Brooklyn, N. Y.
Partridge, William Ordway, . . 289 Fourth Avenue, New York City
Paulding, James Kirk, ... 130 E. 24th Street, " " "
Pauli, H. G., ... 116 Broad Street, " " "
Peabody, George Foster, . . . 43 Exchange Place, " " "
Pease, George Card, ... Vergennes, Vt.
Peck, George G., ... 117 Chambers Street, New York City
Pedersen, James, ... 20 E. 46th Street, " " "
Pederson, Victor C., ... 45 W. 9th Street, " " "
Pell, Frederick A., ... Lakewood, N. J.
Pendleton, Francis K., ... 25 Broad Street, New York City
Perrine, William A., . . . 2440 N. Marshall Street, Philadelphia, Pa.
Phillips, N. Taylor, ... 51 Chambers Street, New York City
Phoenix, Phillips, ... 68 Broad Street, " " "
Pierce, Franklin, ... 27 Pine Street, " " "
Pierce, Henry H., ... 49 Wall Street, " " "
Pierrepont, Henry E., . . . 216 Columbia Heights, Brooklyn
Pierrepont, Robert Low, ... Box 449, Bay Shore, N. Y.
Pinchot, Amos R. E., . . Criminal Court Building, New York City
Pinchot, Gifford, . . . 1615 Rhode Island Avenue, Washington, D. C.
Planten, John R., ... 44 Eighth Avenue, Brooklyn, N. Y.
Planten, W. R. J., ... 44 Eighth Avenue, " "
Plaut, Albert, ... 120 William Street, New York City
Poillon, Cornelius, ... 125 E. 70th Street, " " "
Polk, W. M., ... 7 E. 36th Street, " " "
Pollak, Francis D., ... 49 Wall Street, " " "

Pope, George A.,	926 St. Paul Street, Baltimore, Md.
Post, Abram S.,	81 Fulton Street, New York City
Potts, W. Rockhill,	143 Liberty Street, " " "
Powell, Wilson M., Jr.,	29 Wall Street. " " "
Pratt, Frederic B.,	215 Ryerson Street, Brooklyn, N. Y.
Pratt, John T.,	43 Exchange Place, New York City
Prentice, William P.,	52 Broadway, " " "
Prentiss, George H.,	108 Pierrepont Street, Brooklyn, N Y.
Price, Joseph M.,	158 West Broadway, New York City
Proskauer, Joseph M.,	170 Broadway, " " "
Pruden, W. Edgar,	162 W. 120th Street, " " "
Pryer, Charles,	New Rochelle, N. Y.
Putnam, George Haven,	27 W. 23d Street, New York City
Putnam, George P.,	160 Fifth Avenue, " " "
Putnam, Harrington,	404 Washington Avenue, Brooklyn
Putnam, Irving,	27 W. 23rd Street, New York City
Putnam, J. Bishop,	27 W. 23rd Street, " " "
Pyne, Moses Taylor,	30 Pine Street, " " "
Rand, William H., Jr.	63 Wall Street, New York City
Raven, A. A.,	51 Wall Street, " " "
Raymond, Charles H.,	11 Pine Street, " " "
Raymond, Rossiter W.	29 W. 39th Street, " " "
Reed, Lansing P.,	15 Broad Street, " " "
Rees, Norman I.,	39 Frankford Street, " " "
Reichhelm, Edward P.,	90 West 84th Street, Bayonne, N. J.
Reid, Wallace,	56 Maiden Lane, New York City
Reynolds, James B.,	500 Fifth Avenue, " " "
Rhoades, John Harsen,	45 Wall Street, " " "
Rice, Edwin T., Jr.,	59 Wall Street, " " "
Richards, C. A. L.,	169 Power Street, Providence, R. I.
Rives, George L.,	69 E. 79th Street, New York City
Robb, J. Hampden,	23 Park Avenue, " " "
Robinson, Beverly R.,	42 W. 37th Street, " " "
Robinson, Moncure,	7 E. 42d Street, " " "
Rogers, Robert,	48 E. 61st Street, " " "
Roome, W. Harris,	287 Fourth Avenue, " " "
Roosevelt, Franklin D.,	125 E. 36th Street, " " "
Roosevelt, Theodore,	Oyster Bay, N. Y.
Root, Elihu,	733 Park Avenue, New York City
Root, Elihu, Jr.,	31 Nassau Street, " " "
Rose, Arthur P.,	Geneva, N. Y.
Rosendale, Simon W.,	57 State Street, Albany, N. Y.
Rosenfeld, George,	58 New Street, New York City
Rossbach, Jacob,	1 W. 86th Street, " " "
Rothschild, Jacob,	31 W. 57th Street, " " "
Rothschild, Ludwig,	466 Broadway, " " "
Rounds, Arthur C.,	96 Broadway

Rowe, Basil W.,	71 Broadway, New York City
Rowe, William V.,	51 Wall Street, " " "
Rublee, George.	30 Pine Street, " " "
Runyon, Carman R,	87 Locust Hill Avenue, Yonkers. N. Y.
Rush, Thomas E,	40 Wall Street, New York City
Russell, J. Townsend,	170 Remsen Street, Brooklyn, N. Y
Sachs, Walter E.,	43 Exchange Place, New York City
Sackett, Henry W.	154 Nassau Street, " " "
Sage, Dean.	49 Wall Street, " " "
Salomon, William,	25 Broad Street, " " "
Sand, Henry A. L.,	120 Broadway, " " "
Sands, B. Aymar,	31 Nassau Street, " " "
Sanger, William Cary,	Sangerfield, N. Y.
Sayer, W. Murray, Jr.,	398 Washington Avenue, Brooklyn
Schafer, Samuel M.,	5 Wall Street, New York City
Scharmann, Hermann B.,	170 W. 59th Street, " " "
Schieren, Charles A.	405 Clinton Avenue, Brooklyn
Schnakenberg, D.,	6 Hanover Street, New York City
Schneidenbach, Arthur Jaques,	75 E. 82d Street, " " "
Schrader, George H. F.,	32 Rose Street, " " "
Schurman, George W.,	15 W. 75th Street, " " "
Schwarzenbach, Robert J. T.,	472 Broome Street, " " "
Schwarzschild, Monroe M.,	340 W. 86th Street, " " "
Schurz, Carl Lincoln,	49 Wall Street, " " "
Scott, J. F.,	11 Overbrook Street, Mount Vernon, N. Y.
Scott, William,	25 Duane Street, New York City
Scribner, Arthur H.,	153 Fifth Avenue, " " "
Scribner, Charles,	153 Fifth Avenue, " " "
Seaman, Louis L.,	247 Fifth Avenue. " " "
Searle, Arthur,	41 Concord Avenue, Cambridge, Mass.
Seaver, Benjamin F.,	111 Pierrepont Street, Brooklyn
Seaver, Oscar S.,	49 Exchange Place, New York City
Sedgwick, Arthur G.,	52 William Street, " " "
Sedgwick, Ellery,	116 E. 26th Street, " " "
Sedgwick, Henry D.,	120 E. 22d Street, " " "
Seligman, E. R. A.,	324 W. 86th Street, " " "
Seligman, George W.,	3 S. William Street, " " "
Seligman, Jefferson,	1 William Street, " " "
Serven, A. Ralph,	1419 "F" Street, N. W., Washington, D. C.
Seward, George F.,	97 Cedar Street, New York City
Sexton, Lawrence E.,	34 Pine Street, " " "
Seymour, Origen S.,	54 William Street, " " "
Shainwald, Ralph L.,	100 William Street, " " "
Shaw, Albert,	13 Astor Place, " " "
Sheldon, Edward W.,	45 Wall Street, " " "
Sheppard, John S., Jr.,	26 Liberty Street, " " "
Shillaber, William Jr.,	1 Broadway, " " "

Shortt, W. A.,	32 Broadway, New York City
Sibley, Harper,	5 Nassau Street, " " "
Siedenberg, Reinhard,	Cotton Exchange, " " "
Silverman, M. J.,	218 Alexander Avenue, " " "
Simes, William,	Box 3084, Boston, Mass.
Simon, Franklin,	414 Fifth Avenue, New York City
Skidmore, William L.,	39 W. 52nd Street, " " "
Skuse, Thomas J,	Naval Office, Customs House, " " "
Slade, Francis Louis,	115 Broadway, " " "
Sleicher, John A.,	225 Fifth Avenue, " " "
Slicer, Thomas R.,	55 W. 44th Street, " " "
Smillie, James C.,	440 West End Avenue, " " "
Smith, Adelbert J.,	15 William Street, " " "
Smith, Bryan H.,	Brooklyn Savings Bank, Brooklyn, N. Y.
Smith, Charles Robinson,	25 Broad Street, New York City
Smith, Charles Stewart,	25 W. 47th Street, " " "
Smith, Clarence B.,	27 William Street, " " "
Smith, Edgar L.,	31 W. 45th Street, " " "
Smith, F. Hopkinson,	150 E. 34th Street, " " "
Smith, Frederick J.,	278 Mulberry Street, " " "
Smith, Howard M.,	Brevoort Savings Bank. Brooklyn, N. Y.
Smith, James E.,	38 Park Row, New York City
Smith J. Waldo,	165 Broadway, " " "
Smith, Nathaniel S.,	68 William Street, " " "
Smith, William Mason,	128 Broadway, " " "
Smith, William Alexander,	412 Madison Avenue, " " "
Smyth, Nathan A.,	5 Nassau Street, " " "
Snow, Elbridge G,	56 Cedar Street, " " "
Snow, Frederick A.,	15 Wall Street, " " "
Spackman, W. M.,	820 Madison Avenue, " " "
Spector, Joseph,	241 E. 68th Street, " " "
Spiegelberg, Frederick,	36 W. 76th Street, " " "
Spingarn, J. E.,	9 W. 73rd Street, " " "
Stebbins. H. C.,	718 Fifth Avenue, " " "
Steers, James R.,	101 Park Avenue, " " "
Steinway, Frederick T.,	53rd Street and Park Avenue, " " "
Stern, Benjamin,	32 W. 23rd Street, " " "
Stern, Henry Root,	40 Wall Street. " " "
Stevens, Gorham P.,	107 E. 16th Street, " " "
Stewart, William R.,	P. O. Box 258, " " "
Stimson, Daniel M.,	28 W. 37th Street, " " "
Stix, Sylvan L.,	Hudson and N. Moore Streets, " " "
Stokes, Anson Phelps, Jr., (Life),	Yale University, New Haven, Conn.
Stokes, Harold M. Phelps, (Life),	229 Madison Avenue, New York City
Stokes, I. N. Phelps, (Life),	118 E. 22nd Street, " " "
Stokes. James,	49 Cedar Street, " " "
Stokes, J. G. Phelps, (Life),	229 Madison Avenue, " " "
Strasbourger, Samuel,	74 Broadway, " " "

Straus, Isador,	Broadway and 34th Street, New York City
Strauss, Albert,	15 Broad Street, " " "
Strauss. Frederick.	15 Broad Street, " " "
Strobel, Emil L ,	307 W. 108rd Street, " " "
Strong, George A.,	50 Wall Street, " " "
Strong, Theron G.,	49 Wall Street, " " "
Stuart, J. P. Whiton,	8 E. 54th Street, " " "
Sturges, S. Perry,	305 Washington Avenue, Brooklyn
Sturgis, F. K.,	36 Broad Street, New York City
Stuyvesant, Rutherford,	32 Liberty Street, " " "
Sulzberger, Cyrus L.,	516 West End Avenue, " " "
Sulzberger, Ferdinand,	802 First Avenue, " " "
Taft, Henry W.,	40 Wall Street, New York City
Taggart, Rush,	195 Broadway, " " "
Tappan, J. B. Coles,	49 Wall Street, " " "
Tatham, Charles,	261 Water Street, " " "
Tatham, Edwin,	82 Beekman Street, " " "
Taussig, Walter M.,	9-15 Murray Street, " " "
Taylor, E. P., Jr.,	7 Pine Street, " " "
Taylor, Thomas Fenton,	130 E. 67th Street, " " "
Taylor, Walter F.,	54 Wall Street, " " "
Terry, Roderick,	Newport, R. I.
Terry, Seth Sprague,	66 Broadway, New York City
Thacher, Thomas,	62 Cedar Street, " " "
Thacher, Thomas, D.,	62 Cedar Street " " "
Thatcher, John S ,	839 Madison Avenue. " " "
Thomas, John H.,	9 Broadway. " " "
Thomson, George G.,	412 Bergen Street, Brooklyn, N. Y.
Thomson. Herbert G.,	145 Broadway, New York City
Thorne, Robert,	30 Broad Street, " " "
Thorne, Samuel,	43 Cedar Street, " " "
Thorne, Samuel, Jr.,	43 Cedar Street, " " "
Thornton, William,	117 Prince Street, " " "
Tiebout, Charles H.,	31 Grand Street, Brooklyn
Tinker, Edward L.,	70 West 55th Street. New York City
Tinkham, Julian R.,	42 Broadway. " " "
Tison, Alexander,	11 William Street, " " "
Tod, J. Kennedy,	5 Nassau Street, " " "
Todd, Henry A.,	824 West End Avenue, " " "
Tomkins, Calvin,	17 Battery Place, " " "
Tompkins, Hamilton B.,	229 Broadway, " " "
Tower, George H.,	2 Rector Street, " " "
Train, Arthur C.,	30 Broad Street, " " "
Trowbridge, Alexander B.,	114 E. 28th Street, " " "
Trowbridge, Mason,	1 Liberty Street, " " "
Tuckerman, Alfred,	Metropolitan Club, Washington, D. C.
Tuckerman, Eliot,	44 Pine Street, New York City

Tuckerman, Paul. . . . . Tuxedo, N. Y.
Tuttle, George M., ... 38 W. 52nd Street, New York City
Tweedy, J. F., ... 11 Pine Street, " " "

Unckles, D. S., ... 957 St. Mark's Avenue, Brooklyn
Ulbrich, Gustav, ... 30 Broad Street, New York City

Vail, Charles D., ... Geneva, N. Y.
Valentine, Charles A., ... 1 E. 27th Street, New York City
Valentine, Henry C., (Life), ... 257 Broadway, " " "
Valentine, Robert G. . . . Office of Indian Affairs, Washington, D. C.
Van Dusen, Samuel C., ... 32 Cliff Street, New York City
Van Ingen, Edward H., ... 9 E. 71st Street, " " "
Van Nest, George W., ... 20 Broad Street, " " "
Van Santvoord, R., . . . 10 W. 122nd Street, " " "
Vidal, J. E., ... 68 Beach Street, Stapleton, S. I.
Villard, Harold G. . . . . . 43 Cedar Street, New York City
Villard, Oswald Garrison, (Life), . . 20 Vesey Street, " " "

Wadsworth, James W., ... Geneseo, N. Y.
Wagener, August P., . . . 51 Chambers Street, New York City
Walker, John, . . . 1231 Western Avenue, Allegheny City, Pa.
Walker, William, ... Harbison & Walker, Pittsburg, Pa.
Wallace, William H., ... 66 Broadway, New York City
Wallace, W. J., ... 209 W. 81st Street, " " "
Walling, William English, . . . 3 Fifth Avenue, " " "
Warburg, F. M., (Life), . . . 52 William Street, " " "
Warburg, Paul M., . . . 52 William Street, " " "
Ward, Henry Galbreath, ... 79 Wall Street, " " "
Wardwell, Allen, ... 15 Broad Street, " " "
Warren, George A., 1443 Massachusetts Avenue, N. W., Washington, D. C.
Warren, H. Langford, ... 120 Boylston Street, Boston, Mass.
Watson, Charles W., . . . 500 Madison Avenue, New York City
Webb, Willoughby L., ... 63 Wall Street, " " "
Weber, Leonard, ... 25 W. 46th Street, " " "
Weed, John W., ... 62 William Street, " " "
Weeks, John E., ... 46 E. 57th Street, " " "
Weir, R. F., ... 30 W. 50th Street, " " "
Welch, Archibald A., ... Woodland Street, Hartford, Conn.
Weld, Francis M., ... 5 Nassau Street, New York City
Welling, R. W. G., ... 2 Wall Street, " " "
Werthein, H. P., ... 27 William Street, " " "
Wetmore, Edmund, ... 34 Pine Street, " " "
Wheeler, Everett P., ... 27 William Street, " " "
Wheeler, James R., ... Columbia College, " " "
White, Alexander M., ... 52 Remsen Street, Brooklyn
White, Andrew D., (Life), ... Ithaca, N. Y.
White, Harold T., ... 5 Nassau Street, New York City

Whiteside, George W., . . District Attorney's Office, New York City
Whiton, John M., ... 73 William Street, " " "
Whitridge, Frederick W., ... 59 Wall Street, " " "
Wickersham, C. W., ... Hastings Hall, Cambridge, Mass.
Wickersham, George W., . . Department Justice, Washington, D. C.
Wilcox, Ansley, ... 295 Main Street, Buffalo, N. Y.
Wilder, William R., ... 45 Cedar Street, New York City
Wilds, Howard Payson, ... University Club, " " "
Wilcox, William G., . . . 3 South William Street, " " "
Williams, Benjamin A., ... 22 E. 82nd Street, " " "
Williams, L. L., . Care E. C. Williams, 135 Broadway, " " "
Williams, Norman A., ... 165 Broadway, " " "
Williams, Perry P., . . . Produce Exchange, " " "
Williams, Richard H., ... 1 Broadway, " " "
Williams, Roger H., ... 31 W. 12th Street, " " "
Williams, Stephen G., . . . 953 Madison Avenue, " " "
Williams, William, ... 35 Wall Street, " " "
Willis, Albert L., ... 124 W. 183rd Street, " " "
Wilson, George Augustus, . . . 37 Liberty Street, " " "
Wilson, Richard T., ... 511 Fifth Avenue, " " "
Wingate, George W., ... 1100 Dean Street, Brooklyn, N. Y.
Winston, G. Owen, ... 936 Broadway, New York City
Winters, Joseph E., ... 25 W. 37th Street, " " "
Winthrop, Bronson, ... 32 Liberty Street, " " "
Wise, E. E., ... 19 William Street, " " "
Wisner, Charles, ... Cotton Exchange, " " "
Wisner, H. G., ... 18 W. 12th Street, " " "
Witherbee F. S., ... 71 Broadway, " " "
Wolff, Emil, ... 171 W. 71st Street, " " "
Wolff, Lewis S., ... 12 E. 70th Street, " " "
Wood, L. Hollingsworth, . . , . . 2 Wall Street, " " "
Woodbridge, Charles E., ... 17 Battery Place, " " "
Worcester, Edwin D., Jr., . . . 35 Nassau Street, " " "
Wright, Jonathan, ... 44 W. 49th Street, " " "

Yonge, Henry, ... 391 Fulton Street, Brooklyn

Zabriskie, George, ... 49 Wall Street, New York City
Zollikoffer, Oscar F., ... 49 W. 54th Street, " " "

ARTICLES OF INCORPORATION

OF

THE NEW YORK CIVIL SERVICE REFORM ASSOCIATION

[Filed May 11, 1900.]

KNOW ALL MEN BY THESE PRESENTS: That we, the undersigned, being persons of full age and all citizens of the United States, a majority of whom are also citizens of the State of New York, and being now Directors of an unincorporated association known as the New York Civil Service Reform Association, and organized for the purposes hereinafter mentioned; being desirous of incorporation for the same purposes under the Membership Corporations Law of the State of New York, do hereby, pursuant to unanimous vote of all the members of the said Association, present and voting at a regularly called meeting thereof, and pursuant to authority given by the said unanimous vote at the said meeting, of which meeting notice of the intention so to incorporate was given personally or by mail to each member of such Association whose residence or Post Office address was known, at least thirty days before said meeting, and at which meeting the corporate name stated in paragraph First was by unanimous vote adopted, do hereby certify as follows:

FIRST.—The name or title by which the Association in which we desire to form ourselves as aforesaid shall be known in law, shall be the Civil Service Reform Association.

SECOND.—The territory in which its operations are to be principally conducted shall be the City of New York.

THIRD.—The city in which its principal office is to be located is the City of New York.

FOURTH.—The objects of the Association shall be to further the establishment of a system of appointment, promotion and removal in the civil service, founded upon the principle that public office is a public trust, admission to and retention in which should depend upon proven fitness; and to take such action as may tend to secure the honest and efficient execution of laws and rules relating to the civil service, and to the proper administration thereof.

FIFTH.—The number of its directors shall be twenty-eight.

SIXTH.—The names of the persons to be its directors until its first annual meeting are as follows:

Samuel P. Avery, Truman J. Backus, Henry De Forest Baldwin, Edward Cary, Charles Collins, W. Bayard Cutting, Horace E. Deming, A. S. Frissell, Richard Watson Gilder, Edwin L. Godkin, J. Warren Greene, George McAneny, James McKeen, Jacob F. Miller, Samuel H. Ordway, William A. Perrine, George Foster Peabody, William J. Schieffelin, Carl Schurz, Charles A. Schieren, Thomas R. Slicer, Henry Sanger Snow, Anson Phelps Stokes, S. Perry Sturges, Henry W. Taft, William H. Thomson, Charles W. Watson and Everett P. Wheeler.

In WITNESS WHEREOF we have made, signed, acknowledged and filed this certificate in duplicate.

Dated this Eighth day of May, 1900.

C. SCHURZ,	WILLIAM H. THOMSON,
JACOB F. MILLER,	A. S. FRISSELL,
ANSON PHELPS STOKES,	GEORGE MCANENY,
EVERETT P. WHEELER,	CHARLES A. SCHIEREN,
CHARLES COLLINS,	SAMUEL P. AVERY,
SAMUEL H. ORDWAY,	GEORGE FOSTER PEABODY.
J. WARREN GREENE,	

STATE OF NEW YORK, } ss.
COUNTY OF NEW YORK,

On this eighth day of May, one thousand and nine hundred, before me personally came Carl Schurz, Jacob F. Miller, Anson Phelps Stokes, Everett P. Wheeler, Charles Collins, J. Warren Greene, William H. Thomson, Samuel H. Ordway, A. S. Frissell, George McAneny, Charles A. Schieren, Samuel P. Avery and George Foster Peabody, to me personally known to be the persons described in and who made and signed the foregoing certificate, and severally duly acknowledged to me that they had made, signed and executed the same for the uses and purposes therein set forth.

F. W. HOERSCHGEN,
Notary Public, Kings County. (149)
(Certificate filed in New York County.)

Approved, May 9, 1900.

DAVID LEVINTRITT,
Justice of the Supreme Court of the State of New York.

REPORT

OF THE

Executive Committee

OF THE

New York

Civil Service Reform Association

Submitted at the Annual Meeting,
May 10, 1911.

LIST OF MEMBERS, ETC.

NEW YORK
PUBLISHED FOR THE
CIVIL SERVICE REFORM ASSOCIATION
79 Wall Street
1911

PRESS OF
GEORGE G. PECK
117 CHAMBERS STREET
NEW YORK

CONTENTS

Annual Report of the Executive Committee	5
Appendix: Report of the Special Committee on Retirement Legislation	25
Annual Report of the Treasurer	32
Constitution and By-Laws	34
Roll of Officers and Members	42
Articles of Incorporation	65

ANNUAL REPORT

OF THE

Executive Committee of the Civil Service Reform Association.

The work of the Association since its last Annual Meeting on May 11, 1910, divides itself sharply into two parts. Until the end of the calendar year both the personnel and the policy of the administration of the civil service law in New York State and New York City remained unchanged. That policy was in the main distinctly favorable to the advancement of the merit system and its conservative extension to new branches, and to the growth of public confidence in the fairness of its administration and public recognition of its fundamental usefulness. The activity of the Association was therefore largely confined to encouraging and suggesting improved methods of examination and administration and bringing violations or evasions of the law to the attention of the proper authorities. Since the advent on January 1, 1911, of a new party control in State administration the whole atmosphere has changed; the merit system is no longer advancing but distinctly retrograding, and the Association has been engaged in a bitter struggle to hold as much as possible of the ground gained in the past. Before, however, entering upon a discussion of the detailed work done by the Association in this State and City, this Committee desires to call attention to the marked progress which the merit system has made in other parts of the country.

THE FEDERAL SERVICE AND OTHER STATES.

By the attitude which within the past year President Taft has publicly assumed toward the merit system he has placed the federal service on a higher plane than it has ever before reached. By order of September 30, the President extended the competitive service to include the high grade positions of assistant postmasters. In his message to Congress last December, after stating that officers responsible for the policy of the administration and their immediate personal assistants or deputies should not be included in the classified service, he declared in favor of the classification of all purely administrative positions. This program for extension, he did his utmost to carry into effect by securing the introduction of bills in Congress to give to the President power to classify all postmasters, collectors of customs and internal revenue and similar officers whose appointment is now subject to confirmation by the Senate. None of these bills secured passage, but that could not have reasonably been expected on the first announcement of so far reaching a program for extension and at a short session of Congress. That this program met with such wide-spread public approval and with so little expressed criticism even from Senators and Representatives is an indication of how strong the hold of the merit system as the necessary basis of decent public administration has become.

An even more striking illustration of this popular support of the merit system is to be found in the majorities by which it has been carried wherever submitted to the people by referendum. Nowhere when submitted as a separate issue has it been defeated. Last fall a proposition for a state wide civil service law was submitted to the voters of Illinois and propositions for the adoption of the competitive system in municipal government to the voters of Detroit, Michigan, Newark, East Orange and Essex County, New Jersey. These, in every case, were carried by large majorities. Civil service bills were presented this year in the legislatures of California, Michigan, Ohio and Pennsylvania, while the rapid extension of city government by commission has, in most cases, carried with it the merit system as an integral part of the plan.

A change in party control is recognized as meaning a critical period for the merit system. But whether at such a critical period the merit system will advance or retreat depends on the attitude that the chief executive takes toward it on assuming office. In our neighbor state of New Jersey there has been no retrograde movement such as has occurred on a like change in party control in New York; Governor Wilson made no change in the State Civil Service Commission until recently when the term of one member who was unwilling to serve again, expired, while by the legislation which he has advocated he has increased the scope of the commission's jurisdiction. No disturbance of the administration of the federal civil service law has followed a change in party control in the House of Representatives; on the contrary, the Democratic majority has started out with a particularly noteworthy act, in the nature of a self-denying ordinance, by making a decided reduction in the amount of House patronage.

The administration of the federal offices in New York has been less affected by outside political influences than in former years. Marked improvements in method of administration have been introduced. But few changes in heads of local offices have occurred. The recent appointment of Hon. Francis W. Bird as Appraiser of the Port of New York is particularly to be commended. To the members of this Committee, in which he has been an active worker for some years, he is known by his record both in the United States District Attorney's office and in politics as able and energetic and in thorough accord with the principles of the merit system and of efficient administration.

THE STATE SERVICE.

THE NEW YORK STATE CIVIL SERVICE COMMISSION.

The Democratic platform in the last state election was unequivocal in its support of civil service reform.

"We believe that for the promotion of greater efficiency in the public service, the merit system should be extended wherever it is found practical and protection given to civil service employees from unjust dismissal."

The Republican platform was silent on the subject. Both candidates declared themselves in favor of the merit system; Governor Dix had been a member of the Association, Mr. Stimson as U. S. District Attorney, had in the absence of legal requirement, applied the principles of merit and fitness in the selection of his immediate subordinates. The maintenance and support of the merit system was not, therefore, considered to be at issue in the campaign.

Just prior to election Governor Dix authorized the following statement in reply to questions as to his attitude:

Q. Are you in sympathy with the policy of maintaining the civil service as now constituted and of promoting the reasonable extension thereof?

A. I am in complete sympathy with the policy of maintaining the civil service as now constituted and of promoting the reasonable extension thereof.

Q. Are you in favor of retaining in their present positions faithful employees of the state, now in the classified service?

A. Decidedly so.

Q. If elected governor, would it be your policy, as has been stated, to exempt from the civil service positions now under its protection and would you be disposed to appoint as civil service commissioners men in sympathy with such a purpose?

A. No such statement has been made with my consent or knowledge. *If I am elected governor, the civil service commission appointed by me will be in complete sympathy with the letter and spirit of the civil service law and the merit system.*

After election the Association made use of every legitimate means in its power for calling the attention of Governor Dix to the importance of securing a strong and efficient civil service commission, thoroughly in sympathy with the principles underlying the civil service law. In view of all these facts it was with intense surprise that the public heard the announcement on February 7 of the new Commission, composed of former Commissioner John E. Kraft of Kingston, Ex-Senator Walter C. Burton of Brooklyn and Elek John Ludvigh of New York. To accomplish these changes the resignations of Commissioners Milliken and Brown had been called for in January.

Commissioner Kraft has seen long service in the commission, but his course in office has not commended him favorably to those who watch the administration of the law. When Colonel Silas W. Burt, now President of the Association, was summarily removed from the commission by Governor Odell on assuming office in January, 1901, Mr. Kraft was selected to succeed him. He has never displayed any real sympathy with the merit system and this Committee has frequently had occasion in previous reports to call attention to the petty and partisan attitude assumed by him on important matters.

Commissioner Burton was appointed at the behest of the Democratic organization of Brooklyn, of which John H. McCooey is the leader. An investigation of the Senate Journal for the years 1903 and 1904 during which he served in the State Senate disclosed the fact that he had been recorded as voting in favor of every bill which the Association opposed, on the ground that they would injure the merit system, that passed the Senate during these years. There were five of these bills, all of which were vetoed either by the Governor or the Mayor.

Commissioner Ludvigh, the minority member, had never held public office nor had he been identified in any way with the movement for the merit system. The courageous stand he has taken in opposition to his colleagues on requests for wholesale exemptions from competition entitle him to great credit.

THE RAID ON THE STATE SERVICE.

The Commission held its first meeting on February 21 and organized by the election of Commissioner Kraft as President. Much of their subsequent action must be attributed to him personally, for the other members, lacking previous experience, have relied largely on his judgment. At this first meeting they were confronted with requests for the exemption from competition of 54 positions in the offices of the State Comptroller, the State Engineer and Surveyor and the Attorney-General representing a total annual patronage value of $117,000. All of these requests have since been granted by the Commission.

Forty-nine of these exemptions were requested by State Comptroller William Sohmer, a representative of Tammany Hall. They covered 22 transfer tax appraisers, with salaries ranging from $1,000 to $4,000, 13 stock transfer tax examiners, $1,700; 8 court and trust fund examiners, $8 per day; 3 prison clerks, $2,000 to $2,500; 3 assistant prison clerks, $1,500 to $1,800. All of these positions had been placed in the competitive class (with the assent of Commissioner Kraft, except in the case of the prison clerks) during 1909 and 1910 at the request of Comptroller Clark Williams, a banker of high reputation who had never taken an active part in politics, who was appointed by Governor Hughes in November, 1909, to fill the vacancy caused by the death of Comptroller Gaus. For all these positions except the prison clerks successful competitive examinations had been held and in four cases appointments had been made from them of men who have proved satisfactory and who are still in the service. Comptroller Sohmer attacked neither the competency of the men in office, whom he had not had time to become acquainted with, nor the eligible lists created for the filling of vacancies, but made use of the time-worn and barnacled plea of confidentiality.

The Constitution of the State makes practicability of competition the only question which the State Commission has the right to consider in classifying any position or acting on any request for exemption. The practicability of competition in these cases,—if indeed any question could be raised as to it in the face of successful eligible lists drawn up as the result of competition,—has been pointed out to the Commission at public hearings and in the public press. So have also the real reasons underlying the plea of confidentiality,—if indeed the majority of the Commission can be presumed to have been ignorant of it. Nevertheless, the Commission, on March 14, Commissioner Ludvigh dissenting, granted the exemption of all but the transfer tax appraisers. The appraisers, forming the choicest and most desired patronage, were held over until the senatorial fight was settled and then were granted on April 5, Commissioner Ludvigh again voting in the negative.

A barefaced attempt, which as soon as discovered proved abortive, was made to increase the value of the patronage thus granted. Although after its meeting of March 14 the Commission announced that they had exempted 8 court and trust · fund examiners and 13 examiners of transfers of stock, at the request of the Comptroller the resolution sent to the Governor for approval provided for the exemption of 16 court and trust fund examiners and 26 examiners of transfers of stock. When this was discovered by the Association the resolution was hastily recalled from the Governor by authority of the Democratic members of the Commission and retransmitted, with the original numbers restored.

All these resolutions of the State Commission providing for exemptions are now in the hands of Governor Dix awaiting his action. He has very courteously acceded to a request for a hearing which has not as yet been held as the Governor has been understood to be awaiting the outcome of a suit brought in behalf of one of the examiners of transfers of stock by Albert de

Roode, formerly Assistant Secretary of the Association, but acting in this case solely as private counsel retained by the examiners. Although the Court of Appeals in the leading case of People ex rel. Schau v. McWilliams stated that a writ of mandamus would not be granted to review the action of the Commission on a classification as to which reasonable men might differ, the classification by the majority of the Commission of the position of examiner of transfers of stock as exempt was so clearly against reason that Justice Rudd of the Supreme Court, Albany County, in a carefully considered opinion has granted the writ, and commanded the Commission to rescind its action. The Governor has set the hearing for May 5.

The complaisant attitude of the majority of the Commission toward demands from Democratic officeholders for increased patronage has encouraged further requests. State Commissioner of Excise W. W. Farley has recently asked for the exemption of all the excise agents, basing his plea on the confidential character of the position. By law, not more than 60 such agents are to be employed and there were on January 1, 1911, 59 in office, all but two or three receiving a salary of $1,500, so that this request involves between eighty and ninety thousand dollars of patronage annually. This position was created in 1896. That same year it was placed in the competitive class and of the 59 serving on January 1, 1911, 57 were appointed as the result of competitive examination and only 2 entered the service under non-competitive examination prior to the position being classified as competitive. Better proof of practicability of competition cannot reasonably be asked than 15 years of its successful operation under a number of different appointing officers. The request has not been acted on as yet.

No extensions of the competitive service have been made by the new Commission and no action has been taken looking in any way toward material improvement in the administration of the law. The attitude of the majority of the Commission has indicated so clearly a lack of sympathy with the spirit and purpose of the civil service law and so marked a willingness to use their powers to further partisan ends that this Committee has felt fully justified in publishing resolutions calling for the removal of Commissioners Kraft and Burton.

This Committee has not instituted or encouraged any suit to interfere with the exercise of the discretion lodged in the commission and the governor in the administration of the civil service law. It believes in resorting to such action only when it is made clear that those charged with the administration of the law have failed to enforce it. In these cases, in spite of the action of his Commissioners, this Committee has preferred to await the action of Governor Dix and to place its main reliance on his unequivocal pledge to maintain the merit system, to promote its reasonable extension, and to retain faithful employees now in the classified service.

ACTION OF THE ASSOCIATION OF CIVIL EMPLOYEES.

In its efforts to maintain the integrity of the merit system in the state service the Association has had the hearty co-operation and assistance of the recently formed organization of civil employees which originated in New York City and has now developed into a state association with constituent organizations in the various cities of the state. That organization has adopted a three fold program: the extension of the merit system, protection against unjust removal, and civil pensions. Differences of opinion as to the proper method and legislation by which the last two objects should be accomplished have not prevented a cordial working together for the primary object of civil service reformers and employees alike—the maintenance and extension of the merit system.

WORK OF THE LAST STATE COMMISSION.

During the last eight months of 1910, the State Commission made comparatively few changes of classication. The important extensions to additional counties and to seven villages made prior to the last report of this Committee carried the classified service as far as in the judgment of the Commission it was practicable to apply it at present. Its report shows that during the six years it had been retained in office the classified service under its immediate jurisdiction had grown to over 16,000 positions, an increase of 45 per cent, the number of competitive positions had increased from 4,080 to 7,720 and the number of candidates in examinations from 6,923 to 13,658. Many important improvements in methods of examination and administration were adopted under this regime. This Committee desires to express its appreciation of the energy and devotion of purpose of Commissioner Roscoe C. E. Brown of New York City, who took the lead in measures for strengthening and extending the administration of the merit system and with whom Commissioner Charles F. Milliken of Canandaigua, with but few exceptions, worked in entire accord.

LEGISLATION.

None of the bills introduced by the Association at the last session of the Legislature secured passage, but the Association was instrumental in defeating a number of measures detrimental to the administration of the merit system as well as an inexcusably crude civil pension bill. Upon its pointing out defects in a bill for a new charter for the city of Amsterdam by which the Legislature, in defiance of the constitutional provision, had attempted to classify certain positions as non-competitive, Governor Hughes vetoed the measure. One measure for extending the privileges of a trial on removal to veterans of the regular army in the Spanish War was signed by the Governor although opposed by the Association on the ground that all such class privileges in the civil service are detrimental to good administration. In the case of the Minor Criminal Courts Bill for New York City, which was opposed by the Association because it contained a clause declaring probation officers to be the confidential agents of the justices, Governor Hughes attached to his approval a memorandum stating that in his opinion the use of such language was insufficient to require the classification of these positions in the exempt class. This went far toward meeting the only objection which the Association had raised to the bill.

This year the Association has introduced but three bills; a bill to increase the right of a taxpayer to bring suit to set aside appointments made in violation of law; a bill to extend the power of the civil service commission to prevent payment of salary to employees assigned to positions to which they are not entitled and a bill to extend the protection against unjust removal, now granted to employees in New York City and the counties included therein, to competitive employees in all other parts of the state. The taxpayers action bill has passed the Assembly and there is ground for believing that the Association's second bill may also secure passage. The Association of Civil Employees objects to the third bill as not giving sufficient protection against unjust removal and has introduced its own bill providing for a trial in case of removal, with a right to review by the courts. This our Association has felt it necessary to oppose and, as a result, probably neither bill will pass.

Our Association has also found it necessary to oppose the pension bill introduced on behalf of the civil employees as not in accord with sound principles for retirement legislation. Assemblyman Smith of New York, the floor leader, also opposes the bill and has advocated the appointment of a commission to make a thorough investigation of the subject and to draft legislation. This coincides precisely with the view expressed in the report of the Association's special committee on Retirement

Legislation. The Association is closely following, through its special counsel, Mr. Albert de Roode, the progress of a considerable number of bills which, intentionally or unintentionally, would be detrimental to the administration of the merit system. None of these has as yet secured passage.

THE NEW CHARTER.

The proposed new charter for New York City which is popularly known as the "Gaynor Charter," although the Mayor has pointed out that he took but little part in the actual drafting of it, was introduced by Senator Cullen and Assemblyman Foley on March 31. The fact that the charter is not Mayor Gaynor's own work may account for its startling civil service provisions which are so diametrically opposed to the views he has hitherto expressed on the merit system. The Association is utterly opposed to the proposed charter in its present form and its Law Committee has been authorized to act for it in conjunction with other civic bodies in the effort to defeat it unless the objectionable civil service provisions are eliminated. They are wholly destructive of the merit system as it has been built up through a long series of years in this city.

The avowed object of the clauses under the headings "Municipal civil service commission" and "The classified service" is to eliminate the supervision and control now exercised by the state civil service commission over the local commission. Such supervision is absolutely essential to prevent the merit system from becoming the football in the game of local politics. Experience elsewhere,—in Philadelphia, at the present time, for instance,—has shown this beyond any doubt. Massachusetts and New Jersey have but one commission appointed by the governor, exercising jurisdiction in all classified cities. State supervision does not seriously interfere with local administration and does not impair local initiative. The state has an absolute right to provide for the carrying out of a general policy established by general law and founded on a provision of the Constitution embracing all cities and other civil divisions. Such supervision is no more obnoxious to the theory of home rule than supervision over local authorities by state boards of education, health and charities and is equally necessary to uniform and efficient administration. It extends to every city of the State, but the new charter would make it inoperative in New York City alone. This is the *reductio ad absurdum* of Home Rule.

But the Charter goes much further than this in demolishing the merit system in New York City. In their attempt to eliminate the supervision of the state civil service commission its framers have found it necessary to destroy entirely the authority of the civil service law itself. Should they succeed in this, nothing would remain in the way of civil service reform regulations but the brief and general mandate contained in the Constitution and a set of mere administrative rules founded on it but supported by no statute and established by the mayor and the civil service commission appointed and removed at will by the mayor. These rules would be changeable at will by like authority; complete changes might be expected with each change in party administration and incidental changes whenever the shoe pinched the appointing officer. In the chapter on school administration also, while the board of examiners is retained, the appointment of teachers is placed in the hands of a paid board of education appointed by the mayor instead of in the expert educator, the superintendent of schools, and the present provision requiring competitive examination for appointment,—the provision that requires the appointment of one of the three standing highest on the eligible list,—has been eliminated.

The Association also opposes the pension and retirement provisions of the proposed Charter because they do not properly safe-guard the interests of the taxpayers on the one hand and the employees on the other. They eliminate the board of estimate and apportionment, the proper body to decide what financial burdens should be placed upon the taxpayers, and contain no requirement for a thorough preliminary investigation and ascertainment of the cost of any new system of pensions. A board of retirement and pensions, of which the mayor and his appointees constitute a majority, is given power, subject only to approval by the board of aldermen, to establish new pension systems and to give pensionable status to individual employees as well as to administer existing systems. The requirement of a flat 2 per cent deduction from the salary of every employee interested in a pension fund is wholly unscientific as the rate of deduction has no relation to the cost of pensions, and is manifestly unfair in that persons not now required to contribute at all, or required to contribute 1 per cent only, are all alike to be required to contribute 2 per cent, without receiving in return any increased benefits. The investment of this board of retirement and pensions with power to pass finally upon all applications for pensions and to reduce or terminate any pension seems to open the door wide for the arbitrary exercise of power.

REPORT OF SPECIAL COMMITTEE ON RETIREMENT LEGISLATION.

The Association is not opposed to the creation of a retirement system for civil employees; on the contrary, it will lend its aid in securing retirement legislation which without imposing an undue burden on the taxpayers will tend to increase the efficiency of the public service by the elimination of the superannuated and the consequent opening of the way to promotion for efficient and energetic younger men. The matter has been the subject of careful study by a special committee on Retirement Legislation which has recently made its report in favor of what is known as the contributory system, providing for a separate account to be kept with each employee and requiring each new entrant to the service to contribute to that account a sufficient percentage of his monthly salary to secure to him, at a reasonable rate of interest, annually compounded, an adequate retirement allowance, or annuity, upon reaching the retirement age. Provision is made for the withdrawal of the amount so contributed on separation from the service before reaching the age of retirement. The question, however, of how to deal with those already in the service who have made no contributions in the past is a distinct and difficult problem. The committee recommends the appointment of a commission with an adequate staff of competent assistants for the purpose of ascertaining the cost of establishing upon a sound actuarial basis a retirement system applicable to employees already in the public service and reporting its recommendations for retirement legislation. The report of the special committee is printed in full as an appendix to this report.

NEW YORK CITY.

THE MUNICIPAL CIVIL SERVICE COMMISSION.

No change has occurred in the membership of the Municipal Civil Service Commission until within the last week, when Mayor Gaynor announced the appointment of Hon. John C. McGuire, President of the Commission, as a city magistrate and the selection of Hon. James Creelman, a well known war correspondent and newspaper and magazine writer on political and other subjects, to fill the vacancy. Mr. Creelman becomes the President of the Commission.

ADMINISTRATION OF THE CIVIL SERVICE LAW.

The firm and advanced attitude of Mayor Gaynor in favor of thorough enforcement of the civil service law in accordance with the principles underlying it has been maintained. His civil service commissioners are manifestly to be considered as in entire sympathy with the purposes of the law and the faults which have come to light in their administration of it are in the main to be attributed to a lack of experience with, and knowledge of, its working prior to their assuming office.

Through its standing committee on Administration the Association has conducted a thorough investigation into the Commission's work during 1910, the results of which have been transmitted to the Commission for their consideration. The report commends the new work undertaken for the better keeping and inspection of efficiency record, the effective operation of the system of investigating statements of candidates as to previous employment and experience and the marked success which has followed the extension of practical examinations to new branches of skilled labor. It finds, however, grounds for just criticism in the lax and vacillating policy of the Commission, particularly in the matter of the classification of probation officers, in the delay in holding examinations and making up eligible lists and in the enormous increase in the number of appointments without examination to positions classified as competitive.

The Minor Criminal Courts Bill was passed in June, 1910. It provided for the appointment of probation officers in the Courts of Special Sessions and the Magistrates' Courts on September 1. Both Mayor Gaynor and Governor Hughes in signing the bill had expressed the opinion that the peculiar language used in regard to the probation officers, declaring them to be the confidential agents of the justices, did not of itself require the classification of the positions as exempt. The Commission, after a hearing at which both sides of the question were fully presented, announced a competitive examination for August 11. This they cancelled after the applications had been received and then held another hearing on August 31. No further action was taken until October 5, when the Commission reversed itself and sent to the Mayor a resolution exempting the positions. The resolution was vetoed by the Mayor on October 21 and the Commission then proceeded with the examination on December 1, but the list was not promulgated until March 22. Meanwhile, however, the justices had been compelled by mandamus to make appointments, pending the preparation of the list, and now suits have been instituted on behalf of these appointees which will require a decision by the highest court before the question of classification and proper method of appointment is settled. It is a fair presumption that this question would not have been raised had not the justices been driven to the point of exasperation by the inexcusable failure of the Commission to provide an eligible list within a reasonable time.

A clause in the rules which permits appointment without examination of "some designated person of high and recognized attainments" to a competitive position demanding "peculiar and exceptional qualifications of a scientific, professional or educational character" and then only "upon satisfactory evidence that competition in such special case is impracticable" was resorted to by the Commission to cover 23 appointments in 1910, as against 3 in 1909 and 3 in 1908. Such positions as interpreter, telephone operator and statistician, investigator, assistant medical superintendent and auditor have been filled without examination under this clause. By resort to this rule the Commission avoided the necessity for the approval of their action by the Mayor and the State Commission which would have been essential to the placing of these positions in the exempt class. The most flagrant case of the abuse of this rule was in the appointment of Dr. Daniel C. Potter as Director of the Ambulance Service. So far was Dr. Potter from being a person of "high and recognized attainments," that the board itself which appointed him was not unanimous and the Civil Service Commission in order to justify its action thought it advisable to compel him to submit to a non-competitive examination in order to ascertain whether in fact he possessed a claim to "high and recognized attainments."

The report of the committee on Administration also criticises the number of appointments to competitive positions without examination under the clause of the rules permitting the commission to except from competition a person engaged in private business who shall render professional, scientific, technical or expert services of an occasional and exceptional character. There were 559 such appointments during 1910, as compared with 263 in 1909 and 275 in 1908. Eighty-three of these exceptions were for positions carrying a salary of more than $750 and it is difficult to understand why in many cases, particularly of those positions with higher salaries, appointment could not have been made from the eligible lists. Attention is called to the practice of permitting reinstatements from the preferred list for one day, not because there is actual need for the services of the employee, but merely in order to continue his name upon the preferred list for an additional year. Such reinstatements were not contemplated by Section 1543 of the Charter and are, in fact, a fraud upon the law.

CONTROVERSY BETWEEN THE MAYOR AND THE COMPTROLLER.

Last November the Association requested the Municipal Commission to transfer a large number of positions in the Finance Department from the exempt to the competitive class, basing its request on the fact that experience with competitive examinations for similar positions in New York State and elsewhere had proved the practicability of competition and exemption was therefore no longer justifiable. These positions were 24 auditors, 3 deputy auditors, 13 examining inspectors, 17 expert accountants, 10 bank messengers, 5 deputy collectors of assessments and arrears, 10 deputy receivers of taxes, 20 cashiers and 7 examiners of accounts of institutions; 109 positions in all. Action was postponed at the request of the Secretary of the Association and the matter did not come up for consideration until April 5, when the Comptroller appeared and opposed the transfers in the case of the auditors, deputy auditors, deputy collectors of assessments and arrears and deputy receivers of taxes. A week later the Commission adopted a resolution which they transmitted to the Mayor, transferring 88 of the positions to the competitive class. This resolution the Mayor vetoed and at the same time issued a public statement in which he severely criticised the Comptroller for making political removals and appointments and attempting by this means to cover his political appointees into the protected service. Comptroller Prendergast issued a hot-tempered reply.

That the Comptroller has made both political removals and political appointments this Association has been well aware. In a case recently brought by Peter J. Garvey, a deputy city paymaster removed by Comptroller Prendergast, a jury decided that the removal was for political purposes and the court ordered his reinstatement. Since assuming office on January 1st, 1910, the Comptroller has made 114 new appointments to positions in the exempt class. An investigation of the enrollment books shows 19 of these appointees enrolled as Democrats, 63 as Republicans, 6 as members of the Independence League and 26 whose enrollment was not found. In initiating the request for the transfer of exempt positions to the competitive class the Association took the most practical method for putting a stop to a grave abuse by making political appointments to these positions impossible in future. The Association recognizes a certain degree of injustice in giving to personal or political appointees a competitive status without requiring them to submit to competitive examination, but it is an injustice that is remedied in a comparatively short time, and is far preferable to leaving the positions subject to the same abuse with each recurring change in party administration. There is no requirement of law for the examination of persons legally holding an office at the time the commission transfers it from the exempt to the competitive class nor, in our judgment, can the commission compel them to submit to examination as a condition of continuing in their positions. Whether the law should be amended to include such a requirement is debatable. The Association desires to see a reconsideration and readjustment of the whole matter with a view solely to the best interests of the city service.

On February 1, Mr. Albert de Roode resigned as Assistant Secretary after six years of continuous, faithful and efficient service to enter the practice of the law in which this Committee wishes him success. During the winter he has acted as counsel for the Association in matters of legislation under the direction of the Law Committee which has had occasion to give careful consideration to many difficult questions of litigation and legislation.

The Association during the past year has increased its membership to 957, of whom 15 are life members, 88 sustaining members and 854 regular members. Its standing committees on Law, Administration and Membership have been active and the Executive Committee thanks their members for the services they have performed for the Association at considerable sacrifice. It also thanks the Women's Auxiliary for the support and assistance it has rendered in furthering the movement for civil service reform.

Respectfully submitted,

SAMUEL H. ORDWAY,
Chairman.

ELLIOT H. GOODWIN,
Secretary.

May 3, 1911.

APPENDIX

Report of the Special Committee on Retirement Legislation.

To the Executive Committee:

Your committee appointed to consider the subject of retirement legislation in this state herewith submits its report.

If a retirement system can be devised, and it seems to your committee that one can be devised, which without imposing an undue burden upon the taxpayers will tend to increase the efficiency of the public service through caring for the old age of those who have served long and faithfully, the New York Civil Service Reform Association should heartily favor the establishment of such a system and should aid in securing the necessary legislation to that end. In so far, however, as any proposed retirement system fails either to increase the efficiency of the public service or to be just and fair to the employees, or to be just and fair to the taxpayers, the Association should oppose the proposal. And this, because unless a retirement system does increase the efficiency of the service it has no excuse for existence, and because a retirement system that imposes unjust or unfair burdens either upon the employees or upon the taxpayers who employ them will prove progressively demoralizing in its operation.

Approaching the subject from this point of view makes clear and sharp the distinction between a straight pension and a retiring allowance for superannuated employees. The former should be confined to civil employees engaged in hazardous occupations who suffer injury or death in the performance of duty. The entire expense of allowances or annuities granted in such cases should be paid out of the public treasury. They should be regarded as a part of the legitimate cost to the public of conducting a hazardous business. The ordinary civil employee is in a very different situation. He should be paid a proper and adequate compensation for the services he performs, and there would seem no valid reason why government employees who have been in receipt of such compensation should be erected into a special class to be supported in their old age at public expense. On the other hand, if the public employee is not paid a proper and adequate compensation for his services, any method which seeks to supply the deficiency by pensioning him when superannuated is unjust to the employee, economically wasteful, politically demoralizing and detrimental to the efficiency of the service.

A retiring pension provided in whole or in part at the public expense as a reward for long and faithful services inadequately paid for at the time they are rendered is inevitably regarded as merely the deferred payment of moneys already earned. This works a double injustice; for it helps to make and keep the pay for current work inadequate and the death of the employee before his superannuation will prevent his ever receiving the deferred portion of his compensation. It is equally unfair to the public, for it has been shown by experience that each year an employee remains in the service with a portion of his pay held back until he shall reach the age of superannuation is an added obstacle to his discharge though his work may have sensibly deteriorated. It would be far better from every point of view for the government to pay adequately and contemporaneously for the services as rendered than to weaken the discipline and impair the efficiency of the public service by deferring the payment of any portion of the earnings of its employees on the promise that if they desired to remain and were not discharged before they reached the age of superannuation they would thereafter be pensioned.

Your Committee is unreservedly in favor of the following propositions:

> Each employee in the civil service of the government should receive proper and adequate compensation for his services at the time the services are rendered;
>
> If the salaries of the government's civil employees are adequate, as compared with salaries for similar employment outside the public service, so that the employees can properly be expected to lay by a sufficient amount year by year to provide for their own old age, it is not reasonable, nor does it tend towards personal thrift and economy for the government to add to such salary a pension for life, at great expense to the taxpayers.

It is quite possible and, indeed, probable, that in certain cases the salary remaining to the employee after deduction has been made to provide for his support in old age will not be sufficient to permit him to maintain the standard of living to which his position entitles him.

In such cases, however, it is clear that the salaries as now fixed are inadequate and your committee therefore recommends that all such cases be inquired into and the necessary advances in salary made.

That some private corporations have of late been establishing various pension systems represented to be wholly or in part at the expense of the employing corporation does not seem to your Committee a convincing or even a strong argument for introducing such a system in the public service. In the first place, assuming it to be honestly believed that the expense of these pensions is borne in whole or in part by the employing corporation, we may be very sure that, if it turns out that any part of the pension is paid out of the capital of the corporation, that part of the pension will stop. We may be equally sure that, by so much as the payment of any part of the pension diminishes the normal return upon capital, the pension will stop. In the second place, in each of these instances a private corporation is simply risking its own money to try an experiment that may or may not prove to be successful as the years go on; while the government has neither savings nor investments nor earnings of its own and, if it ventures upon such an experiment must pay the expense out of forced contributions from the taxpayers. The government lacks the stimulus to keen watchfulness and economical management constantly present when one who fails in either respect must bear the loss occasioned. It would be rashly imprudent in these circumstances to create a large dependent class of voters directly interested in influencing legislation for its pecuniary profit.

Your committee therefore recommends that the following principles be observed in drafting retirement legislation applicable to employees in the civil service:

1. A system of retiring annuities based upon length of service and an attained age of retirement should be provided by compulsory contributions from the employee's salary which, invested by or under the supervision of the government at a reasonable rate of interest, compounded annually, will be sufficient to provide the annuity at the age of retirement. The safety of the contributions and the reasonable rate of interest should be guaranteed by the government.

2. An individual and separate account should be kept of the contributions of each employee. In case of his voluntary separation from the service before the age of retirement, these should be repaid to him.

3. In order that the retirement system should increase the stability of the service and add an inducement to capable men to remain in it, those who separate themselves from the service prior to the age of retirement should receive somewhat less than the full accumulation of interest upon their deposits with the government.

It is apparent that a system of retiring annuities embodying the principles favored in this report can be made to rest upon a sound actuarial basis and in the case of a new entrant into the civil service need not require the contribution of an undue proportion of his salary in order to secure the benefits sought. At the present time, however, the data are almost wholly lacking for devising a sound plan for retiring, at reasonable cost to the taxpayers, the civil employees already in the public service. Those who are still young enough to provide for their own retiring annuities without contributing an unreasonable amount of their salaries should be required to do so; but it is obvious that those already above a certain age cannot afford to contribute from their salaries an amount sufficient to provide an adequate annuity on retirement. In the opinion of the committee, the government should make up the balance between what such employees may reasonably be called upon to contribute and the amount needed to secure them an adequate annuity on retirement. Such investigations as have already been made into the conditions of employment in the federal service lead us to hazard the opinion that a thorough investigation of the problem here will show that the amount which the government is called upon to contribute in order to carry out this plan will not much exceed the loss to the government occasioned by the retention of superannuated employees and the consequent loss in efficiency all along the line through the blocking of the way to promotion.

What is needed at the present time is a thorough investigation which shall ascertain and set forth accurately the facts essential to determining the cost to the taxpayers of establishing upon a sound actuarial basis a retirement system applicable to employees already in the public service. We need to know, for example, the length of service and the age of each such employee, his salary at entrance, all increases since and his present salary. It is not necessary to emphasize the unwisdom of enacting any retiring system into law without the prior official collation and publication of such necessary statistical information. Your Committee, therefore, recommends the creation of a Commission to be appointed by the governor for the purpose of making a thorough study and investigation of the entire subject and to report thereon with its recommendations. The Commission should have power to subpœna and examine witnesses and have an adequate staff of competent experts.

Respectfully submitted,

H. DE F. BALDWIN,
CHARLES A. CONANT,
ELLIOT H. GOODWIN,
RUSSELL H. LOINES,
HORACE E. DEMING, *Chairman.*

Special Committee on Retirement Legislation.
Dated, April 12, 1911.

ANNUAL REPORT OF THE TREASURER.

MAY 1, 1911.

Balance on hand May 1, 1910 .... $ 56.56

RECEIPTS:
  From Annual Dues........................ $3,580.00
  " Sustaining Membership Dues......... 2,075.00
  " Subscriptions........................ 960.00
  " Title Guarantee & Trust Company, Interest on Elial F. Hall Bequest... 320 00
  " Women's Auxiliary.................... 100.00   7,035.00
                                                    ─────────
                                                    $7,091.56

DISBURSEMENTS:
  Salary of Secretary $1,416.61
  "   " Assistant Secretary.............. 1,124.94
  "   " Second Assistant Secretary....... 447.92
  "   " Clerks 1,129.23
  Compensation of Counsel in matters of Legislation............................ 260.00
  Expenses of Litigation 18.66
  Subscription to GOOD GOVERNMENT........ 565.68
  Legislative Information................... 150.00
  Stationery 86.64
  Printing.................................. 237.38
  Postage and Stamped Envelopes............ 289.48
  Telephone Service........................ 163.50
  Office Rent.............................. 825.02
  Travelling Expenses...................... 92.52
  Office Expenses.......................... 161.20
  Expenses of Annual Meeting............... 37.50
  Subscription to National League.......... 11.76   7,018.04
                                                     ─────────
Balance on hand... $ 73.52

E. & O. E.   A. S. FRISSELL, *Treasurer.*

ELIAL F. HALL FUND.

Held as a special deposit at the Fifth Avenue Bank, certificate No. 5844 for sixteen shares Title Guarantee & Trust Company stock. The above stock pays dividends of 20% per annum, namely $320.

A. S. FRISSELL, *Treasurer.*

The above account examined and found correct.
New York, May 9, 1911.

P. J. McCOOK, } *Auditing Committee.*
ALFRED B. MEACHAM,

ORGANIZATION

OF

THE NEW YORK CIVIL SERVICE REFORM ASSOCIATION

CONSTITUTION.

ARTICLE I.

The name of this organization shall be The Civil Service Reform Association.

ARTICLE II.

The object of the Association shall be to establish a system of appointment, promotion, and removal in the civil service, founded upon the principle that public office is a public trust, admission to which should depend upon proven fitness. To this end the Association will demand that appointments to subordinate executive offices, with such exceptions as may be expedient, not inconsistent with the principle already mentioned, shall be made from persons whose fitness has been ascertained by competitive examinations open to all applicants properly qualified, and that removals shall be made for legitimate cause only, such as dishonesty, negligence, or inefficiency, but not for political opinion or refusal to render party service; and the Association will advocate all other appropriate measures for securing integrity, intelligence, efficiency, good order, and due discipline in the civil service.

ARTICLE III.

The Association will hold meetings, raise funds, publish and circulate appropriate information, correspond and co-operate with associations organized elsewhere for the objects set forth in this Constitution, and support all executive and legislative action which promote its purposes.

Article IV.

The conditions of membership shall be wholly independent of party preference. Questions shall not be discussed in the debate or in the publications of the Association upon party grounds. Neither the name nor influence of the Association shall be used on behalf of any party, or for procuring office or promotion for any person. But nothing in this article shall be construed to prevent the Association from opposing any candidate when in its opinion, or in that of three-fourths of the members of the Executive Committee, such course is demanded by the objects of the Association.

Article V.

There shall be a President, to be elected by the Association at the annual meeting, who shall perform the usual and prescribed duties of that office. He shall be, ex-officio, a member of all committees, with a casting vote only, and he may call special meetings of the Executive Committee whenever he thinks it necessary, and, with the assent of two members of the Executive Committee, special meetings of the Association.

There shall be ten Vice-Presidents, to be annually elected by the Association.

There shall be a Treasurer and Secretary and such other officers as the Executive Committee may from time to time designate, who shall perform the usual and prescribed duties of such officers. They shall be respectively appointed by the Executive Committee, and may be removed by them. The Treasurer shall be, ex-officio, a member of the Finance Committee of the Association.

There shall be an Executive Committee of twenty-five members, to be elected annually by the Association. Subject to these articles, the Executive Committee shall manage the affairs of the Association, direct and dispose of its funds, and from time to time make and modify by-laws for the Association and for its own action. The Executive Committee shall keep a record of its proceedings, and shall make a report to the Association at the annual meeting. No appropriation of

money by the Executive Committee beyond the amount in the hands of the Treasurer at the time shall bind any member of the Association, excepting those members of the Executive Committee who shall vote for it. Vacancies in the Executive Committee may be filled by the President for the remainder of the term. Other vacancies may be filled by the Executive Committee.

All the officers of the Association and members of the several Standing Committees shall be, ex-officio, members of the Executive Committee.

Article VI.

Each officer of the Association shall continue to hold office until his successor has been selected and is ready to enter upon the duties of the office.

Article VII.

There shall be an annual meeting of the Association on the second Wednesday of May, at which officers shall be elected for the ensuing year, and other appropriate business may be transacted; except in the year 1898, when the annual meeting shall be held on the second Wednesday of January.

Article VIII.

Any person may be proposed in writing for membership by any member of the Association, and shall be admitted upon approval of the Executive Committee. Members failing to pay their dues may be dropped from the roll by the Executive Committee.

Article IX.

The annual dues of each member shall be $5, payable on the 1st of May, and each member shall receive the annual report and all other publications of the Association. Sustaining members, on payment of twenty-five dollars annually, and Life members, exempt from annual dues on payment of one hundred dollars, may be elected by the Executive Committee at any regular meeting thereof.

Article X.

All provisions of this Constitution, except those relating to the rights of members, and the term of officers, may be suspended or amended by a vote of two-thirds of the Executive Committee, subject to the approval of the Association by a two-thirds vote of the members present either at the annual meeting or at a special meeting duly called. Due notice shall be given before any such annual or special meeting that the approval of the Association will, thereat, be asked for such action of the Executive Committee, and the notice shall clearly state the effect of such suspension or amendment in the text of the Constitution. Any member of the Association may propose amendments to the Constitution, which may be approved under the same conditions.

BY-LAWS.

FOR THE GOVERNMENT OF THE ASSOCIATION AND ITS COMMITTEES.

§ 1. The Annual meeting of the Association shall be held at such hour and place as the Executive Committee shall designate. The election of officers shall be by ballot, but any member not present may declare his vote by letter to the Secretary and it shall be counted.

§ 2. The meetings of each committee, unless otherwise especially provided for, shall be at half-past eight P. M., at which time the chairman shall direct the call of the names of its members and the Secretary shall record the names of those present and others as they appear.

§ 3. The order of business, before each committee shall be:
1. The reading and correction of the records of the last meeting.

And, thereafter, unless otherwise ordered, as follows:
2. Any statement due from the Treasurer.
3. Unfinished business from the last meeting.
4. Report from the Secretary's office.
5. Reports of standing committees.
6. Reports of special committees.
7. Proposals of new members and their election.
8. Miscellaneous business.

§ 4. Regular meetings of the Executive Committee shall be held on the second Wednesday of every month except July and August, but if that day be a holiday, then on the third Wednesday. Ten members of the Executive Committee shall constitute a quorum.

§ 5. Neither in the meetings of the Association nor of any committee shall any member speak more than once on any motion nor more than ten minutes at one time, without unanimous consent, nor shall any person, or his actions, be characterized on party grounds.

§ 6. Special meetings of any committee may be called by its chairman or by any three members, and due notice thereof shall be given by the Secretary.

§ 7. All notices to a member shall be sent to his address filed with the Secretary.

§ 8. On the demand of one-fifth of the members present, at any meeting of the Association or of a committee, the ayes and nays shall be called and recorded on any motion.

§ 9. All committees shall be appointed by the chair unless their selection shall be otherwise provided for.

§ 10. At each regular meeting of the Executive Committee, it shall be the duty of the Treasurer to make a statement of the amount of money in the treasury and of the place of its deposit, and, at the annual meeting, he shall state the source of all moneys received and the use made of the same during the past year.

§ 11. The Secretary shall keep a record of the proceedings of the Association and of the Executive Committee, and perform the other duties assigned him.

§ 12. Without the consent of three-fourths of the members present, no vote which will declare or fill a vacancy or elect a member of the Association shall be deemed carried, at the same meeting in which it was first moved.

§ 13. It shall require a vote of two-thirds of the members of the Executive Committee present to pass any vote under which more than $100 will be appropriated or the Association be pledged for more than that amount, and the Executive Committee alone shall have authority to create any charge upon the funds of the Association. But neither said committee nor any officer or officers of the Association shall be authorized to create a personal liability against any members but themselves.

§ 14. There shall be the following Standing Committees, of seven members each, which shall be selected annually by the Executive Committee:

(1) A Finance Committee, whose duty it shall be to devise and carry into effect, subject to the direction of the Executive Committee, suitable measures for raising funds, and to supervise and report upon the income and expenditures of the Association. The Chairman of the Executive Committee shall, in advance of each annual meeting of the Association, appoint an Auditing Committee from among the members of the Association, whose duty it shall be to examine all vouchers and audit the accounts of the Treasurer, and to report thereon at the annual meeting.

(2) A Publication Committee, whose duty it shall be to prepare and recommend matters suitable for publication by the Association, and to take charge of the printing and distribution of whatever may be ordered printed.

(3) A Committee on Correspondence, whose duty it shall be to promote the objects of the Association through correspondence and co-operation with other organizations.

(4) A Committee on Administration, whose duty it shall be to investigate and report upon the administration of the civil service law and rules and to consider and recommend suitable methods of examination for admission to and promotion in the public service, and suitable procedure tending to make the system more efficient.

There shall also be a Standing Committee on Law of nine members, which shall be selected annually by the Executive Committee. Its duty shall be to consider all legislation affecting the civil service, to promote such as may be approved, and to oppose such as may be disapproved by the Executive Committee, and to prepare and recommend such amendments to the law as in their opinion will advance the purposes of the Association. The Law Committee shall have power to represent the Association in any legal proceedings which may be necessary in order to maintain or enforce the laws affecting the State or Municipal civil service.

There shall also be a Standing Committee on Membership

of fifteen members, which shall be selected annually by the Executive Committee. Its duties shall be to devise and carry into effect measures for increasing the membership of the Association.

Each Standing Committee shall be competent to fix the number of its own quorum; but such quorum shall in no case be less than three.

§ 15. These By-Laws may be amended, or new By-Laws added, by a four-fifths vote at any meeting of the Executive Committee; or by a two-thirds vote, provided a statement of the proposed change had been entered on the minutes at the last meeting.

§ 16. Amendments proposed under the last clause of the tenth section of the constitution shall be first submitted to the Executive Committee.

OFFICERS—1911-1912.

PRESIDENT:

SILAS W. BURT

VICE-PRESIDENTS:

DAVID H. GREER
ABRAHAM JACOBI
WILLIAM G. LOW
LEVI P. MORTON
ELIHU ROOT

EDWARD M. SHEPARD
ANSON PHELPS STOKES
OSCAR S. STRAUS
EVERETT P. WHEELER
HORACE WHITE

EXECUTIVE COMMITTEE:

SAMUEL H. ORDWAY, *Chairman*
HENRY DE FOREST BALDWIN
GEORGE R. BISHOP
ROSCOE C. E. BROWN
CHARLES C. BURLINGHAM
EDWARD CARY
LEANDER T. CHAMBERLAIN
CHARLES COLLINS
JOSEPH P. COTTON, JR.
HORACE E. DEMING
A. S. FRISSELL
J. WARREN GREENE

GEORGE J. GREENFIELD
LEARNED HAND
HENRY W. HARDON
RUSSELL H. LOINES
JACOB W. MACK
JOHN G. MILBURN
LUDWIG NISSEN
CARL L. SCHURZ
ISAAC N. SELIGMAN
NELSON S. SPENCER
WILLIAM H. THOMSON
CHARLES W. WATSON

SECRETARY:
ELLIOT H. GOODWIN

ASSISTANT SECRETARY:
ROBT. W. BELCHER

TREASURER:
A. S FRISSELL

STANDING COMMITTEES.

FINANCE:

CHARLES A. CONANT, *Chairman*.
L. T. CHAMBERLAIN
A. S. FRISSELL, *ex-officio*
ISAAC N. SELIGMAN
JACOB W. MACK
ALFRED BISHOP MASON
HORACE WHITE

PUBLICATION:

EDWARD CARY, *Chairman*.
ROBERT S. BINKERD
H. A. CUSHING
CHARLES J. FAY
FRANCIS D. POLLAK
WILSON M. POWELL, JR.
JOHN A. SLEICHER

CORRESPONDENCE:

————————————, *Chairman*.
ELBRIDGE L. ADAMS
ALBERT S. BARD
WILLIAM M. CHADBOURNE
NATHAN A. SMYTH
CORNELIUS B. SMITH
WALTER F. TAYLOR

ADMINISTRATION:

NELSON S. SPENCER, *Chairman*.
FELIX FRANKFURTER
ELLWOOD HENDRICK
FRANCIS H. KINNICUTT
RUSSELL H. LOINES
PHILIP J. McCOOK
CLARENCE BISHOP SMITH

LAW:

SAMUEL H. ORDWAY, *Chairman*.
HENRY DE FOREST BALDWIN
CHARLES C. BURLINGHAM
JOSEPH P. COTTON, JR.
ALBERT DE ROODE
A. LEO EVERETT
J. WARREN GREENE
HENRY W. HARDON
CHARLES P. HOWLAND

MEMBERSHIP:

ALFRED B. MEACHAM, *Chairman*,
CHARLES BURLINGHAM
CHARLES WHITNEY DALL
ALAN FOX
ROY C. GASSER
HERBERT L. GUTTERSON
JOHN G. JACKSON
PERCY H. JENNINGS
NICHOLAS KELLEY
LEONARD G. McANENY
CHARLES W. McCANDLESS
WILLIAM MASON SMITH
THOMAS D. THACHER
ROGER H. WILLIAMS

MEMBERSHIP ROLL.

SUSTAINING MEMBERS.

AMEND, BERNARD G.,	205 Third Avenue, New York City
APPLETON, R. ROSS,	146 Joralemon Street, Brooklyn, N. Y.
BEHR, HERMAN,	75 Beekman Street, New York City
BURLINGHAM, CHARLES C.,	27 William Street, " " "
CARY, EDWARD,	The "Times," New York City
CHUBB, PERCY,	Glen Cove, L. I.
CLYDE, WILLIAM P.,	24 State Street, New York City
COCHRAN, ALEX. SMITH.	10 East 41st Street, " " "
COLLINS, CHARLES,	33 E. 17th Street, " " "
CONNOR, W. E.,	31 Nassau Street, " " "
CRANE, RICHARD T.,	2541 Michigan Avenue, Chicago, Ill.
CURTIS, W. J.,	49 Wall Street, New York City
CUTTING, R. FULTON,	32 Nassau Street. " " "
DAY, WILLIAM S.,	220 Hobart Avenue, Summit, N. J.
DE COPPET, E. J.,	42 Broadway, New York City
DEERING, JAMES,	Fullerton and Clybourne Avenues, Chicago, Ill.
DE LAMAR, J. R.,	43 Exchange Place, New York City
DELANO, WARREN Jr.,	1 Broadway, " " "
DEMUTH, WILLIAM,	524 Fifth Avenue, " " "
DENISON, WINFRED T.,	Department of Justice, Washington, D. C.
FINCH, EDWARD R.,	37 Fifth Avenue New York City
FLEITMAN, FRED T.,	484 Broome Street, " " "
FORD, JAMES B.,	4 E. 43rd Street, " " "
FRISSELL, A. S.,	530 Fifth Avenue, " " "
FROTHINGHAM, JOHN W.,	5 Nassau Street, " " "
GOODMAN, A. L.,	263 W. 113th Street' " " "
GOODWIN, J. J.,	11 W. 54th Street, " " "
GREENE, J. WARREN,	111 Broadway, " " "
GREENFIELD, GEORGE J.,	32 Broadway, " " "
HARRIOT, S. CARMAN,	57 W. 39th Street, New York City
HEMENWAY, AUGUSTUS,	10 Tremont Street, Boston, Mass.
HENTZ, HENRY,	769 St. Mark's Avenue, Brooklyn
HOPKINS, GEORGE B.,	52 Broadway, New York City
ISELIN, ADRIAN, Jr.,	711 Fifth Avenue, New York City
JACOBI, A.,	19 E. 47th Street, New York City
LOEB, JAMES,	52 William Street, New York City
LOEB, MORRIS,	273 Madison Avenue, " " "
LOINES, STEPHEN,	152 Columbia Heights, Brooklyn
LOW, SETH,	30 E. 64th Street, New York City
LOW, WILLIAM G.,	58 Remsen Street, Brooklyn
LUSTGARTEN, WILLIAM,	68 William Street, New York City

MACK, JACOB W.,	85 Liberty Street, New York City
MACY, V. EVERIT,	68 Broad Street, " " "
MARTIN, BRADLEY, Jr.,	6 E. 87th Street, " " "
MINTURN, ROBERT SHAW,	116 E. 22d Street, " " "
MORTON, LEVI P.,	38 Nassau Street, " " "
MOSLE, GEORGE, R.,	16-18 Exchange Place, " " "
MUSCHENHEIM, WILLIAM C.,	Hotel Astor, " " "
McANENY, GEORGE,	19 E. 47th Street, New York City
McKIM, JOHN A.,	6 E. 74th Street, " " "
ORDWAY, SAMUEL H.,	27 William Street, New York City
OSBORN, WILLIAM CHURCH,	71 Broadway, " " "
PAGE, EDWARD D.,	Oakland, New Jersey
PAGENSTECHER, A.,	P. O. Box 683, New York City
PAYNE, GEORGE E.,	251 Nott Avenue, Long Island City
PERKINS, GEORGE W.,	71 Broadway, New York City
PHIPPS, HENRY,	6 E. 87th Street, " " "
PIERCE, H. CLAY,	25 Broad Street, " " "
PULITZER, JOSEPH,	7 East 73rd Street, " " "
PUTNEY, EDMONDS,	2 Rector Street, " " "
RANDOLPH, STUART F.,	31 Nassau Street, New York City
READ, WILLIAM A.,	25 Nassau Street, " " "
ROBINSON, NELSON,	23 E. 55th Street, " " "
ROSSBACH, LEOPOLD,	42 E. 75th Street, " " "
RUSSELL, CHARLES H.,	15 Broad Street, " " "
SCHEFER, CARL,	476 Broome Street, New York City
SCHIEFFELIN, WILLIAM JAY,	5 E. 66th Street, " " "
SCHIFF, JACOB H.,	P. O. Box 1198, " " "
SCHWAB, GUSTAV H.,	5 Broadway, " " "
SELIGMAN, ISAAC N.,	1 William Street, " " "
SHEPARD, EDWARD M.,	128 Broadway, " " "
SMITH, CORNELIUS B.,	101 E. 69th Street, " " "
SMITH, J. HOPKINS,	17 E. 47th Street, " " "
SPENCER, NELSON S.,	27 William Street, " " "
SPEYER, JAMES,	257 Madison Avenue, " " "
STETSON, FRANCIS LYNDE,	15 Broad Street, " " "
STEVENS, BYAM R.,	11 E. 78th Street, " " "
STOKES, ANSON PHELPS,	100 William Street, " " "
STOWELL, HARLEY L.,	96 Broadway, " " "
STURHAHN, C. F.,	84 William Street, " " "
THOMSON, WILLIAM H.,	70 E. 54th Street, New York City
THORNE, SAMUEL,	43 Cedar Street. " " "
VANDERBILT, HAROLD S.,	Grand Central Terminal, New York City
VOSS, F. G.,	123 Pall Mall, London, S. W., England
WHITE, ALFRED T.,	5 Nassau Street, New York City
WHITE, HORACE,	18 W. 69th Street, " " "
WUNDERLICH, F. W.,	165 Remsen Street, Brooklyn

Abbot, Everett V.,	45 Cedar Street, New York City
Abbott, Lawrence F.,	"The Outlook," " " "
Abbott, Lyman,	287 Fourth Avenue, " " "
Achelis, John,	68 Leonard Street, " " "
Adams, Edward D.,	71 Broadway, " " "
Adams, Elbridge L.,	299 Broadway, " " "
Adams, Joseph,	Union Stock Yards, Chicago, Ill.
Adams, Thatcher M.,	36 Wall Street, New York City
Adler, Felix,	152 W. 77th Street, " " "
Affeld, Francis O.,	873 President Street, Brooklyn
Agar, John G.,	31 Nassau Street, New York City
Agnew, Andrew Gifford,	22 William Street, " " "
Allen, Calvin H.,	1 W. 72nd Street, " " "
Allen, Elmer A.,	42 Broadway, " " "
Allen. Franklin,	371 Fulton Street, Brooklyn
Alling, Joseph T.,	400 Oxford Street, Rochester, N. Y.
Allison, Charles R.,	60 Wall Street, New York City
Alsop, Reese F.,	96 Remsen Street, Brooklyn
Ambrose, John F.,	10 E. 130th Street, New York City
Ames, John McE.,	165 Broadway, " " "
Anderson, Frank E.,	486 Broadway, " " "
Andrews, J. Sherlock,	111 St. Paul Street, Rochester, N. Y.
Arend, F. J.,	165 Broadway, New York City
Armstrong, James,	71 Nassau Street, " " "
Armstrong, S. T.,	Milburn Farms, Katonah, N. Y.
Atterbury, Grosvenor,	20 W. 43rd Street, New York City
Auchincloss, John,	27 Pine Street, " " "
Avery, Samuel P.,	61 Woodland Street, Hartford, Conn.
Babbott, Frank L.,	346 Broadway, New York City
Backus, Grosvenor H,	Englewood, N. J.
Bacon, Gorham,	47 W. 54th Street, New York City
Bagley, Valentine N.,	641 Washington Street, " " "
Baker. William F.,	379 Washington Avenue, Brooklyn, N. Y.
Baldwin, Elbert F.,	"The Outlook," New York City
Baldwin, Henry de Forest,	49 Wall Street, " " "
Baldwin, William D.,	175 W. 58th Street, " " "
Bangs, L. Bolton,	32 E. 51st Street, " " "
Bannard, Otto T.,	24 Broad Street, " " "
Banta, Theodore M.,	348 Broadway, " " "
Bard, Albert Sprague,	25 Broad Street, " " "
Barkley, C. B.,	14 E. 60th Street, " " "
Barnes, Henry B., Jr.,	52 William Street, " " "
Barney, A. H., (Life)	101 E. 38th Street, " " "
Barrett, Frank R.,	Box 105, Portland
Barrett, John D.	49 Wall Street, New
Bartlett, P. G.,	62 Cedar Street, "
Baruch, Bernard M.,	111 Broadway, N

Batterman, Henry,	Hotel Bossert, Brooklyn
Bausch, J. J.,	13 Hyde Park, Rochester, N.Y.
Bausch, William,	745 St. Paul Street, " "
Baylies, Edmund L.,	54 Wall Street, New York City
Beekman, Gerard,	7 E. 42d Street, " " "
Beer, George Lewis,	329 W. 71st Street, " " "
Beers, E. Le Grand,	131 Remsen Street, Brooklyn
Beers, Lucius H.,	49 Wall Street, New York City
Belcher, Robt. W.,	79 Wall Street, " " "
Bell, Gordon Knox,	22 William Street, " " "
Bellamy, Frederick P.,	204 Montague Street, Brooklyn
Benedict, Elliot S.,	60 Wall Street, New York City
Bennecke, Henry,	219 Congress Street, Brooklyn
Bernard, William,	149 Broadway, New York City
Betts, Samuel R.,	52 William Street, " " "
Bijur, Nathan,	160 West 75th Street, " " "
Binkerd, R. S.,	City Club, " " "
Bird, Francis W.,	101 E. 62nd Street, " " "
Bisbee, Ralph,	63 Wall Street, " " "
Bishop, George R.,	142 E. 18th Street, " " "
Blagden, Arthur C.,	Hyde Park, Mass.
Boas, Franz,	Columbia University, New York City
Bodman, Herbert L.,	835 Madison Avenue, " " "
Boller, Alfred P.,	149 Broadway, " " "
Borden, M. C. D.,	Box 1794, " " "
Borkel, John,	42 E. Houston Street, " " "
Bowen, C. Winthrop,	5 E. 63rd Street, " " "
Bowker, R. R.,	298 Broadway, " " "
Bowler, R. P.,	2 Rector Street, " " "
Brachhausen, G. A.,	Rahway, N. J.
Brackett, George C.,	50 Remsen Street, Brooklyn
Bradt, Herbert S.,	120 Broadway, New York City
Brady, William H.,	17 Battery Place, " " "
Briesen, Arthur von, (Life)	49 Wall Street, " " "
Briscoe, S. William,	Valley Cottage, N. Y.
Brookfield, Frank,	2 Rector Street, New York City
Brown, Addison,	45 W. 89th Street, " " "
Brown, Edwin H.,	141 Broadway, " " "
Brown, Franklin Q.,	33 Pine Street, " " "
Brown, Roscoe C. E.,	"Tribune" Office, " " "
Brown, Thatcher M.,	1024 Park Avenue, Plainfield, N. J.
Brownell, William C.,	153 Fifth Avenue, New York City
Brush, W. Franklin,	16 E. 37th Street, " " "
Bulkley, Edwin M.,	54 William Street, " " "
Bulkley, Johathan,	75 Duane Street, " " "
Burlingham, Charles,	52 William Street, " " "
Burr, George L.,	Hartley Hall, Columbia University, " " "
Burr, Winthrop,	7 Wall Street, " " "

Burt, Silas W., The Allenhurst, Broadway and 100th Street, New York City
Butler, Howard R., ... 131 E. 66th Street, " " "
Buttfield, William J., . . . 96 Wall Street, " " "
Byrne, James, ... 26 Broad Street, " " "

Cadwalader, John L., . . . 40 Wall Street, New York City
Cahen, L J., ... 1 Madison Avenue, " " "
Campbell, Frederick B., . . . 54 Wall Street, " " "
Campbell, John A., ... New Cumberland, West Va.
Canfield, George F., ... 49 Wall Street, New York City
Carey, Samuel, ... 170 Broadway, " " "
Carnegie, Andrew, (Life) . . . 2 E. 91st Street, " " "
Carroll, Lauren, ... 2 Wall Street, " " "
Cassatt, George M., ... 327 Broadway, " " "
Cauldwell, S. Millbank, . . . Pelham Manor, N. Y.
Cerf, L. A., ... 135 Broadway, New York City
Chadbourne, William M., . . . 49 Wall Street, " " "
Chaffee, J. Irwin, . Sedgwick Avenue, Fordham Heights, " " "
Chamberlain, L. T., ... 222 W. 23 Street, " " "
Chaplin, Duncan D., ... 817 Broadway, " " "
Chapman, John Jay, ... 35 Wall Street, " " "
Chapman, Henry G., ... 135 Madison Avenue, " " "
Chase, George, ... 174 Fulton Street, " " "
Chauncey, Daniel, ... 129 Joralemon Street, Brooklyn
Chauncey, Elihu, ... 208 Madison Avenue, New York City
Childs, Edwards H., ... 59 Wall Street, " " "
Childs, Richard S., ... 383 Fourth Avenue, " " "
Choate, Joseph H., ... 60 Wall Street, " " "
Choate, Joseph H. Jr., . . . 60 Wall Street, " " "
Choate, William G., ... 40 Wall Street, " " "
Cillis, Hubert, ... 20 Nassau Street, " " "
Claflin, John, ... 224 Church Street, " " "
Clark, Grenville, ... 500 Madison Avenue, " " "
Clarke, Samuel B., ... 32 Nassau Street, " " "
Clarkson, Banyer, ... 26 W. 50th Street, " " "
Clay, George E., ... 9 Jackson Avenue, Long Island City
Clement, Arthur W., ... 150 Nassau Street, New York City
Cleveland, Treadwell, . . . 27 William Street, " " "
Clinch, Edward S., ... 41 Park Row, " " "
Codington, Perley M., . . . 1487 Broadway, " " "
Coffin, C A., ... 30 Church Street, " " "
Coffin, I. Sherwood, ... 30 Cliff Street, " " "
Cohen, William N., ... 22 William Street, " " "
Colby, Bainbridge, ... 111 Broadway, " " "
Coleman, Edwin S., ... 17 Battery Place, " " "
Coley, William B., ... 40 East 41st Street, " " "
Collard, George W., ... 260 West 73rd Street, " " "
Collins, Atwood, ... Asylum Avenue, Hartford, Conn.

Collins, Minturn Post, ... 1 W. 34th Street, New York City
Collins, Stephen W., ... 63 Wall Street, " " "
Comstock, C. B., ... 124 E. 27th Street, " " "
Conant, Charles A., ... 38 Nassau Street, " " "
Conner, Lewis A., ... 53 E. 49th Street, " " "
Conrad, W. Davis, ... 49 Wall Street, " " "
Cook, Walter, ... 3 W. 29th Street, " " "
Cooley, Alford Warriner, . . , . . . Mountain Park, N. M.
Copeland, Henry C., . . . 242 W. 101st Street, New York City
Cornell, Edward, ... 32 Nassau Street, " " "
Corning, C. R., ... 36 Wall Street, " " "
Corrigan, Joseph E., ... 39 E. 10th Street, " " "
Corwine, William R., ... 11 Broadway, " " "
Cotton, Joseph P., Jr., ... 32 Liberty Street, " " "
Coudert, Frederick R., Jr., . . . , 2 Rector Street, " " "
Cowperthwait, J. Howard, . . . 195 Park Row, " " "
Coxe, Macgrane, ... 50 Church Street, " " "
Coykendall, S. D., ... Rondout, N. Y.
Crandall, Floyd M., ... 113 W. 95th Street, New York City
Crane, Frederick, . . "The Schuyler," 46th Street. " " "
Crane, Leroy B., ... 277 Broadway, " " "
Cranford, Walter V., ... 215 Montague Street, Brooklyn
Cravath, Paul D., ... 52 William Street, New York City
Crawford, Gilbert H., ... 32 Liberty Street, " " "
Croly, Herbert D., ... 11 E. 24th Street, " " "
Cromwell, Frederic, ... 32 Nassau Street, " " "
Cromwell, Lincoln, ... 1 Greene Street, " " "
Crosby, John Schuyler, . . . 206 W. 50th Street, " " "
Croswell, J. G., ... 17 W. 44th Street, " " "
Curtis, F. Kingsbury, . , . . . 30 Broad Street, " " "
Curtis, Warren, Sr., ... 30 Broad Street, " " "
Curtis, William E., ... 30 Broad Street, " " "
Cushing, H. A , ... 43 Cedar Street, " ' "
Cushing, William E., . . . Society for Savings Bldg., Cleveland, O.
Cutting, R. Bayard, ... 32 Nassau Street, New York City
Cutting, W. Bayard, ... 24 E. 72nd Street, " " "

Dall, C. Whitney, ... 44 Leonard Street, New York City
Damrosch, Frank, . . , . 181 East 75th Street, " " "
Dana, Charles A., ... 55 West 51st Street, " " "
Dana, Charles L., ... 53 W. 53rd Street, " " "
Dana, Richard H., Jr., . . . 103 Park Avenue, " " "
Davidge, William H., ... 49 Wall Street, " " "
Davies, J. Clarence, . . 149th Street and 3rd Avenue, " " "
Davies, Julien T., ... 32 Nassau Street, " " "
Davis, G. Pierrepont, ... Woodland Street, Hartford, Conn,
Davis, Horace A., ... 135 Broadway, New York City
Davison, Charles Stewart, . . . 60 Wall Street, " " "

Day, Clarence S.,	45 Wall Street, New York City
de Coppet, H.	754 Park Avenue, " " "
DeForest, R. W.,	30 Broad Street, " " "
Deming, Horace E.,	13 William Street, " " "
Demorest, William C.,	60 Liberty Street, " " "
Derby, James Lloyd,	925 Park Avenue, " " "
de Roode, Albert,	52 Wall Street, " " "
Despard, W. D.,	6 Hanover Street, " " "
DeWitt, Theodore,	88 Nassau Street, " " "
Dickinson, A. Lowes,	54 William Street, " " "
Dickinson, Robert L.,	168 Clinton Street, Brooklyn
Dickson, James B.,	49 Wall Street, New York City
Dittenhoefer, A. J.,	96 Broadway, " " "
Dix, John A.,	Executive Chamber, Albany, N. Y.
Dodd, Lee W.,	257 W. 86th Street, New York City
Dodge, Cleveland H.,	99 John Street, " " "
Dommerich, L. F.,	57 Greene Street, " " "
Dormitzer, Henry,	27 E. 74th Street, " " "
Dougherty, J. Hampden,	27 William Street, " " "
Dows, David,	102 Produce Exchange, " " "
Dows, Tracy,	Room 102, Produce Exchange, " " "
Dreier, H. E.,	129 West 20th Street, " " "
Drescher, William A. E.,	715 St. Paul Street, Rochester, N. Y.
Drew, John,	Racquet and Tennis Club, New York City
Driggs, Laurence,	32 Liberty Street, " " "
Drucklieb Charles G.,	178 Washington Street, " " "
Dunham, Edward K.,	338 E. 26th Street, " " "
Dunning, S. Wright,	80 Madison Avenue, " " "
Dutcher, Charles M.,	248 Sixth Avenue, " " "
Dutton, George D.,	101 E. 62nd Street, " " "
Dwight, Edmund,	5 Maiden Lane, " " "
Eastman, George,	400 East Avenue, Rochester, N. Y.
Eaton, Henry W.,	45 William Street, New York City
Ehrich, Louis R.,	463 Fifth Avenue, " " "
Elderkin, John.	Lotos Club, 558 Fifth Avenue, " " "
Eliot, Charles W.,	Cambridge, Mass.
Elliot, Daniel G.,	77th Street and 8th Avenue, New York City
Ely, Arthur H.,	56 Wall Street, " " "
Ely, Robert E.,	23 West 44th Street, " " "
Emmons, Arthur B.,	1743 Twenty-Second Street, Washington, D. C.
Emmons, Samuel F.,	U. S. Geological Survey, Washington, D. C.
Erbe, Gustav,	344 St. Paul Street, Rochester, N. Y.
Erbslöh, R.,	Box 16, Station A, New York City
Estes, Webster C.,	74 Warren Street. " " "
Evans, George,	55 West 39th Street, " " "
Evans, Selah O.,	118 W. Houston Street, " " "
Everett, A. Leo,	49 Wall Street, " " "

Ewart, Richard H., ... 115 Franklin Street, New York City
Ewing, Thomas, Jr., ... 67 Wall Street, " " "

Fabbri, Alessandro, ... 11 E. 62d Street, New York City
Fabbri, Ernesto G., ... 11 E. 62d Street, " " "
Fairchild, Benjamin T., . . . P. O. Box 1120, " " "
Fairchild, Charles S., ... Cazenovia, N. Y.
Fancher, B. N., . . . 21 Ridgeview Avenue, White Plains, N. Y.
Fay, Charles J., ... 31 Nassau Street, New York City
Ferguson, William C., ... Garden City, New York
Field, Hamilton E., ... 106 Columbia Heights, Brooklyn
Fish, Sidney W., ... 25 East 78th Street, New York City
Folks, Homer, ... 105 E. 22nd Street, " " "
Forrest, C. R., ... Asylum Avenue, Hartford, Conn.
Foster, Macom G., ... P. O. Box 1120, New York City
Fox, Alan, ... 50 Pine Street, " " "
Fox, Austen G., (Life), . . . 37 E. 39th Street, " " "
Francis, C. D., ... 60 Wall Street, " " "
Frankenheimer, John, ... 25 Broad Street, " " "
Frankfort, M., . . . C 22 Produce Exchange, " " "
Frankfurter, Felix, ... 32 Liberty Street, " " "
Franklin, George S., . . . 32 Liberty Street, " " "
French, Daniel E., . . . 125 W. 11th Street, " " "
Frissell, H. B., ... Hampton, Va.
Fuld, Leonard Felix, . . . 130 E. 110th Street, New York City
Fuller, Frank, . . . , . 61 Fifth Avenue, " " "
Fuller, Paul, ... 71 Broadway, " " "
Fullerton, Alexander, (Life), . . 5 W. 8th Street, " " "
Funk, I. K., ... 22 Upper Mountain Ave., Montclair, N. J.

Gaillard, William D., ... 141 Broadway, New York City
Gallagher, Patrick, ... 1181 Broadway, " " "
Garver, John A., ... 44 Wall Street, " " "
Gasser, Roy C., ... 85 Wall Street, " " "
Germond, H. S., ... 44 Broad Street, " " "
Gerrish, Frank Scott, ... 17 E. 76th Street, " " "
Getzelsohn, J. A., . . . 1065 Prospect Avenue, " " "
Gibbons, George W., ... 198 Broadway, " " "
Gilbert, Cass, ... 11 E. 24th Street, " " "
Gilliss, Walter, ... 150 Fifth Avenue, " " "
Glenn, John M., ... 136 E. 19th Street, " " "
Goadby, Clarence, ... 21 W. 35th Street, " " "
Goddard, Henry W., ... 52 Wall Street, " " "
Godkin, Laurence, ... 36 W. 10th Street, " " "
Goetze, Otto, ... 60 Remsen Street, Brooklyn, N. Y.
Goldman, Julius, ... 31 Nassau Street, New York City
Goldmark, James, ... 83 Warren Street, " " "
Goodnow, Frank J., ... 49 Riverside Drive, " " "

Goodrich, David M.,	2 Rector Street, New York City
Goodwin, Elliot H.,	79 Wall Street, " " "
Goodwin, H. L.,	170 Broadway, " " "
Gottheil, Paul,	8-10 Bridge Street, " " "
Gottsberger, Francis,	156 Broadway, " " "
Gould, Elgin R. L.,	281 Fourth Avenue, " " "
Grant, De Forest,	22 E. 46th Street, " " "
Grant, Percy S.,	7 W. 10th Street, " " "
Gray, Henry G.,	161 Madison Avenue, " " "
Greene, Jerome D.,	Rockefeller Inst., " " "
Green, Noah,	478 Central Park, West, " " "
Greene, Francis V.,	816 Fidelity Building, Buffalo, N. Y.
Greenough, John,	38 E. 63rd Street, New York City
Greer, David H.,	7 Gramercy Park, " " "
Gregory, E. C.,	54 W. 47th Street, " " "
Gunther, J. J.,	48 E. 81st Street, " " "
Guthrie, William D.,	28 Park Place, " " "
Gutterson, Herbort L.,	49 Wall Street, " " "
Gwynne, Arthur C.,	Rye, N. Y.
Haan, R. M.,	Hotel St. Regis, New York City
Hale, Robert L.,	15 Dey Street, " " "
Hall, Frank L.,	30 Broad Street, " " "
Hall, Thomas C.,	700 Park Avenue, " " "
Hall, Willis E.,	30 Pine Street, " " "
Halsey, Robert H.,	118 W. 58th Street, " " "
Halsted, John F.,	93 Remsen Street, Brooklyn, N. Y.
Hamlin, Frank H.,	Canandaigua, N. Y.
Hammond, John Henry,	40 Wall Street, New York City
Hand, Learned,	2 Wall Street, " " "
Hand, O. K.,	68 Columbia Heights, Brooklyn
Hand, Richard L.,	Elizabethtown, N. Y.
Hansmann, Carl A.,	96 Broadway, New York City
Harbeck, Charles T.,	306 Lexington Avenue, " " "
Hard, Anson W.,	107 Wall Street, " " "
Harding, Edward,	43 Exchange Place, " " "
Hardon, Henry Winthrop,	60 Wall Street, " " "
Harrison, Robert L.,	59 Wall Street, " " "
Hart, John Wilson,	District Attorney's Office, " " "
Hasslacher, Jacob,	100 William Street, " " "
Haupt, Louis,	232 E. 19th Street, " " "
Hayes, J. Noble,	68 William, " " "
Healy, A. Augustus,	196 Columbia Heights, Brooklyn
Heath, Frank E.,	95 Liberty Street, New York City
Heckscher, A.,	576 Fifth Avenue, " " "
Heimann, Julius,	315 W. 105th Street, " " "
Heinze, Arthur P.,	31 Nassau Street, " " "
Henderson, Harold G.,	80 Irving Place, " " "

Hendrick, Ellwood, ... 139 E. 40th Street, New York City
Hentz, Leonard S., ... 769 St. Mark's Avenue, Brooklyn
Herbert, William, ... 11 Pine Street, New York City
Hermann, Ferdinand, ... 24 Pine Street, " " "
Hess, Selmar, ... 151 W. 25th Street, " " "
Hewlett, Mortimer C., ... 900 Broadway, " " "
Hey, George, ... 3630 Park Avenue, " " "
Hildreth, P. S , ... 135 Broadway, " " "
Hinkley, Samuel Neilson, ... Lawrence, L. I.
Hinrichs, Frederick W., . . . 76 William Street, New York City
Hitchcock, Welcome G., (Life) . . 69 E. 11th Street, " " "
Hobart, Henry L., ... 120 Front Street, " " "
Hodges, Harrison B., ... 16 Gramercy Park, " " "
Hoe, Richard M., . . . Room 102, Produce Exchange, " " "
Holt, Henry, ... 34 W. 33rd Street, " " "
Holt, Roland, ... 34 W. 33rd Street, " " "
Holter, Edwin O , ... 40 Wall Street, " " "
Hooper, Parker Morse, . . . 527 Fifth Avenue, " " "
Hoppin, Frederick S., ... 29 Waverly Place, " " "
Hoppin, William W., ... 54 William Street, " " "
Hornblower, William B., . . . 24 Broad Street, " " "
Howe, Daniel R., ... Asylum Avenue, Hartford, Conn.
Howe, J. Morgan, ... 12 W. 46th Street, New York City
Howe, Wirt, ... 135 Broadway, " " "
Howell, Wilson S., . . . 80th Street, East End Avenue, " " "
Howland, Charles P., ... 35 Wall Street, " " "
Hoyt, Allen G., ... 49 Wall Street, " " "
Hoyt, Francis D., ... 69 Wall Street, " " "
Hubbard, Thomas H., . . . 16 W. 58th Street, " " "
Hughes, Charles E., ... Washington, D. C.
Hull, Charles A., ... 95 William Street, New York City
Hunt, Leavitt J., ... 165 Broadway, " " "
Huntington, Francis C., . . . 54 William Street, " " "
Huntington, Samuel, ... 176 Broadway, " " "
Hyde, A. F., ... 55 Liberty Street, " " "
Hyslop, John, 4 Riverview Terrace, foot East 58th Street, " " "

Ide, Robert L., ... 7 Nassau Street, New York City
Ijams, J. Horton, ... 56 William Street, " " "
Ingraham, Edward, ... 69 Worth Street, " " "
Insley, Robert B.. . . . . Westfield, N. J.
Ireland, F. G., , ... 299 Broadway, New York City
Ireland, John B., ... 15 E. 47th Street, " " "
Iselin, C. Oliver, ... 36 Wall Street, " " "
Iselin, John H., ... , 25 Broad Street, " " "
Isham, Samuel. . . . . . 471 Park Avenue, " " "

Jackson, John G., ... 71 Broadway, New York City
Jacob, Lawrence, ... 68 Broad Street, " " "

Jacobson, Samuel A.,	132 Nassau Street,	New York City
James, Walter B.,	17 W. 54th Street,	" " "
Jameson, E. C.,	76 William Street,	" " "
Jaretzki, Alfred,	49 Wall Street,	" " "
Jay, William,	48 Wall Street,	" " "
Jellenix, Felix,	111 Broadway,	" " "
Jennings, Frederick B.,	15 Broad Street,	" " "
Jennings, Percy H.,	25 Broad Street,	" " "
Johnson, Burgess,	3 E. 14th Street,	" " "
Johnson, Robert Underwood,	33 E. 17th Street,	" " "
Johnson, Willis Fletcher,	154 Nassau Street,	" " "
Joline, Adrian, H.,	54 Wall Street,	" " "
Jones, Oliver Livingston, Jr.,	116 W. 72d Street,	" " "
Josephthal, Sidney L.,	43 Cedar Street,	" " "
Kahn, Otto H., (Life),	54 William Street,	New York City
Kelley, Nicholas,	52 William Street,	" " "
Kellogg, Francis B,	Temple Auditorium,	Los Angeles, Cal.
Kelsey, Clarence H.,	146 Broadway,	New York City
Kemp, Edward,	135 Water Street,	" " "
Kenneson, Thaddeus D.,	13 William Street,	" " "
Kenyon, Alan D.,	49 Wall Street,	" " "
Kenyon, William Houston,	49 Wall Street,	" " "
Keppler, Rudolph,	25 Broad Street,	" " "
Kernan, John D.,		Utica, N.Y.
Kernochan, J. Frederic,	44 Pine Street,	New York City
Kidder, Camillus G.,	27 William Street,	" " "
Kiernan, Patrick,	14 E. 83rd Street,	" " "
Kilbreth, James T.,	45 Broadway,	" " "
Kilmer, Alfred G.,	15 William Street,	" " "
Kimball, A. R.,		Orange, N. J.
Kimball, Daniel T.,	198 Broadway,	New York City
King, Le Roy,	20 E. 84th Street,	" " "
Kinnicutt, Francis H.,	165 Broadway,	" " "
Kinnicutt, Francis P.,	39 E. 35th Street,	" " "
Kinnicutt, G Herman,	39 E. 35th Street,	" " "
Kirchhoff, Charles,	14 & 16 Park Place,	" " "
Klein, Isaac H.,	30 Broad Street,	" " "
Knapp, Horace Greeley,	5 E. 42nd Street,	" " "
Knapp, James R.,	60 Wall Street,	" " "
Knapp, Shepherd,	8 Institute Road,	Worcester, Mass.
Knauth, Antonio,	39 West 76th Street,	New York City
Knauth, Theodor W.,	15 William Street,	" " "
Koehler, Jerome H,	47 Cedar Street,	" " "
Kohler, Max J.,	30 Broad Street,	" " "
Kudlich, Herman C.,	299 Broadway,	" " "
Kuehnle, Frederick C.,	629 W. 51st Street,	" " "
Kuhne, Percival,	13 William Street,	" " "

Kunhardt, William B.,		100 Broadway, New York City
Kunstlich, Samuel H.,		256 Broadway, " " "
Laimbeer, Francis E.,		292 Broadway, New York City
Lambert, William B.,		Highland Street, Cambridge Mass.
Landes, Leonard,		140 E. 22nd Street, New York City
Landsman, S. M.,		220 E. 19th Street, " " "
Langmann, G.,		121 W. 57th Street, " " "
Lansing, J. Townsend,		82 State Street, Albany, N. Y.
Larremore, Wilbur,		32 Nassau Street, New York City
Law, James,		15 E. 127th Street, " " "
Lawrence, John Burling,		136 E. 30th Street, " " "
Lawrence, Walter B.,		35 Wall Street, " " "
Leavitt, John Brooks,		30 Broad Street, " " "
Leaycraft, J. Edgar,		19 W. 42nd Street, " " "
Lederle, Ernest J.,		471 W. 143d Street, " " "
Ledoux, Albert R.,		9 Cliff Street, " " "
Lee, Frederick S.,		125 E. 65th Street, " " "
Lee, Henry T.,		54 W. 52nd Street, " " "
Lee, W. H. L.,		45 Pine Street, " " "
Leech, John E.,		94 Remsen Street, Brooklyn, N. Y.
Leech, Robinson,		94 Remsen Street, " "
Leffingwell, R. C.,		52 William Street, New York City
Le Gendre, William,		59 Wall Street, " " "
Lehmaier, James M.,		215 E. 22nd Street, " " "
Lehmaier, Louis A.,		78 Beekman Street, " " "
LeRoy, E. A.,		200 West 57th Street, " " "
Levi, Albert A.,		52 Broadway, " " "
Lewis, Richard V.,		130 W. 42d Street, " " "
Lewisohn, Sam A.,		42 Broadway, " " "
Lichtenstein, Paul,		304 W. 78th Street, " " "
Lindsay, Alexander M.,		373 East Avenue, Rochester, N. Y.
Littauer, Lucius N.,		Gloversville, N. Y.
Livingston, Goodhue,		38 E. 65th Street, New York City
Lobenstein, William C.,		245 Central Park West, " " "
Loines, Russell H.,		131 E. 66th Street, " " "
Lomb, Adolph,		48 Cumberland Street, Rochester, N. Y.
Lomb, Henry C.,		281 Barrington Street, " "
Lord, Franklin B.,		49 Wall Street, New York City
Lord, Frederic W.,		126 E. 65th Street, " " "
Lounsbery, Richard P.,		15 Broad Street, " " "
Low, Josiah O.,		56 William Street, " " "
Ludington, A. C.,		56 W. 10th Street, " " "
Ludlow, James B.,		45 Cedar Street, " " "
Luther, George Martin,		25 Broad Street, " " "
Lyman, Frank,		88 Wall Street, " " "
Lyman, Theodore,		Woodland Street, Hartford, Conn.
Lynch, J. De P.,		Utica, N. Y.

Macfarlane, Wallace,	32 Liberty Street, New York City
MacKellar, George M.,	43 Cedar Street. " " "
MacVeagh, Charles,	15 Broad Street, " " "
MacKenzie, James C.,	Dobbs Ferry. N. Y.
Mallet-Prevost, Severo,	30 Broad Street, New York City
Mallinckrodt, Edward,	Mallinckrodt Chemical Works, St. Louis, Mo.
Mansfield, Howard,	49 Wall Street, New York City
Marble, Charles B.,	58 Morningside Avenue, " " "
Marling, Alfred E.,	21 Liberty Street, " " "
Marsh, Robert McC,	45 West 11th Street, " " "
Marshall, Charles H.,	45 William Street, " " "
Marshall, Fielding L.,	4141 Sheridan Road. Chicago, Ill.
Marshall, Louis,	37 Wall Street, New York City
Marsters, A., A.,	15 Dey Street, " " "
Martin, Alfred W.,	995 Madison Avenue, " " "
Martin, John,	Grymes Hill, Staten Island, N. Y.
Martin, Newell,	20 Exchange Place, New York City
Martin, T. Comerford,	29 West 39th Street, " " "
Mason, Alexander T.,	13 William Street, " " "
Mason, Alfred Bishop,	University Club, " " "
Mather, Robert,	165 Broadway, " " "
Mathews, Robert,	135 Spring Street, Rochester, N. Y.
Matthew, William B.,	319 W. 112th Street, New York City
Matthews, Brander,	661 West End Avenue, " " "
Matthewson, Arthur,	South Woodstock, Conn.
Maxwell, William H.,	500 Park Avenue, New York City
May, Charles,	62 Nassau Street, " " "
Maynard, Walter E.,	Fifth Avenue Building, " " "
Meacham, Alfred B.,	59 Wall Street, " " "
Mellen, Chase,	32 Nassau Street, " " "
Merck, George,	Llewelyn Park, West Orange, N. J.
Merrill, Charles E.,	44 E. 23d Street, New York City
Merrill, Payson,	31 Nassau Street, " " "
Metcalfe, Henry,	147 Fourth Avenue, " " "
Meyer, Alfred,	785 Madison Avenue, " " "
Milbank, Albert G.,	49 Wall Street, " " "
Milburn, John G.,	54 Wall Street, " " "
Miller, Clifford L.,	62 West 89th Street, " " "
Miller, Daniel S.,	150 Central Park S., " " "
Miller, George Douglas,	125 State Street, Albany, N. Y
Milliken, Hugh K.,	51 Leonard Street, New York City
Mills, L. H.,	473 Broome Street, " " "
Mills, Ogden L.,	15 Broad Street, " " "
Moen, Edward C.,	52 William Street, " " "
Moffat, George B.,	5 Nassau Street, " " "
Moffat, R. Burnham,	63 Wall Street, " "
Montgomery, R. M.,	27 Pine Street, " "
Morgan, W. Fellows,	Arch 5, Brooklyn Bridge, " " "

Morgan, W. Forbes, Jr.,	. . . .	71 Broadway, New York City
Morris, Ray,	. . . . .	81 Fulton Street, " " "
Morrow, Dwight,	. . . . . .	Englewood, N. J.
Morse, Horace J.,	. . . . .	820 St. Mark's Avenue, Brooklyn
Morse, Richard C.,	. . . . . .	35 Sidney Place, "
Mortimer, Richard,	. . . . . .	11 Wall Street, New York City
Mosenthal, P. J.,	. . . . .	95 William Street, " " "
Mosle, A. Henry,	. . . . .	30 Broad Street, " " "
Mott, William F.,	. . . .	Toms River, N. J.
Munro, J. G.,	. . .	61 Erie County Bank Building, Buffalo, N. Y.
Munro, John R.,	. . . .	132 Remsen Street, Brooklyn, N. Y.
Munroe, Vernon,	. . . .	45 William Street, New York City
Murphy, Daniel F.,	. . . . .	165 Broadway, " " "
Murray, Joseph K.,	.	Broadway, opposite 10th Street, Flushing, N. Y.
McAlpin, George L.,	. . . .	55 W. 33d Street, New York City
McAneny, Leonard G.,	. . . .	2 Rector Street, " " "
McCagg, Louis Butler,	. . . .	18 E. 84th Street, " " "
McCandless, Charles W.,	. . .	15 William Street, " " "
McCarroll, William,	. . . .	Tribune Building, " " "
McCobb, James S.,	. . . .	44 W. 44th Street, " " "
McCook, Philip J.,	. . . .	15 William Street, " " "
McGinness, Remsen,	. . .	42 East 41st Street, " " "
McKeever, J. Lawrence,	. .	164 Lexington Avenue, " " "
McMahon, Fulton,	. . .	54 William Street, " " "
Nadal, Charles C.,	. . .	142 E. 35th Street, New York City
Nash, Francis Philip,	. . . . .	Geneva, N. Y.
Naumberg, Elkan,	. . .	48 W. 58th Street, New York City
Neilson, Robert H.,	. . . .	52 William Street, " " "
Nelson, H. W., Jr.,	. . . . . .	Marshfield Hills, Mass.
Newton Albro J.,	. . . .	528 Union Street, Brooklyn, N. Y.
Newton, R. Heber,	. . . . .	East Hampton, N. Y.
Nichols, George M.,	. . .	277 Adelphi Street, Brooklyn, N. Y.
Nichols, W. N.,	. . . .	25 Broad Street, New York City
Nicoll, James C.,	. . . .	51 W. 10th Street, " " "
Nissen, Ludwig,	. . . .	182 Broadway, " " "
Norris, Henry S.,	. . . .	10 W. 49th Street, " " "
Norton, Charles D.,	. . . .	2 Wall Street, " " "
Notman, George,	. . . .	99 John Street, " " "
Oakes, Charles,	. . . .	49 Wall Street, " " "
O'Connor, John A.,	. . . . .	, Box H. Tarrytown, N. Y.
Ogden, Charles W.,	. . . .	14 E. 79th Street, New York City
Ogden, Rollo,	. . . .	20 Vesey Street, " " "
Olin, Stephen H.,	. . . .	32 Nassau Street, " " "
Olney, Peter B., Jr.,	. . . .	68 William Street, " " "
Oltman, H. H.,	. . . . .	42 Broadway, " " "
Olyphant, Robert,	. . . .	17 Battery Place, " " "

Opdyke, William S., ... 20. Nassau Street, New York City
Oppenheim, Edward L., ... 30 Broad Street, " " "
Oppenheimer, Henry S., ... 5 E. 43rd Street, " " "
Orcutt C. Blake, ... Hudson River Day Line, " " "
Ordway, Edward W., ... 1093 Dean Street, Brooklyn
Orr, Alexander E., ... 102 Remsen Street, "
Osborn, Perry, ... 52 Brattle Street, Cambridge, Mass.
Osborne, Thomas M., ... Auburn, N. Y.
Ottley, James H., ... 236 West 37th Street. New York City

Paffard, Frederic C., ... 238 Clinton Street, Brooklyn, N. Y.
Page, Walter H., ... 130 East 67th Street, New York City
Page, William H., ... 32 Liberty Street, " " "
Parker, Frédéric S., ... 32 Garden Place, Brooklyn
Parsons, Herbert, ... 52 William Street, " " "
Parsons, John E., ... 52 William Street, " " "
Partridge John N , ... Hamilton Club, Brooklyn, N. Y.
Partridge, William Ordway, . . 289 Fourth Avenue. New York City
Paulding, James Kirk, ... 130 E. 24th Street, " " "
Peabody, George Foster, ... 43 Exchange Place, " " "
Peck, George G., ... 117 Chambers Street, " " "
Pedersen, James, ... 20 E. 46th Street, " " "
Pendleton, Francis K., . . . 25 Broad Street, " " "
Perrine, William A., . . . 2440 N. Marshall Street, Philadelphia, Pa.
Phillips, Louis S., ... 49 Broadway, New York City
Phillips, N. Taylor, ... 51 Chambers Street, " " "
Phoenix, Phillips, ... 68 Broad Street, " " "
Pierce, Franklin, ... 2 Rector Street, " " "
Pierce, Henry H., ... 49 Wall Street, " " "
Pierrepont, Henry E., ... 216 Columbia Heights, Brooklyn
Pierrepont, Robert Low, ... Box 449, Bay Shore, N. Y,
Pierson, James R., ... 29 Broadway, New York City
Pinchot, Amos R. E., . . Criminal Court Building, " " "
Pinchot, Gifford, . . . 1615 Rhode Island Avenue, Washington, D. C.
Planten, John R., ... 44 Eighth Avenue. Brooklyn, N. Y.
Planten, W. R. J., ... 44 Eighth Avenue, " "
Plaut, Albert, ... 120 William Street, New York City
Poillon, Cornelius, ... 125 E. 70th Street, " " "
Polk, W. M., ... 7 E. 36th Street, " " "
Pollak, Francis D., ... 49 Wall Street, " " "
Pope, George A., ... 926 St. Paul Street, Baltimore, Md.
Post, Abram S., ... 81 Fulton Street, New York City
Potter, Frederick. . . . . 71 Broadway, " " "
Potts, W. Rockhill, ... 143 Liberty Street, " " "
Powell, Wilson M., Jr., ... 29 Wall Street. " " "
Pratt, Frederic B., ... 215 Ryerson Street, Brooklyn, N. Y.
Pratt, John T., ... 43 Exchange Place, New York City
Prentice, William P., ... 52 Broadway, " " "

Prentiss, George H.,	108 Pierrepont Street, Brooklyn, N Y
Price, Joseph M.,	158 West Broadway, New York City
Proskauer, Joseph M.,	170 Broadway, " " "
Pruden, W. Edgar,	162 W. 120th Street, " " "
Pryer, Charles,	New Rochelle, N. Y.
Putnam, George Haven,	27 W. 23d Street, New York City
Putnam, George P.,	160 Fifth Avenue, " " "
Putnam, Harrington,	404 Washington Avenue, Brooklyn
Putnam, Irving,	27 W. 23rd Street, New York City
Putnam, J. Bishop,	27 W. 23rd Street, " " "
Pyne, Moses Taylor,	30 Pine Street, " " "
Pyle, James McAlpin,	55 Wall Street, " " "
Quereau, C. H.,	Grand Central Terminal, New York City
Rand, William H., Jr.	39 Wall Street, New York City
Raven, A. A.,	51 Wall Street, " " "
Raymond, Charles H.,	11 Pine Street, " " "
Raymond, Rossiter W.	29 W. 39th Street, " " "
Reed, Lansing P.,	15 Broad Street, " " "
Reichhelm, Edward P.,	90 West 34th Street, Bayonne, N. J.
Reid, Wallace,	56 Maiden Lane, New York City
Reynolds, James B.,	151 Central Park West, " " "
Rhoades, John Harsen,	66 Beaver Street, " " "
Rice, Edwin T., Jr.,	59 Wall Street, " " "
Richards, C. A. L.,	169 Power Street, Providence, R. I.
Richards, George,	141 Broadway, New York City
Rives, George L.,	69 E. 79th Street, " " "
Robinson, Beverly R.,	42 W. 37th Street, " " "
Robinson, Moncure,	7 E. 42d Street, " " "
Rogers, Robert,	48 E. 61st Street, " " "
Roome, W. Harris,	287 Fourth Avenue, " " "
Roosevelt, Franklin D.,	125 E. 36th Street, " " "
Roosevelt, Theodore,	Oyster Bay, N. Y.
Root, Elihu,	733 Park Avenue, New York City
Root, Elihu, Jr.,	31 Nassau Street, " " "
Rose, Arthur P.,	Geneva, N. Y.
Rosendale, Simon W.,	57 State Street, Albany, N. Y.
Rosenfeld, George,	58 New Street, New York City
Rossbach, Jacob,	1 W. 86th Street, " " "
Rothschild, Jacob,	31 W. 57th Street, " " "
Rothschild, Ludwig,	466 Broadway, " " "
Rounds, Arthur C.,	96 Broadway, " " "
Rowe, Basil W.,	71 Broadway, " " "
Rowe, William V.,	51 Wall Street, " " "
Rublee, George,	32 Liberty Street, " " "
Runyon, Carman R.,	87 Locust Hill Avenue, Yonkers, N. Y.
Rush, Thomas E,	40 Wall Street, New York City
Russell, J. Townsend,	220 Columbia Heights, Brooklyn, N. Y.

Sachs, Walter E.,	43 Exchange Place, New York City
Sackett, Henry W.	154 Nassau Street, " " "
Sage, Dean.	49 Wall Street, " " "
Salomon, William.	25 Broad Street, " " "
Sand, Henry A. L.,	120 Broadway, " " "
Sands, B. Aymar,	31 Nassau Street, " " "
Sanger, William Cary,	Sangerfield, N. Y.
Sayer, W. Murray, Jr.,	398 Washington Avenue, Brooklyn
Schafer, Samuel M.,	5 Wall Street, New York City
Scharmann, Hermann B.,	170 W. 59th Street, " " "
Schieren, Charles A.	405 Clinton Avenue, Brooklyn
Schnakenberg, D.,	6 Hanover Street, New York City
Schneidenbach, Arthur Jaques,	75 E. 82d Street, " " "
Schrader, George H. F.,	32 Rose Street, " " "
Schurman, George W.,	15 W. 57th Street, " " "
Schurz, Carl Lincoln,	49 Wall Street, " " "
Schwarz, Herbert F., The Manchester,	255 W. 108th Street, " " "
Schwarzenbach, Robert J. T.,	472 Broome Street, " " "
Schwarzschild, Monroe M.,	340 W. 86th Street, " " "
Scott, J. F.,	11 Overbrook Street, Mount Vernon, N. Y.
Scott, William,	25 Duane Street, New York City
Scribner, Arthur H.,	153 Fifth Avenue. " " "
Scribner, Charles,	153 Fifth Avenue, " " "
Seaman, Louis L.,	247 Fifth Avenue, " " "
Searle, Arthur,	41 Concord Avenue, Cambridge, Mass.
Seaver, Benjamin F.,	111 Pierrepont Street, Brooklyn
Sedgwick, Arthur G.,	52 William Street, New York City
Sedgwick, Ellery,	116 E. 26th Street, " " "
Sedgwick, Henry D.,	120 E. 22d Street, " " "
Seligman, E. R. A.,	324 W. 86th Street, " " "
Seligman, George W.,	3 S. William Street, " " "
Seligman, Jefferson,	1 William Street, " " "
Serven, A. Ralph,	1419 "F" Street, N. W., Washington, D. C.
Sexton, Lawrence E.,	34 Pine Street, New York City
Seymour, Origen S.,	54 William Street, " " "
Shainwald, Ralph L.,	100 William Street, " " "
Shaw, Albert,	13 Astor Place, " " "
Sheldon, Edward W.,	45 Wall Street, " " "
Sheppard, John S., Jr.,	26 Liberty Street, " " "
Shortt, W. A.,	32 Broadway, " " "
Sibley, Harper,	5 Nassau Street, " " "
Siedenberg, Reinhard,	Cotton Exchange, " " "
Silverman, M. J.,	218 Alexander Avenue, " " "
Simes, William.	Box 3084, Boston, Mass.
Simon, Franklin,	414 Fifth Avenue, New York City
Skidmore, William L.,	39 W. 52nd Street, " " "
Skuse, Thomas J,	Naval Office, Customs House. " " "
Slade, Francis Louis,	115 Broadway, " " "

Sleicher, John A.,	225 Fifth Avenue,	New York City
Slicer, Thomas R.,	55 W. 44th Street,	" " "
Slicer, Benson B.,	38 Wall Street,	" " "
Sloan, Benson B.,	38 Wall Street,	" " "
Small, A.,	20 Pike Street,	" " "
Smillie, James C.,	440 West End Avenue,	" " "
Smith, Adelbert J.,	15 William Street,	" " "
Smith, Bryan H.,	Brooklyn Savings Bank,	Brooklyn, N. Y.
Smith, Charles Robinson,	25 Broad Street,	New York City
Smith, Clarence B.,	27 William Street,	" " "
Smith, Edgar L.,	31 W. 45th Street,	" " "
Smith, F. Hopkinson,	150 E. 34th Street,	" " "
Smith, Frederick J.,	278 Mulberry Street,	" " "
Smith, Howard M.,	Brevoort Savings Bank,	Brooklyn, N. Y.
Smith, James E.,	38 Park Row,	New York City
Smith, J. Waldo,	165 Broadway,	" " "
Smith, Nathaniel S.,	68 William Street,	" " "
Smith, William Alexander,	412 Madison Avenue,	" " "
Smith, William Mason,	128 Broadway,	" " "
Smyth, Nathan A.,	5 Nassau Street,	" " "
Snow, Elbridge G.,	56 Cedar Street,	" " "
Snow, Frederick A.,	15 Wall Street,	" " "
Spackman, W M.,	820 Madison Avenue,	" " "
Spector, Joseph,	241 E. 68th Street,	" " "
Spiegelberg, Frederick,	36 W. 76th Street,	" " "
Spingarn, J. E.,	9 W. 73rd Street,	" " "
Stebbins. H. C.,	718 Fifth Avenue,	" " "
Steers, James R.,	101 Park Avenue,	" " "
Steinway F. T.,	Orchard St. and Jackson Ave.,	Long Island City, N. Y.
Stern, Benjamin,	32 W. 23rd Street,	New York City
Stern, Henry Root,	40 Wall Street,	" " "
Stevens, Gorham P.,	107 E. 16th Street,	" " "
Stewart, William R.,	P. O. Box 258,	" " "
Stimson, Daniel M.,	28 W. 37th Street,	" " "
Stix, Sylvan L.,	Hudson and N. Moore Streets,	" " "
Stokes, Anson Phelps, Jr., (Life),	Yale University,	New Haven, Conn.
Stokes, Harold M. Phelps, (Life),	229 Madison Avenue,	New York City
Stokes, I. N. Phelps, (Life),	118 E. 22nd Street,	" " "
Stokes, James,	49 Cedar Street,	" " "
Stokes, J. G. Phelps, (Life),	229 Madison Avenue,	" " "
Strasbourger, Samuel,	74 Broadway	" " "
Straus, Isador,	Broadway and 34th Street,	" " "
Straus, Oscar S.,	42 Warren Street,	" " "
Strauss, Albert,	15 Broad Street,	" " "
Strauss, Frederick,	15 Broad Street,	" " "
Strong, George A.,	50 Wall Street,	" " "
Stuart, J. P. Whiton,	8 E. 54th Street,	" " "
Wilds, Howard Payson,	University Club,	" " "

Sturgis, F. K.,	36 Broad Street, New York City
Sturges, S. Perry,	305 Washington Avenue, Brooklyn
Stuyvesant, Rutherford,	32 Liberty Street, New York City
Sulzberger, Cyrus L.,	516 West End Avenue, " " "
Sulzberger, Ferdinand,	802 First Avenue, " " "
Taft, Henry W.,	40 Wall Street, New York City
Taggart, Rush,	195 Broadway, " " "
Tappan, J. B. Coles,	49 Wall Street, " " "
Tatham, Charles,	261 Water Street, " " "
Tatham, Edwin,	133 East 36th Street, " " "
Taussig, Walter M.,	9-15 Murray Street, " " "
Taylor, E. P., Jr.,	7 Pine Street, " " "
Taylor, Thomas Fenton,	130 E. 67th Street, " " "
Taylor, Walter F.,	54 Wall Street, " " "
Terry, Roderick,	Newport, R. I.
Terry, Seth Sprague,	66 Broadway, New York City
Thacher, Archibald,	49 East 51st Street, " " "
Thacher, Thomas,	62 Cedar Street, " " "
Thacher, Thomas, D.,	62 Cedar Street " " "
Thatcher, John S.,	839 Madison Avenue. " " "
Thomas, John H.,	9 Broadway, " " "
Thomas, Arthur V.,	68 William Street, " " "
Thomson, Herbert G.,	145 Broadway, " " "
Thorne, Robert,	30 Broad Street, " " "
Thorne, Samuel,	43 Cedar Street, " " "
Thorne, Samuel, Jr.,	43 Cedar Street, " " "
Thornton, William,	18 Thomas Street, " " "
Tiebout, Charles H.,	31 Grand Street, Brooklyn
Tinker, Edward L.,	40 Wall Street. New York City
Tinkham, Julian R.,	42 Broadway. " " "
Tison, Alexander,	11 William Street, " " "
Tod, J. Kennedy,	5 Nassau Street, " " "
Todd, Henry A.,	824 West End Avenue, " " "
Tomkins, Calvin,	17 Battery Place, " " "
Tompkins, Hamilton B.,	80 Broadway, " " "
Tower, George H.,	2 Rector Street. " " "
Train, Arthur C.,	30 Broad Street, " " "
Trowbridge, Alexander B.,	114 E. 28th Street, " " "
Tuckerman, Alfred,	University Club, " " "
Tuckerman, Eliot,	32 Liberty Street, " " "
Tuckerman, Paul.	Tuxedo, N. Y.
Tuttle, George M,	38 W. 52nd Street, New York City
Tweedy, J. F.,	11 Pine Street, " " "
Ulbrich, Gustav,	30 Broad Street, New York City
Unckles, D. S.,	957 St. Mark's Avenue, Brooklyn
Vail, Charles D.,	Geneva, N. Y.

Valentine, Charles A., ... 1 E. 27th Street, New York City
Valentine, Henry C., (Life), ... 257 Broadway, " " "
Valentine, Robert G. . . . Office of Indian Affairs, Washington, D. C.
Van Dusen, Samuel C., . . . 32 Cliff Street, New York City
Van Ingen, Edward H., ... 9 E. 71st Street, " " "
Van Nest, George W., ... 20 Broad Street, " " "
Van Rensselare, William S., . . 1 East 51st Street, " " "
Van Santvoord, R., ... 10 W. 122nd Street, " " "
Vidal, J. E., ... 393 St. Paul's Avenue, Stapleton, S. I.
Villard, Harold G. . . . . 43 Cedar Street, New York City
Villard, Oswald Garrison, (Life), . . 20 Vesey Street, " " "

Wadsworth, James W., ... Geneseo, N. Y.
Wagener, August P., . . . 51 Chambers Street, New York City
Walker, John, . . . 1231 Western Avenue, Allegheny City, Pa.
Walker, William, ... Harbison & Walker, Pittsburg, Pa.
Wallace, William H., ... 66 Broadway, New York City
Wallace, W. J., ... 209 W. 81st Street, " " "
Walling, William English, . . . 3 Fifth Avenue, " " "
Warburg, F. M., (Life), . . . 52 William Street, " " "
Warburg, Paul M., ... 52 William Street, " " "
Ward, Henry Galbreath, ... 79 Wall Street, " " "
Wardwell, Allen, ... 15 Broad Street, " " "
Warren, Frank S., Jr., ... 54 Wall Street, " " "
Warren, George A., 1443 Massachusetts Avenue, N. W., Washington, D. C.
Warren, H. Langford, ... 120 Boylston Street, Boston, Mass.
Watson, Charles W., ... 500 Madison Avenue, New York City
Webb, Willoughby L., ... 63 Wall Street, " " "
Weber, Leonard, ... 25 W. 46th Street, " " "
Weed, John W., ... 62 William Street, " " "
Weeks, John E., ... 46 E. 57th Street, " " "
Weir, R. F., ... Plaza Hotel, " " "
Welch, Archibald A., ... Woodland Street, Hartford, Conn.
Weld, Francis M., ... 5 Nassau Street, New York City
Welling, R. W. G., ... 2 Wall Street, " " "
Werthein, H. P., ... 1 William Street, " " "
Wetmore, Edmund, ... 34 Pine Street, " " "
Wheeler, Everett P., ... 27 William Street, " " "
Wheeler, James R., ... Columbia College, " " "
White, Alexander M., ... 52 Remsen Street, Brooklyn
White, Andrew D., (Life), ... Ithaca, N. Y.
White, Harold T., ... 5 Nassau Street, New York City
Whiteside, George W., . . . 27 William Street, " " "
Whiton, John M., ... 73 William Street, " " "
Whitridge, Frederick W., ... 59 Wall Street, " " "
Wickersham, C. W., ... Hastings Hall, Cambridge, Mass.
Wickersham, George W., . . Department Justice, Washington, D. C.
Wilcox, Ansley, ... 295 Main Street, Buffalo, N. Y.

Wilcox, William G.,	3 South William Street.	New York City
Williams, Benjamin A.,	22 E. 82nd Street,	" " "
Williams, L. L.,	Care E. C. Williams, 135 Broadway,	" " "
Williams, Perry P.,	Produce Exchange,	" " "
Williams, Richard H.,	1 Broadway,	" " "
Williams, Roger H.,	31 W. 12th Street,	" " "
Williams, Stephen G.,	953 Madison Avenue,	" " "
Williams, William,	1 West 54th Street.	" " "
Willis, Albert L.,	124 W. 133rd Street,	" " "
Wilson, George Augustus,		Celeron, N. Y.
Wilson, Richard T.,	511 Fifth Avenue,	New York City
Wingate, George W.,	1100 Dean Street,	Brooklyn, N. Y.
Winston, G. Owen,	936 Broadway,	New York City
Winters, Joseph E.,	25 W. 37th Street,	" " "
Winthrop, Bronson,	32 Liberty Street,	" " "
Wise, E. E.,	19 William Street,	" " "
Wisner, Charles,	Cotton Exchange,	" " "
Wisner, H. G.,	18 W. 12th Street,	" " "
Witherbee, F. S.,	71 Broadway,	" " "
Wolff, Emil,	171 W. 71st Street,	" " "
Wolff, Lewis S.,	12 E. 70th Street,	" " "
Wood, J. Leverne,	Care State Ins. Dept., 165 Broadway,	" " "
Wood, L. Hollingsworth,	2 Wall Street,	" " "
Woodbridge, Charles E.,	17 Battery Place,	" " "
Worcester, Edwin D., Jr.,	35 Nassau Street,	" " "
Wotherspoon, Henry H.,	1170 Broadway,	" " "
Wright, Jonathan,	44 W. 49th Street,	" " "
Yonge, Henry,	391 Fulton Street,	Brooklyn
Zabriskie, George,	49 Wall Street,	New York City
Zollikoffer, Oscar F.,	49 W. 54th Street,	" " "

ARTICLES OF INCORPORATION

OF

THE NEW YORK CIVIL SERVICE REFORM ASSOCIATION

[Filed May 11, 1900.]

KNOW ALL MEN BY THESE PRESENTS: That we, the undersigned, being persons of full age and all citizens of the United States, a majority of whom are also citizens of the State of New York, and being now Directors of an unincorporated association known as the New York Civil Service Reform Association, and organized for the purposes hereinafter mentioned; being desirous of incorporation for the same purposes under the Membership Corporations Law of the State of New York, do hereby, pursuant to unanimous vote of all the members of the said Association, present and voting at a regularly called meeting thereof, and pursuant to authority given by the said unanimous vote at the said meeting, of which meeting notice of the intention so to incorporate was given personally or by mail to each member of such Association whose residence or Post Office address was known, at least thirty days before said meeting, and at which meeting the corporate name stated in paragraph First was by unanimous vote adopted, do hereby certify as follows:

FIRST.—The name or title by which the Association in which we desire to form ourselves as aforesaid shall be known in law, shall be the Civil Service Reform Association.

SECOND.—The territory in which its operations are to be principally conducted shall be the City of New York.

THIRD.—The city in which its principal office is to be located is the City of New York.

FOURTH.—The objects of the Association shall be to further the establishment of a system of appointment, promotion and removal in the civil service, founded upon the principle that public office is a public trust, admission to and retention in which should depend upon proven fitness; and to take such action as may tend to secure the honest and efficient execution of laws and rules relating to the civil service, and to the proper administration thereof.

FIFTH.—The number of its directors shall be twenty-eight.

SIXTH.—The names of the persons to be its directors until its first annual meeting are as follows:

Samuel P. Avery, Truman J. Backus, Henry De Forest Baldwin, Edward Cary, Charles Collins, W. Bayard Cutting, Horace E. Deming, A. S. Frissell, Richard Watson Gilder, Edwin L. Godkin, J. Warren Greene, George McAneny, James McKeen, Jacob F. Miller, Samuel H. Ordway, William A. Perrine, George Foster Peabody, William J. Schieffelin, Carl Schurz, Charles A. Schieren, Thomas R. Slicer, Henry Sanger Snow, Anson Phelps Stokes, S. Perry Sturges, Henry W. Taft, William H. Thomson, Charles W. Watson and Everett P. Wheeler.

In WITNESS WHEREOF we have made, signed, acknowledged and filed this certificate in duplicate.

Dated this Eighth day of May, 1900.

C. SCHURZ,	WILLIAM H. THOMSON,
JACOB F. MILLER,	A. S. FRISSELL,
ANSON PHELPS STOKES,	GEORGE MCANENY,
EVERETT P. WHEELER,	CHARLES A. SCHIEREN,
CHARLES COLLINS,	SAMUEL P. AVERY,
SAMUEL H. ORDWAY,	GEORGE FOSTER PEABODY.
J. WARREN GREENE,	

STATE OF NEW YORK, } ss.
COUNTY OF NEW YORK,

On this eighth day of May, one thousand and nine hundred, before me personally came Carl Schurz, Jacob F. Miller, Anson Phelps Stokes, Everett P. Wheeler, Charles Collins, J. Warren Greene, William H. Thomson, Samuel H. Ordway, A. S. Frissell, George McAneny, Charles A. Schieren, Samuel P. Avery and George Foster Peabody, to me personally known to be the persons described in and who made and signed the foregoing certificate, and severally duly acknowledged to me that they had made, signed and executed the same for the uses and purposes therein set forth.

F. W. HOERSCHGEN,
Notary Public, Kings County. (149)
(Certificate filed in New York County.)

Approved, May 9, 1900.

DAVID LEVINTRITT,
Justice of the Supreme Court of the State of New York.